D0121591

GNU *Autoconf, Automake, and Libtool*

Gary V. Vaughan, Ben Elliston,
Tom Tromey, and Ian Lance Taylor

New Riders

GNU Autoconf, Automake, and Libtool

Copyright © 2001 by Gary V. Vaughan, Ben Elliston, Tom Tromey, and Ian Lance Taylor

FIRST EDITION: *October, 2000*

This material may be distributed only subject to the terms and conditions set forth in the Open Publication License, v.1.0 or later (the latest version is presently available at http://www.opencontent.org/openpub/). For version 1.0 of the Open Publication License, see Appendix E.

International Standard Book Number: 1-57870-190-2

Library of Congress Catalog Card Number: 99-067439

05 04   7 6 5 4

Interpretation of the printing code: The rightmost double-digit number is the year of the book's printing; the rightmost single-digit number is the number of the book's printing. For example, the printing code 01-1 shows that the first printing of the book occurred in 2001.

Composed in Sabon and MCPdigital by New Riders Publishing

Printed in the United States of America

Trademarks

All terms mentioned in this book that are known to be trademarks or service marks have been appropriately capitalized. New Riders Publishing cannot attest to the accuracy of this information. Use of a term in this book should not be regarded as affecting the validity of any trademark or service mark.

Warning and Disclaimer

This book is designed to provide information about Autoconf, Automake, and Libtool. Every effort has been made to make this book as complete and as accurate as possible, but no warranty or fitness is implied.

The information is provided on an as-is basis. The authors and shall have neither liability nor responsibility to any person or entity with respect to any loss or damages arising from the information contained in this book or from the use of the discs or programs that may accompany it.

Publisher
David Dwyer

Associate Publisher
Al Valvano

Executive Editor
Stephanie Wall

Managing Editor
Gina Brown

Product Marketing Manager
Stephanie Layton

Publicity Manager
Susan Petro

Acquisitions Editor
Ann Quinn

Development Editor
Leah Williams

Project Editor
Lisa M. Thibault

Copy Editor
Keith Cline

Indexer
Cheryl Lenser

Manufacturing Coordinator
Chris Moos

Book Designer
Louisa Klucznik

Cover Designer
Aren Howell

Composition
Scan Communications Group, Inc.

Contents at a Glance

Table of Contents

About the Authors

Gary V. Vaughan spent three years as a Computer Systems Engineering undergraduate at the University of Warwick and then two years at Coventry University studying Computer Science. He has been employed as a professional C programmer in several industry sectors for the past seven years, but most recently as a scientist for the Defence Evaluation and Research Agency. Over the past 10 years or so, Gary has contributed to several free software projects, including AutoGen, Cygwin, Enlightenment, and GNU M4. He currently helps maintain GNU Libtool for the Free Software Foundation.

Ben Elliston works at Red Hat Inc., telecommuting from his home in Canberra, Australia. He develops instruction set simulators and adapts the GNU development tools to new microprocessors. He has worked with GNU tools for many years and is a past maintainer of GNU Autoconf. He has a bachelor's degree in Computer Engineering from the University of Canberra.

Tom Tromey works at Red Hat Inc., where he works on GCJ, the Java front end to the GNU Compiler Collection. Patches of his appear in GCC, emacs, Gnome, Autoconf, GDB, and probably other packages he has forgotten about. He is the primary author of GNU Automake.

Ian Lance Taylor is co-founder and CTO of Zembu Labs. Previously, he worked at Cygnus Solutions, where he designed and wrote features and ports for many free software programs, including the GNU Compiler Collection and the GNU binutils. He was the maintainer of the GNU binutils for several years. He is the author of GNU/Taylor UUCP. He was one of the first contributors to Autoconf, and has also made significant contributions to Automake and Libtool.

About the Technical Reviewers

These reviewers contributed their considerable hands-on expertise to the entire development process for *GNU Autoconf, Automake, and Libtool*. As the book was being written, these dedicated professionals reviewed all the material for technical content, organization, and flow. Their feedback was critical to ensuring that this book fits our reader's need for the highest quality technical information.

Akim Demaille maintains Autoconf, Bison, and a2ps. He graduated from the *E´cole Nationale Supe´rieure des Te´le´ommunications* (ENST), and has a Ph.D. in Logic. He teaches at the *E´cole Pour l'Informatique et les Techniques Avance´es* (EPITA), and is a researcher at the EPITA *Research and Development Laboratory* (LRDE).

Phil Edwards is a maintainer of GNU libstdc++-v3, and sometimes hacks around on small open-source utilities. He currently works in Dayton, Ohio, as a "C++ guy" and Unix sysadmin. He is pursuing a master's degree in Computer Science in his copious free time.

Bruce Korb received his bachelor's degree in Computer Science from the University of California at Berkeley in 1976. Since that time, he has done both operating systems and applications development for various major computer manufacturers. He has also developed and released *Automated Option Processing* (AutoOpts), AutoGen, and a new GCC-fixincludes. All these are released under the GPL and LGPL licensing terms. He is currently employed by SCO and can be reached at bkorb@sco.com.

Alexandre Oliva is one of the maintainers of Autoconf, Automake, and Libtool, as well as a couple of other free software projects. He works for Red Hat as a GCC engineer, and is a Ph.D. student at the Institute of Computing of the State University of Campinas, Brazil, where he earned his bachelor's degree in Computational Engineering and his master's degree in Computer Science.

Didier Verna is one of the core maintainers of XEmacs and is also a regular contributor to other free software projects such as the Autotools. He graduated from the *E´cole Nationale Supe´rieure des Te´le´communications de Paris* (ENST) and has a Ph.D. in Computer Science. He works as a teacher at the *E´cole Pour l'Informatique et les Techniques Avance´es* (EPITA) and as a researcher at *EPITA Research and Development Laboratory* (LRDE).

Benjamin Koznik is one of the maintainers of libstdc++. On occasion, he hacks on g++. He received his bachelor's degree in Mathematics from the University of Texas at Austin in 1995. He works for Red Hat as a GCC engineer.

Jason Molenda is a Technical Yahoo with Yahoo!, Inc. in the San Francisco Bay area. He worked on GNU tools for six years while at Cygnus Solutions, and has been an avid GNU user for the past decade. Recently, he has been working on the infrastructure used by free software developers, and has made significant improvements in the support available to many GNU programs.

Dedication

I dedicate this book to Karen, my wonderful wife, who has endured eight months of watching television over the sound of my typing, and waiting until 3am for me to go to bed. And to my children, Daniel ("Yes, I have finished the book now!") and Zoe ("Yes, you can play a game on my computer now!").

Gary V. Vaughan

I dedicate this book to my family and recently neglected friends. I am indebted to Michael Tiemann for the opportunity to work on GNU software and to Lisa for keeping my kitchen appliances in order.

Ben Elliston

For Janet.

Tom Tromey

For Elisabeth.

Ian Lance Taylor

Acknowledgments

Our thanks to the following people, without whom this book would never have happened (or at least it would have been rather thin): Richard Stallman and the Free Software Foundation, Gord Matzigkeit, David Mackenzie, Akim Demaille, Phil Edwards, Bruce Korb, Alexandre Oliva, Didier Verna, Benjamin Koznik, Jason Molenda, the Gnits group, and the New Riders staff.

Tell Us What You Think

As the reader of this book, you are the most important critic and commentator. We value your opinion and want to know what we are doing right, what we could do better, what areas you would like to see us publish in, and any other words of wisdom you are willing to pass our way.

I welcome your comments. You can email or write me directly to let me know what you did or did not like about this book—as well as what we can do to make our books stronger.

Please note that I cannot help you with technical problems related to the topic of this book, and that due to the high volume of mail I receive, I might not be able to reply to every message.

When you write, please be sure to include this book's title and author as well as your name and phone or fax number. I will carefully review your comments and share them with the author and editors who worked on the book.

Email: `nrfeedback@newriders.com`
Mail: Mark Taber
       Associate Publisher
       Pearson Technology Group
       800 East 96th Street
       Indianapolis, IN 46240 USA

Foreword

Do you remember the 1980s? Veteran users of free software on Unix could testify that although there were a lot of programs distributed as source code back then (over USENET), there was not a lot of consistency in how to compile and install them. The more complicated a package was, the more likely it was to have its own unique build procedure that had to be learned first. And there were no widely used approaches to portability problems. Each software author handled them in a different way, if they did at all.

Fast forward to the present. A de facto standard is in widespread use for solving those problems, and it is not just free software packages that are using it; some proprietary programs from the largest computer companies are built using this software. It even does Windows.

As it evolved in the 1990s, it demonstrated the power of some good ideas: sharing expertise, automating repetitive work, and having consistency where it is helpful without sacrificing flexibility where it is helpful.

What is "it?" GNU Autotools, a group of utilities developed in the 1990s for the GNU Project. The authors of this book and I were some of its principal developers, but it turned out to help solve many other people's problems as well, and many other people contributed to it. It is one of the many projects that developed by cooperation while making what is now often called GNU/Linux. The community made GNU Autotools widespread, as people adopted it for their own programs and extended it where they found that was needed. The creation of Libtool is that type of contribution.

Autoconf, Automake, and Libtool were developed separately, to make tackling the problem of software configuration more manageable by partitioning it. They were designed to be used as a system, however, and they make more sense when you have documentation for the whole system. This book stands a level above the software packages, giving the expertise of its authors in using this whole system to its fullest. It was written by people who have lived closest to the problems and their solutions in software.

Magic happens under the hood, where experts have tinkered until The GNU Autotools engine can run on everything from jet fuel to whale oil. But there is a different kind of magic, in the cooperation and sharing that built a widely used system over the Internet, for anyone to use and improve. Now, as the authors share their knowledge and experience, you are part of the community, too. Perhaps its spirit will inspire you to make your own contributions.

David MacKenzie
Germantown, Maryland
June 2000

Introduction

Autoconf, Automake, and Libtool are packages for making your software more portable and to simplify building it—usually on someone else's system. Software portability and effective build systems are crucial aspects of modern software engineering practice. It is unlikely that a software project would be started today with the expectation that the software would run on only one platform. Hardware constraints may change the choice of platform, new customers with different kinds of systems may emerge, or your vendor might introduce incompatible changes in newer versions of their operating system. In addition, tools that make building software easier and less error-prone are valuable.

Autoconf is a tool that makes your packages more portable by performing tests to discover system characteristics before the package is compiled. Your source code can then adapt to these differences.

Automake is a tool for generating `Makefile`'s—descriptions of what to build—that conform to a number of standards. Automake substantially simplifies the process of describing the organization of a package and performs additional functions such as dependency tracking between source files.

Libtool is a command-line interface to the compiler and linker that makes it easy to portably generate static and shared libraries, regardless of the platform on which it is running.

I.1 What This Book Is

This book is a tutorial for Autoconf, Automake, and Libtool, hereafter referred to as the GNU Autotools. The GNU manuals that accompany each tool adequately document each tool in isolation. Until now, a guide has not described how these tools work *together*.

As these tools have evolved over the years, contributors who clearly understand the associated problems have made design decisions, but little documentation exists that captures why things are the way they are. By way of example, one might wonder why some Autoconf macros use shell constructs such as this:

```
if test "x$var" = xbar; then
  echo yes 1>&5
fi
```

rather than the simpler

```
if [ $var = bar ]; then
  echo yes 1>&5
fi
```

This book records much of this reasoning.

I.2 What This Book Is Not

This book is not a definitive reference to Autoconf, Automake, or Libtool. Attempting to be so would fill this book with information doomed to obsolescence. For instance, you will not find a description of every predefined macro provided by Autoconf. Instead, this book attempts to help you understand any macro you encounter and influence how you approach software portability and package building. You should consult the GNU manual for each tool as a reference.

This book briefly introduces pertinent concepts, but does not attempt to teach them comprehensively. You will find an introduction to writing 'Makefile's and Bourne shell scripts, but you should consult other references to become familiar with these broader topics.

I.3 Who Should Read This Book

Demystifying the GNU Autotools should raise the interest of a wide audience of software developers, system administrators, and technical managers.

Software developers, especially those involved with free software projects, will find it valuable to understand how to use these tools. The GNU Autotools are enjoying growing popularity in the free software community. Developers of in-house projects can reap the same benefits by using these tools.

System administrators can benefit from a working knowledge of these tools—a common task for system administrators is to compile and install packages that use the GNU Autotools framework. Occasionally, a feature test may produce a false result, leading to a compilation error or a misbehaving program. Some hacking is usually sufficient to get the package to compile, but knowing the correct way to fix the problem can assist the package maintainer.

Finally, technical managers may find the discussion to be an insight into the complex nature of software portability and the process of building a large project.

I.4 How This Book Is Organized

Like any good tutorial, this book starts with an explanation of simple concepts and builds on these fundamentals to progress to advanced topics.

The first chapter of this book provides a history of the development of these tools and why they exist.

The next 18 chapters contain most of the book's content, starting with an introduction to concepts such as `Makefile`'s and configuration triplets. Later chapters introduce each tool and how to manage projects of varying sizes using the tools in concert. Programs written in C and C++ can be non-portable if written carelessly. Chapters 14, "Writing Portable C with GNU Autotools," and 15, "Writing Portable C++ with GNU Autotools," offer guidelines for writing portable programs in C and C++, respectively.

Chapters 20 through 25 provide information that you are unlikely to find in any other documentation; this information is based on extensive experience with the tools. It embodies chapters that treat some advanced, yet essential, concepts such as the `m4` macro processor and how to write portable Bourne shell scripts. Chapter 23 outlines how to migrate an existing package to the GNU Autotools framework and will be of interest to many developers. One of the most mystifying aspects of using the GNU Autotools relates to building packages in a cross-compilation environment. Chapter 25 demystifies this.

The appendixes include instructions on installing GNU Autotools, platforms, generated file dependencies, and an Autoconf macro reference. Appendix E contains the Open Publication License.

I.5 Conventions Used in This Book

Typographical conventions used in this book are as follows:

- A monospaced (Mono) font is used for commands, command-line options, functions, and all code examples. This font is also used for interactive shell logs where the results of commands are interspersed with lines typed at a CLI prompt by the user.
- Bold is used for the emphasis of terms and function names.
- Italics are used for emphasized terms, fields in code examples, variable tags, and words that are being defined.
- Text following a => symbol indicates a result which is output.

1

History

This chapter summarizes the history of the tools described in this book. Although you do not need to know this history to use the tools, the history of how the tools developed over time helps explain why the tools act the way that they do today. Also, in a book such as this, it is only fair for us to credit the original authors and sources of inspiration and to explain what they did.

1.1 The Diversity of Unix Systems

Of the programs discussed in this book, the first to be developed was autoconf. The history of the Unix operating system determined its development.

Dennis Ritchie and Ken Thompson of Bell Labs wrote the first version of Unix in 1969. During the 1970s, Bell Labs was not permitted to sell Unix commercially, but did distribute Unix to universities at relatively low cost. The University of California at Berkeley added their own improvements to the Unix sources; the result was known as the BSD version of Unix.

In the early 1980s, AT&T signed an agreement permitting them to sell Unix commercially. The first AT&T version of Unix was known as System III.

As the popularity of Unix increased during the 1980s, several other companies modified the Unix sources to create their own variants. Examples include SunOS from Sun Microsystems, Ultrix from Digital Equipment Corporation, and HP-UX from Hewlett Packard.

Although all the Unix variants were fundamentally similar, various differences existed between them. They had slightly different sets of header files and slightly different lists of functions in the system libraries, as well as more significant differences in areas such as terminal handling and job control.

The emerging POSIX standards helped to eliminate some of these differences. In some areas, however, POSIX introduced new features, leading to more variants.

Also, different systems adopted the POSIX standard at different times, leading to further disparities.

All these variations caused problems for programs distributed as source code. Even a function as straightforward as memcpy was not available everywhere; the BSD system library provided the similar function bcopy instead, but the order of arguments was reversed.

Program authors who wanted their programs to run on a wide variety of Unix variants had to be familiar with the detailed differences between the variants. They also had to worry about the ways in which the variants changed from one version to another, as variants on the one hand converged on the POSIX standard and on the other continued to introduce new and different features.

Although it was generally possible to use #ifdef to identify particular systems and versions, it became increasingly difficult to know which versions had which features. It became clear that some more organized approach was needed to handle the differences between Unix variants.

1.2 The First *configure* Programs

By 1992, four different systems had been developed to help with source-code portability:

- The metaconfig program, by Larry Wall, Harlan Stenn, and Raphael Manfredi.
- The Cygnus 'configure' script, by K. Richard Pixley, and the original GCC 'configure' script, by Richard Stallman. These are quite similar, and the developers communicated regularly. GCC is the GNU Compiler Collection (formerly the GNU C compiler).
- The GNU Autoconf package, by David MacKenzie.
- Imake, part of the X Window system.

These systems all split building a program into two steps: a configuration step and a build step. For all the systems, the build step used the standard Unix make program. The make program reads a set of rules in a 'Makefile', and uses them to build a program. The configuration step generates 'Makefile's, and perhaps other files, which are then used during the build step.

Metaconfig and Autoconf both use feature tests to determine the capabilities of the system. They use Bourne shell scripts (all variants of Unix support the Bourne shell in one form or another) to run various tests to see what the system can support.

The Cygnus 'configure' script and the original GCC 'configure' script are also Bourne shell scripts. They rely on little configuration files for each system variant, both header files and 'Makefile' fragments. In early versions, the user compiling the program had to tell the script which type of system the program should be built for; they were later enhanced with a shell script written by Per Bothner, which determines the system type based on the standard Unix uname program and other information.

imake is a portable C program. imake can be customized for a particular system, and run as part of building a package. It is more normally distributed with a package, however, including all the configuration information needed for supported systems.

metaconfig and autoconf are programs used by program authors. They produce a shell script distributed with the program's source code. A user who wants to build the program runs the shell script to configure the source code for the particular system on which it is to be built.

The Cygnus and GCC 'configure' scripts, and imake, do not have this clear distinction between use by the developer and use by the user.

The Cygnus and GCC 'configure' scripts included features to support cross development, both to support building a cross-compiler (which compiles code to be run on another system) and to support building a program using a cross-compiler.

autoconf, metaconfig, and imake did not have these features (they were later added to autoconf); they worked only for building a program on the system on which they were to run.

The scripts generated by metaconfig are interactive by default: They ask questions of the users as they go along. This permits them to determine certain characteristics of the system, which it is difficult or impossible to test, such as the behavior of setuid programs.

The Cygnus and GCC 'configure' scripts, and the scripts generated by autoconf, and the imake program, are not interactive; they determine everything themselves. When using autoconf, the package developer normally writes the script to accept command-line options for features that cannot be tested for, or sometimes requires the user to edit a header file after the 'configure' script has run.

1.3 *configure* Development

The Cygnus 'configure' script and the original GCC 'configure' script both had to be updated for each new Unix variant they supported. This meant that packages that used them were continually out of date as new Unix variants appeared. It was not hard for the developer to add support for a new system variant; however, package users could not do so easily themselves.

The same was true of Imake as it was commonly used. Although it was possible for a user to build and configure Imake for a particular system, it was not commonly done. In practice, packages that use Imake (such as the X Window system) are shipped with configuration information detailed for specific Unix variants.

Because Metaconfig and Autoconf used feature tests, the scripts they generated could often work correctly on new Unix variants without modification. This made them more flexible and easier to work with over time, and led to the wide adoption of Autoconf.

In 1994, David MacKenzie extended Autoconf to incorporate the features of the Cygnus 'configure' script and the original GCC 'configure' script. This included support for using system-specified header file and 'Makefile' fragments, and support for cross-compilation.

GCC has since been converted to use Autoconf, eliminating the GCC 'configure' script. Most programs that use the Cygnus 'configure' script have also been converted, and no new programs are being written to use the Cygnus 'configure' script.

The metaconfig program is still used today to configure Perl and a few other programs. imake is still used to configure the X Window system. However, these tools are not generally used for new packages.

1.4 Automake Development

By 1994, Autoconf was a solid framework for handling the differences between Unix variants. However, program developers still had to write large 'Makefile.in' files to use it. The 'configure' script generated by autoconf would transform the 'Makefile.in' file into a 'Makefile' used by the make program.

A 'Makefile.in' file has to describe how to build the program. In the Imake equivalent of a 'Makefile.in', known as an 'Imakefile', it is only necessary to describe which source files are used to build the program. When Imake generates a 'Makefile', it adds the rules for how to build the program itself. Later versions of the BSD make program also include rules for building a program.

Because most programs are built in much the same way, there was a great deal of duplication in 'Makefile.in' files. Also, the GNU project developed a reasonably complex set of standards for 'Makefile's, and it was easy to get some of the details wrong.

These factors led to the development of Automake. `automake`, like `autoconf`, is a program run by a developer. The developer writes files named `'Makefile.am'`; these use a simpler syntax than ordinary `'Makefile'`s. `automake` reads the `'Makefile.am'` files and produces `'Makefile.in'` files. The idea is that a script generated by `autoconf` converts these `'Makefile.in'` files into `'Makefile'`s.

As with Imake and BSD `make`, the `'Makefile.am'` file needs only to describe the files used to build a program. `automake` automatically adds the necessary rules when it generates the `'Makefile.in'` file. `automake` also adds any rules required by the GNU `'Makefile'` standards.

David MacKenzie wrote the first version of Automake in 1994. Tom Tromey rewrote it completely in 1995.

1.5 Libtool Development

Over time, Unix systems added support for shared libraries.

Conventional libraries, or static libraries, are linked into a program image. This means that each program that uses a static library includes some or all of the library in the program binary on disk.

Shared libraries, on the other hand, are separate files. A program that uses a shared library does not include a copy of the library; it includes only the name of the library. Many programs can use a single shared library.

Using a shared library reduces disk-space requirements. Because the system can generally share a single executable instance of the shared library among many programs, it also reduces swap-space requirements at runtime. Another advantage is that it is possible to fix a bug by updating the single shared library file on disk, without requiring all the programs that use the library to be rebuilt.

The first Unix shared library implementation was in System V release 3 from AT&T. Other Unix vendors rapidly adopted the idea, and it appeared in SunOS, HP-UX, AIX, and Digital Unix among others. Unfortunately, each implementation differed in the creation and use of shared libraries and in the specific features that were supported.

Naturally, packages distributed as source code that included libraries wanted to be able to build their own shared libraries. Several different implementations were written in the Autoconf/Automake framework.

In 1996, Gordon Matzigkeit began work on a package known as Libtool. Libtool is a collection of shell scripts that handle the differences between shared library generation and use on different systems. It is closely tied to Automake, although it is possible to use it independently.

Over time, Libtool has been enhanced to support more Unix variants and to provide an interface for standardizing shared library features.

1.6 Microsoft Windows

In 1995, Microsoft released Windows 95, which soon became the most widely used operating system in the world. Autoconf and Libtool were written to support portability across Unix variants, but they provided a framework to support portability to Windows as well. This made it possible for a program to support both Unix and Windows from a single source-code base.

The key requirement of both Autoconf and Libtool was the Unix shell. The GNU bash shell was ported to Windows as part of the Cygwin project, which was originally written by Steve Chamberlain. The Cygwin project implements the basic Unix API in Windows, making it possible to port Unix programs directly.

After the shell and the Unix make program (also provided by Cygwin) became available, it was possible to make Autoconf and Libtool support Windows directly, using either the Cygwin interface or the Visual C++ tools from Microsoft. This compatibility involved handling details such as the different file extensions used by the different systems as well as yet another set of shared library features. Ian Lance Taylor produced the first version of this work in 1998. Automake has also been ported to Windows. It requires Perl to be installed. (For more information, see Section A.1, "Prerequisite Tools.")

2

How to Run Configure, and The Most Useful Standard Makefile Targets

A package constructed using Autoconf comes with a `'configure'` script. Users who want to build and install the package must run this script to prepare their source tree for building on their particular system. The actual build is performed using the `make` program.

The `'configure'` script tests system features. For example, it might test whether the C library defines the `time_t` data type for use by the `time()` C library function. The `'configure'` script then makes the results of those tests available to the program while it is being built.

This chapter explains how to invoke a `'configure'` script from the perspective of a user—someone who just wants to take your package and compile it on his system with a minimum of fuss. Because Autoconf works as well as it does, it is usually possible to build a package on any kind of machine with a simple `configure; make` command line. The topics covered in this chapter include how to invoke `configure`, the files that `configure` generates, and the most useful `Makefile` targets—actions that you want `make` to perform—that will be available when computing the package. (See Chapter 3, "Introducing 'Makefiles'.")

2.1 Configuring

A `'configure'` script takes a large number of command-line options. The set of options can vary from one package to the next, although a number of basic options are always present. The available options can be discovered by running `'configure'` with the `'-help'` option. Although many of these options are esoteric, it's worthwhile knowing of their existence when configuring packages with special installation requirements. Each option is briefly described as follows:

`'--cache-file=file'`   `'configure'` runs tests on your system to determine the availability of features (or bugs!). The results of these tests can be stored in a *cache file* to speed up subsequent invocations of `configure`. The presence of a well-primed cache file makes a big improvement when configuring a complex tree that has `'configure'` scripts in each subtree.

`'--help'`   This option outputs a help message. Even experienced users of `'configure'` need to use `'--help'` occasionally, because complex projects will include additional options for per-project configuration. For example, `'configure'` in the GCC package enables you to control whether the GNU assembler will be built and used by GCC in preference to a vendor's assembler.

`'--no-create'`   One of the primary functions of `'configure'` is to generate output files. This option prevents `'configure'` from generating such output files. You can think of this as a kind of *dry run*, although the cache will still be modified.

`'--quiet'`, `'--silent'`   As `'configure'` runs its tests, it outputs brief messages telling the user what the script is doing. This is done because `'configure'` can be slow. If there is no such output, the user is left wondering what is happening. By using this option, you too can be left wondering!

`'--version'`   This option prints the version of Autoconf that was used to generate the `configure` script.

`'--prefix=prefix'`   The `'--prefix'` option is one of the most frequently used. If generated `Makefiles` choose to observe the argument you pass with this option, it is possible to entirely relocate the architecture-independent portion of a package when it is installed. When installing a package such as Emacs, for example, the following command line causes the Emacs Lisp files to be installed in /opt/gnu/share:

```
$ ./configure --prefix=/opt/gnu
```

It is important to stress that this behavior depends on the generated files making use of this information. For developers writing these files, Automake simplifies this process a great deal. See Section 7.1, "GNU Autotools in Practice."

`'--exec-prefix=eprefix'`

This option is similar to `--prefix`, except that it sets the location of installed files that are architecture dependent. The compiled `'emacs'` binary is such a file. If this option is not given, the default `'exec-prefix'` value inserted into generated files is set to the same values as the `'prefix'`.

`'--bindir=dir'`

This option specifies the location of installed binary files. Although there may be other generated files that are binary in nature, binary files here are defined to be programs run directly by users.

`'--sbindir=dir'`

This option specifies the location of installed superuser binary files. These are programs usually run only by the superuser.

`'--libexecdir=dir'`

This option specifies the location of installed executable support files. Contrasted with "binary files," these files are never run directly by users, but may be executed by the binary files mentioned earlier.

`'--datadir=dir'`

This option specifies the location of generic data files.

`'--sysconfdir=dir'`

This option specifies the location of read-only data used on a single machine.

`'--sharedstatedir=dir'`

This option specifies the location of data that may be modified, and which may be shared across several machines.

`'--localstatedir=dir'`

This option specifies the location of data that may be modified, but which is specific to a single machine.

`'--libdir=dir'`

This option specifies where the object code library should be installed.

`'--includedir=dir'`

This option specifies where C header files should be installed. Header files for other languages, such as C++, may be installed here also.

`'--oldincludedir=dir'`

This option specifies where C header files should be installed for compilers other than GCC.

`'--infodir=dir'`   This option specifies where Info format documentation files should be installed. Info is the documentation format used by the GNU project.

`'--mandir=dir'`   This option specifies where manual pages should be installed.

`'--srcdir=dir'`   This option does not affect installation. Instead, it tells `'configure'` where the source files may be found. Generally, you do not have to specify this, because the `'configure'` script is usually in the same directory as the source files.

`'--program-prefix=prefix'`   This option specifies a prefix that should be added to the name of a program when installing it. For example, using `--program-prefix=g` when configuring a program usually named `tar` causes the installed program to be named `gtar` instead. As with the other installation options, this `'configure'` option works only if it is used by the `'Makefile.in'` file.

`'--program-suffix=suffix'`   This option specifies a suffix that should be appended to the name of a program when installing it.

`'--program-transform-name=program'`   Here, *program* is a `sed` program. When a program is installed, its name is run through `'sed -e program'` to select the installed name.

`'--build=BUILD'`   Specifies the type of system on which the package will be built. If not specified, the default is the same configuration name as the host.

`'--host=HOST'`   Specifies the type of system on which the package will run, or *be hosted*. If not specified, the host triplet is determined by executing `'config.guess'`.

`'--target=TARGET'`   Specifies the type of system to which the package is to be targeted. This makes the most sense in the context of programming language tools such as compilers and assemblers. If not specified, the default is the same configuration name as the host.

`'--disable-FEATURE'`   Some packages may choose to provide compile-time configurability for large-scale options such as using the Kerberos authentication system or an experimental compiler optimization pass. If the default is to provide such features, you can disable them with `'--disable-FEATURE'`, where `'FEATURE'` is the feature's designated name. For example:

```
$ ./configure --disable-gui
```

`'--enable-FEATURE[=ARG]'`	Conversely, some packages may provide features disabled by default. To enable them, use `'--enable-FEATURE'`, where `'FEATURE'` is the feature's designated name. A feature may accept an optional argument. For example:

```
$ ./configure --enable-buffers=128
```

Using `'--enable-FEATURE=no'` is synonymous with `'--disable-FEATURE'`, described earlier.

`'--with-PACKAGE[=ARG]'`	In the free software community, there is a healthy tendency to reuse existing packages and libraries where possible. At the time when a source tree is configured by `'configure'`, it is possible to provide hints about other installed packages. For example, the BLT widget toolkit relies on Tcl and Tk. To configure BLT, you may have to give `'configure'` some hints about where you have installed Tcl and Tk:

```
$ ./configure --with-tcl=/usr/local
➥ --with-tk=/usr/local
```

Using `'--with-PACKAGE=no'` is synonymous with `'--without-PACKAGE'`, described next.

`'--without-PACKAGE'`	Sometimes, you may not want your package to interoperate with some preexisting package installed on your system. For example, you might not want your new compiler to use GNU ld. You can prevent this by using an option such as this:

```
$ ./configure --without-gnu-ld
```

`'--x-includes=DIR'`	This option is really a specific instance of a `'--with-package'` option. When Autoconf was initially being developed, it was common to use `'configure'` to build programs to run on the X Window system as an alternative to Imake. The `'--x-includes'` option provides a way to guide the configure script to the directory containing the X11 header files.
`'--x-libraries=DIR'`	Similarly, the `'--x-libraries'` option provides a way to guide `'configure'` to the directory containing the X11 libraries.

It is unnecessary, and often undesirable, to run 'configure' from within the source tree. Instead, a well-written 'Makefile' generated by 'configure' can build packages whose source files reside in another tree. The advantages of building derived files in a separate tree to the source code are fairly obvious: The derived files, such as object files, would clutter the source tree. This would also make it impossible to build those same object files on a different system or with a different configuration. Instead, you should use three trees: a source tree, a build tree, and an *install tree*. Here is a closing example of how to build the GNU malloc package in this way:

```
$ gtar zxf mmalloc-1.0.tar.gz
$ mkdir build && cd build
$ ../mmalloc-1.0/configure
  creating cache ../config.cache
  checking for gcc... gcc
  checking whether the C compiler (gcc  ) works... yes
  checking whether the C compiler (gcc  ) is a cross-compiler... no
  checking whether we are using GNU C... yes
  checking whether gcc accepts -g... yes
  checking for a BSD compatible install... /usr/bin/install -c
  checking host system type... i586-pc-linux-gnu
  checking build system type... i586-pc-linux-gnu
  checking for ar... ar
  checking for ranlib... ranlib
  checking how to run the C preprocessor... gcc -E
  checking for unistd.h... yes
  checking for getpagesize... yes
  checking for working mmap... yes
  checking for limits.h... yes
  checking for stddef.h... yes
  updating cache ../config.cache
  creating ./config.status
```

Now that this build tree is configured, you can build the package and install it into the default location of '/usr/local':

```
$ make all && make install
```

2.2 Files Generated by *'configure'*

After you have invoked configure, you will discover a number of generated files in your build tree. The build directory structure created by 'configure' and the number of files vary from package to package. The following list describes each of the generated files. Appendix C, "Generated File Dependencies," illustrates their relationships.

'config.cache'   'configure' can cache the results of system tests that have been performed to speed up subsequent tests. This file contains the cache data and is a plain-text file that can be hand-modified or removed if desired.

'config.log'

As 'configure' runs, it outputs a message describing each test it performs and the result of each test. Substantially more output is produced by the shell and utilities that 'configure' invokes, but it is hidden from the user to keep the output understandable. The output is instead redirected to 'config.log'. This file is the first place to look when 'configure' goes haywire or a test produces a nonsense result. A common scenario is that configure, when run on a Solaris system, tells you it was unable to find a working C compiler. An examination of config.log shows that Solaris's default /usr/ucb/cc is a program that informs the user that the optional C compiler is not installed.

'config.status'

'configure' generates a shell script called 'config.status' that you can use to re-create the current configuration. That is, all generated files will be regenerated. You can also use this script to re-run 'configure' if the '--recheck' option is given.

'config.h'

Many packages that use 'configure' are written in C or C++. Some of the tests that 'configure' runs involve examining variability in the C and C++ programming languages and implementations thereof. So that source code can programmatically deal with these differences, #define preprocessor directives can be optionally placed in a *config header*, usually called 'config.h', as 'configure' runs. Source files may then include the 'config.h' file and act accordingly:

```
#if HAVE_CONFIG_H
#   include <config.h>
#endif /* HAVE_CONFIG_H */

#if HAVE_UNISTD_H
#   include <unistd.h>
#endif /* HAVE_UNISTD_H */
```

Best Practice

We recommend always using a config header. ◆

'Makefile'	One of the common functions of 'configure' is to generate 'Makefile's and other files. As it has been stressed, a 'Makefile' is just a file often generated by 'configure' from a corresponding input file (usually called 'Makefile.in'). There are other cases where generating files in this way can be helpful. For instance, a Java developer might want to make use of a 'defs.java' file generated from 'defs.java.in'.

The following section will describe how you can use make to process the preceding Makefile.

2.3 The Most Useful *'Makefile'* Targets

At this point, 'configure' has generated the output files (such as a 'Makefile'). Most projects include a 'Makefile' with a basic set of well-known *targets* (see Section 3.1, "Targets and Dependencies"). A *target* is a task you want make to perform—usually, it is to build all of the programs belonging to your package (commonly known as the *all* target). From your build directory, the following commands are likely to work with any configured package:

make all	Builds all derived files sufficient to declare the package built.
make check	Runs any self-tests that the package may have.
make install	Installs the package in a predetermined location.
make clean	Removes all derived files.

Other less commonly used targets are likely to be recognized, particularly if the package includes a 'Makefile' that conforms to the GNU 'Makefile' standard or is generated by automake. You may want to inspect the generated 'Makefile' to see what other targets have been included.

2.4 Configuration Names

The GNU Autotools name all types of computer systems using a *configuration name*. This is a name for the system in a standardized format. Some example configuration names are 'sparc-sun-solaris2.7', 'i586-pc-linux-gnu', or 'i386-pc-cygwin'.

All configuration names used to have three parts, and some documentation still calls them *configuration triplets*. A three-part configuration name is *cpu-manufacturer-operating_system*. Currently configuration names are permitted to have four parts on systems that distinguish the kernel and the operating system, such as GNU/Linux. In these cases, the configuration name is *cpu-manufacturer-kernel-operating_system*.

When using a configuration name in option to a tool such as `configure`, usually you do not have to specify an entire name. In particular, the middle field (*manufacturer*, described later) is often omitted, leading to strings such as `i386-linux` or `sparc-sunos`. The shell script `config.sub` is used to translate these shortened strings into the canonical form.

On most Unix variants, the shell script `config.guess` prints the correct configuration name for the system on which it is run. It does this by running the standard `uname` program, and by examining other characteristics of the system. On some systems, `config.guess` requires a working C compiler or an assembler.

Because `config.guess` can normally determine the configuration name for a machine, a user or developer has to specify only a configuration name in unusual cases, such as when building a cross-compiler.

The following list describes each field in a configuration name:

cpu

The type of processor used on the system. This is typically something like `i386` or `sparc`. More specific variants are used as well, such as `mipsel` to indicate a little endian MIPS processor.

manufacturer

A somewhat freeform field that indicates the manufacturer of the system. This is often just `unknown`. Other common strings are `pc` for an IBM PC-compatible system, or the name of a workstation vendor, such as `sun`.

operating_system

The name of the operating system run on the system. This will be something like `solaris2.5` or `winnt4.0`. No particular restriction applies to the version number, and strings such as `aix4.1.4.0` are seen. You can use configuration names to describe all sorts of systems, including embedded systems that do not run any operating system. In this case, the field is generally used to indicate the object file format, such as `elf` or `coff`.

kernel   This is used mainly for GNU/Linux
                                            systems. A typical GNU/Linux configura-
                                            tion name is `i586-pc-linux-gnulibc1`.
                                            In this case, the kernel, `linux`, is sepa-
                                            rated from the operating system,
                                            `gnulibc1`.

`configure` allows fine control over the format of binary files. It is not necessary
to build a package for a given kind of machine on that machine natively.
Instead, a cross-compiler can be used. Moreover, if the package you are trying
to build is itself capable of operating in a cross configuration, then the build
system need not be the same kind of machine used to host the cross-configured
package once the package is built! Consider some examples:

Compiling a simple package for a GNU/Linux system:	`host = build = target = i586-pc-linux-gnu`
Cross-compiling a package on a GNU/Linux system that is intended to run on an IBM AIX machine:	`build = i586-pc-linux-gnu`, `host = target = rs6000-ibm-aix3.2`
Building a Solaris-hosted MIPS-ECOFF cross-compiler on a GNU/Linux system:	`build = i586-pc-linux-gnu`, `host = sparc-sun-solaris2.4`, `target = mips-idt-ecoff`

3

Introducing 'Makefile's

A 'Makefile' is a specification of dependencies between files and how to resolve those dependencies such that an overall goal, known as a *target*, can be reached. 'Makefile's are processed by the make utility. Other references describe the syntax of 'Makefile's and the various implementations of make in detail. This chapter provides an overview into 'Makefile's and gives just enough information to write custom rules in a 'Makefile.am' (see Chapter 6, "Introducing GNU Automake") or 'Makefile.in'.

3.1 Targets and Dependencies

The make program attempts to bring a target up-to-date by bringing all the target's dependencies up-to-date. These dependencies may have further dependencies. Thus, a potentially complex dependency graph forms when processing a typical 'Makefile':

```
all: foo

foo: foo.o bar.o baz.o

.c.o:
        $(CC) $(CFLAGS) -c $< -o $@@

.l.c:
        $(LEX) $< && mv lex.yy.c $@@
```

From a simple file that looks like this one, we can draw a dependency graph such as the one in Figure 3.1.

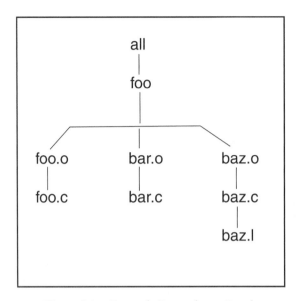

Figure 3.1   *Example Dependency Graph.*

Unless the 'Makefile' contains a directive to make, all targets are assumed to be filenames, and rules must be written to create these files or somehow bring them up-to-date.

When leaf nodes are found in the dependency graph, the 'Makefile' must include a set of shell commands to bring the dependent up-to-date with the dependency. Much to the chagrin of many make users, "up-to-date" means the dependent has a more recent time stamp than the target. Moreover, each of these shell commands are run in their own subshell and, unless the 'Makefile' instructs make otherwise, each command must exit with an exit code of 0 to indicate success.

You can write target rules that are executed unconditionally. To do so, you must specify that the target has no dependents. The following simple rule should be familiar to most users:

```
clean:
    -rm *.o core
```

3.2 *'Makefile'* Syntax

'Makefile's have a rather particular syntax that can trouble new users. There are many implementations of make, some of which provide non-portable extensions. An abridged description of the syntax follows. For portability, this syntax may be stricter than you might be used to.

Comments start with a '#' and continue until the end of line. They may appear anywhere except in command sequences—if they do, they will be interpreted by the shell running the command. The following Makefile shows three individual targets with dependencies on each:

```
target1:  dep1 dep2 ... depN
<tab>     cmd1
<tab>     cmd2
<tab>     ...
<tab>     cmdN

target2:  dep4 dep5
<tab>     cmd1
<tab>     cmd2

dep4 dep5:
<tab>     cmd1
```

Target rules start at the beginning of a line and are followed by a colon. Following the colon is a white space separated list of dependencies. A series of lines follow that contain shell commands to be run by a subshell. (The default is the Bourne shell.) Each of these lines *must* be prefixed by a horizontal tab character. This is the most common mistake made by new make users.

These commands may be prefixed by an '@' character to prevent make from echoing the command line prior to executing it. They may also optionally be prefixed by a '-' character to allow the rule to continue if the command returns a non-zero exit code. The combination of both characters is permitted.

3.3 Macros

You can use a number of helpful macros anywhere throughout the 'Makefile'. Macros start with a dollar sign, like shell variables. Our first 'Makefile' example used a few:

```
$(CC) $(CFLAGS) -c $< -o $@
```

Here, syntactic forms of '$(..)' are make variable expansions. You can define a make variable using a 'VAR=VALUE' syntax, as follows:

```
CC=ec++
```

In a 'Makefile', $(CC) is then literally replaced by 'ec++'. make has a number of built-in variables and default values. The default value for $(CC) is 'cc'.

Other built-in macros exist with fixed semantics. The two most common macros are $@ and $<. They represent the names of the target and the first dependency for the rule in which they appear. $@ is available in any rule, but for some versions of make $< is only available in suffix rules. Here is a simple Makefile:

```
all:    dummy
        @echo "$@ depends on dummy"

dummy:
        touch $@
```

This is what make outputs when processing the Makefile:

```
$ make
touch dummy
all depends on dummy
```

The GNU Make manual documents these macros in more detail.

4

Using GNU Autotools to Manage a "Minimal Project"

This chapter describes how to manage a minimal project using the GNU Autotools. For this discussion, a minimal project refers to the smallest possible project that can still illustrate a sufficient number of principles related to using the tools. Studying a smaller project makes it easier to understand the more complex interactions between these tools when larger projects require advanced features.

The example project used throughout this chapter is a fictitious command interpreter called 'foonly'. 'foonly' is written in C, but like many interpreters, uses a lexical analyzer and a parser expressed using the lex and yacc tools. The package is developed to adhere to the GNU 'Makefile' standard, which is the default behavior for Automake.

This project does not use many features of the GNU Autotools. The most noteworthy one is libraries; this package does not produce any libraries of its own, so Libtool does not feature them in this chapter. The more complex projects presented in Chapter 7, "A Small GNU Autotools Project" and Chapter 11, "A Large GNU Autotools Project" illustrate how Libtool participates in the build system. The essence of this chapter is to provide a high-level overview of the user-written files and how they interact.

4.1 User-Provided Input Files

The smallest project requires the user to provide only two files. The GNU Autotools generate the remainder of the files needed to build the package are in Section 4.2, "Generated Output Files." The files are as follows:

'Makefile.am'	An input to automake
'configure.in'	An input to autoconf

I like to think of 'Makefile.am' as a high-level, bare-bones specification of the project's build requirements: what needs to be built, and where does it go when it is installed? This is probably Automake's greatest strength—the description is about as simple as it could possibly be, yet the final product is a 'Makefile' with an array of convenient make targets.

The 'configure.in' is a template of macro invocations and shell code fragments used by autoconf to produce a 'configure' script (see Appendix C, "Generated File Dependencies"). autoconf copies the contents of 'configure.in' to 'configure', expanding macros as they occur in the input. Other text is copied verbatim.

Let's take a look at the contents of the user-provided input files relevant to this minimal project. Here is the 'Makefile.am':

```
bin_PROGRAMS = foonly
foonly_SOURCES = main.c foo.c foo.h nly.c scanner.l parser.y
foonly_LDADD = @LEXLIB@
```

This 'Makefile.am' specifies that we want a program called 'foonly' to be built and installed in the 'bin' directory when make install is run. The source files used to build 'foonly' are the C source files 'NLY.C', 'main.c', 'foo.c', and 'foo.h'; the lex program 'scanner.l'; and a yacc grammar in 'parser.y'. This points out a particularly nice aspect about Automake: Because lex and yacc both generate intermediate C programs from their input files, Automake knows how to build such intermediate files and link them into the final executable. Finally, we must remember to link a suitable lex library, if 'configure' concludes that one is needed.

And here is the 'configure.in':

```
dnl Process this file with autoconf to produce a configure script.
AC_INIT(main.c)
AM_INIT_AUTOMAKE(foonly, 1.0)
AC_PROG_CC
AM_PROG_LEX
AC_PROG_YACC
AC_OUTPUT(Makefile)
```

This 'configure.in' invokes some mandatory Autoconf and Automake initialization macros, and then calls on some Autoconf macros from the AC_PROG family to find suitable C compiler, lex, and yacc programs. Finally, the AC_OUTPUT macro is used to cause the generated 'configure' script to output a 'Makefile'—but from what? It is processed from 'Makefile.in', which Automake produces for you based on your 'Makefile.am' (see Appendix C).

4.2 Generated Output Files

By studying the diagram in Appendix C, you can see which commands must be run to generate the required output files from the input files shown in the preceding section.

First, we generate `'configure'`:

```
$ aclocal
$ autoconf
```

Because `'configure.in'` contains macro invocations that are not known to Autoconf itself—AM_INIT_AUTOMAKE being a case in point—it is necessary to collect all the macro definitions for Autoconf to use when generating `'configure'`. This is done using the aclocal program, so called because it generates `'aclocal.m4'` (see Appendix C). If you were to examine the contents of `'aclocal.m4'`, you would find the definition of the AM_INIT_AUTOMAKE macro contained within.

After running autoconf, you will find a `'configure'` script in the current directory. It is important to run aclocal first, because automake relies on the contents of `'configure.in'` and `'aclocal.m4'`. Now on to automake:

```
$ automake --add-missing
automake: configure.in: installing ./install-sh
automake: configure.in: installing ./mkinstalldirs
automake: configure.in: installing ./missing
automake: Makefile.am: installing ./INSTALL
automake: Makefile.am: required file ./NEWS not found
automake: Makefile.am: required file ./README not found
automake: Makefile.am: installing ./COPYING
automake: Makefile.am: required file ./AUTHORS not found
automake: Makefile.am: required file ./ChangeLog not found
```

The `'--add-missing'` option copies some boilerplate files from your Automake installation into the current directory. Files such as `'COPYING'`, which contain the GNU General Public License, change infrequently, and so can be generated without user intervention. A number of utility scripts are also installed—these are used by the generated `'Makefile'`'s, particularly by the install target. Notice that some required files are still missing. These are as follows:

`'NEWS'`	The `'NEWS'` file is a record of user-visible changes to a package. The format is not strict, but the changes to the most recent version should appear at the top of the file.
`'README'`	A `'README'` file is the first place a user will look to get an overview for the purpose of a package, and perhaps special installation instructions.
`'AUTHORS'`	The `'AUTHORS'` file lists the names, and usually mail addresses, of individuals who worked on the package.

continues ▶

▶ *continued*

'ChangeLog'

The 'ChangeLog' is an important file—it records the changes made to a package. The format of this file is quite strict (see Section 4.5, "Documentation and ChangeLogs").

For now, we will do enough to placate Automake:

```
$ touch NEWS README AUTHORS ChangeLog
$ automake --add-missing
```

Automake has now produced a 'Makefile.in'. At this point, you may want to take a snapshot of this directory before we really let loose with automatically generated files.

By now, the contents of the directory are looking fairly complete and reminiscent of the top-level directory of a GNU package you may have installed in the past:

```
AUTHORS     INSTALL      NEWS        install-sh    mkinstalldirs
COPYING     Makefile.am  README      configure     missing
ChangeLog   Makefile.in  aclocal.m4  configure.in
```

It should now be possible to package up your tree in a tar file and give it to other users for them to install on their own systems. One of the make targets that Automake generates in 'Makefile.in' makes it easy to generate distributions (see Chapter 12, "Rolling Distribution Tarballs"). A user would merely have to unpack the tar file, run configure (see Chapter 2, "How to Run Configure, and The Most Useful Standard Makefile Targets"), and finally type make all:

```
$ ./configure
creating cache ./config.cache
checking for a BSD compatible install... /usr/bin/install -c
checking whether build environment is sane... yes
checking whether make sets $@{MAKE@}... yes
checking for working aclocal... found
checking for working autoconf... found
checking for working automake... found
checking for working autoheader... found
checking for working makeinfo... found
checking for gcc... gcc
checking whether the C compiler (gcc  ) works... yes
checking whether the C compiler (gcc  ) is a cross-compiler... no
checking whether we are using GNU C... yes
checking whether gcc accepts -g... yes
checking how to run the C preprocessor... gcc -E
checking for flex... flex
checking for flex... (cached) flex
checking for yywrap in -lfl... yes
```

```
checking lex output file root... lex.yy
checking whether yytext is a pointer... yes
checking for bison... bison -y
updating cache ./config.cache
creating ./config.status
creating Makefile

$ make all
gcc -DPACKAGE=\"foonly\" -DVERSION=\"1.0\" -DYYTEXT_POINTER=1  -I. -I. \
  -g -O2 -c main.c
gcc -DPACKAGE=\"foonly\" -DVERSION=\"1.0\" -DYYTEXT_POINTER=1  -I. -I. \
  -g -O2 -c foo.c
flex   scanner.l && mv lex.yy.c scanner.c
gcc -DPACKAGE=\"foonly\" -DVERSION=\"1.0\" -DYYTEXT_POINTER=1  -I. -I. \
  -g -O2 -c scanner.c
bison -y   parser.y && mv y.tab.c parser.c
if test -f y.tab.h; then \
  if cmp -s y.tab.h parser.h; then rm -f y.tab.h; \
  else mv y.tab.h parser.h; fi; \
else :; fi
gcc -DPACKAGE=\"foonly\" -DVERSION=\"1.0\" -DYYTEXT_POINTER=1  -I. -I. \
  -g -O2 -c parser.c
gcc  -g -O2  -o foonly  main.o foo.o scanner.o parser.o -lfl
```

4.3 Maintaining Input Files

If you edit any of the GNU Autotools input files in your package, you must regenerate the machine-generated files for these changes to take effect. If you add a new source file to the foonly_SOURCES variable in 'Makefile.am', for instance, you must regenerate the derived file 'Makefile.in'. If you are building your package, you need to rerun configure to regenerate the site-specific 'Makefile', and then rerun make to compile the new source file and link it into 'foonly'.

It is possible to regenerate these files by running the required tools, one at a time. As you can see from the preceding discussion, it can be difficult to compute the dependencies—does a particular change require aclocal to be run? Does a particular change require autoconf to be run? There are two solutions to this problem.

The first solution is to use the autoreconf command. This tool regenerates all derived files by rerunning all the necessary tools in the correct order. It is some-what of a brute-force solution, but it works very well, particularly if you are not trying to accommodate other maintainers, or regular maintenance that would render this command bothersome.

The alternative is Automake's 'maintainer mode'. By invoking the AM_MAINTAINER_MODE macro from 'configure.in', Automake activates an '--enable-maintainer-mode' option in 'configure'. Chapter 8, "Bootstrapping," explains this at length.

4.4 Packaging Generated Files

What to do with generated files is keenly contested on the relevant Internet mailing lists. There are two points of view, and this section presents both of them so that you can try to determine the best policy for your project.

One argument is that generated files should not be included with a package, but rather only the "preferred form" of the source code should be included. By this definition, 'configure' is a derived file, just like an object file, and it should not be included in the package. Therefore, the user should use the GNU Autotools to bootstrap themselves prior to building the package. I believe there is some merit to this purist approach, because it discourages the practice of packaging derived files.

The other argument is that the advantages of providing these files can far outweigh the violation of good software-engineering practice already mentioned. By including the generated files, users have the convenience of not needing to be concerned with keeping up-to-date with all the different versions of the tools in active use. This is especially true for Autoconf, because 'configure' scripts are often generated by maintainers using locally modified versions of autoconf and locally installed macros. If the user were to regenerate 'configure', the result could be different to that intended. Of course, this is poor practice, but it does happen in real life.

I think the answer is to include generated files in the package when the package is going to be distributed to a wide user community (that is, the general public). For in-house packages, the former argument might make more sense, because the tools may also be held under version control.

4.5 Documentation and ChangeLogs

As with any software project, it is important to maintain documentation as the project evolves. The documentation must reflect the current state of the software, but it must also accurately record the changes that have been made in the past. The GNU coding standard rigorously enforces the maintenance of documentation. Automake, in fact, implements some of the standard by checking for the presence of a 'ChangeLog' file when automake is run!

A number of files exist, with standardized filenames, for storing documentation in GNU packages. The complete GNU coding standard, which offers some useful insights, can be found at http://www.gnu.org/prep/standards.html.

Other projects, including in-house projects, can use these same tried-and-true techniques. The purpose of most of the standard documentation files was outlined earlier (see Section 4.2, "Generated Output Files"), but the 'ChangeLog' deserves additional treatment.

When recording changes in a 'ChangeLog', one entry is made per person, per day. Logical changes are grouped together, whereas logically distinct changes (that is, "change sets") are separated by a single blank line. Here is an example from Automake's own 'ChangeLog':

```
1999-11-21  Tom Tromey  <tromey@cygnus.com>

        * automake.in (finish_languages): Only generate suffix rule
        when not doing dependency tracking.

        * m4/init.m4 (AM_INIT_AUTOMAKE): Use AM_MISSING_INSTALL_SH.
        * m4/missing.m4 (AM_MISSING_INSTALL_SH): New macro.

        * depend2.am: Use @SOURCE@, @OBJ@, @LTOBJ@, @OBJOBJ@,
        and @BASE@.  Always use -o.
```

Another important point to make about 'ChangeLog' entries is that they should be brief. It is not necessary for an entry to explain in detail *why* a change was made but rather *what* the change was. If a change is not straightforward, the explanation of *why* belongs in the source code itself. The GNU coding standard offers the complete set of guidelines for keeping 'ChangeLog's. Although any text editor can be used to create ChangeLog entries, Emacs provides a major mode to help you write them.

5

Writing a Portable 'configure.in'

Writing a portable 'configure.in' is a tricky business. Because you can put arbitrary shell code into 'configure.in', your options seem overwhelming. The first-time Autoconf user asks many questions: What constructs are portable and what constructs aren't portable? How do I decide what to check for? What shouldn't I check for? How do I best use Autoconf's features? What shouldn't I put in 'configure.in'? In what order should I run my checks? When should I look at the name of the system instead of checking for specific features?

5.1 What Is Portability?

Before we talk about the mechanics of deciding what to check for and how to check for it, let's ask ourselves a simple question: What is portability? Portability is a quality of the code that enables it to be built and run on a variety of platforms. In the Autoconf context, portability usually refers to the capability to run on Unix-like systems—sometimes including Windows.

When I first started using Autoconf, I had a hard time deciding what to check for in my 'configure.in'. At the time, I was maintaining a proprietary program that ran only on SunOS 4. However, I was interested in porting it to Solaris, OSF/1, and possibly Irix.

The approach I took, while workable, was relatively time-consuming and painful: I wrote a minimal 'configure.in' and then proceeded to just try to build my program on Solaris. Each time I encountered a build problem, I updated 'configure.in' and my source and started again. After it had built correctly, I started testing to see whether there were runtime problems related to portability.

Because I didn't start with a relatively portable base, and because I was unaware of the tools available to help with adding Autoconf support to a package (see Chapter 23, "Migrating an Existing Package to GNU Autotools"), it was much more difficult than it had to be. If at all possible, it is better to write portable code to begin with.

A large number of Unix-like systems exist in the world, including many systems that, although still running, can only be considered obsolete. Although it is probably possible to port some programs to all such systems, typically it is not useful to even try. Porting to everything is a difficult process, especially given that it usually is not possible to test on all platforms, and that new operating systems, with their own bugs and idiosyncrasies, are released every year.

We advocate a pragmatic approach to portability: We write our programs to target a fairly large, but also fairly modern, cross-section of Unix-like systems. As deficiencies are discovered in our portability framework, we update `configure.in` and our sources, and move on. In practice, this is an effective approach.

5.2 Brief Introduction to Portable *sh*

If you read a number of `configure.in`'s, you will quickly notice that they tend to be written in an unusual style. You will notice, for instance, that you hardly ever see the `[` program used; instead you will see `test` invoked. We won't go into all the details of writing a portable shell script here; instead, we leave that for Chapter 21, "Writing Portable Bourne Shell."

Like other aspects of portability, the approach you take to writing shell scripts in `configure.in` and `Makefile.am` should depend on your goals. Some platforms have notoriously broken sh implementations. For instance, Ultrix sh doesn't implement unset. Of course, the GNU Autotools are written in the most portable style possible, so as not to limit your possibilities.

Also, it does not really make sense to talk about portable sh programming in the abstract. sh by itself does very little; most actual work is done by separate programs, each with its own potential portability problems. Some options are not portable between systems, for instance, and some seemingly common programs do not exist on every system—so not only do you have to know which sh constructs are not portable, but you also must know which programs you can (and cannot) use, and which options to those programs are portable.

This seems daunting, but in practice it doesn't seem to be too hard to write portable shell scripts—after you have internalized the rules. Unfortunately, this process can take a long time. Meanwhile, a pragmatic "try-and-see" approach, while noting other portable code you have seen elsewhere, works fairly well. Once again, it pays to be aware of which architectures you will probably care about; you will make different choices if you are writing an extremely portable program such as emacs or gcc than if you are writing something that will run only on various flavors of Linux. Also, the cost of having unportable code in 'configure.in' is relatively low. In general, it is fairly easy to rewrite pieces on demand as unportable constructs are found.

5.3 Ordering Tests

In addition to the problem of writing portable sh code, another problem confronts first-time 'configure.in' writers: determining the order in which to run the various tests. Autoconf indirectly (via the autoscan program covered in Chapter 23) suggests a standard ordering, as described here.

The standard ordering is as follows:

1. **Boilerplate.** This section should include standard boilerplate code, such as the call to AC_INIT (which must be first), AM_INIT_AUTOMAKE, AC_CONFIG_HEADER, and perhaps AC_REVISION.

2. **Options.** The next section should include macros that add command-line options to configure, such as AC_ARG_ENABLE. It is typical to put support code for the option in this section as well, if it is short enough, like this example from libgcj:

```
AC_ARG_ENABLE(getenv-properties,
[  -disable-getenv-properties
                        don't set system properties from GCJ_PROPERTIES])

dnl Whether GCJ_PROPERTIES is used depends on the target.
if test -n "$enable_getenv_properties"; then
   enable_getenv_properties=${enable_getenv_properties_default-yes}
fi
if test "$enable_getenv_properties" = no; then
   AC_DEFINE(DISABLE_GETENV_PROPERTIES)
fi
```

3. **Programs.** Next it is traditional to check for programs that are either needed by the configure process, the build process, or by one of the programs being built. This usually involves calls to macros such as AC_CHECK_PROG and AC_PATH_TOOL.

4. **Libraries.** Checks for libraries come before checks for other objects visible to C (or C++, or anything else). This is necessary because some other checks work by trying to link or run a program; by checking for libraries first, you ensure that the resulting programs can be linked.

5. **Headers.** Next come checks for the existence of headers.

6. **Typedefs and structures.** We do checks for typedefs after checking for headers for the simple reason that typedefs appear in headers, and we need to know which headers we can use before we look inside them.

7. **Functions.** Finally we check for functions. These come last because functions have dependencies on the preceding items: When searching for functions, libraries are needed to correctly link; headers are needed to find prototypes (this is especially important for C++, which has stricter prototyping rules than C); and typedefs are needed for those functions that use or return types not built in.

8. **Output.** This is done by invoking `AC_OUTPUT`.

This ordering should be considered a rough guideline, and not a list of hard-and-fast rules. Sometimes it is necessary to interleave tests, either to make `'configure.in'` easier to maintain, or because the tests themselves do need to be in a different order. If your project uses both C and C++, for instance, you might choose to perform all the C++ checks after all the C checks have been performed, to make `'configure.in'` a bit easier to read.

5.4 What to Check For

Deciding what to check for is really the central part of writing `'configure.in'`. After you have read the Autoconf reference manual, the "how"s of writing a particular test should be fairly clear. The "when"s might remain a mystery—and it is just as easy to check for too many things as it is to check for too few.

One notable area of divergence between various Unix-like systems is that the same programs don't exist on all systems, and, even when they do, they don't always work in the same way. For these problems, we recommend, when possible, following the advice of the GNU coding standards: Use the most common options from a relatively limited set of programs. Failing that, try to stick to programs and options specified by POSIX, perhaps augmenting this approach by doing checks for known problems on platforms you care about.

Checking for tools and their differences is usually a fairly small part of a `'configure'` script; more common are checks for functions, libraries, and the like.

Except for a few core libraries such as `'libc'` and, usually, `'libm'` and libraries such as `'libX11'`, which typically aren't considered system libraries, there is not much agreement about library names or contents between Unix systems. Still, libraries are easy to handle, because decisions about libraries almost always affect only the various `'Makefile'`s. That means that checking for another library typically doesn't require major (or even, sometimes, any) changes to the source code. Also, because adding a new library test has a small impact on the development cycle—effectively just rerunning `'configure'` and then a relink—you can effectively adopt a lax approach to libraries. You can just make things work on the few systems you immediately care about, for instance, and then handle library changes on an as-needed basis.

Suppose you do end up with a link problem. How do you handle it? The first thing to do is use nm to look through the system libraries to see whether the missing function exists. If it does, and it is in a library you can use, the solution is easy: Just add another AC_CHECK_LIB. Note that just finding the function in a library is not enough, because on some systems, some "standard" libraries are undesirable; 'libucb' is the most common example of a library that you should avoid.

If you can't find the function in a system library, you have a somewhat more difficult problem: a non-portable function. There are basically three approaches to a missing function. This chapter discusses functions, but really these same approaches apply, more or less, to typedefs, structures, and global variables.

The first approach is to write a replacement function and either conditionally compile it, or put it into an appropriately named file and use AC_REPLACE_FUNCS. For instance, Tcl uses AC_REPLACE_FUNCS(strstr) to handle systems that have no strstr function.

The second approach is used when there is a similar function with a different name. The idea here is to check for all the alternatives and then modify your source to use whichever one might exist. The idiom here is to use break in the second argument to AC_CHECK_FUNCS; this is used both to skip unnecessary tests and to indicate to the reader that these checks are related. For instance, here is how libgcj checks for inet_aton or inet_addr; it uses only the first one found:

```
AC_CHECK_FUNCS(inet_aton inet_addr, break)
```

Code to use the results of these checks looks something like this:

```
#if HAVE_INET_ATON
   ... use inet_aton here
#else
#if HAVE_INET_ADDR
   ... use inet_addr here
#else
#error Function missing!
#endif
#endif
```

Note how we have made it a compile-time error if the function does not exist. In general, it is best to make errors occur as early as possible in the build process.

The third approach to nonportable functions is to write code such that these functions are only optionally used. If you are writing an editor, for example, you might decide to use `mmap` to map a file into the editor's memory. Because `mmap` is not portable, however, you would also write a function to use the more portable `read`.

Handling known nonportable functions is only part of the problem, however. The pragmatic approach works fairly well, but it is somewhat inefficient if you are primarily developing on a more modern system, such as GNU/Linux, that has few functions missing. In this case, the problem is that you might not notice nonportable constructs in your code until it has largely been finished.

Unfortunately, there's no high road to solving this problem. In the end, you need to have a working knowledge of the range of existing Unix systems. Knowledge of standards such as POSIX and XPG can be useful here, as a first cut—if it isn't in POSIX, you should at least consider checking for it. Standards are not a panacea, however; not all systems are POSIX-compliant, and sometimes there are bugs in systems functions that you must work around.

One final class of problems you might encounter is that it is also easy to check for too much. This is bad because it adds an unnecessary maintenance burden to your program. For instance, sometimes you'll see code that checks for `<sys/types.h>`. However, there is no point in doing that—using this header is mostly portable. Again, this can be addressed only by having a practical knowledge, which is really possible only by examining your target systems.

5.5 Using Configuration Names

Although feature tests are definitely the best approach, a `'configure'` script may occasionally have to make a decision based on a configuration name. This may be necessary if certain code must be compiled differently based on something that cannot be tested using a standard Autoconf feature test. For instance, the `expect` package needs to find information about the system's `'tty'` implementation; this can't reliably be done when cross-compiling without examining the particular configuration name.

It is normally better to test for particular features rather than to test for a particular system type. This is because as Unix and other operating systems evolve, different systems copy features from one another.

When there is no alternative to testing the configuration name in a `'configure'` script, it is best to define a macro that describes the feature instead of defining a macro that describes the particular system. This permits the same macro to be used on other systems which adopt the same feature (see Chapter 22, "Writing New Macros for Autoconf").

Testing for a particular system is normally done using a case statement in the Autoconf 'configure.in' file. The case statement might look something like the following, assuming that 'host' is a shell variable holding a canonical configuration system—which will be the case if 'configure.in' uses the 'AC_CANONICAL_HOST' or 'AC_CANONICAL_SYSTEM' macros:

```
case "${host}" in
i[[3456]]86-*-linux-gnu*) do something ;;
sparc*-sun-solaris2.[[56789]]*) do something ;;
sparc*-sun-solaris*) do something ;;
mips*-*-elf*) do something ;;
esac
```

Note the doubled square brackets in this piece of code. These are used to work around an ugly implementation detail of autoconf; it uses M4 under the hood. Without these extra brackets, the square brackets in the case statement would be swallowed by M4, and would not appear in the resulting 'configure'. Chapter 20, "GNU M4," discusses this nasty detail at more length.

It is particularly important to use '*' after the operating system field to match the version number that will be generated by 'config.guess'. In most cases, you must be careful to match a range of processor types. For most processor families, a trailing '*' suffices, as in 'mips*'. For the i386 family, something along the lines of 'i[34567]86' suffices at present. For the m68k family, you need something like 'm68*'. Of course, if you do not need to match on the processor, it is simpler to just replace the entire field by a '*', as in '*-*-irix*'.

6
Introducing GNU Automake

The primary goal of Automake is to generate 'Makefile.in's compliant with the GNU Makefile standards. Along the way, it tries to remove boilerplate and drudgery. It also helps the 'Makefile' writer by implementing features that most maintainers don't have the patience to implement by hand (for instance, automatic dependency tracking and parallel make support). It also implements some best practices as well as workarounds for vendor make bugs—both of which require arcane knowledge not generally available.

A secondary goal for Automake is that it work well with other free software, and, specifically, GNU tools. For example, Automake has support for DejaGNU-based test suites.

Chances are that you don't care about the GNU coding standards. That's okay. You will still appreciate the convenience that Automake provides, and you will find that the GNU standards-compliance feature, for the most part, assists rather than impedes.

Automake helps the maintainer with five large tasks, and countless minor ones. The basic functional areas are as follows:

- Build
- Check
- Clean
- Install and uninstall
- Distribution

This chapter covers the first three items; the others are covered in later chapters. Before we get into the details, let's talk a bit about some general principles of Automake.

6.1 General Automake Principles

Automake at its simplest turns a file called `'Makefile.am'` into a GNU-compliant `'Makefile.in'` for use with `'configure'`. Each `'Makefile.am'` is written according to `make` syntax; Automake recognizes special macro and target names and generates code based on these.

A few Automake rules differ slightly from `make` rules:

- Ordinary `make` comments are passed through to the output, but comments beginning with `'##'` are Automake comments and are not passed through.

- Automake supports `include` directives. These directives are not passed through to the `'Makefile.in'`, but instead are processed by `automake`—files included this way are treated as if they were textually included in `'Makefile.am'` at that point. This can be used to add boilerplate to each `'Makefile.am'` in a project via a centrally maintained file. The filename to include can start with `'$(top_srcdir)'` to indicate that it should be found relative to the topmost directory of the project; if it is a relative path or if it starts with `'$(srcdir)'`, it is relative to the current directory. Here is how you would reference boilerplate code from the file `'config/Make-rules'`, for example, where `'config'` is a top-level directory in the project:

    ```
    include $(top_srcdir)/config/Make-rules
    ```

- Automake supports conditionals, which are not passed directly through to `'Makefile.in'`. This feature is discussed in Chapter 18, "Advanced GNU Automake Usage."

- Automake supports macro assignment using `'+='`; these assignments are translated by Automake into ordinary `'='` assignments in `'Makefile.in'`.

All macros and targets, including those that Automake does not recognize, are passed through to the generated `'Makefile.in'`—this is a powerful extension mechanism. Sometimes Automake defines macros or targets internally. If these are also defined in `'Makefile.am'`, the definition in `'Makefile.am'` takes precedence. This feature provides an easy way to tailor specific parts of the output in small ways.

> ### Warning
>
> *Note, however, that it is a mistake to override parts of the generated code that are not documented (and therefore "exported" by Automake). Overrides like this stand a good chance of not working with future Automake releases.* ◆

Automake also scans 'configure.in'. Sometimes it uses the information it discovers to generate extra code, and sometimes to provide extra error checking. Automake also turns every AC_SUBST into a 'Makefile' variable. This is convenient in more ways than one: Not only does it mean that you can refer to these macros in 'Makefile.am' without extra work, but, because Automake scans 'configure.in' before it reads any 'Makefile.am', it also means that special variables and overrides Automake recognizes can be defined once in 'configure.in'.

6.2 Frequently Asked Questions

Experience has shown that there are several common questions that arise as people begin to use Automake for their own projects. It seems prudent to mention these issues here.

Users often want to make a library (or program, but for some reason it comes up more frequently with libraries) whose sources live in subdirectories:

```
lib_LIBRARIES = libsub.a
libsub_a_SOURCES = subdir1/something.c ...
```

If you try this with Automake 1.4, you'll get an error:

```
$ automake
automake: Makefile.am: not supported: source file 'subdir1/something.c' is in subdirectory
```

For libraries, this problem is mostly simply solved by using libtool convenience libraries. For programs, there is no simple solution. Many people elect to restructure their package in this case. The next major release of Automake addresses this problem.

Another general problem that comes up is that of setting compilation flags. Most rules have flags—for instance, compilation of C code automatically uses CFLAGS. However, these variables are considered user variables. Setting them in Makefile.am is unsafe, because the user will expect to be able to override them at will.

To handle this, for each flag variable, Automake introduces an AM_ version which can be set in Makefile.am. For instance, we could set some flags for C and C++ compilation like so:

```
AM_CFLAGS = -DFOR_C
AM_CXXFLAGS = -DFOR_CXX
```

Finally, people often ask how to compile a single source file in two different ways. For instance, the etags.c file which comes with Emacs can be compiled with different -D options to produce the etags and ctags programs.

With Automake 1.4, this can only be done by writing your own compilation rules, like this:

```
bin_PROGRAMS = etags ctags
etags_SOURCES = etags.c
ctags_LDADD = ctags.o

etags.o: etags.c
        $(CC) $(CFLAGS) -DETAGS ...

ctags.o: etags.c
        $(CC) $(CFLAGS) -DCTAGS ...
```

This is tedious and hard to maintain for larger programs. Automake 1.5 will support a much more natural approach:

```
bin_PROGRAMS = etags ctags
etags_SOURCES = etags.c
etags_CFLAGS = -DETAGS
ctags_SOURCES = etags.c
ctags_CFLAGS = -DCTAGS
```

6.3 Introduction to Primaries

Each type of object that Automake understands has a special root variable name associated with it. This root is called a *primary*. Many actual variable names put into 'Makefile.am' are constructed by adding various prefixes to a primary.

For instance, scripts—interpreted executable programs—are associated with the SCRIPTS primary. Here is how you would list scripts to be installed in the user's 'bindir':

```
bin_SCRIPTS = magic-script
```

(The mysterious 'bin_' prefix is discussed later.)

The contents of a primary-derived variable are treated as targets in the resulting 'Makefile'. For instance, in the preceding example, we could generate 'magic-script' using sed by just introducing it as a target:

```
bin_SCRIPTS = magic-script
magic-script: magic-script.in
    sed -e 's/whatever//' < $(srcdir)/magic-script.in > magic-script
    chmod +x magic-script
```

6.4 The Easy Primaries

This section describes the common primaries that are relatively easy to understand; the next section discusses the more complicated ones.

DATA

This is the easiest primary to understand. A macro of this type lists a number of files that are installed verbatim. These files can appear either in the source directory or the build directory.

HEADERS

Macros of this type list header files. These are separate from DATA macros because this allows for extra error checking in some cases.

SCRIPTS

This is used for executable scripts (interpreted programs). These differ from DATA because they are installed with different permissions and because they have the program name transform applied to them (for example, the '--program-transform-name' argument to configure). Scripts also differ from compiled programs because the latter can be stripped whereas scripts cannot.

MANS

This lists man pages. Installing man pages is more complicated than you might think due to the lack of a single common practice. One developer might name a man page in the source tree 'foo.man', and then rename to the real name 'foo.1' at install time. Another developer might instead use numeric suffixes in the source tree and install using the same name. Sometimes an alphabetic code follows the numeric suffix (for example, 'quux.3n'); this code must be stripped before determining the correct install directory. (This file must still be installed in '$(man3dir)'.) Automake supports all of these modes of operation:

man_MANS can be used when numeric suffixes are already in place:

```
man_MANS = foo.1 bar.2 quux.3n
```

man1_MANS, man2_MANS, and so on can be used to force renaming at install time. This renaming is skipped if the suffix already begins with the correct number. For instance:

```
man1_MANS = foo.man
man3_MANS = quux.3n
```

Here 'foo.man' will be installed as 'foo.1', but 'quux.3n' will keep its name at install time.

TEXINFOS	GNU programs traditionally use the Texinfo documentation format, not man pages. Automake has full support for Texinfo, including some additional features such as versioning and install-info support. This discussion does not go into that here except to mention that it exists. See the Automake Reference Manual for more information.

Automake supports a variety of lesser-used primaries such as JAVA and LISP (and, in the next major release, PYTHON). See the reference manual for more information on these.

6.5 Programs and Libraries

The preceding primaries have all been relatively easy to use. Now the discussion turns to a more complicated set, namely those used to build programs and libraries. These primaries are more complex because building a program is more complex than building a script (which often doesn't even need building at all).

Use the PROGRAMS primary for programs, LIBRARIES for libraries, and LTLIBRARIES for Libtool libraries (see Chapter 9, "Introducing GNU Libtool"). Here is a minimal example:

```
bin_PROGRAMS = doit
```

This creates the program doit and arranges to install it in bindir. First make compiles 'doit.c' to produce 'doit.o'. Then it links 'doit.o' to create 'doit'.

Of course, if you have more than one source file, and most programs do, you will want to be able to list them somehow. You can do this via the program's SOURCES variable. Each program or library has a set of associated variables whose names are constructed by appending suffixes to the "normalized" name of the program. The *normalized name* is the name of the object with non-alphanumeric characters changed to underscores. The normalized name of 'quux' is 'quux', for instance, but the normalized name of 'install-info' is 'install_info'. Normalized names are used because they correspond to make syntax, and, like all macros, Automake propagates these definitions into the resulting 'Makefile.in'.

Therefore, if 'doit' is to be built from files 'main.c' and 'doit.c', you write the following:

```
bin_PROGRAMS = doit
doit_SOURCES = doit.c main.c
```

The same holds for libraries. In the zlib package, you might make a library called 'libzlib.a', and then write the following:

```
lib_LIBRARIES = libzlib.a
libzlib_a_SOURCES = adler32.c compress.c crc32.c deflate.c deflate.h \
gzio.c infblock.c infblock.h infcodes.c infcodes.h inffast.c inffast.h \
inffixed.h inflate.c inftrees.c inftrees.h infutil.c infutil.h trees.c \
trees.h uncompr.c zconf.h zlib.h zutil.c zutil.h
```

You can also do this with Libtool libraries. Suppose, for instance, that you want to build 'libzlib.la' instead:

```
lib_LTLIBRARIES = libzlib.la
libzlib_la_SOURCES = adler32.c compress.c crc32.c deflate.c deflate.h \
gzio.c infblock.c infblock.h infcodes.c infcodes.h inffast.c inffast.h \
inffixed.h inflate.c inftrees.c inftrees.h infutil.c infutil.h trees.c \
trees.h uncompr.c zconf.h zlib.h zutil.c zutil.h
```

As you can see, making shared libraries with Automake and Libtool is just as easy as making static libraries.

As the preceding example shows, header files are listed in the SOURCES variable. These are ignored (except by make dist[1]) but can serve to make your 'Makefile.am' a bit clearer (and sometimes shorter, if you are not installing headers).

Warning

Note that you cannot use 'configure' *substitutions in a* SOURCES *variable. Automake needs to know the static list of files that can be compiled into your program. There are still various ways to conditionally compile files (for example, Automake conditionals or the use of the* LDADD *variable).* ♦

The static list of files is also used in some versions of Automake's automatic dependency tracking. The general rule is that each source file that might be compiled should be listed in some SOURCES variable. If the source is conditionally compiled, it can be listed in an EXTRA variable. Suppose, for instance, in this example '@FOO_OBJ@' is conditionally set by 'configure' to 'foo.o' when 'foo.c' should be compiled:

```
bin_PROGRAMS = foo
foo_SOURCES = main.c
foo_LDADD = @FOO_OBJ@
foo_DEPENDENCIES = @FOO_OBJ@
EXTRA_foo_SOURCES = foo.c
```

---

[1] *See Chapter 12, "Rolling Distribution Tarballs."*

In this case, 'EXTRA_foo_SOURCES' is used to list sources conditionally compiled; this tells Automake that they exist even though it cannot deduce their existence automatically.

In the preceding example, note the use of the 'foo_LDADD' macro. This macro is used to list other object files and libraries that should be linked into the foo program. Each program or library has several such associated macros that can be used to customize the link step. The following list describes the most common ones:

_DEPENDENCIES	Extra dependencies added to the program's dependency list. If not specified, this is automatically computed based on the value of the program's '_LDADD' macro.
_LDADD	Extra objects passed to the linker. This is used only by programs and shared libraries.
_LDFLAGS	Flags passed to the linker. This is separate from '_LDADD' to allow '_DEPENDENCIES' to be auto-computed.
_LIBADD	Like '_LDADD', but used for static libraries and not programs.

You are not required to define any of these macros.

6.6 Multiple Directories

So far, we have dealt only with single-directory projects. Automake can also handle projects with many directories. The variable 'SUBDIRS' is used to list the subdirectories that should be built. Here is an example from Automake itself:

```
SUBDIRS = . m4 tests
```

Automake does not need to know the list of subdirectories statically, so there is no 'EXTRA_SUBDIRS' variable. You might think that Automake would use 'SUBDIRS' to see which 'Makefile.am's to scan, but it actually gets this information from 'configure.in'. This means that if you have a subdirectory optionally built, you should still list it unconditionally in your call to AC_OUTPUT, and then arrange for it to be substituted (or not, as appropriate) at configure time.

Subdirectories are always built in the order they appear, but cleaning rules (for example, maintainer-clean) are always run in the reverse order. The reason for this odd reversal is that it is wrong to remove a file before removing all the files that depend on it.

You can put '.' into 'SUBDIRS' to control when the objects in the current directory are built, relative to the objects in the subdirectories. In the preceding example, targets in '.' will be built before subdirectories are built. If '.' does not appear in 'SUBDIRS', it is built following all the subdirectories.

6.7 Testing

Automake also includes simple support for testing your program. The most simple form of this is the 'TESTS' variable. This variable holds a list of tests that are run when the user runs make check. Each test is built (if necessary) and then executed. For each test, make prints a single line indicating whether the test has passed or failed. Failure means exiting with a non-zero status, with the special exception that an exit status of '77'[2] means that the test should be ignored. make check also prints a summary showing the number of passes and fails.

Automake also supports the notion of an *xfail*, which is a test expected to fail. Sometimes this is useful when you want to track a known failure, but you are not prepared to fix it right away. Tests which are expected to fail should be listed in both TESTS and XFAIL_TESTS.

You can use the special prefix 'check' with primaries to indicate that the objects should be built only at make check time. For example, here is how you can build a program that will be used only during the testing process:

```
check_PROGRAMS = test-program
test_program_SOURCES = ...
```

Automake also supports the use of DejaGNU, the GNU test framework. You can enable DejaGNU support by using the 'dejagnu' option:

```
AUTOMAKE_OPTIONS = dejagnu
```

The resulting 'Makefile.in' includes code to invoke the runtest program appropriately.

---

[2] *A number chosen arbitrarily by the Automake developers.*

7

A Small GNU Autotools Project

This chapter introduces a small—but real—worked example, to illustrate some of the features and highlight some of the pitfalls of the GNU Autotools discussed so far. You can download all the source from this book's Web page at www.newriders.com/autoconf. The text is peppered with my own pet ideas, accumulated over several years of working with the GNU Autotools, and you should be able to easily apply these to your own projects. I begin by describing some of the choices and problems I encountered during the early stages of the development of this project. Then by way of illustration of the issues covered, move on to showing you a general infrastructure that I use as the basis for all my own projects, followed by the specifics of the implementation of a portable command-line shell library. This chapter then finishes with a sample shell application that uses that library.

Later, in Chapter 11, "A Large GNU Autotools Project," and in Chapter 19, "A Complex GNU Autotools Project," the example introduced here will be gradually expanded as new features of GNU Autotools are revealed.

7.1 GNU Autotools in Practice

This section details some of the specific problems I encountered when starting this project and is representative of the sorts of things you are likely to want to do in projects of your own, but for which the correct solution may not be immediately evident. You can always refer back to this section for some inspiration if you come across similar situations. I discuss some of the decisions I made about the structure of the project and also the tradeoffs for the other side of the argument—you might find the opposite choice to the one I make here is more relevant for a particular project of yours.

7.1.1 Project Directory Structure

Before starting to write code for any project, you need to decide on the directory structure you will use to organize the code. I like to build each component of a project in its own subdirectory and to keep the configuration sources separate from the source code. The great majority of GNU projects I have seen use a similar method, so adopting it yourself will likely make your project more familiar to your developers by association.

The top-level directory is used for configuration files, such as 'configure' and 'aclocal.m4', and for a few other sundry files ('README' and a copy of the project license, for example).

Any significant libraries will have a subdirectory of their own, containing all the sources and headers for that library along with a 'Makefile.am' and anything else specific to just that library. Libraries that are part of a small like group (a set of pluggable application modules, for example) are kept together in a single directory.

The sources and headers for the project's main application will be stored in yet another subdirectory, traditionally named 'src'. Your developers might expect other conventional directories too: a 'doc' directory for project documentation; and a 'test' directory for the project self-test suite.

To keep the project top-level directory as uncluttered as possible, as I like to do, you can take advantage of Autoconf's 'AC_CONFIG_AUX_DIR' by creating another directory ('config', for example), which will be used to store many of the GNU Autotools intermediate files, such as install-sh. I always store all project-specific Autoconf M4 macros to this same subdirectory.

So, this is what you should start with:

```
$ pwd
~/mypackage
$ ls -F
Makefile.am  config/    configure.in  lib/  test/
README       configure* doc/          src/
```

7.1.2 C Header Files

You should add a small amount of boilerplate to all header files, not least of which is a small amount of code to prevent the contents of the header from being scanned multiple times. This is achieved by enclosing the entire file in a preprocessor conditional that evaluates to false after the first time it has been seen by the preprocessor. Traditionally, the macro used is in all uppercase and named after the installation path without the installation prefix. Imagine a header that will be installed to '/usr/local/include/sys/foo.h', for example.

The preprocessor code would be as follows:

```
#ifndef SYS_FOO_H
#define SYS_FOO_H 1
...
#endif /* !SYS_FOO_H */
```

Apart from comments, the entire content of the rest of this header file must be between these few lines. It is worth mentioning that inside the enclosing `ifndef`, the macro `SYS_FOO_H` must be defined before any other files are `#include`'d. It is a common mistake to not define that macro until the end of the file, but mutual dependency cycles are only stalled if the guard macro is defined before the `#include` that starts that cycle.[1]

If a header is designed to be installed, it must `#include` other installed project headers from the local tree using angle brackets. There are some implications to working like this:

- You must be careful that the names of header file directories in the source tree match the names of the directories in the install tree. When I plan to install the aforementioned `'foo.h'` to `'/usr/local/include/project/foo.h'`, from which it will be included using `'#include <project/foo.h>'`, for the same include line to work in the source tree, I must name the source directory it is installed from `'project'` too, or other headers that use it will not be able to find it until after it has been installed.

- When you come to developing the next version of a project laid out in this way, you must be careful about finding the correct header. Automake takes care of that for you by using `'-I'` options that force the compiler to look for uninstalled headers in the current source directory before searching the system directories for installed headers of the same name.

- You don't have to install all your headers to `'/usr/include'`—you can use subdirectories. And all without having to rewrite the headers at install time.

7.1.3 C++ Compilers

For a C++ program to use a library compiled with a C compiler, any symbols exported from the C library must be declared between `'extern "C" {'` and `'}'`. This code is important, because a C++ compiler *mangles*[2] all variable and

---

[1] *An* `#include` *cycle is the situation where file* `'a.h'` `#include`'s *file* `'b.h'`, *and* `'b.h'` `#include`'s *file* `'a.h'`—*either directly or through some longer chain of* `#includes`.

[2] *For an explanation of name mangling, see Chapter 15, "Writing Portable C++ with GNU Autotools."*

function names, whereas a C compiler does not. On the other hand, a C compiler will not understand these lines, so you must be careful to make them invisible to the C compiler.

Sometimes you will see this method used, written out in long hand in every installed header file, like this:

```
#ifdef __cplusplus
extern "C" {
#endif

...

#ifdef __cplusplus
}
#endif
```

But that is a lot of unnecessary typing if you have a few dozen headers in your project. Also, the additional braces tend to confuse text editors, such as emacs, which do automatic source indentation based on brace characters.

Far better, then, to declare them as macros in a common header file, and use the macros in your headers:

```
#ifdef __cplusplus
#  define BEGIN_C_DECLS extern "C" {
#  define END_C_DECLS   }

#else /* !__cplusplus */

#  define BEGIN_C_DECLS
#  define END_C_DECLS
#endif /* __cplusplus */
```

I have seen several projects that name such macros with a leading underscore—'_BEGIN_C_DECLS'. Any symbol with a leading underscore is reserved for use by the compiler implementation, so you shouldn't name *any* symbols of your own in this way. By way of example, I recently ported the Small language compiler (see http://www.compuphase.com/small.htm) to Unix, and almost all the work was writing a Perl script to rename huge numbers of symbols in the compiler's reserved namespace to something more sensible so that GCC could even parse the sources. Small was originally developed on Windows, and the author had used a lot of symbols with a leading underscore. Although his symbol names didn't clash with his own compiler, in some cases they were the same as symbols used by GCC.

7.1.4 Function Definitions

As a stylistic convention, the return types for all function definitions should be on a separate line. The main reason for this is that it makes it very easy to find the functions in source file, by looking for a single identifier at the start of a line followed by an open parenthesis:

```
$ egrep '^[_a-zA-Z][_a-zA-Z0-9]*[ \t]*\(' error.c
set_program_name (const char *path)
error (int exit_status, const char *mode, const char *message)
sic_warning (const char *message)
sic_error (const char *message)
sic_fatal (const char *message)
```

Some emacs lisp functions and various code analysis tools, such as ansi2knr (see Section 7.1.6, "K&R Compilers"), rely on this formatting convention, too. Even if you don't use those tools yourself, your fellow developers might like to, so it is a good convention to adopt.

7.1.5 Fallback Function Implementations

Due to the huge number of Unix varieties in common use today, many of the C library functions that you take for granted on your preferred development platform are very likely missing from some of the architectures you would like your code to compile on. Fundamentally you can cope with this in two ways:

- Use only the few library calls available everywhere. In reality this is not actually possible because there are two lowest common denominators with mutually exclusive APIs: one rooted in BSD Unix ('bcopy', 'rindex') and the other in SYSV Unix ('memcpy', 'strrchr'). The only way to deal with this is to define one API in terms of the other using the preprocessor. The newer POSIX standard deprecates many of the BSD-originated calls (with exceptions such as the BSD socket API). Even on non-POSIX platforms, there has been so much cross pollination that often both varieties of a given call may be provided; however, you would be wise to write your code using POSIX-endorsed calls, and where they are missing, define them in terms of whatever the host platform provides.

  This approach requires a lot of knowledge about various system libraries and standards documents, and can leave you with reams of preprocessor code to handle the differences between APIs. You also need to perform a lot of checking in 'configure.in' to figure out which calls are available. To allow the rest of your code to use the 'strcpy' call with impunity, for example, you need the following code in 'configure.in':

  ```
  AC_CHECK_FUNCS(strcpy bcopy)
  ```

And the following preprocessor code in a header file that is seen by every source file:

```
#if !HAVE_STRCPY
#  if HAVE_BCOPY
#    define strcpy(dest, src)    bcopy (src, dest, 1 + strlen (src))
#  else /* !HAVE_BCOPY */
      error no strcpy or bcopy
#  endif /* HAVE_BCOPY */
#endif /* HAVE_STRCPY */
```

- Alternatively you can provide your own fallback implementations of function calls you know are missing on some platforms. In practice, you do not need to be as knowledgeable about problematic functions when using this approach. You can look in GNU libiberty (ftp://sourceware.cygnus.com/pub/binutils/) or François Pinard's libit project (distributed from http://www.iro.umontreal.ca/~pinard/libit) to see for which functions other GNU developers have needed to implement fallback code. The libit project is especially useful in this respect because it comprises canonical versions of fallback functions and suitable Autoconf macros assembled from across the entire GNU project. I won't give an example of setting up your package to use this approach, because that is how I have chosen to structure the project described in this chapter.

Rather than writing code to the lowest common denominator of system libraries, I am a strong advocate of the latter school of thought in the majority of cases. As with all things, it pays to take a pragmatic approach; don't be afraid of the middle ground—weigh the options on a case-by-case basis.

7.1.6 K&R Compilers

K&R C is the name now used to describe the original C language specified by Brian Kernighan and Dennis Ritchie (hence, *K&R*). I have yet to see a C compiler that doesn't support code written in the K&R style, yet it has fallen very much into disuse in favor of the newer ANSI C standard. Although it is increasingly common for vendors to *unbundle* their ANSI C compiler, the GCC project[3] is available for all the architectures I have ever used.

There are four differences between the two C standards:

- ANSI C expects full type specification in function prototypes, such as you might supply in a library header file:

  ```
  extern int functionname (const char *parameter1, size_t parameter2);
  ```

---

[3] *GCC must be compilable by K&R compilers so that it can be built and installed in an ANSI compiler free environment.*

The nearest equivalent in K&R style C is a forward declaration, which
enables you to use a function before its corresponding definition:

```
extern int functionname ();
```

As you can imagine, K&R has very bad type safety, and does not
perform any checks that only function arguments of the correct type
are used.

- The function headers of each function definition are written differently.
  Where you might see the following written in ANSI C:

```
int
functionname (const char *parameter1, size_t parameter2)
{
  ...
}
```

K&R expects the parameter type declarations separately, like this:

```
int
functionname (parameter1, parameter2)
     const char *parameter1;
     size_t parameter2;
{
  ...
}
```

- There is no concept of an untyped pointer in K&R C. Where you
  might be used to seeing 'void *' pointers in ANSI code, you are forced
  to overload the meaning of 'char *' for K&R compilers.

- Variadic functions are handled with a different API in K&R C,
  imported with '#include <varargs.h>'. A K&R variadic function definition looks like this:

```
int
functionname (va_alist)
     va_dcl
{
  va_list ap;
  char *arg;

  va_start (ap);
  ...
  arg = va_arg (ap, char *);
  ...
  va_end (ap);

  return arg ? strlen (arg) : 0;
}
```

ANSI C provides a similar API, imported with `'#include <stdarg.h>'`, although it cannot express a variadic function with no named arguments such as the one above. In practice, this isn't a problem because you always need at least one parameter, either to specify the total number of arguments somehow or else to mark the end of the argument list. An ANSI variadic function definition looks like this:

```
int
functionname (char *format, ...)
{
  va_list ap;
  char *arg;

  va_start (ap, format);
  ...
  arg = va_arg (ap, char *);
  ...
  va_end (ap);

  return format ? strlen (format) : 0;
}
```

Except in very rare cases in which you are writing a low-level project (GCC, for example), you probably do not need to worry about K&R compilers too much. However, supporting them can be very easy, and if you are so inclined, can be handled either by employing the ansi2knr program supplied with Automake or by careful use of the preprocessor.

Using ansi2knr in your project is described in some detail in the section "Automatic de-ANSI-fication" in The Automake Manual, but boils down to the following:

1. Add this macro to your `'configure.in'` file:

   ```
   AM_C_PROTOTYPES
   ```

2. Rewrite the contents of `'LIBOBJS'` and/or `'LTLIBOBJS'` in the following fashion:

   ```
   # This is necessary so that .o files in LIBOBJS are also built via
   # the ANSI2KNR-filtering rules.
   Xsed='sed -e 's/^X//''
   LIBOBJS='echo X"$LIBOBJS"|\
     [$Xsed -e 's/\.[^.]* /.\$U&/g;s/\.[^.]*$/.\$U&/']'
   ```

Personally, I dislike this method, because every source file is filtered and rewritten with ANSI function prototypes and declarations converted to K&R style adding a fair overhead in additional files in your build tree, and in compilation time. This would be reasonable were the abstraction sufficient to enable you to forget about K&R entirely, but ansi2knr is a simple program, and does not address any of the other differences between compilers that I raised previously, and it cannot handle macros in your function prototypes of definitions. If you decide to use ansi2knr in your project, you must make the decision before you write any code, and be aware of its limitations as you develop.

For my own projects, I prefer to use a set of preprocessor macros along with a few stylistic conventions so that all the differences between K&R and ANSI compilers are actually addressed, and so that the unfortunate few who have no access to an ANSI compiler (and who cannot use GCC for some reason) needn't suffer the overheads of ansi2knr.

The four differences in style listed at the beginning of this subsection are addressed as follows:

- The function prototype argument lists are declared inside a PARAMS macro invocation so that K&R compilers will still be able to compile the source tree. PARAMS removes ANSI argument lists from function prototypes for K&R compilers. Some developers continue to use __P for this purpose, but strictly speaking, macros starting with '_' (and especially '__') are reserved for the compiler and the system headers, so using PARAMS, as follows, is safer:

```
#if __STDC__
#  ifndef NOPROTOS
#    define PARAMS(args)      args
#  endif
#endif
#ifndef PARAMS
#  define PARAMS(args)        ()
#endif
```

  This macro is then used for all function declarations like this:

```
extern int functionname PARAMS((const char *parameter));
```

- When the PARAMS macro is used for all function declarations, ANSI compilers are given all the type information they require to do full compile-time type checking. The function definitions proper must then be declared in K&R style so that K&R compilers don't choke on ANSI syntax. There is a small amount of overhead in writing code this way, however: The ANSI compile-time type checking can work only in conjunction with K&R function definitions if it first sees an ANSI function prototype. This forces you to develop the good habit of proto-typing *every single* function in your project. Even the static ones.

- The easiest way to work around the lack of void * pointers is to define a new type conditionally set to void * for ANSI compilers, or char * for K&R compilers. You should add the following to a common header file:

```
#if __STDC__
typedef void *void_ptr;
#else /* !__STDC__ */
typedef char *void_ptr;
#endif /* __STDC__ */
```

- The difference between the two variadic function APIs poses a stickier problem, and the solution is ugly. But it *does* work. First you must check for the headers in 'configure.in':

```
AC_CHECK_HEADERS(stdarg.h varargs.h, break)
```

Having done this, add the following code to a common header file:

```
#if HAVE_STDARG_H
#   include <stdarg.h>
#   define VA_START(a, f)    va_start(a, f)
#else
#   if HAVE_VARARGS_H
#     include <varargs.h>
#     define VA_START(a, f)  va_start(a)
#   endif
#endif
#ifndef VA_START
   error no variadic api
#endif
```

You must now supply each variadic function with both a K&R and an ANSI definition, like this:

```
int
#if HAVE_STDARG_H
functionname (const char *format, ...)
#else
functionname (format, va_alist)
     const char *format;
     va_dcl
#endif
{
  va_alist ap;
  char *arg;

  VA_START (ap, format);
  ...
  arg = va_arg (ap, char *);
  ...
  va_end (ap);

  return arg : strlen (arg) ? 0;
}
```

7.2 A Simple Shell Builders Library

An application that most developers try their hand at sooner or later is a Unix shell. There is a lot of functionality common to all traditional command-line shells, which I thought I would push into a portable library to get you over the first hurdle when that moment is upon you. Before elaborating on any of this, I need to name the project. I have called it *Sic*, from the Latin "*so it is*"; because like all good project names, it is somewhat pretentious and it lends itself to the recursive acronym "*Sic is cumulative.*"

The gory detail of the minutia of the source is beyond the scope of this book. To convey a feel for the need for Sic, however, some of the goals that influenced the design follow:

- Sic must be very small so that in addition to being used as the basis for a full-blown shell, it can be linked (unadorned) into an application and used for trivial tasks, such as reading startup configuration.

- It must not be tied to a particular syntax or set of reserved words. If you use it to read your startup configuration, I don't want to force you to use my syntax and commands.

- The boundary between the library ('libsic') and the application must be well defined. Sic will take strings of characters as input, and internally parse and evaluate them according to registered commands and syntax, returning results or diagnostics as appropriate.

- It must be extremely portable—that is what I am trying to illustrate here, after all.

7.2.1 Portability Infrastructure

As I explained in Section 7.1.1, "Project Directory Structure," I will first create the project directories, a top-level directory and a subdirectory to put the library sources into. I want to install the library header files to '/usr/local/include/sic', so the library subdirectory must be named appropriately (see Section 7.1.2, "C Header Files").

I will describe the files I add in this section in more detail than the project-specific sources, because they comprise an infrastructure that I use relatively unchanged for all my GNU Autotools projects. You could keep an archive of these files and use them as a starting point each time you begin a new project of your own.

Error Management

A good place to start with any project design is the error-management facility. In Sic, I will use a simple group of functions to display simple error messages. Here is 'sic/error.h':

```
#ifndef SIC_ERROR_H
#define SIC_ERROR_H 1

#include <sic/common.h>

BEGIN_C_DECLS

extern const char *program_name;
extern void set_program_name (const char *argv0);

extern void sic_warning     (const char *message);
extern void sic_error       (const char *message);
extern void sic_fatal       (const char *message);

END_C_DECLS

#endif /* !SIC_ERROR_H */
```

This header file follows the principles set out in Section 7.1.2, "C Header Files."

I am storing the 'program_name' variable in the library that uses it so that I can be sure that the library will build on architectures that don't allow undefined symbols in libraries (AIX and Windows being the main culprits).

Keeping those preprocessor macro definitions designed to aid code portability together (in a single file) is a good way to maintain the readability of the rest of the code. For this project, I will put that code in 'common.h':

```
#ifndef SIC_COMMON_H
#define SIC_COMMON_H 1

#if HAVE_CONFIG_H
#  include <sic/config.h>
#endif

#include <stdio.h>
#include <sys/types.h>

#if STDC_HEADERS
#  include <stdlib.h>
#  include <string.h>
#elif HAVE_STRINGS_H
#  include <strings.h>
#endif /*STDC_HEADERS*/
```

```
#if HAVE_UNISTD_H
#  include <unistd.h>
#endif

#if HAVE_ERRNO_H
#  include <errno.h>
#endif /*HAVE_ERRNO_H*/
#ifndef errno
/* Some systems #define this! */
extern int errno;
#endif

#endif /* !SIC_COMMON_H */
```

You may recognize some snippets of code from The Autoconf Manual here—in particular the inclusion of the project 'config.h', which will be generated shortly. Notice that I have been careful to conditionally include any headers that are not guaranteed to exist on every architecture. The rule of thumb here is that only 'stdio.h' is ubiquitous (although I have never heard of a machine that has no 'sys/types.h'). You can find more details of some of these in the section "Existing Tests" in The GNU Autoconf Manual.

Here is a little more code from 'common.h':

```
#ifndef EXIT_SUCCESS
#  define EXIT_SUCCESS 0
#  define EXIT_FAILURE 1
#endif
```

The implementation of the error-handling functions goes in 'error.c' and is very straightforward:

```
#if HAVE_CONFIG_H
#  include <sic/config.h>
#endif

#include "common.h"
#include "error.h"

static void error (int exit_status, const char *mode,
                   const char *message);

static void
error (int exit_status, const char *mode, const char *message)
{
  fprintf (stderr, "%s: %s: %s.\n", program_name, mode, message);

  if (exit_status >= 0)
    exit (exit_status);
}
```

```
void
sic_warning (const char *message)
{
  error (-1, "warning", message);
}

void
sic_error (const char *message)
{
  error (-1, "ERROR", message);
}

void
sic_fatal (const char *message)
{
  error (EXIT_FAILURE, "FATAL", message);
}
```

I also need a definition of `program_name`; `set_program_name` copies the filename
component of path into the exported data, program_name. The xstrdup function
just calls strdup, but abort's if there is not enough memory to make the copy:

```
const char *program_name = NULL;

void
set_program_name (const char *path)
{
  if (!program_name)
    program_name = xstrdup (basename (path));
}
```

Memory Management

A useful idiom common to many GNU projects is to wrap the memory-
management functions to localize *out-of-memory handling,* naming them with
an `x` prefix. By doing this, the rest of the project is relieved of having to
remember to check for `NULL` returns from the various memory functions.
These wrappers use the error API to report memory exhaustion and abort the
program. I have placed the implementation code in `xmalloc.c`:

```
#if HAVE_CONFIG_H
#  include <sic/config.h>
#endif

#include "common.h"
#include "error.h"

void *
xmalloc (size_t num)
{
  void *new = malloc (num);
  if (!new)
    sic_fatal ("Memory exhausted");
  return new;
```

```
}

void *
xrealloc (void *p, size_t num)
{
  void *new;

  if (!p)
    return xmalloc (num);

  new = realloc (p, num);
  if (!new)
    sic_fatal ("Memory exhausted");

  return new;
}

void *
xcalloc (size_t num, size_t size)
{
  void *new = xmalloc (num * size);
  bzero (new, num * size);
  return new;
}
```

Notice in the preceding code that xcalloc is implemented in terms of xmalloc, because calloc itself is not available in some older C libraries. Also, the bzero function is actually deprecated in favor of memset in modern C libraries—I'll explain how to take this into account in section 7.2.3, "Beginnings of a 'configure.in'."

Rather than create a separate 'xmalloc.h' file, which would need to be #include'd from almost everywhere else, the logical place to declare these functions is in 'common.h', because the wrappers will be called from most everywhere else in the code:

```
#ifdef __cplusplus
# define BEGIN_C_DECLS          extern "C" {
# define END_C_DECLS            }
#else
# define BEGIN_C_DECLS
# define END_C_DECLS
#endif

#define XCALLOC(type, num)                              \
        ((type *) xcalloc ((num), sizeof(type)))
#define XMALLOC(type, num)                              \
        ((type *) xmalloc ((num) * sizeof(type)))
#define XREALLOC(type, p, num)                          \
        ((type *) xrealloc ((p), (num) * sizeof(type)))
#define XFREE(stale)                            do {    \
        if (stale) { free (stale);  stale = 0; }        \
                                    } while (0)
```

```
BEGIN_C_DECLS

extern void *xcalloc    (size_t num, size_t size);
extern void *xmalloc    (size_t num);
extern void *xrealloc   (void *p, size_t num);
extern char *xstrdup    (const char *string);
extern char *xstrerror  (int errnum);

END_C_DECLS
```

By using the macros defined here, allocating and freeing heap memory is reduced from:

```
char **argv = (char **) xmalloc (sizeof (char *) * 3);
do_stuff (argv);
if (argv)
  free (argv);
```

To the simpler and more readable:

```
char **argv = XMALLOC (char *, 3);
do_stuff (argv);
XFREE (argv);
```

In the same spirit, I have borrowed 'xstrdup.c' and 'xstrerror.c' from project GNU's libiberty (see Section 7.1.5, "Fallback Function Implementations").

Generalized List Data Type
In many C programs, you will see various implementations and re-implementations of lists and stacks, each tied to its own particular project. It is surprisingly simple to write a catchall implementation, as I have done here with a generalized list operation API in 'list.h':

```
#ifndef SIC_LIST_H
#define SIC_LIST_H 1

#include <sic/common.h>

BEGIN_C_DECLS

typedef struct list {
  struct list *next;   /* chain forward pointer*/
  void *userdata;      /* in case you want to use raw Lists */
} List;

extern List *list_new    (void *userdata);
extern List *list_cons   (List *head, List *tail);
extern List *list_tail   (List *head);
extern size_t list_length (List *head);

END_C_DECLS

#endif /* !SIC_LIST_H */
```

The trick is to ensure that any structures you want to chain together have their forward pointer in the first field. Having done that, the generic functions declared above can be used to manipulate any such chain by casting it to List * and back again as necessary.

For example:

```
struct foo {
  struct foo *next;

  char *bar;
  struct baz *qux;
  ...
};

...

struct foo *foo_list = NULL;

  foo_list = (struct foo *) list_cons ((List *) new_foo (),
                                       (List *) foo_list);
...
```

The implementation of the list manipulation functions is in 'list.c':

```
#include "list.h"

List *
list_new (void *userdata)
{
  List *new = XMALLOC (List, 1);

  new->next = NULL;
  new->userdata = userdata;

  return new;
}

List *
list_cons (List *head, List *tail)
{
  head->next = tail;
  return head;
}
```

```
List *
list_tail (List *head)
{
  return head->next;
}

size_t
list_length (List *head)
{
  size_t n;

  for (n = 0; head; ++n)
    head = head->next;

  return n;
}
```

7.2.2 Library Implementation

To set the stage for later chapters that expand on this example, this subsection describes the purpose of the sources that combine to implement the shell library. I do not dissect the code introduced here—you can download the sources from this book's Web page at www.newriders.com/autoconf.

The remaining sources for the library, beyond the support files described in the preceding subsection, are divided into four pairs of files, as discussed in the following sections.

'sic.c' and 'sic.h'

Here are the functions for creating and managing Sic parsers:

```
#ifndef SIC_SIC_H
#define SIC_SIC_H 1

#include <sic/common.h>
#include <sic/error.h>
#include <sic/list.h>
#include <sic/syntax.h>

typedef struct sic {
  char *result;                    /* result string */
  size_t len;                      /* bytes used by result field */
  size_t lim;                      /* bytes allocated to result field */
  struct builtintab *builtins;     /* tables of builtin functions */
  SyntaxTable **syntax;            /* dispatch table for syntax of input */
  List *syntax_init;               /* stack of syntax state initializers */
  List *syntax_finish;             /* stack of syntax state finalizers */
  SicState *state;                 /* state data from syntax extensions */
} Sic;

#endif /* !SIC_SIC_H */
```

This structure has fields to store registered command (builtins) and syntax (syntax) handlers, along with other state information (state) that can be used to share information between various handlers, and some room to build a result or an error string (result).

'builtin.c' and 'builtin.h'

Here are the functions for managing tables of built-in commands in each Sic structure:

```
typedef int (*builtin_handler) (Sic *sic,
                                int argc, char *const argv[]);

typedef struct {
  const char *name;
  builtin_handler func;
  int min, max;
} Builtin;

typedef struct builtintab BuiltinTab;

extern Builtin *builtin_find (Sic *sic, const char *name);
extern int builtin_install   (Sic *sic, Builtin *table);
extern int builtin_remove    (Sic *sic, Builtin *table);
```

'eval.c' and 'eval.h'

Having created a Sic parser and populated it with some Builtin handlers, a user of this library must tokenize and evaluate its input stream. These files define a structure for storing tokenized strings (Tokens) and functions for converting char * strings both to and from this structure type:

```
#ifndef SIC_EVAL_H
#define SIC_EVAL_H 1

#include <sic/common.h>
#include <sic/sic.h>

BEGIN_C_DECLS

typedef struct {
  int   argc;            /* number of elements in ARGV */
  char **argv;           /* array of pointers to elements */
  size_t lim;            /* number of bytes allocated */
} Tokens;

extern int eval       (Sic *sic, Tokens *tokens);
extern int untokenize (Sic *sic, char **pcommand, Tokens *tokens);
extern int tokenize   (Sic *sic, Tokens **ptokens, char **pcommand);

END_C_DECLS

#endif /* !SIC_EVAL_H */
```

These files also define the `eval` function, which examines a `Tokens` structure in the context of the given `Sic` parser, dispatching the `argv` array to a relevant `Builtin` handler, also written by the library user.

'syntax.c' and 'syntax.h'

When `tokenize` splits a `char *` string into parts, by default it breaks the string into words delimited by white space. These files define the interface for changing this default behavior, by registering callback functions that the parser will run when it meets an "interesting" symbol in the input stream. Here are the declarations from `'syntax.h'`:

```
BEGIN_C_DECLS

typedef int SyntaxHandler (struct sic *sic, BufferIn *in,
                           BufferOut *out);

typedef struct syntax {
  SyntaxHandler *handler;
  char *ch;
} Syntax;

extern int syntax_install (struct sic *sic, Syntax *table);
extern SyntaxHandler *syntax_handler (struct sic *sic, int ch);

END_C_DECLS
```

A `'SyntaxHandler'` is a function called by `tokenize` as it consumes its input to create a `Tokens` structure; the two functions associate a table of such handlers with a given `Sic` parser, and find the particular handler for a given character in that `Sic` parser, respectively.

7.2.3 Beginnings of a 'configure.in'

Now that I have some code, I can run `autoscan` to generate a preliminary `'configure.in'`. `autoscan` examines all the sources in the current directory tree looking for common points of non-portability, adding macros suitable for detecting the discovered problems. `autoscan` generates the following in `'configure.scan'`:

```
# Process this file with autoconf to produce a configure script.
AC_INIT(sic/eval.h)

# Checks for programs.

# Checks for libraries.

# Checks for header files.
AC_HEADER_STDC
AC_CHECK_HEADERS(strings.h unistd.h)

# Checks for typedefs, structures, and compiler characteristics.
```

```
AC_C_CONST
AC_TYPE_SIZE_T

# Checks for library functions.
AC_FUNC_VPRINTF
AC_CHECK_FUNCS(strerror)

AC_OUTPUT()
```

> ### *autoscan*
>
> Because the generated 'configure.scan' does not overwrite your project's 'configure.in', it is a good idea to run autoscan periodically even in established project source trees and compare the two files. Sometimes autoscan will find some portability issue you have overlooked, or weren't aware of. ♦

Looking through the documentation for the macros in this 'configure.scan', AC_C_CONST and AC_TYPE_SIZE_T will take care of themselves (provided I ensure that 'config.h' is included into every source file), and AC_HEADER_STDC and AC_CHECK_HEADERS(unistd.h) are already taken care of in 'common.h'.

autoscan is no silver bullet! Even here in this simple example, I need to manually add macros to check for the presence of 'errno.h':

```
AC_CHECK_HEADERS(errno.h strings.h unistd.h)
```

I also need to manually add the Autoconf macro for generating 'config.h', a macro to initialize automake support, and a macro to check for the presence of ranlib. These should go close to the start of 'configure.in':

```
...
AC_CONFIG_HEADER(config.h)
AM_INIT_AUTOMAKE(sic, 0.5)

AC_PROG_CC
AC_PROG_RANLIB
...
```

Recall the use of bzero in the Memory Management subsection, of section 7.2.1, is not entirely portable. The trick is to provide a bzero work-alike, depending on which functions Autoconf detects. Add the following towards the end of configure.in:

```
...
AC_CHECK_FUNCS (bzero memset, break)
...
```

With the addition of this small snippet of code to common.h, I can now make use of bzero even when linking with a C library that has no implementation of its own:

```
#if !HAVE_BZERO && HAVE_MEMESET
# define bzero (buf, bytes)     ((void) memset (buf, 0, bytes))
#endif
```

An interesting macro suggested by autoscan is AC_CHECK_FUNCS(strerror). This tells me that I need to provide a replacement implementation of strerror for the benefit of architectures that do not have it in their system libraries. This is resolved by providing a file with a fallback implementation for the named function and creating a library from it and any others that 'configure' discovers to be lacking from the system library on the target host.

Recall that 'configure' is the shell script the end user of this package will run on his machine to test that it has all the features the package wants to use. The library that is created will allow the rest of the project to be written in the knowledge that any functions required by the project but missing from the installers' system libraries will be available nonetheless. GNU 'libiberty' comes to the rescue again—it already has an implementation of 'strerror.c' that I was able to use with a little modification.

Being able to supply a simple implementation of strerror, as the 'strerror.c' file from 'libiberty' does, relies on there being a well-defined sys_errlist variable. It is a fair bet that if the target host has no strerror implementation, however, that the system sys_errlist will be broken or missing. I need to write a configure macro to check whether the system defines sys_errlist and tailor the code in 'strerror.c' to use this knowledge.

To avoid clutter in the top-level directory, I am a great believer in keeping as many of the configuration files as possible in their own subdirectory. First of all, I will create a new directory called 'config' inside the top-level directory, and put 'sys_errlist.m4' inside it:

```
AC_DEFUN(SIC_VAR_SYS_ERRLIST,
[AC_CACHE_CHECK([for sys_errlist],
sic_cv_var_sys_errlist,
[AC_TRY_LINK([int *p;], [extern int sys_errlist; p = &sys_errlist;],
        sic_cv_var_sys_errlist=yes, sic_cv_var_sys_errlist=no)])
if test x"$sic_cv_var_sys_errlist" = xyes; then
  AC_DEFINE(HAVE_SYS_ERRLIST, 1,
    [Define if your system libraries have a sys_errlist variable.])
fi])
```

I must then add a call to this new macro in the 'configure.in' file, being careful to put it in the right place—somewhere between *typedefs and structures* and *library functions* according to the comments in 'configure.scan':

```
SIC_VAR_SYS_ERRLIST
```

GNU Autotools can also be set to store most of their files in a subdirectory, by calling the AC_CONFIG_AUX_DIR macro near the top of 'configure.in', preferably right after AC_INIT:

```
AC_INIT(sic/eval.c)
AC_CONFIG_AUX_DIR(config)
AM_CONFIG_HEADER(config.h)
...
```

Having made this change, many of the files added by running autoconf and automake --add-missing will be put in the *aux_dir*.

The source tree now looks like this:

```
sic/
  +-- configure.scan
  +-- config/
  |      +-- sys_errlist.m4
  +-- replace/
  |      +-- strerror.c
  +-- sic/
         +-- builtin.c
         +-- builtin.h
         +-- common.h
         +-- error.c
         +-- error.h
         +-- eval.c
         +-- eval.h
         +-- list.c
         +-- list.h
         +-- sic.c
         +-- sic.h
         +-- syntax.c
         +-- syntax.h
         +-- xmalloc.c
         +-- xstrdup.c
         +-- xstrerror.c
```

To correctly utilize the fallback implementation, AC_CHECK_FUNCS(strerror) needs to be removed and strerror added to AC_REPLACE_FUNCS:

```
# Checks for library functions.
AC_REPLACE_FUNCS(strerror)
```

This will be clearer if you look at the 'Makefile.am' for the 'replace' subdirectory:

```
## Makefile.am -- Process this file with automake to produce Makefile.in

INCLUDES           = -I$(top_builddir) -I$(top_srcdir)

noinst_LIBRARIES   = libreplace.a
libreplace_a_SOURCES =
libreplace_a_LIBADD  = @LIBOBJS@
```

The code tells automake that I want to build a library for use within the build tree (that is, not installed—'noinst'), and that has no source files by default. The clever part here is that when someone comes to install Sic, he will run configure, which will test for strerror and add 'strerror.o' to LIBOBJS if the

target host environment is missing its own implementation. Now, when
'configure' creates 'replace/Makefile' (as I asked it to with AC_OUTPUT),
'@LIBOBJS@' is replaced by the list of objects required on the installer's machine.

Having done all this at configure time, when my user runs make, the files
required to replace functions missing from their target machine are added to
'libreplace.a'.

Unfortunately this is not quite enough to start building the project. First I need
to add a top-level 'Makefile.am' from which to ultimately create a top-level
'Makefile' that will descend into the various subdirectories of the project:

```
## Makefile.am -- Process this file with automake to produce Makefile.in

SUBDIRS = replace sic
```

And 'configure.in' must be told where it can find instances of 'Makefile.in':

```
AC_OUTPUT(Makefile replace/Makefile sic/Makefile)
```

I have written a bootstrap script for Sic; for details see Chapter 8,
"Bootstrapping":

```
#! /bin/sh

set -x
aclocal -I config
autoheader
automake --foreign --add-missing --copy
autoconf
```

The '--foreign' option to automake tells it to relax the GNU standards for
various files that should be present in a GNU distribution. Using this option
saves me from having to create empty files as we did in Chapter 4, "Using
GNU Autotools to Manage a 'Minimal Project'."

Right. Let's build the library! First, I run bootstrap:

```
$ ./bootstrap
+ aclocal -I config
+ autoheader

+ automake --foreign --add-missing --copy
automake: configure.in: installing config/install-sh
automake: configure.in: installing config/mkinstalldirs
automake: configure.in: installing config/missing

+ autoconf
```

The project is now in the same state that an end user would see, having
unpacked a distribution tarball. What follows is what an end user might expect
to see when building from that tarball:

```
$ ./configure
creating cache ./config.cache

checking for a BSD compatible install... /usr/bin/install -c
checking whether build environment is sane... yes
checking whether make sets ${MAKE}... yes
checking for working aclocal... found
checking for working autoconf... found
checking for working automake... found
checking for working autoheader... found
checking for working makeinfo... found
checking for gcc... gcc
checking whether the C compiler (gcc  ) works... yes
checking whether the C compiler (gcc  ) is a cross-compiler... no
checking whether we are using GNU C... yes
checking whether gcc accepts -g... yes
checking for ranlib... ranlib
checking how to run the C preprocessor... gcc -E
checking for ANSI C header files... yes
checking for unistd.h... yes
checking for errno.h... yes
checking for string.h... yes
checking for working const... yes
checking for size_t... yes
checking for strerror... yes

updating cache ./config.cache
creating ./config.status
creating Makefile
creating replace/Makefile
creating sic/Makefile
creating config.h
```

Compare this output with the contents of 'configure.in', and notice how each macro is ultimately responsible for one or more consecutive tests (via the Bourne shell code generated in 'configure'). Now that the 'Makefile's have been successfully created, it is safe to call make to perform the actual compilation:

```
$ make
make all-recursive
make[1]: Entering directory `/tmp/sic'

Making all in replace
make[2]: Entering directory `/tmp/sic/replace'
rm -f libreplace.a
ar cru libreplace.a
ranlib libreplace.a
make[2]: Leaving directory `/tmp/sic/replace'

Making all in sic
make[2]: Entering directory `/tmp/sic/sic'
gcc -DHAVE_CONFIG_H -I. -I. -I.. -I..    -g -02 -c builtin.c
gcc -DHAVE_CONFIG_H -I. -I. -I.. -I..    -g -02 -c error.c
gcc -DHAVE_CONFIG_H -I. -I. -I.. -I..    -g -02 -c eval.c
gcc -DHAVE_CONFIG_H -I. -I. -I.. -I..    -g -02 -c list.c
```

```
gcc -DHAVE_CONFIG_H -I. -I. -I.. -I..    -g -O2 -c sic.c
gcc -DHAVE_CONFIG_H -I. -I. -I.. -I..    -g -O2 -c syntax.c
gcc -DHAVE_CONFIG_H -I. -I. -I.. -I..    -g -O2 -c xmalloc.c
gcc -DHAVE_CONFIG_H -I. -I. -I.. -I..    -g -O2 -c xstrdup.c
gcc -DHAVE_CONFIG_H -I. -I. -I.. -I..    -g -O2 -c xstrerror.c

rm -f libsic.a
ar cru libsic.a builtin.o error.o eval.o list.o sic.o syntax.o xmalloc.o
xstrdup.o xstrerror.o
ranlib libsic.a

make[2]: Leaving directory `/tmp/sic/sic'
make[1]: Leaving directory `/tmp/sic'
```

On this machine, as you can see from the preceding output of 'configure', I
have no need of the fallback implementation of strerror, so 'libreplace.a' is
empty. On another machine this might not be the case. In any event, I now
have a compiled 'libsic.a'—so far, so good.

7.3 A Sample Shell Application

What I need now is a program that uses 'libsic.a', if only to give me confi-
dence that it is working. In this section, I write a simple shell that uses the
library. But first, I create a directory to put it in:

```
$ mkdir src
$ ls -F
COPYING  Makefile.am  aclocal.m4  configure*    config/   sic/
INSTALL  Makefile.in  bootstrap*  configure.in  replace/  src/
$ cd src
```

To put this shell together, we need to provide just a few things for integration
with 'libsic.a'.

7.3.1 'sic_repl.c'

In 'sic_repl.c' (Read Eval Print Loop), there is a loop for reading strings typed
by the user, evaluating them, and printing the results. GNU readline is ideally
suited to this, but it is not always available—or sometimes people just may not
want to use it.

With the help of GNU Autotools, it is very easy to cater for building with and
without GNU readline. 'sic_repl.c' uses this function to read lines of input
from the user:

```
static char *
getline (FILE *in, const char *prompt)
{
  static char *buf = NULL;      /* Always allocated and freed
                                   from inside this function. */
  XFREE (buf);
```

```
  buf = (char *) readline ((char *) prompt);

#ifdef HAVE_ADD_HISTORY
  if (buf && *buf)
    add_history (buf);
#endif

  return buf;
}
```

To make this work, I must write an Autoconf macro that adds an option to
'configure' so that when the package is installed, it will use the readline library
if '--with-readline' is used:

```
AC_DEFUN([SIC_WITH_READLINE],
[AC_ARG_WITH(readline,
[  --with-readline          compile with the system readline library],
[if test x"${withval-no}" != xno; then
  sic_save_LIBS=$LIBS
  AC_CHECK_LIB(readline, readline)
  if test x"${ac_cv_lib_readline_readline}" = xno; then
    AC_MSG_ERROR(libreadline not found)
  fi
  LIBS=$sic_save_LIBS
fi])
AM_CONDITIONAL(WITH_READLINE, test x"${with_readline-no}" != xno)
])
```

Having put this macro in the file 'config/readline.m4', I must also call the new
macro (SIC_WITH_READLINE) from 'configure.in'.

7.3.2 'sic_syntax.c'
The syntax of the commands in the shell I am writing is defined by a set of
syntax handlers loaded into 'libsic' at startup. I can get the C preprocessor to
do most of the repetitive code for me, and just fill in the function bodies:

```
#if HAVE_CONFIG_H
#  include <sic/config.h>
#endif

#include "sic.h"

/* List of builtin syntax. */
#define syntax_functions                \
        SYNTAX(escape,  "\\")           \
        SYNTAX(space,   " \f\n\r\t\v")  \
        SYNTAX(comment, "#")            \
        SYNTAX(string,  "\"")           \
        SYNTAX(endcmd,  ";")            \
        SYNTAX(endstr,  "")

/* Prototype Generator. */
#define SIC_SYNTAX(name)                \
        int name (Sic *sic, BufferIn *in, BufferOut *out)
```

```
#define SYNTAX(name, string)                \
        extern SIC_SYNTAX (CONC (syntax_, name));
syntax_functions
#undef SYNTAX

/* Syntax handler mappings. */
Syntax syntax_table[] = {

#define SYNTAX(name, string)                \
        { CONC (syntax_, name), string },
  syntax_functions
#undef SYNTAX

  { NULL, NULL }
};
```

This code writes the prototypes for the syntax handler functions and creates a
table that associates each with one or more characters that might occur in the
input stream. The advantage of writing the code this way is that when I want
to add a new syntax handler later, it is a simple matter of adding a new row to
the syntax_functions macro, and writing the function itself.

7.3.3 'sic_builtin.c'

In addition to the syntax handlers I have just added to the Sic shell, the
language of this shell is also defined by the built-in commands it provides. The
infrastructure for this file is built from a table of functions fed into various C
preprocessor macros, just as I did for the syntax handlers.

One built-in handler function has special status, builtin_unknown. This is the
built in that is called if the Sic library cannot find a suitable built-in function to
handle the current input command. At first this does not sound especially
important—but it is the key to any shell implementation. When there is no
built-in handler for the command, the shell searches the user's command path,
'$PATH', to find a suitable executable. And this is the job of 'builtin_unknown':

```
int
builtin_unknown (Sic *sic, int argc, char *const argv[])
{
  char *path = path_find (argv[0]);
  int status = SIC_ERROR;

  if (!path)
    {
      sic_result_append (sic, "command \"");
      sic_result_append (sic, argv[0]);
      sic_result_append (sic, "\" not found");
    }
  else if (path_execute (sic, path, argv) != SIC_OKAY)
    {
      sic_result_append (sic, "command \"");
      sic_result_append (sic, argv[0]);
```

```c
        sic_result_append (sic, "\" failed: ");
        sic_result_append (sic, strerror (errno));
    }
  else
    status = SIC_OKAY;

  return status;
}

static char *
path_find (const char *command)
{
  char *path = xstrdup (command);

  if (*command == '/')
    {
      if (access (command, X_OK) < 0)
        goto notfound;
    }
  else
    {
      char *PATH = getenv ("PATH");
      char *pbeg, *pend;
      size_t len;

      for (pbeg = PATH; *pbeg != '\0'; pbeg = pend)
        {
          pbeg += strspn (pbeg, ":");
          len = strcspn (pbeg, ":");
          pend = pbeg + len;
          path = XREALLOC (char, path, 2+ len + strlen(command));
          *path = '\0';
          strncat (path, pbeg, len);
          if (path[len -1] != '/') strcat (path, "/");
          strcat (path, command);

          if (access (path, X_OK) == 0)
              break;
        }

      if (*pbeg == '\0')
          goto notfound;
    }

  return path;

 notfound:
  XFREE (path);
  return NULL;
}
```

Running autoscan again at this point adds AC_CHECK_FUNCS(strcspn strspn) to
configure.scan. This tells me that these functions are not truly portable. As
before I provide fallback implementations for these functions in case they are
missing from the target host—and as it turns out, they are easy to write:

```
/* strcspn.c — implement strcspn() for architectures without it */

#if HAVE_CONFIG_H
# include <sic/config.h>
#endif

#include <sys/types.h>

#if STDC_HEADERS
# include <string.h>
#elif HAVE_STRINGS_H
# include <strings.h>
#endif

#if !HAVE_STRCHR
# ifndef strchr
#   define strchr index
# endif
#endif

size_t
strcspn (const char *string, const char *reject)
{
  size_t count = 0;
  while (strchr (reject, *string) == 0)
    ++count, ++string;

  return count;
}
```

There is no need to add any code to 'Makefile.am', because the configure script
automatically adds the names of the missing function sources to '@LIBOBJS@'.

This implementation uses the autoconf-generated 'config.h' to get information
about the availability of headers and type definitions. It is interesting that
autoscan reports that strchr and strrchr, which are used in the fallback implementations of strcspn and strspn respectively, are themselves not portable!
Luckily, the Autoconf manual tells me exactly how to deal with this: by adding
some code to my 'common.h' (paraphrased from the literal code in the manual):

```
#if !STDC_HEADERS
# if !HAVE_STRCHR
#   define strchr index
#   define strrchr rindex
# endif
#endif
```

And another macro in 'configure.in':

```
AC_CHECK_FUNCS(strchr strrchr)
```

7.3.4 'sic.c' and 'sic.h'

Because the application binary has no installed header files, there is little point in maintaining a corresponding header file for every source. All the structures shared by these files and non-static functions in these files are declared in 'sic.h':

```
#ifndef SIC_H
#define SIC_H 1

#include <sic/common.h>
#include <sic/sic.h>
#include <sic/builtin.h>

BEGIN_C_DECLS

extern Syntax syntax_table[];
extern Builtin builtin_table[];
extern Syntax syntax_table[];

extern int evalstream   (Sic *sic, FILE *stream);
extern int evalline     (Sic *sic, char **pline);
extern int source       (Sic *sic, const char *path);
extern int syntax_init  (Sic *sic);
extern int syntax_finish (Sic *sic, BufferIn *in, BufferOut *out);

END_C_DECLS

#endif /* !SIC_H */
```

To hold together everything you have seen so far, the main function creates a Sic parser and initializes it by adding syntax handler functions and built-in functions from the two tables defined earlier, before handing control to evalstream, which will eventually exit when the input stream is exhausted.

```
int
main (int argc, char * const argv[])
{
  int result = EXIT_SUCCESS;
  Sic *sic = sic_new ();

  /* initialize the system */
  if (sic_init (sic) != SIC_OKAY)
      sic_fatal ("sic initialisation failed");
  signal (SIGINT, SIG_IGN);
  setbuf (stdout, NULL);

  /* initial symbols */
  sicstate_set (sic, "PS1", "] ", NULL);
  sicstate_set (sic, "PS2", "- ", NULL);
```

```
/* evaluate the input stream */
evalstream (sic, stdin);

exit (result);
}
```

Now, the shell can be built and used:

```
$ bootstrap
...

$ ./configure --with-readline
...

$ make
...

make[2]: Entering directory `/tmp/sic/src'
gcc -DHAVE_CONFIG_H -I. -I.. -I../sic -I.. -I../sic -g -c sic.c
gcc -DHAVE_CONFIG_H -I. -I.. -I../sic -I.. -I../sic -g -c sic_builtin.c
gcc -DHAVE_CONFIG_H -I. -I.. -I../sic -I.. -I../sic -g -c sic_repl.c
gcc -DHAVE_CONFIG_H -I. -I.. -I../sic -I.. -I../sic -g -c sic_syntax.c
gcc   -g -02  -o sic  sic.o sic_builtin.o sic_repl.o sic_syntax.o \
../sic/libsic.a ../replace/libreplace.a -lreadline
make[2]: Leaving directory `/tmp/sic/src'
...

$ ./src/sic
] pwd
/tmp/sic

] ls -F
Makefile     aclocal.m4   config.cache   configure*   sic/
Makefile.am  bootstrap*   config.log     configure.in src/
Makefile.in  config/      config.status* replace/

] exit
$
```

This chapter has developed a solid foundation of code, which I return to in Chapter 11, when Libtool will join the fray. The chapters leading up to that explain what Libtool is for, how to use it and integrate it into your own projects, and the advantages it offers over building shared libraries with Automake (or even just Make) alone.

8

Bootstrapping

The GNU Autotools contain many programs, each of which has a complex set of inputs. When one of these inputs changes, it is important to run the proper programs in the proper order. Unfortunately, it is hard to remember both the dependencies and the ordering.

Whenever you edit `'configure.in'`, for instance, you must remember to rerun `aclocal` in case you added a reference to a new macro. You must also rebuild `'configure'` by running `autoconf`; `'config.h'` by running `autoheader`, if you added a new `AC_DEFINE`; and `automake` to propagate any new `AC_SUBST`s to the various `'Makefile.in'`s. If you edit a `'Makefile.am'`, you must rerun `automake`. In both these cases, you must then remember to rerun `config.status --recheck` if `'configure'` changed, followed by `config.status` to rebuild the `'Makefile'`s.

When doing active development on the build system for your project, these dependencies quickly become painful. Of course, Automake knows how to handle this automatically. By default, `automake` generates a `'Makefile.in'` that knows all these dependencies and that automatically reruns the appropriate tools in the appropriate order. These rules assume that the correct versions of the tools are all in your `PATH`.

It helps to have a script ready to do all this for you once—before you have generated a `'Makefile'` that will automatically run the tools in the correct order, or when you make a fresh checkout of the code from a CVS repository where the developers don't keep generated files under source control. There are at least two opposing schools of thought regarding how to go about this: the `autogen.sh` school and the `bootstrap` school:

`autogen.sh`
From the outset, this is a poor name for a bootstrap script, because there is already a GNU automatic text-generation tool called AutoGen. Often packages that follow this convention have the script automatically run the generated

▶ *continued*

configure script after the bootstrap process, passing autogen.sh arguments through to configure—except you don't know which options you want yet, because you can't run 'configure --help' until configure has been generated. I suggest that if you find yourself compiling a project set up in this way that you type the following:

```
$ /bin/sh ./autogen.sh --help
```

and ignore the spurious warning that tells you configure will be executed.

bootstrap

Increasingly, projects are starting to call their bootstrap scripts 'bootstrap'. Such scripts just run the various commands required to bring the source tree into a state in which the end user can do the following:

```
$ configure
$ make
$ make install
```

Unfortunately, proponents of this school of thought don't put the bootstrap script in their distributed tarballs, because the script is unnecessary except when the build environment of a developer's machine has changed. This means the proponents of the autogen.sh school may never see the advantages of the other method.

Autoconf comes with a program called autoreconf, which essentially does the work of the bootstrap script. autoreconf is rarely used because historically it has not been very well known, and only in Autoconf 2.13 did it acquire the capability to work with Automake. Unfortunately, even the Autoconf 2.13 autoreconf does not handle libtoolize and some automake-related options that are frequently nice to use.

We recommend the bootstrap method, until autoreconf is fixed. At this point bootstrap has not been standardized, so here is a version of the script we used while writing this book.[1]

```
#! /bin/sh

aclocal \
&& automake --gnu --add-missing \
&& autoconf
```

---

[1] *This book is built using* automake *and* autoconf. *We couldn't find a use for* libtool.

We don't use autoreconf here because that script (as of Autoconf 2.13) also does not handle the '--add-missing' option, which we want. A typical bootstrap might also run libtoolize or autoheader.

It is also important for all developers on a project to have the same versions of the tools installed so that these rules don't inadvertently cause problems due to differences between tool versions. This version-skew problem turns out to be fairly significant in the field. So, automake provides a way to disable these rules by default, while still allowing users to enable them when they know their environment is set up correctly.

To enable this mode, you must first add AM_MAINTAINER_MODE to 'configure.in'. This adds the '--enable-maintainer-mode' option to 'configure'; when specified, this flag causes these so-called maintainer rules to be enabled.

Note that maintainer mode is a controversial feature. Some people like to use it because it causes fewer bug reports in some situations. For instance, CVS does not preserve relative time stamps on files. If your project has both 'configure.in' and 'configure' checked in, and maintainer mode is not in use, sometimes make decides to rebuild 'configure' even though it is not really required. This in turn means more headaches for your developers—on a large project most developers won't touch 'configure.in' and many may not even want to install the GNU Autotools.[2]

The other camp claims that end users should use the same build system that developers use, that maintainer mode is simply unaesthetic, and furthermore that the modality of maintainer mode is dangerous—you can easily forget what mode you are in and therefore forget to rebuild, and therefore correctly test, a change to the configure or build system. When maintainer mode is not in use, the Automake-supplied missing script is used to warn users when it appears that they need a maintainer tool that they do not have.

The approach you take depends strongly on the social structures surrounding your project.

---

[2] *Shock, horror.*

9

Introducing GNU Libtool

Libtool takes care of all the peculiarities of creating, linking, and loading shared and static libraries across a great number of platforms, providing a uniform command-line interface to the developer. By using Libtool to manage your project libraries, you need only to concern yourself with *Libtool's* interface: When someone else builds your project on a platform with a different library architecture, Libtool invokes that platform's compiler and linker with the correct environment and command-line switches. It installs libraries and library-using binaries according to the conventions of the host platform, and follows that platform's rules for library versioning and library interdependencies.

Libtool enables you to treat a library as an implementation of a well-defined interface of your choosing. This *Libtool library* may be manifest as a collection of compiler objects, a static ar archive, or a position-independent runtime-loadable object. By definition, native libraries are fully supported by Libtool because they are an implementation detail of the Libtool library abstraction. It is just that until Libtool achieves complete world domination, you might need to bear in mind what is going on behind the command-line interface when you first add Libtool support to your project.

Terminology

The sheer number of uses of the word "library" in this book could easily be very confusing. In this chapter and throughout the rest of the book, I refer to various kinds of libraries as follows:

"native"
  Low-level libraries that is, libraries provided by the host architecture.

"Libtool library"
  The kind of library built by Libtool. This encompasses both the shared and static native components of the implementation of the named library.

"pseudo-library"
> The high-level `'.la'` file produced by Libtool. The 'pseudo-library is not a library in its own right, but is treated as if it were from outside the Libtool interface.

Furthermore, in the context of Libtool, there is another subtle (but important) distinction to be drawn:

"static library"
> A Libtool library which has no shared archive component.

"static archives"
> The static component of a Libtool library. ◆

Many developers use Libtool as a black box that requires adding a few macros to `'configure.in'` and tweaking a project's `'Makefile.am'`. The next chapter addresses that school of thought in more detail. This chapter talks a little about the inner workings of Libtool, and shows how you can use it directly from your shell prompt—how to build various kinds of libraries and how an application can use those libraries. Before you can do any of this, you need to create a libtool script tailored to the platform from which you are using it.

9.1 Creating *libtool*

When you install a distribution of Libtool on your development machine, a host-specific libtool program is installed. The examples in the rest of this chapter use this installed instance of libtool.

When you start to use Libtool in the build process of your own projects, you should not require that libtool be installed on the user's machine, particularly because they may have a different libtool version to the one used to develop your project. Instead, distribute some of the files installed by the Libtool distribution along with your project, and custom build a libtool script on the user's machine before invoking ./libtool to build any objects. If you use Autoconf and Automake, these details are taken care of automatically (see Chapter 10, "Using GNU Libtool with `'configure.in'` and `'Makefile.am'`"). Otherwise, you should copy the following files from your own Libtool installation into the source tree of your own project:

```
$ ls /usr/local/share/libtool
config.guess   config.sub   libltdl   ltconfig   ltmain.in

$ cp /usr/local/share/libtool/config.* /usr/local/share/libtool/lt* .

$ ls
config.guess   config.sub   ltconfig   ltmain.in
```

You must then arrange for your project build process to create an instance of libtool on the user's machine so that it is dependent on the user's target system and not your development machine. The creation process requires the four files you just added to your project. Let's create a libtool instance by hand so that you can see what is involved:

```
$ ./config.guess
hppa1.1-hp-hpux10.20

$ ./ltconfig --disable-static --with-gcc ./ltmain.sh hppa1.1-hp-hpux10.20
checking host system type... hppa1.1-hp-hpux10.20
checking build system type... hppa1.1-hp-hpux10.20
checking whether ln -s works... yes
checking for ranlib... ranlib
checking for BSD-compatible nm... /usr/bin/nm -p
checking for strip... strip
checking for gcc... gcc
checking whether we are using GNU C... yes
checking for objdir... .libs
checking for object suffix... o
checking for executable suffix... no
checking for gcc option to produce PIC... -fPIC
checking if gcc PIC flag -fPIC works... yes
checking if gcc static flag -static works... yes
checking if gcc supports -c -o file.o... yes
checking if gcc supports -c -o file.lo... yes
checking if gcc supports -fno-rtti -fno-exceptions ... no
checking for ld used by GCC... /opt/gcc-lib/hp821/2.7.0/ld
checking if the linker (/opt/gcc-lib/hp821/2.7.0/ld) is GNU ld... no
checking whether the linker (/opt/gcc-lib/hp821/2.7.0/ld) supports \
shared libraries... yes
checking how to hardcode library paths into programs... relink
checking whether stripping libraries is possible... yes
checking for /opt/gcc-lib/hp821/2.7.0/ld option to reload object \
files... -r
checking dynamic linker characteristics... hpux10.20 dld.sl
checking command to parse /usr/bin/nm -p output... ok
checking if libtool supports shared libraries... yes
checking whether to build shared libraries... yes
checking whether to build static libraries... yes
creating libtool

$ ls
config.guess    config.sub    ltconfig
config.log      libtool       ltmain.sh

$ ./libtool --version
ltmain.sh (GNU libtool) 1.3c (1.629 1999/11/02 12:33:04)
```

The examples in this chapter are all performed on an HP-UX system, but the principles depicted are representative of any of the platforms to which Libtool has been ported (see Appendix B, "Platforms").

Often you do not need to specify any options. And, if you omit the configuration triplet (see Section 2.4, "Configuration Names"), ltconfig runs config.guess itself. You can specify several options that affect the generated libtool (see section ltconfig in The Libtool Manual). Unless your project has special requirements, you can simplify things by using the following:

```
$ ./ltconfig ./ltmain.sh
```

With the current release of Libtool, you must be careful that '$CC' is set to the same value when you call ltconfig as when you invoke the libtool it generates; otherwise libtool uses the compiler specified in '$CC' currently, but with the semantics probed by ltconfig for the compiler specified in '$CC' at the time *it* was executed.

9.2 The Libtool Library

A Libtool library is built from Libtool objects in the same way that a native (non-Libtool) library is built from native objects. Building a Libtool library with libtool is as easy as building an old-style static archive. Generally, each of the sources is compiled to a *Libtool object*, and then these objects are combined to create the library.

> ### Hands On
>
> *If you want to try this to see what* libtool *does on your machine, put the following code in a file* 'hello.c' *in a directory of its own, and run the example shell commands from there:*
>
> ```
> #include <stdio.h>
>
> void
> hello (who)
>      char *who;
> {
>   printf ("Hello, %s!\n", who);
> }
> ```

The traditional way to make a (native) static library is as follows:

```
$ gcc -c hello.c
$ ls
hello.c  hello.o

$ ar cru libhello.a hello.o
$ ranlib libhello.a
$ ls
hello.c   hello.o    libhello.a
```

---

[1] *Generally this involves indexing the symbols exported from the archive for faster linking and to allow the archived objects to reference symbols from other objects earlier in the same archive.*

Notice that even when I just want to build an old static archive, I need to know that, in common with most Unices, I have to *bless*[1] my library with `ranlib` to make it work optimally on HP-UX.

Essentially, Libtool supports the building of three types of library: shared libraries, static libraries, and convenience libraries. The following sections discuss each in turn, but first you need to understand how to create and use *position-independent* code, as explained in the next section.

9.2.1 Position-Independent Code

On most architectures, when you compile source code to object code, you need to specify whether the object code should be *position-independent*. Occasional architectures don't make the distinction, usually because all object code is position-independent by virtue of the ABI,[2] or less often because the load address of the object is fixed at compile time (which implies that shared libraries are not supported by such a platform).

If an object is compiled as *position-independent code* (PIC), the operating system can load the object at *any* address in preparation for execution. This involves a time overhead, in replacing direct address references with relative addresses at compile time, and a space overhead, in maintaining information to help the runtime loader fill in the unresolved addresses at runtime. Consequently, PIC objects are usually slightly larger and slower at runtime than the equivalent non-PIC object. The advantage of sharing library code on disk and in memory outweighs these problems as soon as the PIC object code in shared librariesis reused.

PIC compilation is exactly what is required for objects that will become part of a shared library. Consequently, `libtool` builds PIC objects for use in shared libraries and non-PIC objects for use in static libraries. Whenever `libtool` instructs the compiler to generate a PIC object, it also defines the preprocessor symbol, `'PIC'`, so that assembly code can be aware of whether it will reside in a PIC object.

Typically, as `libtool` is compiling sources, it generates a `'.lo'` object, as PIC, and a `'.o'` object, as non-PIC, and then it uses the appropriate one of the pair when linking executables and libraries of various sorts. On architectures where there is no distinction, the `'.lo'` file is just a soft link to the `'.o'` file.

In practice, you can link PIC objects into a static archive for a small overhead in execution and load speed, and often you can similarly link non-PIC objects into shared archives. If you find that you need to do this, `libtool` provides several ways to override the default behavior (see Section 9.1, "Creating `libtool`").

---

[2] *Application Binary Interface. The layout of the bytes that comprise binary objects and executables: 32- or 64-bit words; procedure-calling conventions; memory-alignment rules; system-call interface; order and type of the binary sections (such as data and code); and so on.*

9.2.2 Creating Shared Libraries

From Libtool's point of view, the term "shared library" is somewhat of a misnomer. Because Libtool is intended to abstract away the details of library building, it doesn't matter whether Libtool is building a shared library or a static archive. Of course, Libtool always tries to build a shared library by default on the platforms to which it has been ported (see Appendix B), but equally falls back to building a static archive if the host architecture does not support shared libraries or if the project developer deliberately configures Libtool to always build static archives only. These libraries are more properly called *Libtool libraries*; the underlying native library is usually a shared library, except as described earlier.

To create a Libtool library on my HP-UX host, or indeed anywhere else that libtool works, run the following commands:

```
$ rm hello.o libhello.a
$ libtool gcc -c hello.c
mkdir .libs
gcc -c  -fPIC -DPIC hello.c -o .libs/hello.lo
gcc -c hello.c -o hello.o >/dev/null 2>&1
mv -f .libs/hello.lo hello.lo

$ ls
hello.c    hello.lo    hello.o

$ libtool gcc -rpath /usr/local/lib -o libhello.la hello.lo
rm -fr .libs/libhello.la .libs/libhello.* .libs/libhello.*
/opt/gcc-lib/hp821/2.7.0/ld -b +h libhello.sl.0 +b /usr/local/lib \
-o .libs/libhello.sl.0.0  hello.lo
(cd .libs && rm -f libhello.sl.0 && ln -s libhello.sl.0.0 libhello.sl.0)
(cd .libs && rm -f libhello.sl && ln -s libhello.sl.0.0 libhello.sl)
ar cru .libs/libhello.a  hello.o
ranlib .libs/libhello.a
creating libhello.la
(cd .libs && rm -f libhello.la && ln -s ../libhello.la libhello.la)

$ ls
hello.c    hello.lo    hello.o    libhello.la
```

This example illustrates several features of libtool. Compare the command-line syntax with the preceding example (see Section 9.2, "The Libtool Library"). They are both very similar. Notice, however, that when compiling the 'hello.c' source file, libtool creates *two* objects. The first, 'hello.lo', is the *Libtool object* that we use for Libtool libraries, and the second, 'hello.o', is a standard object. On HP-UX, libtool knows that Libtool objects should be compiled with *position-independent code*, hence the extra switches when creating the first object.

Which Compiler Does Libtool Use?

When you run libtool *from the command line, you must also specify a compiler for it to call. Similarly, when you create a* libtool *script with* ltconfig, *a compiler is chosen and interrogated to discover what characteristics it has (see Section 9.1, "Creating* libtool*").*

Prior to release 1.4 of Libtool, ltconfig *probed the build machine for a suitable compiler, by searching first for* gcc *and then* cc. *The functionality of* ltconfig *is being migrated into the* 'AC_PROG_LIBTOOL' *macro, such that there will be no* ltconfig *script in Libtool release 1.5. The current release is part way between the two. In all cases, you can specify a particular compiler by setting the* 'CC' *environment variable.*

It is important to continue to use the same compiler when you run libtool *as the compiler that was used when you created the* libtool *script. If you create the script with* 'cc' *set to* gcc, *and subsequently try to compile using, for example, the following:*

```
$ libtool c89 -rpath /usr/local/lib -c hello.c
```

libtool *tries to call* c89 *using the options it discovered for* gcc. *Needless to say, that doesn't work!* ◆

The link command specifies a Libtool library target, 'libhello.la', compiled from a single Libtool object, 'hello.lo'. Even so, libtool knows how to build both static and shared archives on HP-UX—underneath the libtool abstraction, both are created. libtool also understands the particulars of library linking on HP-UX: The static archive, 'libhello.a', is *blessed*; the system (and compiler) - dependent compiler and linker flags, versioning scheme, and .sl extension are utilized for the shared archive, 'libhello.sl'. On another host, all these details may differ completely, yet have exactly the same invocation. libtool calls the native tools with the appropriate options to achieve the same result. Try it on your own machines to see any differences.

The '-rpath' switch tells libtool that you want to build a Libtool library (with both the shared and static components where possible). If you omit the '-rpath' switch, libtool builds a convenience library instead (see Section 9.2.4, "Creating Convenience Libraries"). The '-rpath' switch is doubly important, because it tells libtool that you intend to install 'libhello.la' in '/usr/local/lib'. This allows libtool to finalize the library correctly after installation on the architectures that need it (see Section 9.6, "Installing a Library").

Finally, notice that only the Libtool library, 'libhello.la', is visible after a successful link. The various files that form the local implementation details of the Libtool library are in a hidden subdirectory, but for the abstraction to work cleanly you shouldn't need to worry about these too much.

9.2.3 Creating Static Libraries

In contrast, libtool creates a static library if either the '-static' or '-all-static' switches are specified on the link line for a Libtool library:

```
$ libtool gcc -static -o libhello.la hello.lo
rm -fr .libs/libhello.la .libs/libhello.* .libs/libhello.*
ar cru .libs/libhello.a  hello.o
ranlib .libs/libhello.a
creating libhello.la
(cd .libs && rm -f libhello.la && ln -s ../libhello.la libhello.la)
```

Note that because libtool creates only a static archive, the '-rpath' switch is not required: After a static library has been installed, there is no need to perform additional finalization for the library to be used from the installed location[3] or to track runtime search paths when installing a static archive.

When you link an executable against this 'libhello.la', the objects from the static archive are statically linked into the executable. The advantage of such a library over the traditional native static archive is that all the dependency information from the Libtool library is used (see Section 9.2.4, "Creating Convenience Libraries").

> **When to Use Libtool?**
>
> libtool *is useful as a* general *library-building toolkit, yet people still seem to regress to the old way of building libraries whenever they want to use static archives. You should exploit the consistent interface of* libtool *even for static archives. If you don't want to use shared archives, use the* '-static' *switch to build a static Libtool library.* ◆

9.2.4 Creating Convenience Libraries

The third type of library that can be built with libtool is the *convenience library*. Modern compilers can create *partially linked* objects: intermediate compilation units that comprise several compiled objects, but are neither an executable nor a library. Such partially linked objects must be subsequently linked into a library or executable to be useful. Libtool convenience libraries *are* partially linked objects, but are emulated by libtool on platforms with no native implementation.

---

[3] *As is often the case, AIX is peculiar in this respect*—ranlib *adds path information to a static archive, and must be run again after the archive has been installed.* libtool *knows about this and automatically blesses the installed library again on AIX.*

Hands On

If you want to try this to see what libtool *does on your machine, put the following code in a file* 'trim.c' *in the same directory as* 'hello.c' *and* 'libhello.la', *and run the example shell commands from there:*

```c
#include <string.h>

#define WHITESPACE_STR  " \f\n\r\t\v"

/**
 * Remove whitespace characters from both ends of a copy of
 *  '\0' terminated STRING and return the result.
 **/
char *
trim (string)
     char *string;
{
  char *result = 0;

  /* Ignore NULL pointers.  */
  if (string)
    {
      char *ptr = string;

      /* Skip leading whitespace.  */
      while (strchr (WHITESPACE_STR, *ptr))
        ++ptr;

      /* Make a copy of the remainder.  */
      result = strdup (ptr);

      /* Move to the last character of the copy.  */
      for (ptr = result; *ptr; ++ptr)
        /* NOWORK */;
      --ptr;

      /* Remove trailing whitespace.  */
      for (--ptr; strchr (WHITESPACE_STR, *ptr); --ptr)
        *ptr = '\0';
    }

  return result;
}
```

To compile the convenience library with libtool, you would do this:

```
$ libtool gcc -c trim.c
rm -f .libs/trim.lo
gcc -c -fPIC -DPIC trim.c -o .libs/trim.lo
gcc -c trim.c -o trim.o >/dev/null 2>&1
mv -f .libs/trim.lo trim.lo

$ libtool gcc -o libtrim.la trim.lo
rm -fr .libs/libtrim.la .libs/libtrim.* .libs/libtrim.*
ar cru .libs/libtrim.al trim.lo
ranlib .libs/libtrim.al
creating libtrim.la
(cd .libs && rm -f libtrim.la && ln -s ../libtrim.la libtrim.la)
```

Additionally, you can use a convenience library as an alias for a set of zero or more object files and some dependent libraries. If you need to link several objects against a long list of libraries, it is much more convenient to create an alias:

```
$ libtool gcc -o libgraphics.la -lpng -ltiff -ljpeg -lz
rm -fr .libs/libgraphics.la .libs/libgraphics.* .libs/libgraphics.*
ar cru .libs/libgraphics.al
ranlib .libs/libgraphics.al
creating libgraphics.la
(cd .libs && rm -f libgraphics.la && \
ln -s ../libgraphics.la libgraphics.la)
```

Having done this, whenever you link against 'libgraphics.la' with libtool, all the dependent libraries are linked too. In this case, there are no actual objects compiled into the convenience library, but you can do that too, if need be.

9.3 Linking an Executable

Continuing the parallel between the syntax used to compile with libtool and the syntax used when building old static libraries, linking an executable is a matter of combining compilation units into a binary in both cases. We tell the compiler which objects and libraries are required, and it creates an executable for us.

Hands On

If you want to try this to see what libtool *does on your machine, put the following code in a file* 'main.c' *in the same directory as* 'hello.c' *and* 'libhello.la', *and run the example shell commands from there:*

```
void hello ();

int
main (argc, argv)
    int argc;
    char *argv[];
{
  hello ("World");
  exit (0);
}
```

To compile an executable that uses the non-Libtool 'libhello.a' library built previously, I would use the following commands:

```
$ gcc -o hello main.c libhello.a
$ ./hello
Hello, World!
```

To create a similar executable on the HP-UX host, using libtool this time:

```
$ libtool gcc -o hello main.c libhello.la
libtool: link: warning: this platform does not like uninstalled
libtool: link: warning: shared libraries.
libtool: link: hello will be relinked during installation
gcc -o .libs/hello main.c /tmp/hello/.libs/libhello.sl  \
-Wl,+b -Wl,/tmp/hello/.libs:/usr/local/lib
creating hello

$ ls
hello      hello.lo    libhello.la
hello.c    hello.o     main.c

$ ./hello
Hello, World!
```

Notice that you linked against the Libtool library, 'libhello.la', but otherwise the link command you used was not really very different from non-Libtool static library link command used earlier. Still, libtool does several things for you: It links with the shared archive rather than the static archive; and it sets the compiler options so that the program can be run in place, even though it is linked against the uninstalled Libtool library. Using a make rule *without* the benefit of libtool, it would be almost impossible to reliably link a program against an uninstalled shared library in this way, because the particular switches needed would differ among the various platforms with which you want the project to work. Also without the extra compiler options libtool adds for you, the program searches only the standard library directories for a shared 'libhello'.

The link warning tells you that libtool knows, that on HP-UX, the program will stop working if it is copied directly to the installation directory; to prevent it from breaking, libtool relinks the program when it is installed (see Section 9.6, "Installing a Library").

You can find a discussion of the creation of static Libtool libraries in Section 9.2.3, "Creating Static Libraries." If you link an executable against such a library, the library objects, by definition, can only be statically linked into your executable. Often this is what you want, if the library is not intended for installation or if you have temporarily disabled building of shared libraries in your development tree to speed up compilation while you are debugging.

Sometimes, this isn't what you want. You might need to install a complete Libtool library with shared and static components, but need to generate a static executable linked against the same library, like this:

```
$ libtool gcc -static -o hello main.c libhello.la
gcc -o hello main.c ./.libs/libhello.a
```

In this case, the '-static' switch instructs libtool to choose the static component of any uninstalled Libtool library.

You could have specified '-all-static' instead, which instructs libtool to link the executable with only static libraries (wherever possible), for any Libtool or native libraries used.

Finally, you can also link executables against convenience libraries. This makes sense when the convenience library is being used as an alias (see Section 9.2.4, "Creating Convenience Libraries"). Notice how 'libgraphics.la' expands to its own dependencies in the link command:

```
$ libtool gcc -o image loader.o libgraphics.la
libtool: link: warning: this platform does not like uninstalled
libtool: link: warning: shared libraries
libtool: link: image will be relinked during installation
gcc -o .libs/image loader.o -lpng -ltiff -ljpeg -lz \
-Wl,+b -Wl,/tmp/image/.libs:/usr/local/lib
creating image
```

You can also link against convenience libraries being used as partially linked objects, as long as you are careful that each is linked only once. Remember that a partially linked object is just the same as any other object, and that if you load it twice (even from different libraries) you will get multiple definition errors when you try to link your executable. This is almost the same as using the '-static' switch on the libtool link line to link an executable with the static component of a normal Libtool library, except that the convenience library comprises PIC objects. When statically linking an executable, PIC objects are best avoided, however (see Section 9.2.1, "Position-Independent Code").

9.4 Linking a Library

Libraries often rely on code in other libraries. Traditionally the way to deal with this is to *know* what the dependencies are and, when linking an executable, be careful to list all the dependencies on the link line in the correct order. If you have ever built an X Window application using a widget library, you are already familiar with this notion.

Even though you use only the functions in the widget library directly, a typical
link command needs to be as follows:

```
$ gcc -o Xtest -I/usr/X11R6/include Xtest.c -L/usr/X11R6/lib \
-lXm -lXp -lXaw -lXmu -lX11 -lnsl -lsocket
```

Modern architectures have solved this problem by allowing libraries to be
linked into other libraries, but this feature is not yet particularly portable. If
you are trying to write a portable project, it is not safe to rely on native
support for interlibrary dependencies, especially if you want to have dependencies between static and shared archives. Some of the features discussed in this
section were not fully implemented before Libtool 1.4, so you should make sure
that you are using this version or newer if you need these features.

Hands On

If you want to try the examples in this section to see what libtool *does on your
machine, you first need to modify the source of* 'hello.c' *to introduce a dependency on* 'trim.c':

```
#include <stdio.h>

extern char *trim ();
extern void free ();

void
hello (who)
     char *who;
{
  char *trimmed = trim (who);
  printf ("Hello, %s!\n", trimmed);
  free (trimmed);
}
```

You might also want to modify the 'main.c' *file to exercise the new* 'trim' *functionality to prove that the newly linked executable is working:*

```
void hello ();

int
main (argc, argv)
     int argc;
     char *argv[];
{
  hello ("\tWorld \r\n");
  exit (0);
}
```

Suppose I want to make two libraries, `'libtrim'` and `'libhello'`. `'libhello'` uses the `'trim'` function in `'libtrim'` but the code in `'main'` uses only the `'hello'` function in `'libhello'`. Traditionally, the two libraries are built like this:

```
$ rm hello *.a *.la *.o *.lo
$ gcc -c trim.c

$ ls
hello.c   main.c   trim.c   trim.o

$ ar cru libtrim.a trim.o
$ ranlib libtrim.a
$ gcc -c hello.c

$ ls
hello.c   hello.o   libtrim.a   main.c   trim.c   trim.o

$ ar cru libhello.a hello.o
$ ranlib libhello.a

$ ls
hello.c   libhello.a   main.c   trim.o
hello.o   libtrim.a    trim.c
```

Notice that there is no way to specify that `'libhello.a'` won't work unless it is also linked with `'libtrim.a'`. Because of this, I need to list both libraries when I link the application. What's more, I need to list them in the correct order:

```
$ gcc -o hello main.c libtrim.a libhello.a
/usr/bin/ld: Unsatisfied symbols:
   trim (code)
collect2: ld returned 1 exit status

$ gcc -o hello main.c libhello.a libtrim.a

$ ls
hello      hello.o      libtrim.a   trim.c
hello.c    libhello.a   main.c      trim.o

$ ./hello
Hello, World!
```

9.4.1 Interlibrary Dependencies

libtool's interlibrary dependency support uses the native implementation if there is one available. If there is no native implementation, or if the native implementation is broken or incomplete, libtool uses an implementation of its own.

You build 'libtrim' as a standard Libtool library (see Section 9.2, "The Libtool
Library") as follows:

```
$ rm hello *.a *.o

$ ls
hello.c   main.c   trim.c

$ libtool gcc -c trim.c
rm -f .libs/trim.lo
gcc -c  -fPIC -DPIC trim.c -o .libs/trim.lo
gcc -c trim.c -o trim.o >/dev/null 2>&1
mv -f .libs/trim.lo trim.lo

$ libtool gcc -rpath /usr/local/lib -o libtrim.la trim.lo
rm -fr .libs/libtrim.la .libs/libtrim.* .libs/libtrim.*
/opt/gcc-lib/hp821/2.7.0/ld -b +h libtrim.sl.0 +b /usr/local/lib \
-o .libs/libtrim.sl.0.0  trim.lo
(cd .libs && rm -f libtrim.sl.0 && ln -s libtrim.sl.0.0 libtrim.sl.0)
(cd .libs && rm -f libtrim.sl && ln -s libtrim.sl.0.0 libtrim.sl)
ar cru .libs/libtrim.a  trim.o
ranlib .libs/libtrim.a
creating libtrim.la
(cd .libs && rm -f libtrim.la && ln -s ../libtrim.la libtrim.la)
```

When you build 'libhello', you can specify the libraries it depends on at the
command line, like this:

```
$ libtool gcc -c hello.c
rm -f .libs/hello.lo
gcc -c  -fPIC -DPIC hello.c -o .libs/hello.lo
gcc -c hello.c -o hello.o >/dev/null 2>&1
mv -f .libs/hello.lo hello.lo

$ libtool gcc -rpath /usr/local/lib -o libhello.la hello.lo libtrim.la
rm -fr .libs/libhello.la .libs/libhello.* .libs/libhello.*

*** Warning: inter-library dependencies are not known to be supported.
*** All declared inter-library dependencies are being dropped.
*** The inter-library dependencies that have been dropped here will be
*** automatically added whenever a program is linked with this library
*** or is declared to -dlopen it.
/opt/gcc-lib/hp821/2.7.0/ld -b +h libhello.sl.0 +b /usr/local/lib \
-o .libs/libhello.sl.0.0  hello.lo
(cd .libs && rm -f libhello.sl.0 && ln -s libhello.sl.0.0 libhello.sl.0)
(cd .libs && rm -f libhello.sl && ln -s libhello.sl.0.0 libhello.sl)
ar cru .libs/libhello.a  hello.o
ranlib .libs/libhello.a
creating libhello.la
(cd .libs && rm -f libhello.la && ln -s ../libhello.la libhello.la)

$ ls
hello.c    hello.o      libtrim.la    trim.c    trim.o
hello.lo   libhello.la  main.c        trim.lo
```

Although, on HP-UX, `libtool` warns that it doesn't know how to use the native interlibrary dependency implementation, it tracks the dependencies and makes sure they are added to the final link line, so that you need to specify only the libraries that you use directly.

Now you can rebuild `'hello'` exactly as in the earlier example in Section 9.3, "Linking an Executable," as follows:

```
$ libtool gcc -o hello main.c libhello.la
libtool: link: warning: this platform does not like uninstalled
libtool: link: warning: shared libraries
libtool: link: hello will be relinked during installation
gcc -o .libs/hello main.c /tmp/intro-hello/.libs/libhello.sl \
/tmp/intro-hello/.libs/libtrim.sl \
-Wl,+b -Wl,/tmp/intro-hello/.libs:/usr/local/lib
creating hello

$ ./hello
Hello, World!
```

Notice that even though you specified only the `'libhello.la'` library at the command line, `libtool` remembers that `'libhello.sl'` depends on `'libtrim.sl'` and links that library too.

You can also link a static executable, and the dependencies are handled similarly:

```
$ libtool gcc -o hello-again -static main.c libhello.la
gcc -o hello main.c ./.libs/libhello.a /tmp/intro-hello/.libs/libtrim.a

$ ./hello-again
Hello, World!
```

For your own projects, provided that you use `libtool` and that you specify the libraries you want to link using the `'.la'` pseudo-libraries, these dependencies can be nested as deeply as you like. You can also register dependencies on native libraries, although you will of course need to specify any dependencies that the native library itself has at the same time.

9.4.2 Using Convenience Libraries
To rebuild `'libtrim'` as a convenience library (see Section 9.2.4, "Creating Convenience Libraries"), use the following commands:

```
$ rm hello *.la

$ ls
hello.c   hello.lo   hello.o   main.c   trim.c   trim.lo   trim.o

$ libtool gcc -o libtrim.la trim.lo
rm -fr .libs/libtrim.la .libs/libtrim.* .libs/libtrim.*
```

```
ar cru .libs/libtrim.al trim.lo
ranlib .libs/libtrim.al
creating libtrim.la
(cd .libs && rm -f libtrim.la && ln -s ../libtrim.la libtrim.la)
```

Then, rebuild 'libhello', with an interlibrary dependency on 'libtrim', like this:

```
$ libtool gcc -rpath `pwd`/_inst -o libhello.la hello.lo libtrim.la
rm -fr .libs/libhello.la .libs/libhello.* .libs/libhello.*

*** Warning: inter-library dependencies are not known to be supported.
*** All declared inter-library dependencies are being dropped.
*** The inter-library dependencies that have been dropped here will be
*** automatically added whenever a program is linked with this library
*** or is declared to -dlopen it.
rm -fr .libs/libhello.lax
mkdir .libs/libhello.lax
rm -fr .libs/libhello.lax/libtrim.al
mkdir .libs/libhello.lax/libtrim.al
(cd .libs/libhello.lax/libtrim.al && ar x /tmp/./.libs/libtrim.al)
/opt/gcc-lib/hp821/2.7.0/ld -b +h libhello.sl.0 +b /tmp/hello/_inst \
-o .libs/libhello.sl.0.0  hello.lo .libs/libhello.lax/libtrim.al/trim.lo
(cd .libs && rm -f libhello.sl.0 && ln -s libhello.sl.0.0 libhello.sl.0)
(cd .libs && rm -f libhello.sl && ln -s libhello.sl.0.0 libhello.sl)
rm -fr .libs/libhello.lax
mkdir .libs/libhello.lax
rm -fr .libs/libhello.lax/libtrim.al
mkdir .libs/libhello.lax/libtrim.al
(cd .libs/libhello.lax/libtrim.al && ar x /tmp/hello/./.libs/libtrim.al)
ar cru .libs/libhello.a  hello.o  .libs/libhello.lax/libtrim.al/trim.lo
ranlib .libs/libhello.a
rm -fr .libs/libhello.lax .libs/libhello.lax
creating libhello.la
(cd .libs && rm -f libhello.la && ln -s ../libhello.la libhello.la)

$ ls
hello.c    hello.o     libtrim.la   trim.c    trim.o
hello.lo   libhello.la main.c       trim.lo
```

Compare this to the preceding example of building 'libhello' and you can see that things are rather different. On HP-UX, partial linking is not known to work, so libtool extracts the objects from the convenience library and links them directly into 'libhello'. That is, 'libhello' is comprised of its own objects *and* the objects in 'libtrim'. If 'libtrim' had had any dependencies, 'libhello' would have inherited them too. This technique is especially useful for grouping source files into subdirectories, even though all the objects compiled in the subdirectories must eventually reside in a big library: Compile the sources in each into a convenience library, and in turn link all of these into a single library that will then contain all the constituent objects and dependencies of the various convenience libraries.

When you relink the `hello` executable, notice that 'libtrim' is *not* linked, because the 'libtrim' objects are already present in 'libhello':

```
$ libtool gcc -o hello main.c libhello.la
libtool: link: warning: this platform does not like uninstalled
libtool: link: warning: shared libraries
libtool: link: hello will be relinked during installation
gcc -o .libs/hello main.c /tmp/intro-hello/.libs/libhello.sl \
-Wl,+b -Wl,/tmp/intro-hello/.libs:/usr/local/lib
creating hello

$ ./hello
Hello, World!
```

9.5 Executing Uninstalled Binaries

If you look at the contents of the `hello` program you built in the preceding section, you will see that it is not actually a binary at all, but a shell script that sets up the environment so that when the real binary is called it finds its shared libraries in the correct locations. Without this script, the runtime loader might not be able to find the uninstalled libraries. Or worse, it might find an old version and load that by mistake!

In practice, this is all part of the unified interface `libtool` presents so you needn't worry about it most of the time. The exception is when you need to look at the binary with another program, to debug it for example:

```
$ ls
hello       hello.lo   libhello.la   main.c   trim.lo
hello.c     hello.o    libtrim.la    trim.c   trim.o

$ libtool gdb hello
GDB is free software and you are welcome to distribute copies of it
under certain conditions; type "show copying" to see the conditions.
There is absolutely no warranty for GDB; type "show warranty" for
details.
GDB 4.18 (hppa1.0-hp-hpux10.20),
Copyright 1999 Free Software Foundation, Inc...
(gdb) bre main
Breakpoint 1 at 0x5178: file main.c, line 6.
(gdb) run
Starting program: /tmp/intro-hello/.libs/hello
Breakpoint 1, main (argc=1, argv=0x7b03aa70) at main.c:6
6           return hello("World");
```

9.6 Installing a Library

Now that the library and an executable that links with it have been successfully built, they can be installed. For the sake of this example, I `cp` the objects to their destination, although `libtool` would be just as happy if I were to use `install` with the long, requisite list of parameters.

It is important to install the library to the '-rpath' destination specified when it was linked earlier, or at least that it be visible from that location when the runtime loader searches for it. This rule is not enforced by libtool, because it is often desirable to install libraries to a *staging* area (when making a binary package from a virtual root directory, for example). Of course, the package must ultimately install the library to the specified '-rpath' destination for it to work correctly, like this:

```
$ libtool cp libtrim.la /usr/local/lib
cp .libs/libtrim.sl.0.0 /usr/local/lib/libtrim.sl.0.0
(cd /usr/local/lib && rm -f libtrim.sl.0 && \
ln -s libtrim.sl.0.0 libtrim.sl.0)
(cd /usr/local/lib && rm -f libtrim.sl && \
ln -s libtrim.sl.0.0 libtrim.sl)
chmod 555 /usr/local/lib/libtrim.sl.0.0
cp .libs/libtrim.lai /usr/local/lib/libtrim.la
cp .libs/libtrim.a /usr/local/lib/libtrim.a
ranlib /usr/local/lib/libtrim.a
chmod 644 /usr/local/lib/libtrim.a


----------------------------------------

Libraries have been installed in:
   /usr/local/lib

If you ever happen to want to link against installed libraries
in a given directory, LIBDIR, you must either use libtool, and
specify the full pathname of the library, or use -LLIBDIR
flag during linking and do at least one of the following:
   - add LIBDIR to the SHLIB_PATH environment variable
     during execution
   - use the -Wl,+b -Wl,LIBDIR linker flag

See any operating system documentation about shared libraries for
more information, such as the ld(1) and ld.so(8) manual pages.
----------------------------------------
```

Again, libtool takes care of the details for you. Both the static and shared archives are copied into the installation directory and their access modes are set appropriately. libtool *blesses* the static archive again with ranlib, which would be easy to forget without the benefit of libtool, especially if I develop on a host where the library will continue to work without this step. Also, libtool creates the necessary links for the shared archive to conform with HP-UX's library-versioning rules. Compare this to what you see with the equivalent commands running on GNU/Linux to see how libtool applies these rules according to the requirements of its host. The block of text libtool shows at the end of the installation serves to explain how to link executables against the newly installed library on HP-UX and how to make sure that the executables linked against it will work. Of course, the best way to ensure this is to use libtool to perform the linking. I leave the details of linking against an installed Libtool library as an exercise—everything you need to know can be extrapolated from the example of linking against an uninstalled Libtool library (see Section 9.3, "Linking an Executable").

On some architectures, even shared archives need to be *blessed* on installation. For example,GNU/Linux requires that `ldconfig` be run when a new library is installed. Typically, a library is installed to its target destination after being built, in which case `libtool` performs any necessary *blessing* during installation. Sometimes, when building a binary package for installation on another machine, for example, it is not desirable to perform the *blessing* on the build machine. No problem; `libtool` takes care of this too! `libtool` detects whether you install the library to a destination other than the one specified in the '`-rpath`' argument passed during the archive link, and just reminds you what needs to be done before the library can be used:

```
$ mkdir -p /usr/local/stow/hello-1.0/lib

$ libtool cp libtrim.la /usr/local/stow/hello-1.0/lib
cp .libs/libtrim.sl.0.0 /usr/local/stow/hello-1.0/lib/libtrim.sl.0.0
(cd /usr/local/stow/hello-1.0/lib && rm -f libtrim.sl.0 && \
ln -s libtrim.sl.0.0 libtrim.sl.0)
(cd /usr/local/stow/hello-1.0/lib && rm -f libtrim.sl && \
ln -s libtrim.sl.0.0 libtrim.sl)
chmod 555 /usr/local/stow/hello-1.0/lib/libtrim.sl.0.0
cp .libs/libtrim.lai /usr/local/stow/hello-1.0/lib/libtrim.la
cp .libs/libtrim.a /usr/local/stow/hello-1.0/lib/libtrim.a
ranlib /usr/local/stow/hello-1.0/lib/libtrim.a
chmod 644 /usr/local/stow/hello-1.0/lib/libtrim.a
libtool: install: warning: remember to run
libtool: install: warning: libtool --finish /usr/local/lib
```

If you will make the installed libraries visible in the destination directory with symbolic links, you need to do whatever it is you do to make the library visible, and then *bless* the library in *that* location with the `libtool --finish /usr/local/lib` command:

```
$ cd /usr/local/stow
$ stow hello-1.0
$ libtool --finish /usr/local/lib
```

If you are following the examples so far, you will also need to install the Libtool library, '`libhello.la`', before you move on to the next section:

```
$ libtool cp libhello.la /usr/local/lib
cp .libs/libhello.sl.0.0 /usr/local/lib/libhello.sl.0.0
(cd /usr/local/lib && rm -f libhello.sl.0 && \
ln -s libhello.sl.0.0 libhello.sl.0)
(cd /usr/local/lib && rm -f libhello.sl && \
```

```
ln -s libhello.sl.0.0 libhello.sl)
chmod 555 /usr/local/lib/libhello.sl.0.0
cp .libs/libhello.lai /usr/local/lib/libhello.la
cp .libs/libhello.a /usr/local/lib/libhello.a
ranlib /usr/local/lib/libhello.a
chmod 644 /usr/local/lib/libhello.a


_____

Libraries have been installed in:
   /usr/local/lib

If you ever happen to want to link against installed libraries
in a given directory, LIBDIR, you must either use libtool, and
specify the full pathname of the library, or use -LLIBDIR
flag during linking and do at least one of the following:
   - add LIBDIR to the SHLIB_PATH environment variable
     during execution
   - use the -Wl,+b -Wl,LIBDIR linker flag

See any operating system documentation about shared libraries for
more information, such as the ld(1) and ld.so(8) manual pages.
_____
```

After a Libtool library has been installed, binaries that link against it hard code the path to the Libtool library, as specified with the '-rpath' switch when the library was built. libtool always encodes the installation directory into a Libtool library for just this purpose. Hard coding directories in this way is a good thing, because binaries linked against such libraries continue to work if several incompatible versions of the library are visible to the runtime loader (a Trojan 'libhello' in a user's LD_LIBRARY_PATH, or a test build of the next release, for example). The disadvantage to this system is that if you move libraries to new directories, executables linked in this way cannot find the libraries they need. Moving any library is a bad idea, however, doubly so for a Libtool library that has its installation directory encoded internally; therefore, the way to avoid problems of this nature is to not move around libraries after installation!

9.7 Installing an Executable

Installing an executable uses exactly the same command line that I used to install the library earlier:

```
$ libtool cp hello /usr/local/bin
gcc -o /tmp/libtool-28585/hello main.c /usr/local/lib/libhello.sl \
/usr/local/lib/libtrim.sl -Wl,+b -Wl,/usr/local/lib
cp /tmp/libtool-28585/hello /usr/local/bin/hello

$ /usr/local/bin/hello
Hello, World!
```

As libtool said earlier, during the initial linking of the hello program in the
build directory, hello must be rebuilt before installation. This is a peculiarity of
HP-UX (and a few other architectures) that you won't see if you are following
the examples on a GNU/Linux system. In the preceding shell trace, libtool has
built an installable version of the hello program, saving me the trouble of
remembering (or worse, coding for) the particulars of HP-UX, which runs
correctly from the installed location.

As a matter of interest, take a look at the attributes of the installed program
using HP-UX's chatr command:

```
$ chatr /usr/local/bin/hello
/usr/local/bin/hello:
        shared executable

        shared library dynamic path search:
            SHLIB_PATH     disabled  second
            embedded path  enabled   first  /usr/local/lib
        internal name:
            /tmp/libtool-28585/hello
        shared library list:
            static   /usr/local/lib/libhello.sl.0
            static   /usr/local/lib/libtrim.sl.0
            dynamic  /lib/libc.1

shared library binding:
        deferred
...
```

You can see that the runtime library search path for the installed hello program
has been set to find the installed 'libhello.sl.0' shared archive, preventing it from
accidentally loading a different library (with the same name) from the default load
path. This is a feature of libtool, and a very important one at that; and although
it may not seem like the right way to do things initially, it saves *a lot* of trouble
when you end up with several versions of a library installed in several locations,
because each program continues to use the version that it was linked with, subject
to library-versioning rules (see Section 10.4, "Library Versioning").

Library Version Safety

Without the help of libtool, *it is very difficult to prevent programs and libraries
in the build tree from loading earlier (compatible) versions of a shared archive
that were previously installed without an intimate knowledge of the build host's
architecture. Making it work portably would be nearly impossible! You should
experiment with changes to the uninstalled library and satisfy yourself that the
previously installed program continues to load the installed library at runtime,
whereas the uninstalled program picks up the modifications in the uninstalled
version of the library.* ◆

Equally importantly, the uninstalled `hello` program continues to load the uninstalled shared archive. This enables me to continue developing in the source directories and perform test builds in the knowledge that `libtool` has built all my executables, including the uninstalled executables in the build tree, to load the correct version of the library. I can check with HP-UX's `chatr` command, like this:

```
$ libtool --mode=execute chatr ./hello
/tmp/hello/.libs/hello:
        shared executable

        shared library dynamic path search:
            SHLIB_PATH      disabled  second
            embedded path   enabled   first  /tmp/intro-hello/.libs:\
                                             /usr/local/lib
        internal name:
            .libs/hello
        shared library list:
            static   /tmp/intro-hello/.libs/libhello.sl.0
            static   /tmp/intro-hello/.libs/libtrim.sl.0
            dynamic  /lib/libc.1

        shared library binding:
            deferred
...
```

This example introduces the concept of Libtool modes. Most of the time, `libtool` can infer a mode of operation from the contents of the command line, but sometimes (as in this example) it needs to be told. In Section 9.5, "Executing Uninstalled Binaries," we already used `libtool` in *execute* mode to run `gdb` against an uninstalled binary. In this example, I am telling `libtool` that I want to pass the `hello` binary to the `chatr` command, particularly because I know that the `'hello'` file is a script to set the local execution environment before running the real binary.

The various modes that `libtool` has are described in the Libtool reference documentation, and are listed in the Libtool help text:

```
$ libtool --help
...
MODE must be one of the following:

        clean       remove files from the build directory
        compile     compile a source file into a libtool object
        execute     automatically set library path, then run a program
        finish      complete the installation of libtool libraries
        install     install libraries or executables
        link        create a library or an executable
        uninstall   remove libraries from an installed directory

MODE-ARGS vary depending on the MODE.  Try `libtool --help --mode=MODE'
for a more detailed description of MODE.
```

9.8 Uninstalling

Having installed all these files to `/usr/local`, it might be difficult to remember which particular files belong to each installation. In the case of an executable, the uninstallation requires no magic; when uninstalling a Libtool library, however, all the files that comprise the implementation of the Libtool library in question must be uninstalled:

```
$ libtool rm -f /usr/local/bin/hello
rm -f /usr/local/bin/hello

$ libtool rm -f /usr/local/lib/libhello.la
rm -f /usr/local/lib/libhello.la /usr/local/lib/libhello.sl.0.0 \
/usr/local/lib/libhello.sl.0 /usr/local/lib/libhello.sl \
/usr/local/lib/libhello.a

$ libtool rm -f /usr/local/lib/libtrim.la
rm -f /usr/local/lib/libtrim.la /usr/local/lib/libtrim.sl.0.0 \
/usr/local/lib/libtrim.sl.0 /usr/local/lib/libtrim.sl \
/usr/local/lib/libtrim.a
```

Using libtool to perform the uninstallation in this way ensures that all the files that it installed, including any additional soft links required by the architecture-versioning scheme for shared archives, are removed with a single command.

Having explored the use of libtool from the command line, the next chapter discusses how to integrate libtool into the configury of your GNU Autotools–based projects.

10

Using GNU Libtool with 'configure.in' *and* 'Makefile.am'

Although Libtool is usable by itself, either from the command line or from a non-make-driven build system, it is also tightly integrated into Autoconf and Automake. This chapter discusses how to use Libtool with Autoconf and Automake and explains how to set up the files you write ('Makefile.am' and 'configure.in') to take advantage of libtool. For a more in-depth discussion of the workings of Libtool, particularly its command-line interface, refer to Chapter 9, "Introducing GNU Libtool." Using libtool for dynamic runtime loading is described in Chapter 17, "Using GNU libltdl."

Using libtool to build the libraries in a project requires declaring your use of libtool inside the project's 'configure.in' and adding the Libtool support scripts to the distribution. You also need to amend the build rules in either 'Makefile.am' or 'Makefile.in', depending on whether you are using Automake.

10.1 Integration with *'configure.in'*

Declaring your use of libtool in the project's 'configure.in' is a simple matter of adding the 'AC_PROG_LIBTOOL' (or 'AM_PROG_LIBTOOL' if you have an older automake or libtool installation) somewhere near the top of the file. I always put it immediately after the other 'AC_PROG_...' macros. If you are converting an old project to use libtool, you also need to remove any calls to 'AC_PROG_RANLIB'. Because Libtool will be handling all the libraries, *it* decides whether to call ranlib as appropriate for the build environment.

> ### Note
>
> The code generated by 'AC_PROG_LIBTOOL' relies on the shell variable
> $top_builddir to hold the relative path to the directory that contains the
> configure script. If you are using Automake, $top_builddir is set in the environ-
> ment by the generated 'Makefile'. If you use Autoconf without Automake, you
> must ensure that $top_builddir is set before the call to 'AC_PROG_LIBTOOL' in
> 'configure.in'.
>
> Adding the following code to 'configure.in' often suffices:
>
> ```
>     for top_builddir in . .. ../.. $ac_auxdir $ac_auxdir/..; do
>       test -f $top_builddir/configure && break
>     done
> ```

Having made these changes to add libtool support to your project, you
need to regenerate the 'aclocal.m4' file to pick up the macro definitions
required for 'AC_PROG_LIBTOOL', and then rebuild your configure script with
these new definitions in place. After you have done that, some new options
are available from configure:

```
$ aclocal
$ autoconf

$ ./configure --help
...
--enable and --with options recognized:
  --enable-shared[=PKGS]  build shared libraries [yes]
  --enable-static[=PKGS]  build static libraries [yes]
  --enable-fast-install[=PKGS]  optimize for fast installation [yes]
  --with-gnu-ld           assume the C compiler uses GNU ld [no]
  --disable-libtool-lock  avoid locking (might break parallel builds)
  --with-pic              try to use only PIC/non-PIC objects [both]
```

These new options give the end users of your project some control over how
they want to build the project's libraries. The opposites of each of these
switches are also accepted, even though they are not listed by configure
--help. You can equally pass '--disable-fast-install' or '--without-gnu-ld',
for example.

10.1.1 Extra Configure Options

The following list describes the more commonly used options automatically
added to configure, by virtue of using 'AC_PROG_LIBTOOL' in your 'configure.in'.
The Libtool manual distributed with Libtool releases always contains the most
up-to-date information about libtool options:

--enable-shared
--enable-static

More often invoked as --disable-shared or equivalently '--enable-shared=no', these switches determine whether libtool should build shared and/or static libraries in this package. If the installer is short of disk space, they might like to build entirely without static archives. To do this, they would use:

```
$ ./configure --disable-static
```

Sometimes it is desirable to configure several related packages with the same command line—from a scheduled build script or where subpackages with their own configure scripts are present, for example. The '--enable-shared' and '--enable-static' switches also accept a list of package names, causing the option to be applied to packages whose name is listed, and the opposite to be applied to those not listed.

By specifying:

```
$ ./configure --enable-static=libsnprintfv,autoopts
```

libtool would pass '--enable-static' to only the packages named *libsnprintfv* and *autoopts* in the current tree. Any other packages configured would effectively be passed '--disable-static'. Note that this doesn't necessarily mean that the packages must honor these options. Enabling static libraries for a package that consists of only dynamic modules makes no sense, and the package author would probably have decided to ignore such requests (see Section 10.1.2, "Extra Macros for Libtool").

--enable-fast-install

On some machines, libtool has to relink executables when they are installed (see Section 9.7, "Installing an Executable"). Generally, when an end user builds your package, he will probably type:

```
$ ./configure
$ make
$ make install
```

libtool builds executables suitable for copying into their respective installation destinations, obviating the need for relinking them on those hosts that would have required it. Whenever libtool links an executable that uses shared libraries, it also creates a *wrapper script* that ensures that the environment is correct for loading the correct libraries (see Section 9.5, "Executing Uninstalled Binaries"). On those hosts that require it, the wrapper script also relinks the executable in the build tree if you attempt to run it from there before installation.

Sometimes this behavior is not what you want, particularly if you are developing the package and not installing between test compilations. By passing '--disable-fast-install', the default behavior is reversed; executables will be built so that they can be run from the build tree without relinking, but during installation they may be relinked.

You can pass a list of executables as the argument to '--enable-fast-install' to determine which set of executables will not be relinked at installation time (on the hosts that require it). By specifying:

```
$ ./configure --enable-fast-install=autogen
```

the autogen executable is linked for fast installation (without being relinked), and any other executables in the build tree are linked for fast execution from their build location. This is useful if the remaining executables are for testing only, and will never be installed.

Most machines do not require that executables be relinked in this way; and in these cases, libtool links each executable once only, no matter whether '--disable-fast-install' is used.

--with-gnu-ld

This option is used to inform libtool that the C compiler is using GNU ld as its linker. It is more often used in the opposite sense when both gcc and GNU ld are installed, but gcc was built to use the native linker. libtool probes the system for GNU ld, and assumes that it is used by gcc if found, unless '--without-gnu-ld' is passed to configure.

--disable-libtool-lock

In normal operation, libtool builds two objects for every source file in a package: one PIC (position- independent code—suitable for shared libraries that might be loaded to different addresses when linked by the runtime loader) and one non-PIC. With gcc and some other compilers, libtool can specify a different output location for the PIC object:

```
$ libtool gcc -c shell.c
gcc -c -pic -DPIC shell.c -o .libs/shell.lo
gcc -c foo.c -o shell.o >/dev/null 2>&1
```

When using a compiler that does not accept both '-o' and '-c' in the same command, libtool must compile first the PIC and then the non-PIC object to the same destination file and then move the PIC object before compiling the non-PIC object. This would be a problem for parallel builds, because one file might overwrite the other. libtool uses a simple shell-locking mechanism to avoid this eventuality.

	If you find yourself building in an environment that has such a compiler, and not using parallel make, you can safely turn off the locking mechanism by using '--disable-libtool-lock' to gain a little extra speed in the overall compilation.
--with-pic	In usual operation, Libtool builds shared libraries from PIC objects and static archives from non-PIC objects, except where one or the other is not provided by the target host. By specifying '--with-pic', you are asking libtool to build static archives from PIC objects, and similarly by specifying '--without-pic' you are asking libtool to build shared libraries from non-PIC objects.
	libtool honors this flag only where it will produce a working library; otherwise it reverts to the default.

10.1.2 Extra Macros for Libtool

Several macros that can be added to 'configure.in' change the default behavior of libtool. If used, they must appear before the call to the 'AC_PROG_LIBTOOL' macro. Note that these macros change only the default behavior, and options passed in to configure on the command line always override the defaults. The most up-to-date information about these macros is available from The Libtool Manual. Some of the simpler macros are described here:

| AC_DISABLE_FAST_INSTALL | This macro tells libtool that on platforms which require relinking at install time, it should build executables so that they can be run from the build tree at the expense of relinking during installation, as if '--disable-fast-install' had been passed on the command line. |
| AC_DISABLE_SHARED AC_DISABLE_STATIC | These macros tell libtool to *not* try and build either shared or static libraries respectively. libtool always tries to build *something*, however; so even if you turn off static library building in 'configure.in', building your package for a target host without shared library support will fall back to building static archives. |

The time spent waiting for builds during development can be reduced a little by including these macros temporarily. Don't forget to remove them before you release the project, however!

In addition to the macros provided with `AC_PROG_LIBTOOL`, you may need to set a few shell variables yourself, depending on the structure of your project:

LTLIBOBJS   If your project uses the `AC_REPLACE FUNCS` macro, or any of the other macros that add object names to the `LIBOBJS` variable, you also need to provide an equivalent `LTLIBOBJS` definition. This is a simple matter of replacing the names of the objects mentioned in `LIBOBJS` with equivalent `.lo`-suffixed Libtool object names. The easiest way to do this is to add the following snippet to your `configure.in` near the end, just before the call to `AC_OUTPUT`:

```
Xsed="sed -e s/^X//"
LTLIBOBJS=`echo X"$LIBOBJS" | \
[$Xsed -e "s,\. [^.]* ,.lo ,g;s,\.[^.]*$,.lo,"]`
AC_SUBST(LTLIBOBJS)
```

The Xsed is not usually necessary, although it can prevent problems with the echo command in the event that one of the `LIBOBJS` files begins with a `-` character. It is also a good habit to write shell code like this to avoid problems in your programs.

LTALLOCA   If your project uses the `AC_FUNC_ALLOCA` macro, you need to provide a definition of `LTALLOCA` equivalent to the `ALLOCA` value provided by the macro:

```
Xsed="sed -e s/^X//"
LTALLOCA=`echo X"$ALLOCA" | [$Xsed -e "s,\.[^.]*$,.lo,"]`
AC_SUBST(LTALLOCA)
```

Obviously you don't need to redefine Xsed if you already used it for `LTLIBOBJS` earlier.

LIBTOOL_DEPS   To help you write make rules for automatic updating of the Libtool configuration files, you can use the value of `LIBTOOL_DEPS` after the call to `AC_PROG_LIBTOOL`:

```
AC_PROG_LIBTOOL
AC_SUBST(LIBTOOL_DEPS)
```

Then add the following to the top-level `Makefile.in`:

```
libtool: @LIBTOOL_DEPS@
        cd $(srcdir) && \
        $(SHELL) ./config.status --recheck
```

If you are using automake in your project, it generates equivalent rules automatically. You don't need to use this except in circumstances in which you want to use libtool and autoconf, but not automake.

10.2 Integration with 'Makefile.am'

Automake supports Libtool libraries in two ways: It can help you to build the Libtool libraries themselves, and also to build executables that link against Libtool libraries.

10.2.1 Creating Libtool Libraries with Automake

Continuing in the spirit of making Libtool library management look like native static archive management, converting a 'Makefile.am' from static archive use to Libtool library use is a matter of changing the name of the library and adding a Libtool prefix somewhere. For example, a 'Makefile.am' for building a static archive might be as follows:

```
lib_LIBRARIES      = libshell.a
libshell_a_SOURCES = object.c subr.c symbol.c
```

This builds a static archive called 'libshell.a' consisting of the objects 'object.o', 'subr.o', and 'bar.o'. To build an equivalent Libtool library from the same objects, you change this as follows:

```
lib_LTLIBRARIES     = libshell.la
libshell_la_SOURCES = object.c subr.c symbol.c
```

The only changes are that the library is now named with a '.la' suffix, and the Automake primary is now 'LTLIBRARIES'. Note that because the name of the library has changed, you also need to use 'libshell_la_SOURCES', and similarly for any other Automake macros that used to refer to the old archive. As for native libraries, Libtool library names should begin with the letters 'lib', so that the linker can find them when passed '-l' options.

Often you will need to add extra objects to the library as determined by configure, but this is also a mechanical process. When building native libraries, the 'Makefile.am' would have contained the following:

```
libshell_a_LDADD = xmalloc.o @LIBOBJS@
```

To add the same objects to an equivalent Libtool library requires this:

```
libshell_la_LDADD = xmalloc.lo @LTLIBOBJS@
```

That is, objects added to a Libtool library must be Libtool objects (with a '.lo' suffix). You should add code to 'configure.in' to ensure that 'LTALLOCA' and 'LTLIBOBJS' are set appropriately (see Section 10.1.2, "Extra Macros for Libtool"). Automake takes care of generating appropriate rules for building the Libtool objects mentioned in an 'LDADD' macro.

If you want to pass any additional flags to `libtool` when it is building, you use the `'LDFLAGS'` macro for that library, like this:

```
libshell_la_LDFLAGS = -version-info 1:0:1
```

For a detailed list of all the available options, see the section "Link Mode" in The Libtool Manual.

> ### Why Use `'-rpath'`?
>
> *Libtool's use of `'-rpath'` has been a point of contention for some users, because it prevents you from moving shared libraries to another location in the library search path. Or, at least, if you do, all the executables that were linked with `'-rpath'` set to the old location need to be relinked.*
>
> *We (the Libtool maintainers) assert that always using `'-rpath'` is a good thing— mainly because you can guarantee that any executable linked with `'-rpath'` will find the correct version of the library, in the rpath directory, that was intended when the executable was linked. Library versions can still be managed correctly, and will be found by the runtime loader, by installing newer versions to the same directory. Additionally, it is much harder for a malicious user to leave a modified copy of the system library in a directory that someone might want to list in his `'LD_LIBRARY_PATH'` in the hope that some code he has written will be executed unexpectedly.*
>
> *The argument against `'-rpath'` was instigated when one of the GNU/Linux distributions moved some important system libraries to another directory to make room for a different version, and discovered that all the executables that relied on these libraries and were linked with Libtool no longer worked. Doing this was, arguably, bad system management; the new libraries should have been placed in a new directory, and the old libraries left alone. Refusing to use `'-rpath'` in case you want to restructure the system library directories is a very weak argument.* ◆

The `-rpath` option (which is required for Libtool libraries) is automatically supplied by `automake` based on the installation directory specified with the library primary:

```
lib_LTLIBRARIES = libshell.la
```

The example would use the value of the `make` macro `'$(libdir)'` as the argument to `'-rpath'`, because that is where the library will be installed.

You can use a few of the other options in the library `'LDFLAGS'`, including the following:

`-no-undefined`	Modern architectures enable us to create shared libraries with undefined symbols, provided those symbols are resolved (usually by the executable that loads the library) at runtime. Unfortunately, some architectures (notably AIX and Windows) require that *all* symbols are resolved

	when the library is linked. If you know that your library has no unresolved symbols at link time, adding this option tells libtool that it will be able to build a shared library, even on architectures that have this requirement.
-static	Using this option forces libtool to build only a static archive for this library.
-release	On occasion, it is desirable to encode the release number of a library into its name. By specifying the release number with this option, libtool will build a library that does this, but will break binary compatibility for each change of the release number. By breaking binary compatibility this way, you negate the possibility of fixing bugs in installed programs by installing an updated shared library. You should probably be using '-version-info' instead.

```
libshell_la_LDFLAGS = -release 27
```

The preceding fragment might create a library called 'libshell-27.so.0.0.0', for example.

-version-info	Set the version number of the library according to the native versioning rules based on the numbers supplied (see Section 10.4, "Library Versioning"). You need to be aware that the library version number is for the use of the runtime loader, and is completely unrelated to the release number of your project. If you really want to encode the project release into the library, you can use '-release' to do it.

If this option is not supplied explicitly, it defaults to '-version-info 0:0:0'.

Why Use -no-undefined?

Historically, the default behavior of Libtool was as if ' -no-undefined' was always passed on the command line, but it proved to be annoying to developers who had to constantly turn it off so that their ELF libraries could be featureful. Now it has to be defined explicitly if you need it.

There are tradeoffs:

- *If you don't specify ' -no-undefined', Libtool will not build shared libraries on platforms that do not allow undefined symbols at link time for such a library.*

- *It is only safe to specify this flag when you know for certain that all the libraries' symbols are defined at link time; otherwise the ' -no-undefined' link will appear to work until it is tried on a platform that requires all symbols to be defined. Libtool will try to link the shared library in this case (because you told it that you have not left any undefined symbols), but the link will fail, because there are undefined symbols in spite of what you told Libtool.*

For more information about this topic, see Section 17.3, "Portable Library Design." ◆

10.2.2 Linking Against Libtool Libraries with Automake

After you have set up your 'Makefile.am' to create some Libtool libraries, you will want to link an executable against them. You can do this easily with automake by using the program's qualified 'LDADD' macro:

```
bin_PROGRAMS = shell
shell_SOURCES = shell.c token.l
shell_LDADD   = libshell.la
```

This chooses either the static or shared archive from the 'libshell.la' Libtool library depending on the target host and any Libtool mode switches mentioned in the 'Makefile.am' or passed to configure. The chosen archive is linked with any objects generated from the listed sources to make an executable. Note that the executable itself is a hidden file, and that in its place libtool creates a wrapper script (see Section 9.5, "Executing Uninstalled Binaries").

As with the Libtool libraries, you can pass additional switches for the libtool invocation in the qualified 'LDFLAGS' macros to control how the shell executable is linked:

-all-static	Always choose static libraries where possible, and try to create a completely statically linked executable.
-no-fast-install	If you really want to use this flag on some targets, you can pass it in an 'LDFLAGS' macro. This is not overridden by the configure '--enable-fast-install' switch. Executables built with this flag do not need relinking to be executed from the build tree on platforms that might have otherwise required it.
-no-install	You should use this option for any executables used only for testing, or for generating other files and are consequently never installed. By specifying this option, you are telling Libtool that the executable it links will only ever be executed from where it is built in the build tree. Libtool can usually considerably speed up the link process for such executables.
-static	This switch is similar to '-all-static', except that it applies to only the uninstalled Libtool libraries in the build tree. Where possible the static archive from these libraries is used, but the default linking mode is used for libraries already installed.

When debugging an executable, for example, it can be useful to temporarily use the following:

```
shell_LDFLAGS = -all-static
```

> **Note**
>
> You can pass Libtool link options to all the targets in a given directory by using the unadorned 'LDFLAGS' macro:
>
> ```
> LDFLAGS = -static
> ```
>
> This is best reserved for directories that have targets of the same type (all Libtool libraries or all executables, for instance). The technique still works in a mixed target type directory, and libtool will ignore switches that don't make sense for particular targets. It is less maintainable and makes it harder to understand what is going on if you do that, however. ◆

10.3 Using libtoolize

Having made the necessary editions in 'configure.in' and 'Makefile.am', all that remains is to add the Libtool infrastructure to your project.

First of all, you must ensure that the correct definitions for the new macros you use in 'configure.in' are added to 'aclocal.m4' (see Appendix C, "Generated File Dependencies"). At the moment, the safest way to do this is to copy 'libtool.m4' from the installed libtool to 'acinclude.m4' in the top-level source directory of your package. This is to ensure that when your package ships, no mismatch errors occur between the M4 macros you provided in the version of libtool you built the distribution with, versus the version of the Libtool installation in another developer's environment. In a future release, libtool will check that the macros in 'aclocal.m4' are from the same Libtool distribution as the generated libtool script:

```
$ cp /usr/share/libtool/libtool.m4 ./acinclude.m4
$ aclocal
```

By naming the file 'acinclude.m4', you ensure that aclocal can see it and will use macros from it, and that automake will add it to the distribution when you create the tarball.

Next, you should run libtoolize, which adds some files to your distribution that are required by the macros from 'libtool.m4'. In particular, you will get 'ltconfig'[1] and 'ltmain.sh', which are used to create a custom libtool script on the installer's machine.

---

[1] The functionality of 'ltconfig' is slated for migration into 'libtool.m4' for a future release of libtool, whereupon this file will no longer be necessary.

If you do not yet have them, `libtoolize` will also add `'config.guess'` and
`'config.sub'` to your distribution. Sometimes you don't need to run `libtoolize`
manually, because `automake` runs it for you when it sees the changes you have
made to `'configure.in'`, as follows:

```
$ automake --add-missing
automake: configure.in: installing ./install-sh
automake: configure.in: installing ./mkinstalldirs
automake: configure.in: installing ./missing
configure.in: 8: required file ./ltconfig not found
```

The error message in the last line is an aberration. If it were consistent with the
other lines, it would say:

```
automake: configure.in: installing ./ltconfig
automake: configure.in: installing ./ltmain.sh
automake: configure.in: installing ./config.guess
automake: configure.in: installing ./config.sub
```

But the effect is the same, and the files are correctly added to the distribution
despite the misleading message.

> **Note**
>
> *Before you release a distribution of your project, it is wise to get the latest versions
> of* `'config.guess'` *and* `'config.sub'` *from the GNU site* (`ftp://ftp.gnu.org/gnu/
> config/`), *because they may be newer than the versions automatically added by*
> `libtoolize` *and* `automake`. *Note that* `automake --add-missing` *will give you its
> own version of these two files if* `'AC_PROG_LIBTOOL'` *is not used in the project*
> `'configure.in'`, *but will give you the versions shipped with* `libtool` *if that
> macro is present!* ◆

10.4 Library Versioning

It is important to note from the outset that the version number of your project
is a very different thing from the version number of any libraries shipped with
your project. It is a common error for maintainers to try to force their libraries
to have the same version number as the current release version of the package
as a whole. At best, they will break binary compatibility unnecessarily, so that
their users won't gain the benefits of the changes in their latest revision without
relinking all applications that use it. At worst, they will allow the runtime
linker to load binary-incompatible libraries, causing applications to crash.

Far better, the Libtool versioning system will build native shared libraries with
the correct *native* library version numbers. Although different architectures use
various numbering schemes, Libtool abstracts these away behind the system
described here. The various native library version-numbering schemes are
designed so that when an executable is started, the runtime loader can, where

appropriate, choose a more recently installed library version than the one with which the executable was actually built. This enables you to fix bugs in your library, and having built it with the correct Libtool version number, have those fixes propagate into any executables that were built with the old buggy version. This can work only if the runtime loader can tell whether it can load the new library into the old executable and expect them to work together. The library version numbers give this information to the runtime loader, so it is very important to set them correctly.

The version scheme used by Libtool tracks *interfaces*, where an interface is the set of exported entry points into the library. All Libtool libraries start with `-version-info` set to `0:0:0`—this will be the default version number if you don't explicitly set it on the Libtool link command line. The meaning of these numbers (from left to right) is as follows:

current	The number of the current interface exported by the library. A *current* value of `0` means that you are calling the interface exported by this library *interface 0*.
revision	The implementation number of the most recent interface exported by this library. In this case, a *revision* value of `0` means that this is the first implementation of the interface.
	If the next release of this library exports the same interface, but has a different implementation (perhaps some bugs have been fixed), the *revision* number will be higher, but the *current* number will be the same. In that case, when given a choice, the the runtime loader always uses the library with the highest *revision*.
age	The number of previous additional interfaces supported by this library. If *age* is `2`, this library can be linked into executables built with a release of this library that exported the current interface number, *current*, or any of the preceding two interfaces.
	By definition, *age* must be less than or equal to *current*. At the outset, only the first ever interface is implemented, so *age* can only be `0`.

For later releases of a library, the `-version-info` argument needs to be set correctly depending on any interface changes you have made. This is quite straightforward when you understand what the three numbers mean:

1. If you have changed any of the sources for this library, the *revision* number must be incremented. *This is a new revision of the current interface.*

2. If the interface has changed, *current* must be incremented, and *revision* reset to `0`. *This is the first revision of a new interface.*

3. If the new interface is a superset of the preceding interface (that is, if the preceding interface has not been broken by the changes in this new release), *age* must be incremented. *This release is backward compatible with the preceding release.*

4. If the new interface has removed elements with respect to the preceding interface, you have broken backward compatibility and *age* must be reset to '0'. *This release has a new, but backward-incompatible, interface.*

Version Example

If the next release of the library included some new commands for an existing socket protocol, you would use -version-info 1:0:1. *This is the first revision of a new interface. This release is backward-compatible with the preceding release.*

Later, you implement a faster way of handling part of the algorithm at the core of the library and release it with -version-info 1:1:1. *This is a new revision of the current interface.*

Unfortunately, the speed of your new implementation can be fully exploited only by changing the API to access the structures at a lower level, which breaks compatibility with the preceding interface, so you release it as -version-info 2:0:0. *This release has a new, but backward-incompatible interface.* ◆

When deciding which numbers to change in the -version-info argument for a new release, you must remember that an interface change is not limited to the API of the library. The notion of an interface must include any method by which a user (code or human) can interact with the library: adding new built-in commands to a shell library; the format used in an output file; the handshake protocol required for a client connecting over a socket; and so on.

Additionally, if you use a development model that has both a stable and an unstable tree being developed in parallel, for example, and you don't mind forcing your users to relink all the applications that use one of your Libtool libraries every time you make a release, libtool provides the '-release' flag to encode the project version number in the name of the library (see Section 10.2.1, "Creating Libtool Libraries with Automake"). This can save you library compatibility problems later if you need to, for example, make a patch release of an older revision of your library, but the library version number that you should use has already been taken by another earlier release. In this case, you could be fairly certain that library releases from the unstable branch will not be binary-compatible with the stable releases, so you could make all the stable releases with '-release 1.0' and begin the first unstable release with '-release 1.1'.

10.5 Convenience Libraries

Sometimes it is useful to group objects together in an intermediate stage of a project's compilation to provide a useful handle for that group without having to specify all the individual objects every time. Convenience libraries are a portable way of creating such a *partially linked* object: Libtool will handle all the low-level details in a way appropriate to the target host. This section describes the use of convenience libraries in conjunction with Automake. The principles of convenience libraries are discussed in Section 9.2.4, "Creating Convenience Libraries."

The key to creating Libtool convenience libraries with Automake is to use the 'noinst_LTLIBRARIES' macro. For the Libtool libraries named in this macro, Automake creates Libtool convenience libraries that can subsequently be linked into other Libtool libraries.

Hands On

In this section, I create two convenience libraries, each in its own subdirectory, and link them into a third Libtool library, which is ultimately linked into an application.

If you want to follow this example, you should create a directory structure to hold the sources by running the following shell commands:

```
$ mkdir convenience
$ cd convenience
$ mkdir lib
$ mkdir replace
```

The first convenience library is built from two source files in the 'lib' subdirectory.

'source.c':

```
#if HAVE_CONFIG_H
#  include <config.h>
#endif

#if HAVE_MATH_H
#  include <math.h>
#endif

void
foo (double argument)
{
  printf ("cos (%g) => %g\n", argument, cos (argument));
}
```

This file defines a single function to display the cosine of its argument on standard output, and consequently relies on an implementation of the `cos` function from the system libraries. Note the conditional inclusion of 'config.h', which will contain a definition of 'HAVE_MATH_H' if 'configure' discovers a 'math.h' system header (the usual location for the declaration of `cos`). The 'HAVE_CONFIG_H' guard is by convention so that the source can be linked by passing the preprocessor macro definitions to the compiler on the command line—if 'configure.in' does not use 'AM_CONFIG_HEADER', for instance.

'source.h':

```
extern void foo     (double argument);
```

For brevity, there is no `#ifndef SOURCE_H` guard. The header is not installed, so you have full control over where it is `#include`'d; and in any case, function declarations can be safely repeated if the header is accidentally processed more than once. In a real program, it is better to list the function parameters in the declaration so that the compiler can do type checking. This limits the code to working only with ANSI compilers, unless you also use a PARAMS macro to conditionally preprocess away the parameters when a K&R compiler is used. These details are beyond the scope of this convenience library example, but are described in full in Section 7.1.6, "K&R Compilers."

You also need a 'Makefile.am' to hold the details of how this convenience library is linked:

```
## Process this file with automake to produce Makefile.in

noinst_LTLIBRARIES       = library.la
library_la_SOURCES       = source.c source.h
library_la_LIBADD        = -lm
```

The 'noinst_LTLIBRARIES' macro names the Libtool convenience libraries to be built in this directory, 'library.la'. Although not required for compilation, 'source.h' is listed in the 'SOURCES' macro of 'library.la' so that correct source dependencies are generated, and so that it is added to the distribution tarball by automake's `dist` rule.

Finally, because the `foo` function relies on the `cos` function from the system math library, '-lm' is named as a required library in the 'LIBADD' macro. As with all Libtool libraries, interlibrary dependencies are maintained for convenience libraries so that you need only list the libraries you are using directly when you link your application later. The libraries used by those libraries are added by Libtool.

The parent directory holds the sources for the main executable, 'main.c', and for a (non-convenience) Libtool library, 'error.c' and 'error.h'.

Like 'source.h', the functions exported from the Libtool library 'liberror.la' are listed in 'error.h':

```
extern void gratuitous       (void);
extern void set_program_name (char *path);
extern void error            (char *message);
```

The corresponding function definitions are in 'error.c':

```
#include <stdio.h>

#include "source.h"

static char *program_name = NULL;

void
gratuitous (void)
{
  /* Gratuitous display of convenience library functionality! */
  double argument = 0.0;
  foo (argument);
}

void
set_program_name (char *path)
{
  if (!program_name)
    program_name = basename (path);
}

void
error (char *message)
{
  fprintf (stderr, "%s: ERROR: %s\n", program_name, message);
  exit (1);
}
```

The gratuitous() function calls the foo() function defined in the 'library.la' convenience library in the 'lib' directory, hence 'source.h' is included.

The definition of error() displays an error message to standard error, along with the name of the program, program_name, which is set by calling set_program_name(). This function, in turn, extracts the basename of the program from the full path using the system function, basename(), and stores it in the library private variable, program_name.

Usually, `basename()` is part of the system C library, although older systems did not include it. Because of this, there is no portable header file that can be included to get a declaration, and you might see a harmless compiler warning due to the use of the function without a declaration. The alternative is to add your own declaration in 'error.c'. The problem with this approach is that different vendors provide slightly different declarations (with or without const, for instance), so compilation will fail on those architectures that *do* provide a declaration in the system headers that differs from the declaration you have guessed.

For the benefit of architectures that do not have an implementation of the `basename()` function, a fallback implementation is provided in the 'replace' subdirectory. The file 'basename.c' follows:

```
#if HAVE_CONFIG_H
#  include <config.h>
#endif

#if HAVE_STRING_H
#  include <string.h>
#elif HAVE_STRINGS_H
#  include <strings.h>
#endif

#if !HAVE_STRRCHR
#  ifndef strrchr
#    define strrchr rindex
#  endif
#endif

char*
basename (char *path)
{
  /* Search for the last directory separator in PATH.  */
  char *basename = strrchr (path, '/');

  /* If found, return the address of the following character,
     or the start of the parameter passed in.  */
  return basename ? ++basename : path;
}
```

For brevity, the implementation does not use any const declarations, which would be good style for a real project, but would need to be checked at configure time in case the end user needs to compile the package with a K&R compiler.

The use of `strrchr()` is noteworthy. Sometimes it is declared in 'string.h'; otherwise, it might be declared in 'strings.h'.

BSD-based Unices, on the other hand, do not have this function at all, but provide an equivalent function, rindex(). The preprocessor code at the start of the file is designed to cope with all these eventualities. The last block of preprocessor code assumes that if strrchr is already defined that it holds a working macro, and does not redefine it.

'Makefile.am' contains:

```
# Process this file with automake to produce Makefile.in

noinst_LTLIBRARIES     = libreplace.la
libreplace_la_SOURCES  =
libreplace_la_LIBADD   = @LTLIBOBJS@
```

Once again, the 'noinst_LTLIBRARIES' macro names the convenience library, 'libreplace.la'. By default, there are no sources, because we expect to have a system definition of basename(). Additional Libtool objects that should be added to the library based on tests at configure time are handled by the 'LIBADD' macro. 'LTLIBOBJS' will contain 'basename.lo' if the system does not provide basename, and will be empty otherwise. Illustrating another feature of convenience libraries: On many architectures, 'libreplace.la' contains no objects.

Back in the top-level project directory, all the preceding objects are combined by another 'Makefile.am':

```
## Process this file with automake to produce Makefile.in

AUTOMAKE_OPTIONS       = foreign

SUBDIRS                = replace lib .

CPPFLAGS               = -I$(top_srcdir)/lib

include_HEADERS        = error.h

lib_LTLIBRARIES        = liberror.la
liberror_la_SOURCES    = error.c
liberror_la_LDFLAGS    = -no-undefined -version-info 0:0:0
liberror_la_LIBADD     = replace/libreplace.la lib/library.la

bin_PROGRAMS           = convenience
convenience_SOURCES    = main.c
convenience_LDADD      = liberror.la
```

The initial 'SUBDIRS' macro is necessary to ensure that the libraries in the subdirectories are built before the final library and executable in this directory.

Notice that I have not listed 'error.h' in 'liberror_la_SOURCES' this time, because 'liberror.la' is an installed library, and 'error.h' defines the public interface to that library. Because the 'liberror.la' Libtool library is installed, I have used the '-version-info' option, and I have also used '-no-undefined' so that the project will compile on architectures that require all library symbols to be defined at link time—the reason program_name is maintained in 'liberror' rather than in 'main.c' is so that the library does not have a runtime dependency on the executable that links it.

The key to this example is that by linking the 'libreplace.la' and 'library.la' convenience libraries into 'liberror.la', all the objects in both convenience libraries are compiled into the single installed library, 'liberror.la'. Additionally, all the interlibrary dependencies of the convenience libraries ('-lm', from 'library.la') are propagated to 'liberror.la'.

> **Note**
>
> *A common difficulty people experience with Automake is knowing when to use a* 'LIBADD' *primary rather than an* 'LDADD' *primary. A useful mnemonic is:* 'LIBADD' *is for **ADD**itional **LIB**rary objects; LDADD is for **ADD**itional linker (LD) objects.* ◆

The executable, 'convenience', is built from 'main.c', and requires only 'liberror.la'. All the other implicit dependencies are encoded within 'liberror.la'. Here is 'main.c':

```
#include <stdio.h>
#include "error.h"

int
main (int argc, char *argv[])
{
  set_program_name (argv[0]);
  gratuitous ();
  error ("This program does nothing!");
}
```

The only file that remains before you can compile the example is 'configure.in':

```
# Process this file with autoconf to create configure.

AC_INIT(error.c)
AM_CONFIG_HEADER(config.h)
AM_INIT_AUTOMAKE(convenience, 1.0)

AC_PROG_CC
AM_PROG_LIBTOOL

AC_CHECK_HEADERS(math.h)
```

```
AC_CHECK_HEADERS(string.h strings.h, break)

AC_CHECK_FUNCS(strrchr)
AC_REPLACE_FUNCS(basename)

Xsed="sed -e s/^X//"
LTLIBOBJS=`echo X"$LIBOBJS"|$Xsed -e "s,\.[^.]*$,.lo,"`
AC_SUBST(LTALLOCA)

AC_OUTPUT(replace/Makefile lib/Makefile Makefile)
```

There are checks for all the features used by the sources in the project:
'math.h' and either 'string.h' or 'strings.h'; the existence of strrchr (*after*
the tests for string headers); adding 'basename.o' to 'LIBOBJS' if there is no
system implementation; and the shell code to set 'LTLIBOBJS'.

With all the files in place, you can now bootstrap the project:

```
$ ls -R
.:
Makefile.am  configure.in  error.c  error.h  lib  main.c  replace

lib:
Makefile.am  source.c  source.h

replace:
Makefile.am  basename.c

$ aclocal
$ autoheader

$ automake --add-missing --copy
automake: configure.in: installing ./install-sh
automake: configure.in: installing ./mkinstalldirs
automake: configure.in: installing ./missing
configure.in: 7: required file ./ltconfig not found

$ autoconf

$ ls -R
.:
Makefile.am   config.h.in   error.c     ltconfig    mkinstalldirs
Makefile.in   config.sub    error.h     ltmain.sh   replace
aclocal.m4    configure     install-sh  main.c
config.guess  configure.in  lib         missing

lib:
Makefile.am  Makefile.in  source.c  source.h

replace:
Makefile.am  Makefile.in  basename.c
```

With these files in place, the package can now be configured:

```
$ ./configure
...
checking how to run the C preprocessor... gcc -E
checking for math.h... yes
checking for string.h... yes
checking for strrchr... yes
checking for basename... yes
updating cache ./config.cache
creating ./config.status
creating replace/Makefile
creating lib/Makefile
creating Makefile
creating config.h
```

Notice that my host has an implementation of basename().

Here are the highlights of the compilation itself:

```
$ make
Making all in replace
make[1]: Entering directory /tmp/replace
/bin/sh ../libtool --mode=link gcc  -g -O2  -o libreplace.la
rm -fr .libs/libreplace.la .libs/libreplace.* .libs/libreplace.*
ar cru .libs/libreplace.al
ranlib .libs/libreplace.al
creating libreplace.la
(cd .libs && rm -f libreplace.la && ln -s ../libreplace.la \
libreplace.la)
make[1]: Leaving directory /tmp/replace
```

Here the build descends into the 'replace' subdirectory and creates 'libreplace.la', which is empty on my host because I don't need an implementation of basename():

```
Making all in lib
make[1]: Entering directory /tmp/lib
/bin/sh ../libtool --mode=compile gcc -DHAVE_CONFIG_H  -I. -I. \
-g -O2 -c source.c
rm -f .libs/source.lo
gcc -DHAVE_CONFIG_H -I. -I. -g -O2 -c -fPIC -DPIC source.c \
-o .libs/source.lo
gcc -DHAVE_CONFIG_H -I. -I. -g -O2 -c source.c \
-o source.o >/dev/null 2>&1
mv -f .libs/source.lo source.lo
/bin/sh ../libtool --mode=link gcc  -g -O2  -o library.la source.lo -lm
rm -fr .libs/library.la .libs/library.* .libs/library.*
ar cru .libs/library.al source.lo
ranlib .libs/library.al
creating library.la
(cd .libs && rm -f library.la && ln -s ../library.la library.la)
make[1]: Leaving directory /tmp/lib
```

Next, the build enters the 'lib' subdirectory to build 'library.la'. The 'configure' preprocessor macros are passed on the command line, because no 'config.h' was created by AC_CONFIG_HEADER:

```
Making all in .
make[1]: Entering directory /tmp
/bin/sh ./libtool --mode=compile gcc -DHAVE_CONFIG_H -I. -I. -I./lib \
-g -O2 -c error.c
mkdir .libs
gcc -DHAVE_CONFIG_H -I. -I. -I./lib -g -O2 -Wp,-MD,.deps/error.pp -c \
-fPIC -DPIC error.c -o .libs/error.lo
error.c: In function set_program_name:
error.c:20: warning: assignment makes pointer from integer without cast

gcc -DHAVE_CONFIG_H -I. -I. -I./lib -g -O2 -Wp,-MD,.deps/error.pp -c \
error.c -o error.o >/dev/null 2>&1
mv -f .libs/error.lo error.lo
/bin/sh ./libtool --mode=link gcc  -g -O2  -o liberror.la -rpath \
/usr/local/lib -no-undefined -version-info 0:0:0 error.lo \
replace/libreplace.la lib/library.la
rm -fr .libs/liberror.la .libs/liberror.* .libs/liberror.*
gcc -shared  error.lo -Wl,--whole-archive replace/.libs/libreplace.al \
lib/.libs/library.al -Wl,--no-whole-archive  \
replace/.libs/libreplace.al lib/.libs/library.al -lc  -Wl,-soname \
-Wl,liberror.so.0 -o .libs/liberror.so.0.0.0
(cd .libs && rm -f liberror.so.0 && ln -s liberror.so.0.0.0 \
liberror.so.0)
(cd .libs && rm -f liberror.so && ln -s liberror.so.0.0.0 liberror.so)
rm -fr .libs/liberror.lax
mkdir .libs/liberror.lax
rm -fr .libs/liberror.lax/libreplace.al
mkdir .libs/liberror.lax/libreplace.al
(cd .libs/liberror.lax/libreplace.al && ar x \
/tmp/replace/.libs/libreplace.al)
rm -fr .libs/liberror.lax/library.al
mkdir .libs/liberror.lax/library.al
(cd .libs/liberror.lax/library.al && ar x \
/tmp/lib/.libs/library.al)
ar cru .libs/liberror.a error.o .libs/liberror.lax/library.al/source.lo
ranlib .libs/liberror.a
rm -fr .libs/liberror.lax
creating liberror.la
(cd .libs && rm -f liberror.la && ln -s ../liberror.la liberror.la)
```

The resulting convenience library is an archive of the resulting PIC objects. The interlibrary dependency, '-lm', is passed to libtool and, although not needed to create the convenience library, *is* stored in the pseudo-archive, 'library.la', to be used when another object links against it.

Also you can see the harmless compiler warning I mentioned earlier, due to the missing declaration for basename(). Notice how libtool uses the '--whole-archive' option of GNU ld to link the convenience library contents directly into 'liberror.so', but extracts the PIC objects from each of the convenience libraries so that a new 'liberror.a' can be made from them. Unfortunately, this means that the resulting static archive component of 'liberror.la' has a mixture of PIC and non-PIC objects. In a future release of Libtool, this will be addressed by tracking both types of objects in the convenience archive if necessary and using the correct type of object, depending on context.

Here, 'main.c' is compiled (not to a Libtool object, because it is not compiled using libtool) and linked with the 'liberror.la' Libtool library:

```
gcc -DHAVE_CONFIG_H -I. -I.  -I./lib  -g -O2 -c main.c
/bin/sh ./libtool --mode=link gcc  -g -O2  -o convenience  main.o \
liberror.la
gcc -g -O2 -o .libs/convenience main.o ./.libs/liberror.so -lm \
-Wl,--rpath -Wl,/usr/local/lib
creating convenience
make[1]: Leaving directory /tmp/convenience
```

libtool calls gcc to link the 'convenience' executable from 'main.o' and the shared library component of 'liberror.la'. libtool also links with '-lm', the propagated interlibrary dependency of the 'library.la' convenience library. Because 'libreplace.la' and 'library.la' were convenience libraries, their objects are already present in 'liberror.la', so they are not listed again in the final link line—the whole point of convenience archives.

This just shows that it all works:

```
$ ls
Makefile      config.h       configure.in  install-sh   main.c
Makefile.am   config.h.in    convenience   lib          main.o
Makefile.in   config.log     error.c       liberror.la  missing
aclocal.m4    config.status  error.h       libtool      mkinstalldirs
config.cache  config.sub     error.lo      ltconfig     replace
config.guess  configure      error.o       ltmain.sh

$ libtool --mode=execute ldd convenience
        liberror.so.0 => /tmp/.libs/liberror.so.0 (0x40014000)
        libm.so.6 => /lib/libm.so.6 (0x4001c000)
        libc.so.6 => /lib/libc.so.6 (0x40039000)
        /lib/ld-linux.so.2 => /lib/ld-linux.so.2 (0x40000000)
$ ./convenience
cos (0) => 1
lt-convenience: ERROR: This program does nothing!
```

Notice that you are running the uninstalled executable, which is in actual fact a wrapper script (see Section 9.5, "Executing Uninstalled Binaries"). That is why you need to use libtool to run ldd on the real executable. The uninstalled executable called by the wrapper script is named lt-convenience, hence the output from basename().

Finally, you can see from the output of ldd that *convenience* really is not linked against either 'library.la' or 'libreplace.la'.

A Large GNU Autotools Project

This chapter develops the worked example described in Chapter 7, "A Small GNU Autotools Project." Again, the example is heavily colored by my own views, and there certainly are other, very different, but equally valid ways of achieving the same objectives.

I explain how I incorporated Libtool into the Sic project, and how to put the project documentation and test suite under the control of GNU Autotools. I pointed out some problems with the project when I first introduced it. This chapter addresses those issues and presents my favored solution to each.

11.1 Using Libtool Libraries

As you have seen, it is very easy to convert automake-built static libraries to automake-built Libtool libraries. To build 'libsic' as a Libtool library, I have changed the name of the library from 'libsic.a' (the *old archive* name in Libtool terminology) to 'libsic.la' (the *pseudo library*), and must use the LTLIBRARIES Automake primary:

```
lib_LTLIBRARIES      = libsic.la
libsic_la_SOURCES    = builtin.c error.c eval.c list.c sic.c \
                       syntax.c xmalloc.c xstrdup.c xstrerror.c
```

Notice the 'la' in libsic_la_SOURCES is new too.

It is similarly easy to take advantage of Libtool *convenience* libraries. For the purposes of Sic, 'libreplace' is an ideal candidate for this treatment—I can create the library as a separate entity from selected sources in their own directory and add those objects to 'libsic'. This technique ensures that the installed library has all the support functions it needs without having to link 'libreplace' as a separate object.

In 'replace/Makefile.am', I have again changed the name of the library
'libreplace.a' to 'libreplace.la', and changed the automake primary from
'LIBRARIES' to 'LTLIBRARIES'. Unfortunately, those changes alone are insuffi-
cient. Libtool libraries are compiled from Libtool objects (which have the
'.lo' suffix), so I cannot use 'LIBOBJS', which is a list of '.o'-suffixed
objects.[1] (See Section 10.1.2, "Extra Macros for Libtool," for more details.)
Here is 'replace/Makefile.am':

```
MAINTAINERCLEANFILES     = Makefile.in

noinst_LTLIBRARIES       = libreplace.la
libreplace_la_SOURCES    =
libreplace_la_LIBADD     = @LTLIBOBJS@
```

And not forgetting to set and use the 'LTLIBOBJS' configure substitution (see the
Section 10.1.2, "Extra Macros for Libtool"):

```
Xsed=" -e s/^X//"
LTLIBOBJS=`echo X"$LIBOBJS" | \
[$Xsed -e "s,\.[^.]* ,.lo ,g;s,\.[^.]*$,.lo,"]`
```

As a consequence of using Libtool to build the project libraries, the increasing
number of configuration files being added to the 'config' directory will grow
to include 'ltconfig' and 'ltmain.sh'. These files will be used on the installer's
machine when Sic is configured, so it is important to distribute them. The naive
way to do it is to give the 'config' directory a 'Makefile.am' of its own.
However, it is not too difficult to distribute these files from the top
'Makefile.am', and it saves clutter, as you can see here:

```
AUX_DIST              = $(ac_aux_dir)/config.guess \
                        $(ac_aux_dir)/config.sub \
                        $(ac_aux_dir)/install-sh \
                        $(ac_aux_dir)/ltconfig \
                        $(ac_aux_dir)/ltmain.sh \
                        $(ac_aux_dir)/mdate-sh \
                        $(ac_aux_dir)/missing \
                        $(ac_aux_dir)/mkinstalldirs
AUX_DIST_EXTRA        = $(ac_aux_dir)/readline.m4 \
                        $(ac_aux_dir)/sys_errlist.m4 \
                        $(ac_aux_dir)/sys_siglist.m4
EXTRA_DIST            = bootstrap

MAINTAINERCLEANFILES  = Makefile.in aclocal.m4 configure config-h.in \
                        stamp-h.in $(AUX_DIST)
```

---

[1] *Actually, the suffix will be whatever is appropriate for the target host, such as '.obj' on*
Windows, for example.

```
dist-hook:
        (cd $(distdir) && mkdir $(ac_aux_dir))
        for file in $(AUX_DIST) $(AUX_DIST_EXTRA); do \
          cp $$file $(distdir)/$$file; \
        done
```

The 'dist-hook' rule is used to make sure the 'config' directory and the files it contains are correctly added to the distribution by the 'make dist' rules (see Section 12.1, "Introduction to Distributions").

I have been careful to use the configure script's location for ac_aux_dir so that it is defined (and can be changed) in only one place. This is achieved by adding the following macro to 'configure.in':

```
AC_SUBST(ac_aux_dir)
```

There is no need to explicitly set a macro in the 'Makefile.am', because Automake automatically creates macros for every value that you 'AC_SUBST' from 'configure.in'.

I have also added the AC_PROG_LIBTOOL macro to 'configure.in' in place of AC_PROG_RANLIB, as described in Chapter 10.

Now I can upgrade the configury to use libtool—the greater part of this is running the libtoolize script that comes with the Libtool distribution. The bootstrap script then needs to be updated to run libtoolize at the correct juncture:

```
#! /bin/sh

set -x
aclocal -I config
libtoolize --force --copy
autoheader
automake --add-missing --copy
autoconf
```

Now I can rebootstrap the entire project so that it can make use of libtool:

```
$ ./bootstrap
+ aclocal -I config
+ libtoolize --force --copy
Putting files in AC_CONFIG_AUX_DIR, config.
+ autoheader
+ automake --add-missing --copy
automake: configure.in: installing config/install-sh
automake: configure.in: installing config/mkinstalldirs
automake: configure.in: installing config/missing
+ autoconf
```

The new macros are evident by the new output seen when the newly regenerated configure script is executed:

```
$ ./configure --with-readline
...
checking host system type... i586-pc-linux-gnu
checking build system type... i586-pc-linux-gnu
checking for ld used by GCC... /usr/bin/ld
checking if the linker (/usr/bin/ld) is GNU ld... yes
checking for /usr/bin/ld option to reload object files... -r
checking for BSD-compatible nm... /usr/bin/nm -B
checking whether ln -s works... yes
checking how to recognise dependent libraries... pass_all
checking for object suffix... o
checking for executable suffix... no
checking for ranlib... ranlib
checking for strip... strip
...
checking if libtool supports shared libraries... yes
checking whether to build shared libraries... yes
checking whether to build static libraries... yes
creating libtool
...

$ make
...
gcc -g -O2 -o .libs/sic sic.o sic_builtin.o sic_repl.o sic_syntax.o \
../sic/.libs/libsic.so -lreadline -Wl,--rpath -Wl,/usr/local/lib
creating sic
...

$ src/sic
] libtool --mode=execute ldd src/sic
    libsic.so.0 => /tmp/sic/sic/.libs/libsic.so.0 (0x40014000)
    libreadline.so.4 => /lib/libreadline.so.4 (0x4001e000)
    libc.so.6 => /lib/libc.so.6 (0x40043000)
    libncurses.so.5 => /lib/libncurses.so.5 (0x40121000)
    /lib/ld-linux.so.2 => /lib/ld-linux.so.2 (0x40000000)
] exit
$
```

As you can see, sic is now linked against a shared library build of 'libsic', but not directly against the convenience library, 'libreplace'.

11.2 Removing '--*foreign*'

Now that I have the bulk of the project in place, I want it to adhere to the
GNU standard layout. By removing the '--foreign' option from the call to
automake in the bootstrap file, automake is able to warn me about missing or, in
some cases,[2] malformed files, as follows:

```
$ ./bootstrap
+ aclocal -I config
+ libtoolize --force --copy
Putting files in AC_CONFIG_AUX_DIR, config.
+ autoheader
+ automake --add-missing --copy
automake: Makefile.am: required file ./NEWS not found
automake: Makefile.am: required file ./README not found
automake: Makefile.am: required file ./AUTHORS not found
automake: Makefile.am: required file ./THANKS not found
+ autoconf
```

The GNU standards book (http://www.gnu.org/prep/standards.html) describes
the contents of these files in more detail. Alternatively, take a look at a few
other GNU packages from ftp://ftp.gnu.org/gnu.

11.3 Installing Header Files

Why Can't I Install 'config.h'?

*One of the more difficult problems with GNU Autotools–driven projects is that
each of them depends on 'config.h' (or its equivalent) and the project-specific
symbols that it defines. The purpose of this file is to be #included from all the
project source files. The preprocessor can then tailor the code in these files to the
target environment.*

*It is often difficult and sometimes impossible to not introduce a dependency on
'config.h' from one of the project's installable header files. It would be nice if
you could just install the generated 'config.h', but even if you name it carefully
or install it to a subdirectory to avoid filename problems, the macros it defines
will clash with those from any other GNU Autotools–based project that also
installs its 'config.h'.*

*If Sic installed its 'config.h' as '/usr/include/sic/config.h', for instance, and
had '#include <sic/config.h>' in the installed 'common.h', when another GNU
Autotools–based project came to use the Sic library it might begin like this:*

continues ▶

---

[2] *For example, when I come to using the* 'make dist' *rule.*

▶ *continued*

```
#if HAVE_CONFIG_H
#  include <config.h>
#endif

#if HAVE_SIC_H
#  include <sic.h>
#endif

static const char version_number[] = VERSION;
```

But, `'sic.h'` *says* `'#include <sic/common.h>'`, *which in turn says* `'#include`
`<sic/config.h>'`. *Even though the other project has the correct value for* `'VERSION'`
in its own `'config.h'`, *by the time the preprocessor reaches the* `'version_number'`
definition, it has been redefined to the value in `'sic/config.h'`. *Imagine the mess*
you could get into if you were using several libraries that each installed its own
`'config.h'` *definitions. GCC issues a warning when a macro is redefined to a*
different value that would help you to catch this error. Some compilers do not issue
a warning, and perhaps worse, other compilers will warn even if the repeated defini-
tions have the same value, flooding you with hundreds of warnings for each source
file that reads multiple `'config.h'` *headers.*

The Autoconf macro, `AC_OUTPUT_COMMANDS`[3], *provides a way to solve this problem.*
The idea is to generate a system-specific, but installable, header from the results of the
various tests performed by `configure`. *There is a one-to-one mapping between*
the preprocessor code that relied on the configure results written to `'config.h'` *and the*
new shell code that relies on the configure results saved in `'config.cache'`. ◆

The following code is a snippet from `'configure.in'`, in the body of the
`AC_OUTPUT_COMMANDS` macro:

```
# Add the code to include these headers only if autoconf has
# shown them to be present.
if test x$ac_cv_header_stdlib_h = xyes; then
  echo '#include <stdlib.h>' >> $tmpfile
fi
if test x$ac_cv_header_unistd_h = xyes; then
  echo '#include <unistd.h>' >> $tmpfile
fi
if test x$ac_cv_header_sys_wait_h = xyes; then
  echo '#include <sys/wait.h>' >> $tmpfile
fi
if test x$ac_cv_header_errno_h = xyes; then
  echo '#include <errno.h>' >> $tmpfile
fi
```

---

[3] *This is for Autoconf version 2.13. Autoconf version 2.50 recommends* `AC_CONFIG_COMMANDS`.

```
      cat >> $tmpfile << '_EOF_'
#ifndef errno
/* Some sytems #define this! */
extern int errno;
#endif
_EOF_
      if test x$ac_cv_header_string_h = xyes; then
         echo '#include <string.h>' >> $tmpfile
      elif test x$ac_cv_header_strings_h = xyes; then
         echo '#include <strings.h>' >> $tmpfile
      fi
      if test x$ac_cv_header_assert_h = xyes; then
         cat >> $tmpfile << '_EOF_'

#include <assert.h>
#define SIC_ASSERT assert

_EOF_
      else
         echo '#define SIC_ASSERT(expr)   ((void) 0)' >> $tmpfile
      fi
```

Compare this with the equivalent C preprocessor code from 'sic/common.h',
which it replaces:

```
#if STDC_HEADERS || HAVE_STDLIB_H
#  include <stdlib.h>
#endif

#if HAVE_UNISTD_H
#  include <unistd.h>
#endif

#if HAVE_SYS_WAIT_H
#  include <sys/wait.h>
#endif

#if HAVE_ERRNO_H
#  include <errno.h>
#endif
#ifndef errno
/* Some systems #define this! */
extern int errno;
#endif

#if HAVE_STRING_H
#  include <string.h>
#else
#  if HAVE_STRING_H
#    include <strings.h>
#  endif
#endif
```

```
#if HAVE_ASSERT_H
#  include <assert.h>
#  define SIC_ASSERT assert
#else
#  define SIC_ASSERT(expr) ((void) 0)
#endif
```

Apart from the mechanical process of translating the preprocessor code, some plumbing is needed to ensure that the 'common.h' file generated by the new code in 'configure.in' is functionally equivalent to the old code and is generated in a correct and timely fashion.

Taking my lead from some of the Automake-generated make rules to regenerate 'Makefile' from 'Makefile.in' by calling 'config.status', I have added some similar rules to 'sic/Makefile.am' to regenerate 'common.h' from 'common-h.in':

```
# Regenerate common.h with config.status whenever common-h.in changes.
common.h: stamp-common
        :
stamp-common: $(srcdir)/common-h.in $(top_builddir)/config.status
        cd $(top_builddir) \
           && CONFIG_FILES= CONFIG_HEADERS= CONFIG_OTHER=sic/common.h \
           $(SHELL) ./config.status
        echo timestamp > $@
```

The way that AC_OUTPUT_COMMANDS works is to copy the contained code into config.status (see Appendix C, "Generated File Dependencies"). It is actually config.status that creates the generated files—for example, automake-generated 'Makefile's can regenerate themselves from corresponding 'Makefile.in's by calling config.status if they become out of date. Unfortunately, this means that config.status doesn't have direct access to the cache values generated while configure was running (because it has finished its work by the time config.status is called). It is tempting to read in the cache file at the top of the code inside AC_OUTPUT_COMMANDS, but that works only if you know where the cache file is saved. Also the package installer can use the '--cache-file' option of configure to change the location of the file, or turn off caching entirely with '--cache-file=/dev/null'.

AC_OUTPUT_COMMANDS accepts a second argument that can be used to pass the variable settings discovered by configure into config.status. It is not pretty, and is a little error-prone. In the first argument to AC_OUTPUT_COMMANDS, you must be careful to check that *every single* configure variable referenced is correctly set somewhere in the second argument.

A slightly stripped down example from the Sic project 'configure.in' looks like this:

```
# ----------------------------------------
# Add code to config.status to create an installable host dependent
# configuration file.
# ----------------------------------------
AC_OUTPUT_COMMANDS([
  if test -n "$CONFIG_FILES" && test -n "$CONFIG_HEADERS"; then
    # If both these vars are non-empty, then config.status wasn't run by
    # automake rules (which always set one or the other to empty).
    CONFIG_OTHER=${CONFIG_OTHER-sic/common.h}
  fi
  case "$CONFIG_OTHER" in
  *sic/common.h*)
    outfile=sic/common.h
    stampfile=sic/stamp-common
    tmpfile=${outfile}T
    dirname="sed s,^.*/,,g"

    echo creating $outfile
    cat > $tmpfile << _EOF_
/*  -*- Mode: C -*-
 *  ----------------------------------------
 *  DO NOT EDIT THIS FILE!  It has been automatically generated
 *  from:    configure.in and `echo $outfile¦$dirname`.in
 *  on host: `(hostname || uname -n) 2>/dev/null ¦ sed 1q`
 *  ----------------------------------------
 */

#ifndef SIC_COMMON_H
#define SIC_COMMON_H 1

#include <stdio.h>
#include <sys/types.h>
_EOF_

    if test x$ac_cv_func_bzero = xno && \
       test x$ac_cv_func_memset = xyes; then
      cat >> $tmpfile << '_EOF_'
#define bzero(buf, bytes) ((void) memset (buf, 0, bytes))
_EOF_
    fi
    if test x$ac_cv_func_strchr = xno; then
      echo '#define strchr index' >> $tmpfile
    fi
    if test x$ac_cv_func_strrchr = xno; then
      echo '#define strrchr rindex' >> $tmpfile
    fi

    # The ugly but portable cpp stuff comes from here
    infile=$srcdir/sic/`echo $outfile | sed 's,.*/,,g;s,\..*$,,g'`-h.in
    sed '/^##.*$/d' $infile >> $tmpfile
```

```
],[
  srcdir=$srcdir
  ac_cv_func_bzero=$ac_cv_func_bzero
  ac_cv_func_memset=$ac_cv_func_memset
  ac_cv_func_strchr=$ac_cv_func_strchr
  ac_cv_func_strrchr=$ac_cv_func_strrchr
])
```

Notice that the contents of 'common-h.in' are copied into 'common.h' verbatim as it is generated. It is just an easy way of collecting together the code that belongs in 'common.h', but which doesn't rely on configuration tests, without cluttering 'configure.in' any more than necessary.

I should point out that although this method has served me well for a number of years now, it is inherently fragile because it relies on undocumented internals of both Autoconf and Automake. There is a very real possibility that if you also track the latest releases of GNU Autotools, it may stop working. Future releases of GNU Autotools will address the interface problems that force us to use code like this, for the lack of a better way to do things.

11.4 Including Texinfo Documentation

Automake provides a few facilities to make the maintenance of Texinfo documentation within projects much simpler than it used to be. Writing a 'Makefile.am' for Texinfo documentation is extremely straightforward:

```
## Process this file with automake to produce Makefile.in

MAINTAINERCLEANFILES    = Makefile.in
info_TEXINFOS           = sic.texi
```

The 'TEXINFOS' primary will not only create rules for generating '.info' files suitable for browsing with the GNU info reader, but also for generating '.dvi' and '.ps' documentation for printing.

You can also create other formats of documentation by adding the appropriate make rules to 'Makefile.am'. Because the more recent Texinfo distributions have begun to support generation of HTML documentation from the '.texi' format master document, for example, I have added the appropriate rules to the 'Makefile.am':

```
SUFFIXES                = .html

html_docs               = sic.html

.texi.html:
        $(MAKEINFO) --html $<

.PHONY: html
html: version.texi $(html_docs)
```

For ease of maintenance, these make rules employ a suffix rule that describes how
to generate HTML from the equivalent '.texi' source—this involves telling make
about the '.html' suffix using the Automake SUFFIXES macro. I have not defined
'MAKEINFO' explicitly (although I could have done so) because I know that
Automake has already defined it for use in the '.info' generation rules.

The 'html' target is for convenience; typing 'make html' is a little easier than
typing 'make sic.html'. I have also added a '.PHONY' target so that featureful
make programs will know that the 'html' target does not actually generate a file
called, literally, 'html'. As it stands, this code is not quite complete, because
the top-level 'Makefile.am' does not know how to call the 'html' rule in the
'doc' subdirectory.

There is no need to provide a general solution here in the way Automake does
for its 'dvi' target, for example. A simple recursive call to 'doc/Makefile' is
much simpler:

```
docdir                  = $(top_builddir)/doc

html:
        echo Making $@ in $(docdir)
        cd $(docdir) && make $@
```

Another useful management function that Automake can perform for you
with respect to Texinfo documentation is to automatically generate the version
numbers for your Texinfo documents. It will add make rules to generate a
suitable 'version.texi', as long as automake sees '@include version.texi' in
the body of the Texinfo source:

```
\input texinfo   @c -*-texinfo-*-
@c %**start of header
@setfilename sic.info
@settitle Dynamic Modular Interpreter Prototyping
@setchapternewpage odd
@c %**end of header
@headings           double

@include version.texi

@dircategory Programming
@direntry
* sic: (sic).    The dynamic, modular, interpreter prototyping tool.
@end direntry

@ifinfo
This file documents sic.

@end ifinfo
```

```
@titlepage
@sp 10
@title Sic
@subtitle Edition @value@{EDITION}, @value@{UPDATED}
@subtitle $Id: sic.texi,v 1.4 2000/05/23 09:07:00 bje Exp $
@author Gary V. Vaughan
@author @email@{gvv@techie.com}

@page
@vskip 0pt plus 1filll
@end titlepage
```

'version.texi' sets Texinfo variables ('VERSION', 'EDITION', and 'UPDATE') that can be expanded elsewhere in the main Texinfo documentation by using @value@{EDITION}, for example. This makes use of another auxiliary file, mdate-sh, which will be added to the scripts in the $ac_aux_dir subdirectory by Automake after adding the 'version.texi' reference to 'sic.texi':

```
$ ./bootstrap
+ aclocal -I config
+ libtoolize --force --copy
Putting files in AC_CONFIG_AUX_DIR, config.
+ autoheader
+ automake --add-missing --copy
doc/Makefile.am:22: installing config/mdate-sh
+ autoconf
$ make html
/bin/sh ./config.status --recheck
...
Making html in ./doc
make[1]: Entering directory /tmp/sic/doc
Updating version.texi
makeinfo --html sic.texi
make[1]: Leaving directory /tmp/sic/doc
```

Hopefully, it now goes without saying that I also need to add the 'doc' subdirectory to 'AC_OUTPUT' in 'configure.in' and to 'SUBDIRS' in the top-level 'Makefile.am'.

11.5 Adding a Test Suite

Automake has very flexible support for automated test suites within a project distribution, which are discussed more fully in The Automake Manual. I have added a simple shell script–based testing facility to Sic using this support—this kind of testing mechanism is perfectly adequate for command-line projects. The tests themselves just feed prescribed input to the uninstalled sic interpreter and compare the actual output with what is expected.

Here is one of the test scripts:

```sh
## -*- sh -*-
## incomplete.test — Test incomplete command handling

# Common definitions
if test -z "$srcdir"; then
    srcdir=echo "$0" | sed s,[^/]*$,,'
    test "$srcdir" = "$0" && srcdir=.
    test -z "$srcdir" && srcdir=.
    test "${VERBOSE+set}" != set && VERBOSE=1
fi
. $srcdir/defs

# this is the test script
cat <<\EOF > in.sic
echo "1
2
3"
EOF

# this is the output we should expect to see
cat <<\EOF >ok
1
2
3
EOF

cat <<\EOF >errok
EOF

# Run the test saving stderr to a file, and showing stdout
# if VERBOSE == 1
$RUNSIC in.sic  2> err | tee -i out >&2

# Test against expected output
if ${CMP} -s out ok; then
    :
else
    echo "ok:" >&2
    cat ok >&2
    exit 1
fi

# Munge error output to remove leading directories, `lt-' or
# trailing '.exe'
sed -e "s,^[^:]*[lt-]*sic[.ex]*:,sic:," err >sederr && mv sederr err

# Show stderr if doesnt match expected output if VERBOSE == 1
if "$CMP" -s err errok; then
    :
```

```
else
    echo "err:" >&2
    cat err >&2
    echo "errok:" >&2
    cat errok >&2
    exit 1
fi
```

The tricky part of this script is the first part, which discovers the location of (and loads) '$srcdir/defs'. It is a little convoluted because it needs to work if the user has compiled the project in a separate build tree—in which case the 'defs' file is in a separate source tree and not in the actual directory in which the test is executed.

The 'defs' file enables me to factor out the common definitions from each of the test files so that it can be maintained once in a single file read by all the tests:

```
#! /bin/sh

# Make sure srcdir is an absolute path.  Supply the variable
# if it does not exist.  We want to be able to run the tests
# stand-alone!!
#
srcdir=${srcdir-.}
if test ! -d $srcdir ; then
    echo "defs: installation error" 1>&2
    exit 1
fi

#  IF the source directory is a Unix or a DOS root directory, ...
#
case "$srcdir" in
    /* | [A-Za-z]:\\*) ;;
    *) srcdir=`cd $srcdir && pwd` ;;
esac

case "$top_builddir" in
    /* | [A-Za-z]:\\*) ;;
    *) top_builddir=`cd ${top_builddir-..} && pwd` ;;
esac

progname=`echo "$0" | sed 's,^.*/,,'`
testname=`echo "$progname" | sed 's,-.*$,,'`
testsubdir=${testsubdir-testSubDir}

SIC_MODULE_PATH=$top_builddir/modules
export SIC_MODULE_PATH

# User can set VERBOSE to prevent output redirection
case x$VERBOSE in
    xNO | xno | x0 | x)
        exec > /dev/null 2>&1
```

```
       ;;
esac

rm -rf $testsubdir > /dev/null 2>&1
mkdir $testsubdir
cd $testsubdir \
   || { echo "Cannot make or change into $testsubdir"; exit 1; }

echo "=== Running test $progname"

CMP="${CMP-cmp}"
RUNSIC="${top_builddir}/src/sic"
```

Having written a few more test scripts, and made sure that they are working by
running them from the command line, all that remains is to write a suitable
'Makefile.am' so that automake can run the test suite automatically:

```
## Makefile.am — Process this file with automake to produce Makefile.in

EXTRA_DIST          = defs $(TESTS)
MAINTAINERCLEANFILES = Makefile.in

testsubdir          = testSubDir

TESTS_ENVIRONMENT   = top_builddir=$(top_builddir)

TESTS               =                   \
                      empty-eval.test   \
                      empty-eval-2.test \
                      empty-eval-3.test \
                      incomplete.test   \
                      multicmd.test

distclean-local:
        -rm -rf $(testsubdir)
```

I have used the 'testsubdir' macro to run the tests in their own subdirectory so
that the directory containing the actual test scripts is not polluted with lots of
fallout files generated by running the tests. For completeness I have used a
hook target[4] to remove this subdirectory when the user types the following:

```
$ make distclean
...
rm -rf testSubDir
...
```

---

[4] *This is a sort of callback function that will be called by the* make *rules generated by Automake.*

Adding more tests is accomplished by creating a new test script and adding it to the list in noinst_SCRIPTS. Remembering to add the new 'tests' subdirectory to 'configure.in' and the top-level 'Makefile.am', and reconfiguring the project to propagate the changes into the various generated files, I can run the whole test suite from the top directory with the following:

```
$ make check
```

It often proves useful to run tests in isolation, either when developing new tests or to examine more closely why a test has failed unexpectedly. Having set this test suite up as I did, individual tests can be executed with the following:

```
$ VERBOSE=1 make check TESTS=incomplete.test
make  check-TESTS
make[1]: Entering directory
/tmp/sic/tests
=== Running test incomplete.test
1
2
3
PASS: incomplete.test
==================
All 1 tests passed
==================
make[1]: Leaving directory /tmp/sic/tests
$ ls testSubDir/
err    errok   in.sic   ok    out
```

The 'testSubDir' subdirectory now contains the expected and actual output from that particular test for both 'stdout' and 'stderr', and the input file that generated the actual output. Had the test failed, I would be able to look at these files to decide whether there is a bug in the program or just a bug in the test script. Being able to examine individual tests like this is invaluable, especially when the test suite becomes very large—because you will, naturally, add tests every time you add features to a project or find and fix a bug.

Another alternative to the pure shell-based test mechanism I have presented here is the Autotest facility by François Pinard, as used in Autoconf after release 2.13.

Later in Chapter 19, "A Complex GNU Autotools Project," the Sic project is revisited to take advantage of some of the more advanced features of GNU Autotools. But first these advanced features are discussed in the next several chapters—starting, in the next chapter, with a discussion of how GNU Autotools can help you to make a tarred distribution of your own projects.

12

Rolling Distribution Tarballs

Something about the word "tarballs" makes you want to avoid them altogether, let alone get involved in the disgusting process of rolling one. And, in the past, that was apparently the attitude of most developers, as witnessed by the strange ways distribution tar archives were created and unpacked. Automake largely automates this tedious process, in a sense providing you with the obliviousness you crave.

12.1 Introduction to Distributions

The basic approach to creating a tar[1] distribution is to run the following:

```
make
make dist
```

The generated tar file is named *package-version*.tar.gz, and unpacks into a directory named *package-version*. These two rules are mandated by the GNU coding standards, and are just good ideas in any case, because it is convenient for the end user to have the version information easily accessible while building a package. It removes any doubt when she goes back to an old tree after some time away from it. Unpacking into a fresh directory is always a good idea—in the old days, some packages would unpack into the current directory, requiring an annoying cleanup job for the unwary system administrator.

The unpacked archive is completely portable, to the extent of Automake's capability to enforce this. That is, all the generated files (for example, 'configure') are newer than their inputs ('configure.in', for instance), and the distributed 'Makefile.in' files should work with any version of make. Of course, some of the responsibility for portability lies with you: You are free to introduce nonportable code into your 'Makefile.am', and Automake cannot diagnose this. No

---

[1] *"tar" is a Unix archiving program and also the name of the format of the files it manipulates. It is akin to zip.*

special tools beyond the minimal tool list, plus whatever your own `'Makefile'` and `'configure'` additions use, are required for the end user to build the package (see "Utilities in Makefiles" in The GNU Coding Standards).

By default Automake creates a `'.tar.gz'` file. It notices if you are using GNU tar[2] and arranges to create portable archives in this case.

People do sometimes want to make other sorts of distributions. Automake allows this through the use of options.

dist-bzip2	Add a `dist-bzip2` target, which creates a `'.tar.bz2'` file. These files are frequently smaller than the corresponding `'.tar.gz'` file.
dist-shar	Add a `dist-shar` target, which creates a `shar` archive.
dist-zip	Add a `dist-zip` target, which creates a `zip` file. These files are popular for Windows distributions.
dist-tarZ	Add a `dist-tarZ` target, which creates a `'.tar.Z'` file. This exists for die-hard old-time UNIX hackers; the rest of the world has moved on to `gzip` or `bzip2`.

12.2 What Goes In

Automake tries to make creating a distribution as easy as possible. The rules are set up by default to distribute those things that Automake knows belong in a distribution. For instance, Automake always distributes your `'configure'` script and your `'NEWS'` file. All the files Automake automatically distributes are shown by `automake --help`:

```
$ automake --help
...
Files which are automatically distributed, if found:
    ABOUT-GNU      README        config.guess     ltconfig
    ABOUT-NLS      THANKS        config.h.bot     ltmain.sh
    AUTHORS        TODO          config.h.top     mdate-sh
    BACKLOG        acconfig.h    config.sub       missing
    COPYING        acinclude.m4  configure        mkinstalldirs
    COPYING.LIB    aclocal.m4    configure.in     stamp-h.in
    ChangeLog      ansi2knr.1    elisp-comp       stamp-vti
    INSTALL        ansi2knr.c    install-sh       texinfo.tex
    NEWS           compile       libversion.in    ylwrap
...
```

---

[2] *By default, GNU* tar *can create non-portable archives in certain (rare) situations. To be safe, Automake arranges to use the* `'-o'` *compatibility flag when GNU* tar *is used.*

Automake also distributes some files about which it has no built-in knowledge, but about which it learns from your 'Makefile.am'. For instance, the source files listed in a '_SOURCES' variable go into the distribution. This is why you should list uninstalled header files in the '_SOURCES' variable; otherwise, you just have to introduce another variable to distribute them—Automake will only know about them if you tell it.

Not all primaries are distributed by default. The rule is arbitrary, but pretty simple: Of all the primaries, only '_TEXINFOS' and '_HEADERS' are distributed by default. (Sources that make up programs and libraries are also distributed by default, but, perhaps confusingly, '_SOURCES' is not considered a primary.)

Although there is no rhyme, there is a reason: Defaults were chosen based on feedback from users. Typically, "enough" reports of the form "I auto-generate my '_SCRIPTS'. How do I prevent them from ending up in the distribution?" would cause a change in the default.

Although the defaults are adequate in many situations, sometimes you have to distribute files that are not covered automatically. It is easy to add additional files to a distribution; just list them in the macro 'EXTRA_DIST'. You can list files in subdirectories here. You can also list a directory's name here and the entire contents will be copied into the distribution by make dist.

Warning

Use this last feature with care. A typical failure is that you will put a "temporary" file in the directory and then it will end up in the distribution when you forget to remove it. Similarly, version-control files, such as a 'CVS' subdirectory, can easily end up in a distribution this way. ♦

If a primary is not distributed by default, but in your case it should be, you can easily correct it with 'EXTRA_DIST':

```
EXTRA_DIST = $(bin_SCRIPTS)
```

Note

The next major Automake release, probably numbered 1.5, will have a better method for controlling whether primaries go into the distribution. In 1.5, you will be able to use the 'dist' and 'nodist' prefixes to control distribution on a per-variable basis. You will even be able to simultaneously use both prefixes with a given primary to include some files and omit others:

```
dist_bin_SCRIPTS = distribute-this
nodist_bin_SCRIPTS = but-not-this
```

12.3 The *distcheck* Rule

The make dist documentation sounds nice, and make dist did do something, but how do you know it really works? It is a terrible feeling when you realize your carefully crafted distribution is missing a file and won't compile on a user's machine.

I would not write such an introduction unless Automake provided a solution. The solution is a smoke test known as make distcheck. This rule performs a make dist as usual, but it doesn't stop there. Instead, it then proceeds to untar the new archive into a fresh directory, build it in a fresh build directory separate from the source directory, install it into a third fresh directory, and finally run make check in the build tree. If any step fails, distcheck aborts, leaving you to fix the problem before it will create a distribution.

> **Best Practice**
>
> *Although not a complete test—it tries only one architecture, after all—*distcheck *nevertheless catches most packaging errors (as opposed to portability bugs), and its use is highly recommended.* ◆

12.4 Some Caveats

Note that currently Automake enables you to make a distribution when maintainer mode is off, or when you do not have all the required maintainer tools. That is, you can make a subtly broken distribution if you are motivated or unlucky. This will be addressed in a future version of Automake.

> **Best Practice**
>
> *Earlier I recommended the use of* make *before* make dist *or* make distcheck. *This practice ensures that all the generated files are newer than their inputs. It also solves some problems related to dependency tracking (see Chapter 18, "Advanced GNU Automake Usage").* ◆

12.5 Implementation

To understand how to use the more advanced dist-related features, you must first understand how make dist is implemented. For most packages, what we have already covered suffices. Few packages need the more advanced features, although I note that many use them anyway.

The dist rules work by building a copy of the source tree and then archiving that copy. This copy is made in stages: A 'Makefile' in a particular directory updates the corresponding directory in the shadow tree. In some cases, automake is run to create a new 'Makefile.in' in the new distribution tree.

After each directory's 'Makefile' has had a chance to update the distribution directory, the appropriate command is run to create the archive. Finally, the temporary directory is removed.

If your 'Makefile.am' defines a dist-hook rule, Automake arranges to run this rule when the copying work for this directory is finished.

> **Warning**
>
> *This rule can do literally anything to the distribution directory, so some care is required—careless use will result in an unusable distribution. For instance, Automake will create the shadow tree using links, if possible. This means that it is inadvisable to modify the files in the* dist *tree in a dist hook.* ◆

One common use for this rule is to remove files that erroneously end up in the distribution. (In rare situations, this can happen.) The variable 'distdir' is defined during the dist process and refers to the corresponding directory in the distribution tree; 'top_distdir' refers to the root of the distribution tree.

Here is an example of removing a file from a distribution:

```
dist-hook:
        -rm $(distdir)/remove-this-file
```

13

Installing and Uninstalling Configured Packages

Have you ever seen a package where, once built, you were expected to keep the build tree around forever, and always cd there before running the tool? You might have to cast your mind way, way back to the bad old days of 1988 to remember such a horrible thing.

The GNU Autotools provide a canned solution to this problem. Although not without flaws, they do provide a reasonable and easy-to-use framework. This chapter discusses the GNU Autotools installation model, how to convince automake to install files where you want them, and finally this chapter concludes with some information about uninstalling, including a brief discussion of its flaws.

13.1 Where Files Are Installed

If you have ever run configure --help, you have probably been frightened by the huge number of options offered. Although nobody ever uses more than two or three of these, they are still important to understand when writing your package; their proper use helps you figure out where each file should be installed. For a background on these standard directories and their uses, refer to Section 2.1, "Configuring."

Note

We recommend using the standard directories as described. Although most package builders use only '--prefix' or perhaps '--exec-prefix', some packages (for example, GNU/Linux distributions) require more control. For instance, if your package 'quux' puts a file into sysconfigdir, *then in the default configuration it will end up in '/usr/local/var'. For a GNU/Linux distribution, however, it would make more sense to configure with '--sysconfigdir=/var/quux'.* ◆

Automake makes it very easy to use the standard directories. Each directory, such as `'bindir'`, is mapped onto a `'Makefile'` variable of the same name. Automake adds three useful variables to the standard list:

`pkgincludedir`	A convenience variable whose value is `'$(includedir)/$(PACKAGE)'`.
`pkgdatadir`	A convenience variable whose value is `'$(datadir)/$(PACKAGE)'`.
`pkglibdir`	A variable whose value is `'$(libdir)/$(PACKAGE)'`.

These cannot be set on the `configure` command line, but are always defined as stated.[1]

In Automake, a directory variable's name, without the `'dir'` suffix, can be used as a prefix to a primary to indicate the install location. Confused yet? An example should help: Items listed in `'bin_PROGRAMS'` are installed in `'bindir'`.

Automake's rules are actually a bit more precise than this: The directory and the primary must agree. It doesn't make sense to install a library in `'datadir'`, so Automake won't let you. Here is a complete list showing primaries and the directories that can be used with them:

`'PROGRAMS'`	`'bindir'`, `'sbindir'`, `'libexecdir'`, `'pkglibdir'`.
`'LIBRARIES'`	`'libdir'`, `'pkglibdir'`.
`'LTLIBRARIES'`	`'libdir'`, `'pkglibdir'`.
`'SCRIPTS'`	`'bindir'`, `'sbindir'`, `'libexecdir'`, `'pkgdatadir'`.
`'DATA'`	`'datadir'`, `'sysconfdir'`, `'sharedstatedir'`, `'localstatedir'`, `'pkgdatadir'`.
`'HEADERS'`	`'includedir'`, `'oldincludedir'`, `'pkgincludedir'`.
`'TEXINFOS'`	`'infodir'`.
`'MANS'`	`'man'`, `'man0'`, `'man1'`, `'man2'`, `'man3'`, `'man4'`, `'man5'`, `'man6'`, `'man7'`, `'man8'`, `'man9'`, `'mann'`, `'manl'`.

---

[1] *There has been some debate in the Autoconf community about extending Autoconf to allow new directories to be set on the* `configure` *command line. Currently the consensus seems to be that there are too many arguments to* `configure` *already.*

Two other useful prefixes, while not directory names, can be used in their place. These prefixes are valid with any primary. The first of these is `noinst`. This prefix tells Automake that the listed objects should not be installed, but should be built anyway. For instance, you can use `noinst_PROGRAMS` to list programs that will not be installed.

The second such non-directory prefix is `check`. This prefix tells Automake that this object should not be installed, and furthermore that it should be built only when the user runs make check.

Early in Automake history, we discovered that even Automake's extended built-in list of directories was not enough—basically anyone who had written a `Makefile.am` sent in a bug report about this. Now Automake enables you to extend the list of directories.

First you must define your own directory variable. This is a macro whose name ends in `dir`. Define this variable however you like.

Note

We suggest that you define it relative to an autoconf directory variable; this gives the user some control over the value. Don't hard code it to something like `/etc`; absolute hard-coded paths are rarely portable. ✦

Now you can attach the base part of the new variable to a primary just as you can with the built-in directories:

```
foodir = $(datadir)/foo
foo_DATA = foo.txt
```

Warning

Automake enables you to attach such a variable to any primary, so you can do things you ordinarily wouldn't want to do or be allowed to do. For instance, Automake won't diagnose this piece of code that tries to install a program in an architecture-independent location:

```
foodir = $(datadir)/foo
foo_PROGRAMS = foo
```

13.2 Fine-Grained Control of Install

The second most common way[2] to configure a package is to set `prefix` and `exec-prefix` to different values. This way, a system administrator on a heterogeneous network can arrange to have the architecture-independent files shared by all platforms. Typically this doesn't save very much space, but it does make in-place bug fixing or platform-independent runtime configuration a lot easier.

To this end, Automake provides finer control to the user than a simple `make install`. The user can strip all the package executables at install time, for instance, by running `make install-strip` (although we recommend setting the various `'INSTALL'` environment variables instead; as discussed later). More importantly, Automake provides a way to install the architecture-dependent and architecture-independent parts of a package independently.

In the preceding scenario, installing the architecture-independent files more than once is just a waste of time. Our hypothetical administrator can install those pieces exactly once, with `make install-data`, and then on each type of build machine install only the architecture-dependent files with `make install-exec`.

Nonstandard directories specified in `'Makefile.am'` are also separated along `'data'` and `'exec'` lines, giving the user complete control over installation. If, and only if, the directory variable name contains the string `'exec'`, items ending up in that directory are installed by `install-exec` and not by `install-data`.

At some sites, the paths referred to by software at runtime differ from those used to actually install the software. Suppose, for instance, that `'/usr/local'` is mounted read-only throughout the network. On the server, where new packages are built, the file system is available read-write as `'/w/usr/local'`—a directory not mounted anywhere else. In this situation, the system administrator can configure and build using the *runtime* values, but use the `'DESTDIR'` trick to temporarily change the paths at install time:

```
./configure --prefix=/usr/local
make
make DESTDIR=/w install
```

Note that `'DESTDIR'` operates as a prefix only. Sometimes this isn't enough. In this situation, you can explicitly override each directory variable:

```
./configure --prefix=/usr/local
make
make prefix=/w/usr/local datadir=/w/usr/share install
```

---

[2] *The most common way being to just set* `prefix`.

Here is a full example,[3] showing how you can unpack, configure, and build a typical GNU program on multiple machines at the same time:

```
sunos$ tar zxf foo-0.1.tar.gz
sunos$ mkdir sunos linux
```

In one window:

```
sunos$ cd sunos
sunos$ ../foo-0.1/configure --prefix=/usr/local \
> --exec-prefix=/usr/local/sunos
sunos$ make
sunos$ make install
```

And in another window:

```
sunos$ rsh linux
linux$ cd ~/linux
linux$ ../foo-0.1/configure --prefix=/usr/local \
> --exec-prefix=/usr/local/linux
linux$ make
linux$ make install-exec
```

In this example, we install everything on the `sunos` machine, but we install only the platform-dependent files on the `linux` machine. We use a different `exec-prefix`; so, for example, GNU/Linux executables end up in `/usr/local/linux/bin/`.

13.3 Install Hooks

As with `dist`, the install process allows for generic targets that can be used when the existing install functionality is not enough. Two types of targets can be used: local rules and hooks.

A local rule is named either `install-exec-local` or `install-data-local`, and is run during the course of the normal install procedure. This rule can be used to install things in ways that Automake usually does not support.

In `libgcj`, for instance, we generate a number of header files, one per Java class. We want to install them in `pkgincludedir`, but we want to preserve the hierarchical structure of the headers (for example, we want `java/lang/String.h` to be installed as `$(pkgincludedir)/java/lang/String.h`, not `$(pkgincludedir)/String.h`), and Automake does not currently support this. Therefore we resort to a local rule, which is a bit more complicated than you might expect:

---

[3] *This example assumes the use of GNU tar when extracting; this is standard on Linux but does not come with Solaris.*

```
install-data-local:
        for f in $(nat_headers) $(extra_headers); do \
## Compute the install directory at runtime.
        d="echo $$f | sed -e s,/[^/]*$$,,'"; \
## Make the install directory.
        $(mkinstalldirs) $(DESTDIR)$(includedir)/$$d; \
## Find the header file — in our case it might be in srcdir or
## it might be in the build directory.  "p" is the variable that
## names the actual file we will install.
        if test -f $(srcdir)/$$f; then p=$(srcdir)/$$f; else p=$$f; fi; \
## Actually install the file.
        $(INSTALL_DATA) $$p $(DESTDIR)$(includedir)/$$f; \
        done
```

A hook is guaranteed to run after the install of objects in this directory has completed. This can be used to modify files after they have been installed. There are two install hooks: install-data-hook and install-exec-hook.

Suppose, for instance, that you have written a program that must be setuid root. You can accomplish this by changing the permissions after the program has been installed:

```
bin_PROGRAMS = su
su_SOURCES = su.c

install-exec-hook:
        chown root $(bindir)/su
        chmod u+s $(bindir)/su
```

Unlike an install hook, an install rule is not guaranteed to be run after all other install rules are run. This lets it be run in parallel with other install rules when a parallel make is used. Ordinarily this is not very important, and in practice you almost always see local hooks and not local rules.

> **Warning**
>
> *The biggest caveat to using a local rule or an install hook is to make sure that it will work when the source and build directories are not the same—many people forget to do this. This means being sure to look in '$(srcdir)' when the file is a source file. ◆*

It is also very important to make sure that you do not use a local rule when install order is important—in this case, your 'Makefile' will succeed on some machines and fail on others.

13.4 Uninstall

As if things aren't confusing enough, there is still one more major installation-related feature not yet mentioned: uninstall. Automake adds an `uninstall` target to your `'Makefile'` that does the reverse of `install`: It deletes the newly installed package.

Unlike `install`, there is no `uninstall-data` or `uninstall-exec`; although possible in theory, we don't think this would be useful enough to actually use. Like `install`, you can write `uninstall-local` or `uninstall-hook` rules.

In our experience, `uninstall` is not a very useful feature. Automake implements it because it is mandated by the GNU standards, but it does not work reliably across packages. Maintainers who write install hooks typically neglect to write uninstall hooks. Also, because it cannot reliably uninstall a *previously* installed version of a package, it isn't useful for what most people would want to use it for anyway. We recommend using a real packaging system, several of which are freely available. In particular, GNU Stow, RPM, and the Debian packaging system seem like good choices.

14

Writing Portable C with GNU Autotools

GNU Autotools enables you to write highly portable programs. However, using GNU Autotools is not by itself enough to make your programs portable. You must also write them portably.

This chapter introduces you to writing portable programs in C. The discussion starts with some notes on the portable use of the C language. The focus then turns to cross-Unix portability. This chapter concludes by examining the portability between Unix and Windows.

Portability is a big topic, and this chapter cannot cover everything related to it. The basic rule of portable code is to remember that every system is in some ways unique. Do not assume that every other system is like yours. It is very helpful to be familiar with relevant standards, such as the ISO C standard and the POSIX.1 standard. Finally, there is no substitute for experience; if you have the opportunity to build and test your program on different systems, do so.

14.1 C Language Portability

The C language makes it easy to write non-portable code. This section discusses these portability issues, and how to avoid them.

This discussion concentrates on differences that can arise on systems in common use today. For example, all common systems today define char to be 8 bits, and define a pointer to hold the address of an 8-bit byte. This examination does not discuss the more exotic possibilities found on historical machines or on certain supercomputers. If your program needs to run in unusual settings, make sure you understand the characteristics of those systems; the system documentation should include a C portability guide describing the problems you are likely to encounter.

14.1.1 ISO C

The ISO C standard first appeared in 1989. (The standard is often called ANSI C.) It added several new features to the C language, most notably function prototypes. This led to many years of portability issues when deciding whether to use ISO C features.

Programs written today can assume the presence of an ISO C compiler. Therefore, this chapter does not discuss issues related to the differences between ISO C compilers and older compilers (often called K&R compilers, from the first book on C by Kernighan and Ritchie). You might, however, see these differences handled in older programs.

A newer C standard exists (called C9X). Because compilers that support it are not widely available as of this writing, this discussion does not cover it.

14.1.2 C Data Type Sizes

The C language defines data types in terms of a minimum size rather than an exact size. This matters mainly for the types int and long. A variable of type int must be at least 16 bits, and is often 32 bits. A variable of type long must be at least 32 bits, and is sometimes 64 bits.

The range of a 16-bit number is –32768 to 32767 for a signed number, or 0 to 65535 for an unsigned number. If a variable may hold numbers larger than 16 bits, use long rather than int. Never assume that int or long have a specific size or that they will overflow at a particular point. When appropriate, use variables of system-defined types rather than int or long, as follows:

size_t	Use this to hold the size of an object, as returned by sizeof.
ptrdiff_t	Use this to hold the difference between two pointers into the same array.
time_t	Use this to hold a time value as returned by the time function.
off_t	On a Unix system, use this to hold a file position as returned by lseek.
ssize_t	Use this to hold the result of the Unix read or write functions.

Some books on C recommend using typedefs to specify types of particular sizes, and then adjusting those typedefs on specific systems. GNU Autotools support this using the 'AC_CHECK_SIZEOF' macro. Although we agree with using typedefs for clarity, we do not recommend using them purely for portability. It is safest to rely only on the minimum size assumptions made by the C language, instead of assuming that a type of a specific size will always be available. Also, most C compilers define int as the most efficient type for the system, so it is normally best to just use int when possible.

14.1.3 C Endianness

When a number longer than a single byte is stored in memory, it must be stored in some particular format. Modern systems do this by storing the number byte by byte, such that the bytes can just be concatenated into the final number. However, the order of storage varies: Some systems store the least significant byte at the lowest address in memory, whereas some store the most significant byte there. These are referred to as *little-endian* and *big-endian* systems, respectively.[1]

This difference means that portable code may not make any assumptions about the order of storage of a number. Code such as this acts differently on different systems, for example:

```
/* Example of non-portable code; don't do this */
  int i = 4;
  char c = *(char *) i;
```

Although this is a contrived example, real problems arise when writing numeric data in a file or across a network connection. If the file or network connection may be read on a different type of system, numeric data must be written in a format that can be unambiguously recovered. This simple code is not portable:

```
/* Example of non-portable code; don't do this */
  write (fd, &i, sizeof i);
```

This example is non-portable both because of endianness and because it assumes that the size of the type of i is the same on both systems.

Instead, you should use something like this:

```
  int j;
  char buf[4];
  for (j = 0; j < 4; ++j)
    buf[j] = (i >> (j * 8)) & 0xff;
  write (fd, buf, 4); /* In real code, check the return value */
```

This unambiguously writes out a little-endian 4-byte value. This code works on any system, and any system can read the result.

Another approach to handling endianness is to use the htons and ntohs functions available on most systems. These functions convert between

---

[1] *These names come from* Gulliver's Travels.

network endianness and host endianness. Network endianness is big endian; it has that name because the standard TCP/IP network protocols use big-endian ordering.

These functions come in two sizes: htonl and ntohl operate on 4-byte quantities, and htons and ntohs operate on 2-byte quantities. The hton functions convert host endianness to network endianness. The ntoh functions convert network endianness to host endianness. On big-endian systems, these functions just return their arguments; on little-endian systems, they return their arguments after swapping the bytes.

Although these functions are used in a lot of existing code, they can be difficult to use in highly portable code, because they require knowing the exact size of your data types. If you know that the type int is exactly 4 bytes long, it is possible to write code such as the following:

```
int j;
j = htonl (i);
write (fd, &j, 4);
```

If int is not exactly 4 bytes long, however, this example will not work correctly on all systems.

14.1.4 C Structure Layout

C compilers on different systems lay out structures differently. In some cases, layout differences can exist even between different C compilers on the same system. Compilers add gaps between fields, and these gaps have different sizes and are at different locations. You can usually assume no gaps occur between fields of type char or array of char. However, you cannot make any assumptions about gaps between fields of any larger type. You also cannot make any assumptions about the layout of bit-field types.

These structure layout issues mean that it is difficult to portably use a C struct to define the format of data that may be read on another type of system, such as data in a file or sent over a network connection. Portable code must read and write such data field by field, instead of trying to read an entire struct at once.

The following example of non-portable code relates to reading data that may have been written to a file or a network connection on another type of system.

Don't do this:

```
/* Example of non-portable code; don't do this */
struct {
  short i;
  int j;
} s;
read (fd, &s, sizeof s);
```

Instead, do something such as this. (The struct s is assumed to be the same as above.)

```
unsigned char buf[6];
read (fd, buf, sizeof buf); /* Should check return value */
s.i = buf[0] | (buf[1] << 8);
s.j = buf[2] | (buf[3] << 8) | (buf[4] << 16) | (buf[5] << 24);
```

Naturally, the code to write out the structure should be similar.

14.1.5 C Floating Point

Most modern systems handle floating point following the IEEE-695 standard. However, portability issues still arise.

Most processors use 64 bits of precision when computing floating-point values. However, the widely used Intel x86 series of processors compute temporary values using 80 bits of precision, as do most instances of the Motorola 68K series. Some other processors, such as the PowerPC, provide fused multiply-add instructions, which perform a multiplication and an addition using high precision for the intermediate value. Optimizing compilers generates such instructions based on sequences of C operations.

For almost all programs, these differences do not matter. For programs that do intensive floating-point operations, however, the differences can be significant. You can write floating-point loops that terminate on one sort of processor, for example, but not on another.

Unfortunately, you cannot just follow a basic rule of thumb to avoid these problems. Most compilers provide an option to disable the use of extended precision. (For GNU cc, for example, the option is '-ffloat-store'). On the one hand, this merely shifts the portability problem elsewhere; and, on the other, the extended precision is often good rather than bad. Although you cannot easily avoid these portability problems, you should at least be aware of them if you write programs that require very precise floating-point operations.

The IEEE-695 standard specifies certain flags that the floating-point processor should make available (for example, overflow, underflow, inexact) and specifies that there should be some control over the floating-point rounding mode. Most processors make these flags and controls available; however, there is no portable way to access them. A portable program should not assume that it will have this degree of control over floating-point operations.

14.1.6 GNU *cc* Extensions

The GNU cc compiler has several useful extensions, which are documented in the GNU cc manual. A program that must be portable to other C compilers must naturally avoid these extensions; you can use the '-pedantic' option to warn about any accidental use of an extension.

The GNU cc compiler is highly portable, however, and it runs on all modern Unix platforms as well as on Windows. Depending on your portability requirements, you may be able to just assume that GNU cc is available (in which case, your program may use extensions when they are useful). Note that some extensions are inherently non-portable, such as inline assembler code or using attributes to specify a particular section for a function or a global variable.

14.2 Cross-Unix Portability

The preceding section discussed issues related to the C language. This section focuses on the portability of C programs across different Unix implementations. All modern Unix systems conform to the POSIX.1 (1990 edition) and POSIX.2 (1992 edition) standards. They also all support the sockets interface for networking code. However, significant differences between systems can still affect portability.

This book does not discuss portability to older Unix systems that do not conform to the POSIX standards. If you need this sort of portability, you can often find some valuable hints in the set of macros defined by autoconf, and in the 'configure.in' files of older programs that use autoconf.

14.2.1 Cross-Unix Function Calls

Functions not mentioned in POSIX.1 may not be available on all systems. If you want to use one of these functions, you should check for its presence by using 'AC_CHECK_FUNCS' in your 'configure.in' script, and adapt to its absence if possible. The following popular functions are available on many, but not all, modern Unix systems:

alloca   alloca entails several portability issues.
                                See the description of 'AC_FUNC_ALLOCA'
                                in The Autoconf Manual. Although this

function can be very convenient, it is generally best to avoid it in highly portable code.

dlopen

GNU libtool provides a portable alternate interface to dlopen. (See Chapter 16, "Dynamic Loading.")

getline

In some cases, you can use fgets as a fall-back. In others, you need to provide your own version of this function.

getpagesize

On some systems, the page size is available as the macro PAGE_SIZE in the header file 'sys/param.h'. On others, the page size is available via the sysconf function. If none of those work, you must generally just guess a value such as 4096.

gettimeofday

When this is not available, fall back to a less precise function such as time or ftime (which itself is not available on all systems).

mmap

In some cases, you can use either mmap or ordinary file I/O. In others, a program that uses mmap will just not be portable to all Unix systems. Note that mmap is an optional part of the 1996 version of POSIX.1, so it is likely to be added to all Unix systems over time.

ptrace

Unix systems without ptrace generally provide some other mechanism for debugging subprocesses, such as /proc. However, there is no widely portable way to control subprocesses, as evidenced by the source code to the GNU debugger, gdb.

setuid

Different Unix systems handle this differently. On some systems, any program can switch between the effective user ID of the executable and the real user ID. On others, switching to the real user ID is final; some of those systems provide the setreuid function instead to switch the effective and real user ID. The effect when a program run by the superuser calls setuid varies among systems.

snprintf

If this is not available, in some cases it is reasonable to just use sprintf; and in others, you must write a little routine to estimate the required length and allocate an appropriate buffer before calling sprintf.

strcasecmp
strdup
strncasecmp

You can usually provide your own version of these simple functions.

| valloc | When this is not available, just use `malloc` instead. |
| vfork | When this is not available, just use `fork` instead. |

14.2.2 Cross-Unix System Interfaces

Several Unix system interfaces have associated portability issues. A discussion of all of these in detail across all Unix systems is beyond the scope of this book. This chapter mentions them, however, to indicate when you might need to consider portability.

`curses` `termcap` `terminfo`	Many Unix systems provide the `curses` interface for simple graphical terminal access, but the name of the library varies. Typical names are `'-lcurses'` or `'-lncurses'`. Some Unix systems do not provide `curses`, but do provide the `'-ltermcap'` or `'-lterminfo'` library. The latter libraries provide only an interface to the `'termcap'` file or `'terminfo'` files. These files contain information about specific terminals, the difference being mainly the manner in which they are stored.
`proc file system`	The `/proc` file system is not available on all Unix systems, and when it is available the actual set of files and their format varies.
`pseudo terminals`	All Unix systems provide pseudo terminals, but the interface to obtain them varies widely. You should examine the configuration of an existing program that uses them, such as GNU emacs or Expect.
`shared libraries`	Shared libraries differ across Unix systems. The GNU libtool program was written to provide an interface to hide the differences. (See Chapter 9, "Introducing GNU Libtool.")
`termios` `termio` `'tty'`	The `termios` interface to terminals is standard on modern Unix systems. Avoid the older, non-portable `termio` and `tty` interfaces. (These interfaces are defined in `termio.h` and `sgtty.h`, respectively.)

`'threads'`	Many, but not all, Unix systems support multiple threads in a single process, but the interfaces differ. One thread interface, `pthreads`, was standardized in the 1996 edition of POSIX.1, so Unix systems are likely to converge on that interface over time.
`utmp` `wtmp`	Most Unix systems maintain the `utmp` and `wtmp` files to record information about which users are logged on to the system. However, the format of the information in the files varies across Unix systems, as does the exact location of the files and the functions that some systems provide to access the information. Programs that merely need to obtain login information are more portable if they invoke a program such as w. Programs that need to update the login information must be prepared to handle a range of portability issues.
`X Window system`	Version 11 of the X Window system is widely available across Unix systems. The actual release number varies somewhat, as does the set of available programs and window managers. Extensions such as OpenGL are not available on all systems.

14.3 Unix/Windows Portability

Unix and Windows are very different operating systems, with very different APIs and functionality. With significant extra work and some sacrifice in functionality, however, you can write programs that run on both Unix and Windows. For more information on how GNU Autotools can help you write programs that run on both Unix and Windows, see Chapter 24, "Using GNU Autotools with Cygnus' Cygwin."

14.3.1 Unix/Windows Emulation

The simplest way to write a program that runs on both Unix and Windows is to use an emulation layer. This generally results in a program that runs, but does not really feel like other programs for the operating system in question.

For example, the Cygwin package (freely available from Cygnus Solutions at http://sourceware.cygnus.com/cygwin/) provides a Unix API that works on Windows. This enables you to compile Unix programs to run on Windows. You can even run an X server in the Cygwin environment, so graphical programs will work as well, although they will not have the Windows look and feel.

You can also use commercial packages to compile Unix programs for Windows (for example, Interix) and to compile Windows programs on Unix (for example, Bristol Technology).

The main disadvantage with using an emulation layer is that the resulting programs have the wrong look and feel. They do not behave as users expect, so they are awkward to use. This is generally not acceptable for high-quality programs.

14.3.2 Unix/Windows Portable Scripting Language

Another approach to Unix/Windows portability is to develop the program using a portable scripting language. An example of such a scripting language is Tcl/Tk (http://www.scriptics.com/). Programs written in Tcl/Tk work on both Unix and Windows (and on the Apple Macintosh operating system as well, for that matter). Graphical programs more or less follow the look and feel for the platform on which they run. Because Tcl/Tk was originally developed on Unix, graphical Tcl/Tk programs typically do not look quite right to experienced Windows users, but they are usable and of reasonable quality. Other portable scripting languages are Perl, Python, and Guile.

One disadvantage of this approach is that scripting languages tend to be less efficient than straight C code, but you can often recode important routines in C. Another disadvantage is the need to learn a new language, one which furthermore may not be well designed for large programming projects.

14.3.3 Unix/Windows User Interface Library

Some programs' main interaction with the operating system is drawing on the screen. You can often write such programs using a cross-platform user interface library.

A cross-platform user interface library is a library that provides basic windowing functions and has been implemented separately for Unix and Windows. The program calls generic routines, which are then translated into the appropriate calls on each platform. These libraries generally provide a good look and feel on each platform, so this can be a reasonable approach for programs that do not require additional services from the system.

The main disadvantage is the least common denominator effect: The libraries often provide only functionality that is available on *both* Unix and Windows. Features specific to either Unix or Windows may be very useful for the program, but they may not be available via the library.

14.3.4 Unix/Windows-Specific Code

When writing a program that should run on both Unix and Windows, you could just write different code for the two platforms. This requires a careful separation of the operating system interface, including the graphical user interface, from the rest of the program. An API must be designed to provide the system needs, and that API must be implemented separately on Unix and Windows. You should set the API at an appropriate level to avoid the least common denominator effect.

This approach can prove useful for a program that has significant platform-independent computation as well as significant user interface or other system needs. It generally produces better results than the other previously discussed approaches. The disadvantage is that this approach requires much more work than the other methods.

14.3.5 Unix/Windows Issues

Whichever approach is used to support the program on both Unix and Windows, certain issues may affect the design of the program, or many specific areas of the program.

Text and Binary Files

Windows supports two different types of files: text files and binary files. On Unix, no such distinction exists. On Windows, any program that uses files must know whether each file is text or binary, and open and use them accordingly.

In a text file on Windows, each line is terminated with a carriage-return character followed by a line-feed character. When a C program in text mode reads the file, the C library converts each carriage-return/line-feed pair into a single line-feed character. If the file is read in binary mode, the program sees both the carriage return and the line feed.

You may have seen this distinction when transferring files between Unix and Window systems via FTP. You need to set the FTP program into binary or text mode as appropriate for the file you want to transfer.

When transferring a binary file, the FTP program just transfers the data unchanged. When transferring a text file, the FTP program must convert each carriage-return/line-feed pair into a single line feed.

When using the C standard library, a binary file is indicated by adding *b* after the *r*, *w*, or *a* in the call to fopen. When reading a text file, the program cannot just count characters and use that when computing arguments to fseek.

File System Issues

The file systems used on Unix and Windows differ in several ways, mainly concerning permissible filenames. You can use the program **doschk**, which you can find in the gcc distribution, on Unix to check for filenames not permitted on DOS or Windows.

DOS Filename Restrictions

The older DOS FAT file systems have severe limitations on filenames. These limitations no longer apply to Windows, but they do apply to DOS-based systems such as DJGPP.

A filename may consist of no more than 8 characters, followed by an optional extension of no more than 3 characters. This is commonly referred to as an 8.3 filename. Filenames are not case-sensitive.

A couple of special rules apply to filenames. You cannot name a file 'aux' or 'prn', for example. In some cases, you cannot even use a certain extension, such as 'aux.c'. These restrictions apply to DOS and also to at least some versions of Windows.

Windows Filename Case

Windows usually folds case when referring to files, unlike Unix. That is, on Windows, the filenames 'file', 'File', and 'FiLe' all refer to the same file. You must be aware of this when porting Unix programs to Windows, because the Unix programs may expect that using different case is reflected in the file system.

The procedure used to build the program perl from source relies on distinguishing between the files PERL and perl, for example. This fails on Windows.

As a matter of interest, the Windows file system stores files under the name with which they were created. The DOS shell displays the names in all uppercase. The Explorer shell displays them with each word in the filename capitalized.

White Space in Filenames

Both Unix and Windows file systems permit white space in filenames. Unix users rarely take advantage of this, however, whereas Windows users often do. For example, many Windows systems use a directory named 'Program Files', whose name has an embedded space. This is a clash of conventions.

Many programs developed on Unix unintentionally assume that there will be no spaces in file and directory names, and behave mysteriously if they encounter any. On Unix, these bugs are almost never seen. On Windows, they pop up immediately.

When writing a program that must run on Windows, consider these issues. Don't forget to test it on directories and files with embedded spaces.

Windows Separators and Drive Letters

On Unix, a forward slash ('/') separates directories in a filename. On Windows, a backward slash ('\') separates directories. For example, the Unix file 'dir/file' on Windows would be 'dir\file'.[2]

On Unix, a colon (':') usually separates a list of directories. On Windows, a semicolon (';') usually separates a list of directories. For example, a simple Unix search path might look like this: '/bin:/usr/bin'. The same search path on Windows would probably look like this: 'c:\bin;c:\usr\bin'.

On Unix, the file system is a single tree rooted at the directory simply named '/'. Windows has multiple file system trees. Absolute filenames often start with a drive letter followed by a colon. Windows maintains a default drive, and a default directory on each drive, which can make it difficult for a program to convert a relative filename into the absolute filename intended by the user. On Windows, you can refer to files on other systems by using a filename that starts with two slashes followed by a system name.

Miscellaneous Issues

Windows shared libraries (DLLs) differ from typical Unix shared libraries. They require special declarations for global variables declared in a shared library. Programs that use shared libraries must generally use special macros in their header files to define these appropriately. GNU libtool can help with some shared library issues, but not all.

---

[2] *Windows does permit a program to use a forward slash to separate directories when calling routines such as* fopen. *However, Windows users do not expect to type forward slashes when they enter filenames, and they do not expect to see forward slashes when a filename is printed.*

Some Unix system features are not supported under Windows: pseudo terminals, effective user ID, file modes with user/group/other permission, named FIFOs, an executable overriding functions called by shared libraries, and `select` on anything other than sockets.

Some Windows system features are not supported under Unix: the Windows event loop, many graphical capabilities, some aspects of the rich set of interthread communication mechanisms, and the `WSAAsyncSelect` function. You should keep these issues in mind when designing and writing a program that should run on both Unix and Windows.

15

Writing Portable C++ with GNU Autotools

My first task in industry was to port a large C++ application from one Unix platform to another. My colleagues immediately offered their sympathies, and I remember my initial reaction: "What's the big deal?" After all, this application used the C++ standard library, a modest subset of common Unix system calls, and C++ was approaching ISO standardization. Little did I know what lay ahead—endless hurdles imposed by differences to C++ implementations in use on those platforms.

Being essentially a superset of the C programming language, C++ suffers from all the machine-level portability issues described in Chapter 14, "Writing Portable C with GNU Autotools." In addition to this, variability in the language and standard libraries present additional trouble when writing portable C++ programs.

Comprehensive guides on C++ portability have been written (see Section 15.5, "Further Reading"). This chapter attempts to draw attention to the less portable areas of the C++ language and to describe how the GNU Autotools can help you overcome these (see Section 15.4, "How GNU Autotools Can Help"). In many instances, the best approach to multiplatform C++ portability is to just reexpress your programs using more widely supported language constructs. Fortunately, this book has been written at a time when the C++ language standard has been ratified and C++ implementations are rapidly conforming. Gladly, as time goes on the necessity for this chapter will diminish.

15.1 Brief History of C++

C++ was developed in 1983 by Bjarne Stroustrup at AT&T. Stroustrup was seeking a new object-oriented language with which to write simulations. C++ has now become a mainstream systems programming language and is increasingly being used to implement free software packages. C++ underwent a lengthy standardization process and was ratified as an ISO standard in 1998.

The first specification of C++ was available in a book titled *The Annotated C++ Reference Manual*, by Stroustrup and Ellis, also known as the "ARM." Since this initial specification, C++ has developed in some areas. These developments are discussed in Section 15.2, "Changeable C++."

The first C++ compiler, known as *cfront*, was produced by Stroustrup at AT&T. Because of its strong ties to C and because C is such a general-purpose systems language, cfront consisted of a translator from C++ to C. After translation, an existing C compiler was used to compile the intermediate C code down to machine code for almost any machine you care to mention. C++ permits overloaded functions—that is, functions with the same name but different argument lists, so cfront implemented a *name-mangling* algorithm to give each function a unique name in the linker's symbol table (see Section 15.3.2, "Name Mangling").

In 1989, Michael Tiemann of Cygnus Support wrote the first true C++ compiler, G++. G++ mostly consisted of a new front end to the GCC portable compiler, so G++ was able to produce code for most of the targets that GCC already supported.

In the years following, a number of new C++ compilers were produced. Unfortunately many could not keep pace with the development of the language being undertaken by the standards committee. This divergence of implementations is the fundamental cause of non-portable C++ programs.

15.2 Changeable C++

The C++ standard encompasses the language and the interface to the standard library, including the Standard Template Library (see Section 15.2.13, "Standard Template Library"). The language has evolved somewhat since the ARM was published, mostly driven by the experience of early C++ users.

This section briefly explains the newer features of C++. Alternatives to these features, where available, are presented when compiler support is lacking. You can use the alternatives if you need to make your code work with older C++ compilers, or you can avoid these features until the compilers you are concerned with are mature. If you are releasing a free software package to the wider community, you might need to specify a minimum level of standards conformance for the end-user's C++ compiler, or use the unappealing alternative of using lowest-common-denominator C++ features.

In covering these, this chapter addresses the following language features:

- Built-in `bool` type
- Exceptions
- Casts
- Variable scoping in `for` loops
- Namespaces
- The `explicit` keyword
- The `mutable` keyword
- The `typename` keyword
- Runtime Type Identification (RTTI)
- Templates
- Default template arguments
- Standard library headers
- Standard Template Library (STL)

15.2.1 Built-in *bool* Type

C++ introduced a built-in Boolean data type called `bool`. The presence of this new type makes it unnecessary to use an `int` with the values `0` and `1` and improves type safety. The two possible values of a `bool` are `true` and `false`— these are reserved words. The compiler knows how to coerce a `bool` into an `int` and vice versa.

If your compiler does not have the `bool` type and `false` and `true` keywords, an alternative is to produce such a type using a `typedef` of an enumeration representing the two possible values:

```
enum boolvals { false, true };
typedef enum boolvals bool;
```

What makes this simple alternative attractive is that it prevents having to adjust the prolific amount of code that might use `bool` objects once your compiler supports the built-in type.

15.2.2 Exceptions

Exception handling is a language feature present in other modern programming languages. Ada and Java both have exception-handling mechanisms. In essence, exception handling is a means of propagating a classified error by unwinding the procedure call stack until the error is caught by a higher procedure in the procedure call chain. A procedure indicates its willingness to handle a kind of error by *catching* it:

```
void foo ();

void
func ()
{
  try {
    foo ();
  }
  catch (...) {
    cerr << "foo failed!" << endl;
  }
}
```

Conversely, a procedure can throw an exception when something goes wrong:

```
typedef int io_error;

void
init ()
{
  int fd;
  fd = open ("/etc/passwd", O_RDONLY);
  if (fd < 0) {
    throw io_error(errno);
  }
}
```

C++ compilers tend to implement exception handling in full, or not at all. If any C++ compiler you may be concerned with does not implement exception handling, you may want to take the lowest-common-denominator approach and eliminate such code from your project.

15.2.3 Casts

C++ introduced a collection of *named* casting operators to replace the conventional C-style cast of the form (type) expr. The new casting operators are static_cast, reinterpret_cast, dynamic_cast, and const_cast. They are reserved words.

These refined casting operators are vastly preferred over conventional C casts for C++ programming. In fact, even Stroustrup recommends that the older style of C casts be banished from programming projects where at all possible. (For more information, refer to *The C++ Programming Language*, 3rd Edition, by Addison-Wesley.) Reasons for preferring the new named casting operators include the following:

- They provide the programmer with a mechanism for more explicitly specifying the kind of type conversion. This assists the compiler in identifying incorrect conversions.

- They are easier to locate in source code, due to their unique syntax: `X_cast<type>(expr)`.

If your compiler does not support the new casting operators, you might have to continue to use C-style casts—and carefully! I have seen one project agree to use macros such as the following one to encourage those involved in the project to adopt the new operators. Although the syntax does not match that of the genuine operators, these macros make it easy to later locate and alter the casts where they appear in source code:

```
#define static_cast(T,e) (T) e
```

15.2.4 Variable Scoping in *for* Loops

C++ has always permitted the declaration of a control variable in the initializer section of for loops:

```
for (int i = 0; i < 100; i++)
{
  ...
}
```

The original language specification allowed the control variable to remain live until the end of the scope of the loop itself:

```
for (int i = 0; i < j; i++)
{
  if (some condition)
    break;
}

if (i < j)
  // loop terminated early
```

In a later specification of the language, the control variable's scope exists only within the body of the for loop. The simple resolution to this incompatible change is to not use the older style. If a control variable needs to be used outside of the loop body, the variable should be defined before the loop:

```
int i;

for (i = 0; i < j; i++)
{
  if (some condition)
    break;
}

if (i < j)
  // loop terminated early
```

15.2.5 Namespaces

C++ namespaces are a facility for expressing a relationship between a set of related declarations such as a set of constants. Namespaces also assist in constraining *names* so that they will not collide with other identical names in a program. Namespaces were introduced to the language in 1993, and some early compilers were known to have incorrectly implemented namespaces. Here's a small example of namespace usage:

```
namespace Animals {
  class Bird {
  public:
    fly (); {} // fly, my fine feathered friend!
  };
};


// Instantiate a bird.
Animals::Bird b;
```

For compilers that do not correctly support namespaces, you can achieve a similar effect by placing related declarations into an enveloping structure. Note that this uses the fact that C++ structure members have public protection by default:

```
struct Animals {
  class Bird {
  public:
    fly (); {} // fly, my find feathered friend!
  };
protected
  // Prohibit construction.
  Animals ();
};


// Instantiate a bird.
Animals::Bird b; ·
```

15.2.6 The *explicit* Keyword

C++ adopted a new explicit keyword to the language. This keyword is a qualifier used when declaring constructors. When a constructor is declared as explicit, it becomes invalid to depend on implicit type conversions to be performed on the constructor arguments. This allows the compiler to perform stricter type checking and to prevent simple programming errors. If your compiler does not support the explicit keyword, you should avoid it and do without the benefits that it provides.

15.2.7 The *mutable* Keyword

You can design C++ classes so that they behave correctly when const objects of those types are declared. Methods that do not alter internal object state can be qualified as const:

```
class String
{
public:
  String (const char* s);
  ~String ();

  size_t Length () const { return strlen (buffer); }

private:
  char* buffer;
};
```

This simple, although incomplete, class provides a Length method that guarantees, by virtue of its const qualifier, to never modify the object state. Therefore, const objects of this class can be instantiated and the compiler will permit callers to use such objects' Length method.

The mutable keyword enables classes to be implemented where the concept of constant objects is sensible, but where details of the implementation make it difficult to declare essential methods as const. A common application of the mutable keyword is to implement classes that perform caching of internal object data. A method may not modify the logical state of the object, but it may need to update a cache—an implementation detail. The data members used to implement the cache storage need to be declared as mutable in order for const methods to alter them.

Let's alter the rather farfetched String class so that it implements a primitive cache that avoids needing to call the strlen library function on each invocation of Length ():

```
class String
{
public:
  String (const char* s) :length(-1) { /* copy string, etc. */ }
  ~String ();

  size_t Length () const
  {
    if (length < 0)
      length = strlen(buffer);
    return length;
  }

private:
  char* buffer;
  mutable size_t length;
}
```

When the `mutable` keyword is not available, your alternatives are to avoid implementing classes that need to alter internal data, like the caching `String` class, or to use the `const_cast` casting operator to cast away the "constness" of the object (see Section 15.2.3, "Casts").

15.2.8 The *typename* Keyword

The `typename` keyword was added to C++ after the initial specification, and not all compilers recognize it. It is a hint to the compiler that a name following the keyword is the name of a type. In the usual case, the compiler has sufficient context to know that a symbol is a defined type, because it must have been encountered earlier in the compilation:

```
class Foo
{
public:
  typedef int map_t;
};

void
func ()
{
  Foo::map_t m;
}
```

Here, `map_t` is a type defined in class `Foo`. If `func` happened to be a function template, however, the class that contains the `map_t` type may be a template parameter. In this case, the compiler just needs to be guided by qualifying `T::map_t` as a *type name*:

```
class Foo
{
public:
  typedef int map_t;
};

template <typename T>
void func ()
{
  typename T::map_t t;
}
```

15.2.9 Runtime Type Identification (RTTI)

Runtime Type Identification (RTTI) is a mechanism for interrogating the type of an object at runtime. Such a mechanism is useful for avoiding the dreaded *switch-on-type* technique used before RTTI was incorporated into the language. Until recently, some C++ compilers did not support RTTI, so it is necessary to assume that it may not be widely available.

Switch-on-type involves giving all classes a method that returns a special type token that an object can use to discover its own type. For example:

```
class Shape
{
public:
  enum types @{ TYPE_CIRCLE, TYPE_SQUARE };
  virtual enum types type () = 0;
};
```

```
class Circle: public Shape
    {
    public:
     enum types type () { return TYPE_CIRCLE; }
    };
```

```
class Square: public Shape
    {
    public:
      enum types type () { return TYPE_SQUARE; }
    };
```

Although switch-on-type is not elegant, RTTI is not particularly object-oriented either. Given the limited number of times you ought to be using RTTI, the switch-on-type technique may be reasonable.

15.2.10 Templates

Templates—known in other languages as *generic types*—enable you to write C++ classes that represent parameterized data types. A common application for *class templates* is container classes. That is, classes that implement data structures that can contain data of any type. For instance, a well-implemented binary tree is not interested in the type of data in its nodes. Templates have undergone a number of changes since their initial inclusion in the ARM. They are a particularly troublesome C++ language element in that it is difficult to implement templates well in a C++ compiler.

Here is a fictitious and overly simplistic C++ class template that implements a fixed-sized stack. It provides a pair of methods for setting (and getting) the element at the bottom of the stack. It uses the modern C++ template syntax, including the new typename keyword (see Section 15.2.8, "The typename Keyword").

```
template <typename T> class Stack
{
public:
  T first () { return stack[9]; }
  void set_first (T t) { stack[9] = t; }

private:
  T stack[10];
};
```

C++ permits this class to be instantiated for any type that you want, using calling code that looks something like this:

```
int
main ()
{
  Stack<int> s;
  s.set_first (7);
  cout << s.first () << endl;
  return 0;
}
```

An old trick for fashioning class templates is to use the C preprocessor. Here is our limited Stack class, rewritten to avoid C++ templates:

```
#define Stack(T) \
  class Stack__##T##__LINE__ \
  { \
  public: \
    T first () { return stack[0]; } \
    void set_first (T t) { stack[0] = t; } \
  \
  private: \
    T stack[10]; \
  }
```

A couple of subtleties used here should be highlighted. This generic class declaration uses the C preprocessor operator '##' to generate a type name unique among stacks of any type. The __LINE__ macro is defined by the preprocessor and is used here to maintain unique names when the template is instantiated multiple times. The trailing semicolon that must follow a class declaration has been omitted from the macro:

```
int
main ()
{
  Stack (int) s;
  s.set_first (7);
  cout << s.first () << endl;
  return 0;
}
```

The syntax for instantiating a Stack differs slightly from modern C++, but it does work relatively well, because the C++ compiler still applies type checking after the preprocessor has expanded the macro. The main problem is that unless you go to great lengths, the generated type name (such as Stack__int) could collide with other instances of the same type in the program.

15.2.11 Default Template Arguments

A later refinement to C++ templates was the concept of *default template arguments*. Templates allow C++ types to be *parameterized*; and, as such, the parameter is in essence a variable that the programmer must specify when instantiating the template. This refinement allows defaults to be specified for the template parameters.

This feature is used extensively throughout the Standard Template Library to relieve the programmer from having to specify a comparison function for sorted container classes (see Section 15.2.13, "Standard Template Library"). In most circumstances, the default less-than operator for the type in question suffices.

If your compiler does not support default template arguments, you might have to suffer without them and require that users of your class and function templates provide the default parameters themselves. Depending on the inconvenience this causes, you might begrudgingly seek some assistance from the C preprocessor and define some preprocessor macros.

15.2.12 Standard Library Headers

Newer C++ implementations provide a new set of standard library header files. These are distinguished from older incompatible header files by their filenames— the new headers omit the conventional '.h' extension. Classes and other declarations in the new headers are placed in the std namespace. Detecting the kind of header files present on any given system is an ideal application of Autoconf. For instance, the header '<vector>' declares the class std::vector<T>. If it is not available, however, '<vector.h>' declares the class vector<T> in the global namespace.

15.2.13 Standard Template Library

The *Standard Template Library* (STL) is a library of containers, iterators, and algorithms. I tend to think of the STL in terms of the container classes it provides, with algorithms and iterators necessary to make these containers useful. By segregating these roles, the STL becomes a powerful library— containers can store any kind of data, and algorithms can use iterators to traverse the containers.

There are about half-dozen STL implementations. Because the STL relies so heavily on templates, these implementations tend to inline all their method definitions. Therefore, there are no precompiled STL libraries; and as an added bonus, you're guaranteed to get the source code to your STL implementation. Hewlett-Packard and SGI produce freely redistributable STL implementations.

It is widely known that the STL can be implemented with complex C++ constructs and is a certain workout for any C++ compiler. The best policy for choosing an STL is to use a modern compiler such as GCC 2.95 or to use the STL that your vendor may have provided as part of their compiler.

Unfortunately, using the STL is pretty much an "all-or-nothing" proposition. If it is not available on a particular system, there are no viable alternatives. The Autoconf macro archive contains a macro that can test for a working STL (see Section 22.5.1, "Autoconf Macro Archive").

15.3 Compiler Quirks

C++ compilers are complex pieces of software. Sadly, sometimes the details of a compiler's implementations leak out and bother the application programmer. The two aspects of C++ compiler implementation that have caused grief in the past are efficient template instantiation and name mangling. The following sections explain each of these aspects.

15.3.1 Template Instantiation

The problem with template instantiation exists because of a number of complex constraints:

- The compiler should generate only an instance of a template once, to speed the compilation process.

- The linker needs to be smart about where to locate the object code for instantiations produced by the compiler.

Separate compilation exacerbates this problem—that is, the method bodies for List<T> might be located in a header file or in a separate compilation unit. These files might even be in a different directory than the current directory!

Life is easy for the compiler when the template definition appears in the same compilation unit as the site of the instantiation; everything needed is known:

```
template <class T> class List
{
private:
  T* head;
  T* current;
};

List<int> li;
```

This becomes significantly more difficult when the site of a template instantiation and the template definition is split between two different compilation units. In *Linkers and Loaders* (published by Morgan Kaufmann), John Levine describes in detail how the compiler driver deals with this by iteratively attempting to link a final executable and noting, from `'undefined symbol'` errors produced by the linker, which template instantiations must be performed to successfully link the program.

In large projects in which templates may be instantiated in multiple locations, the compiler might generate instantiations multiple times for the same type. Not only does this slow down compilation, but it can also result in some difficult problems for linkers that refuse to link object files containing duplicate symbols. Suppose there is the following directory layout:

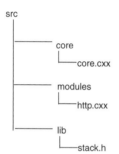

If the compiler generates `'core.o'` in the `'core'` directory and `'libhttp.a'` in the `'http'` directory, the final link might fail because `'libhttp.a'` and the final executable might contain duplicate symbols—those symbols generated as a result of both `'http.cxx'` and `'core.cxx'` instantiating, for example, a `Stack<int>`. Linkers, such as that provided with AIX allow duplicate symbols during a link, but many do not.

Some compilers have solved this problem by maintaining a template repository of template instantiations. Usually, the entire template definition is expanded with the specified type parameters and compiled into the repository, leaving the linker to collect the required object files at link time.

The main concerns about non-portability with repositories center on getting your compiler to do the right thing about maintaining a single repository across your entire project. This often requires a vendor-specific command-line option to the compiler, which can detract from portability. Conceivably, Libtool could come to the rescue here in the future.

15.3.2 Name Mangling

Early C++ compilers mangled the names of C++ symbols so that existing linkers could be used without modification. The cfront C++ translator also mangled names so that information from the original C++ program would not be lost in the translation to C. Today, name mangling remains important for enabling overloaded function names and link-time type checking. The following C++ source file example illustrates name mangling in action:

```
class Foo
{
public:
  Foo ();

  void go ();
  void go (int where);

private:
  int pos;
};

Foo::Foo ()
{
  pos = 0;
}

void
Foo::go ()
{
  go (0);
}

void
Foo::go (int where)
{
  pos = where;
}

int
main ()
{
  Foo f;
  f.go (10);
}
```

```
$ g++ -Wall example.cxx -o example.o

$ nm --defined-only example.o
00000000 T __3Foo
00000000 ? __FRAME_BEGIN__
00000000 t gcc2_compiled.
0000000c T go__3Foo
0000002c T go__3Fooi
00000038 T main
```

Even though Foo contains two methods with the same name, their argument lists (one taking an int, one taking no arguments) help to differentiate them after their names have been mangled. The 'go__3Fooi' is the version that takes an int argument. The '__3Foo' symbol is the constructor for Foo. The GNU binutils package includes a utility called c++filt that can demangle names. Other proprietary tools sometimes include a similar utility, although with a bit of imagination, you can often demangle names in your head:

```
$ nm --defined-only example.o | c++filt
00000000 T Foo::Foo(void)
00000000 ? __FRAME_BEGIN__
00000000 t gcc2_compiled.
0000000c T Foo::go(void)
0000002c T Foo::go(int)
00000038 T main
```

Name-mangling algorithms differ among C++ implementations so that object files assembled by one tool chain may not be linked by another if legitimate reasons exist to prohibit linking. This is a deliberate move, because other aspects of the object file might make them incompatible (such as the calling convention used for making function calls).

This implies that C++ libraries and packages cannot be practically distributed in binary form. Of course, you were intending to distribute the source code to your package anyway, weren't you?

15.4 How GNU Autotools Can Help

Each of the GNU Autotools contribute to C++ portability. Now that you are familiar with the issues, the following subsections will outline precisely how each tool contributes to achieving C++ portability.

15.4.1 Testing C++ Implementations with Autoconf

Of the GNU Autotools, perhaps the most valuable contribution to the portability of your C++ programs will come from Autoconf. You can detect all the portability issues raised in Section 15.2, "Changeable C++," by using Autoconf macros.

Luc Maisonobe has written a large suite of macros for this purpose; you can find them in the Autoconf macro archive (see Section 22.5.1, "Autoconf Macro Archive"). If any of these macros become important enough, they may become incorporated into the core Autoconf release. These macros perform their tests by compiling small fragments of C++ code to ensure that the compiler accepts them. As a side effect, these macros typically use AC_DEFINE to define preprocessor macros of the form HAVE_feature, which may then be exploited through conditional compilation.

15.4.2 Automake C++ Support

Automake provides support for compiling C++ programs. In fact, it makes it practically trivial: Files listed in a SOURCES primary may include '.c++', '.cc', '.cpp', '.cxx', or '.c' extensions, and Automake will know to use the C++ compiler to build them.

For a project containing C++ source code, you must invoke the AC_PROG_CXX macro in 'configure.in' so that Automake knows how to run the most suitable compiler. Fortunately, when little details like this happen to escape you, automake produces a warning:

```
$ automake
automake: Makefile.am: C++ source seen but CXX not defined in
automake: Makefile.am: 'configure.in'
```

15.4.3 Libtool C++ Support

At the moment, Libtool is the weak link in the chain when it comes to working with C++. It is very easy to naively build a shared library from C++ source using libtool:

```
$ libtool -mode=link g++ -o libfoo.la -rpath /usr/local/lib foo.c++
```

This works admirably for trivial examples; with real code, however, several things can go wrong:

- On many architectures, for a variety of reasons, libtool needs to perform object linking using ld. Unfortunately, the C++ compiler often links in standard libraries at this stage, and using ld causes them to be dropped.

- This can be worked around (at the expense of portability) by explicitly adding these missing libraries to the link line in your 'Makefile'. You could even write an Autoconf macro to probe the host machine to discover likely candidates.

- The C++ compiler likes to instantiate static constructors in the library objects, which C++ programmers often rely on. Linking with ld causes this to fail.

- The only reliable way to work around this currently is to not write C++ that relies on static constructors in libraries. You might be lucky enough to be able to link with LD=$CXX in your environment with some projects, but it would be prone to stop working as your project develops.

- Libtool's interlibrary-dependency analysis can fail when it cannot find the special runtime library dependencies added to a shared library by the C++ compiler at link time.

- The best way around this problem is to explicitly add these dependencies to `libtool`'s link line:

```
$ libtool -mode=link g++ -o libfoo.la -rpath /usr/local/lib foo.cxx \
-lstdc++ -lg++
```

Now that C++ compilers on UNIX are beginning to see widespread acceptance and are converging on the ISO standard, it is becoming unacceptable for Libtool to impose such limits. Work is afoot to provide generalized multilanguage and multicompiler support into Libtool—currently slated to arrive in Libtool 1.5. Much of the work for supporting C++ is already finished at the time of writing, pending beta testing and packaging. Visit the Libtool home page at `http://www.gnu.org/software/libtool` for breaking news.

15.5 Further Reading

A number of books devoted to the topic of C++ portability have been published. Unfortunately, the problem with printed publications that discuss the state of C++ is that they date quickly. These publications might also fail to cover inadequacies of your particular compiler, because portability know-how is something that can be acquired only by collective experience.

Instead, online guides such as the Mozilla C++ Portability Guide (`http://www.mozilla.org/hacking/portable-cpp.html`), tend to be a more useful resource. An online guide such as this can accumulate the knowledge of a wider developer community and can be readily updated as new facts are discovered. Interestingly, the Mozilla guide is aggressive in its recommendations for achieving true C++ portability: Item 3, for instance, states, "Don't use exceptions." Although you might not choose to follow each recommendation, this document certainly contains a lot of useful experience.

16

Dynamic Loading

An increasingly popular way of adding functionality to a project is to give a program the capability to dynamically load plug-ins, or modules. By doing this, your users can extend your project in new ways, which even you perhaps hadn't envisioned. *Dynamic loading*, then, is the process of loading compiled objects into a running program and executing some or all of the code from the loaded objects in the same context as the main executable.

This chapter begins with a discussion of the mechanics of dynamic modules and how they are used, and ends with example code for very simple module loading on GNU/Linux, along with the example code for a complementary dynamically loadable module. This chapter examines the principles of dynamic loading, and the next chapter explains how to use GNU Autotools to write portable dynamic module loading code and to address some of the shortcomings of native dynamic loading APIs.

16.1 Dynamic Modules

To dynamically load some code into your executable, that code must be compiled in some special but architecture-dependent fashion. Depending on the compiler you use and the platform you are compiling for, you must observe different conventions in the code for the module, and for the particular combination of compiler options you need to select if the resulting objects are to be suitable for use in a dynamic module. The rest of this chapter concentrates on the conventions used when compiling dynamic modules with GCC on GNU/Linux. Although these are peculiar to this particular combination of compiler and host architecture, they are typical of the sorts of conventions you would need to observe on other architectures or with a different compiler.

With GCC on GNU/Linux, you must compile each of the source files with
'-fPIC'[1], and the resulting objects must be linked into a loadable module with
GCC's '-shared' option:

```
$ gcc -fPIC -c foo.c
$ gcc -fPIC -c bar.c
$ gcc -shared -o baz.so foo.o bar.o
```

This is pretty similar to how you might go about linking a shared library,
except that the 'baz.so' module will never be linked with a '-lbaz' option, so
the 'lib' prefix isn't necessary. In fact, it would probably be confusing if you
used the prefix. Similarly, there is no constraint to use any particular filename
suffix; it is sensible, however, to use the target's native shared library suffix
(GNU/Linux uses '.so') to make it obvious that the compiled file is some sort
of shared object, and not a normal executable.

Apart from that, the only difference between a shared library built for linking
at compile time and a dynamic module built for loading at runtime is that the
module must provide known *entry points* for the main executable to call. That
is, when writing code destined for a dynamic module, you must provide functions or variables with known names and semantics that the main executable
can use to access the functionality of the module. This *is* different to the function and variable names in a regular library, which are already known when
you write the client code, because the libraries are always written *before* the
code that uses them; a runtime module loading system must, by definition, be
able to cope with modules written *after* the code that uses those modules.

16.2 Module Access Functions

To access the functionality of dynamic modules, different architectures provide
various APIs to bring the code from the module into the address space of the
loading program, and to access the symbols exported by that module.

GNU/Linux uses the dynamic module API introduced by Sun's Solaris operating
system and widely adopted (and adapted!) by the majority of modern Unices (HP-
UX being the most notable exception). The interface consists of four functions. In
practice, you really ought not to use these functions, because you would be
locking your project into this single API and the class of machines that supports it.
This description is oversimplified to serve as a comparison with the fully portable
libltdl API described in Chapter 17, "Using GNU libltdl." The minutiae are not
discussed, because therein lie the implementation peculiarities that spoil the portability of this API. As they stand, these descriptions give a good overview of how

---

[1] *Not essential but will be slower without this option; see Section 9.2.1, "Position-
Independent Code."*

the functions work at a high level, and are broadly applicable to the various implementations in use. If you are curious, the details of your machine's particular
dynamic loading API will be available in its system manual pages.

void * **dlopen** (const char *filename, int flag)   Function

> Brings the code from a named module into the address space of the running
> program that calls it, and returns a handle that is used by the other API functions.
> If *filename* is not an absolute path, GNU/ Linux searches for it in directories
> named in the 'LD_LIBRARY_PATH' environment variable, and then in the standard
> library directories before giving up.
>
> The flag argument is made by OR'ing together various flag bits defined in the
> system headers. On GNU/Linux, these flags are defined in 'dlfcn.h':

RTLD_LAZY

> Resolve undefined symbols when they are first used.

RTLD_NOW

> If all symbols cannot be resolved when the module is loaded, dlopen fails and
> returns 'NULL'.

RTLD_GLOBAL

> All the global symbols in the loaded module are available to resolve undefined
> symbols in subsequently loaded modules.

void * **dlsym** (void *handle, char *name)   Function

> Returns the address of the named symbol in the module that returned *handle*
> when it was dlopened. You must cast the returned address to a known type before
> using it.

int **dlclose** (void *handle)   Function

> After you have finished with a particular module, you can remove it from memory
> using this function.

const char * **dlerror** (void)   Function

> If any of the other three API calls fails, this function returns a string that describes
> the last error that occurred.

To use these functions on GNU/Linux, you must #include <dlfcn.h> for the
function prototypes, and link with '-ldl' to provide the API implementation.
Other Unices use '-ldld' or provide the implementation of the API inside the
standard C library.

16.3 Finding a Module

When you are writing a program that will load dynamic modules, a major stumbling block is writing the code to find the modules you want to load. If you are worried about portability (which you must be, or you wouldn't be reading this book!), you can't rely on the default search algorithm of the vendor `dlopen` function, because it varies from implementation to implementation. You can't even rely on the name of the module, because the module suffix varies according to the conventions of the target host (although you could insist on a particular suffix for modules you are willing to load).

Unfortunately, this means that you will need to implement your own searching algorithm and always use an absolute path name when you call `dlopen`. A widely adopted mechanism is to look for each module in directories listed in an environment variable specific to your application, enabling your users to inform the application of the location of any modules they have written. If a suitable module is not yet found, the application would then default to looking in a list of standard locations (in a subdirectory of the user's home directory, for example), and finally a subdirectory of the application installation tree. For application `'foo'`, you might use `'/usr/lib/foo/module.so'`—that is, `'$(pkglibdir)/module.so'` if you are using Automake.

This algorithm can be further improved as follows:

- You can try different module suffixes to the named module for every directory in the search path, which will avoid locking your code into a subset of machines that use the otherwise hard-coded module suffix. With this in place, you can ask the module loader for module `'foomodule'`; and if it is not found in the first search directory, the module loader could try `'foomodule.so'`, `'foomodule.sl'`, and `'foomodule.dll'` before moving on to the next directory.

- You might also provide command-line options to your application to preload modules before starting the program proper or to modify the module search path. For example, GNU M4, version 1.5, will have the following dynamic loading options:

```
$ m4 --help
Usage: m4 [OPTION]... [FILE]...
...
Dynamic loading features:
  -M, --module-directory=DIRECTORY  add DIRECTORY to the search path
  -m, --load-module=MODULE          load dynamic MODULE from M4MODPATH
...
Report bugs to <bug-m4@gnu.org>.
```

16.4 A Simple GNU/Linux Module Loader

Be aware that when your users write dynamic modules for your application, they are subject to the interface you design. It is very important to design a dynamic module interface that is clean and functional before other people start to write modules for your code. If you ever need to change the interface, your users will need to rewrite their modules. Of course you can carefully change the interface to retain backward compatibility to save your users the trouble of rewriting their modules, but that is no substitute for designing a good interface from the outset. If you do get it wrong, and subsequently discover that the design you implemented is misconceived (this is the voice of experience speaking!), you are left with a difficult choice. You could try to tweak the broken API so that it does work while retaining backward compatibility, and suffer the maintenance and performance penalty that brings. Alternatively, you could start again with a fresh design born of the experience gained last time, and rewrite all the modules you have so far.

If other applications have similar module requirements to you, it is worth writing a loader that uses the same interface and semantics. That way, you will (hopefully) be building from a known good API design, and you will have access to all the modules for that other application too, and vice versa.

For the sake of clarity, I have sidestepped any issues of API design for the following example, by choosing this minimal interface:

int **run** (const char *argument)   Function

> When the module is successfully loaded, a function with the following prototype is
> called with the argument given on the command line. If this entry point is found
> and called, but returns '-1', the calling program displays an error message.

You can build the following simplistic, but complete, dynamic module loading application for this interface with the GNU/Linux dynamic loading API:

```
#include <stdio.h>
#include <stdlib.h>
#ifndef EXIT_FAILURE
#  define EXIT_FAILURE    1
#  define EXIT_SUCCESS    0
#endif

#include <limits.h>
#ifndef PATH_MAX
#  define PATH_MAX 255
#endif
```

```
#include <dlfcn.h>
/* This is missing from very old Linux libc. */
#ifndef RTLD_NOW
#  define RTLD_NOW 2
#endif

typedef int entrypoint (const char *argument);

/* Save and return a copy of the dlerror() error  message,
   since the next API call may overwrite the original. */
static char *dlerrordup (char *errormsg);

int
main (int argc, const char *argv)
{
  const char modulepath[1+ PATH_MAX];
  const char *errormsg = NULL;
  void *module = NULL;
  entrypoint *run = NULL;
  int errors = 0;

if (argc != 3)
    {
      fprintf (stderr, "USAGE: main MODULENAME ARGUMENT\n");
      exit (EXIT_FAILURE);
    }

 /* Set the module search path. */
  getcwd (modulepath, PATH_MAX);
  strcat (modulepath, "/");
  strcat (modulepath, argv[1]);

 /* Load the module. */
  module = dlopen (modulepath, RTLD_NOW);
  if (!module)
    {
      strcat (modulepath, ".so");
      module = dlopen (modulepath, RTLD_NOW);
    }
  if (!module)
    errors = 1;

 /* Find the entry point. */
  if (!errors)
    {
      run = dlsym (module, "run");
      /* In principle, run might legitimately be NULL, so
         I don't use run == NULL as an error indicator. */
      errormsg = dlerrordup (errormsg);
```

```
        if (errormsg != NULL)
          errors = dlclose (module);
      }

  /* Call the entry point function. */
  if (!errors)
    {
      int result = (*run) (argv[2]);
      if (result < 0)
        errormsg = strdup ("module entry point execution failed");
      else
        printf ("\t=> %d\n", result);
    }

/* Unload the module, now that we are done with it. */
  if (!errors)
    errors = dlclose (module);

  if (errors)
    {
      /* Diagnose the encountered error. */
      errormsg = dlerrordup (errormsg);

      if (!errormsg)
        {
          fprintf (stderr, "%s: dlerror() failed.\n", argv[0]);
          return EXIT_FAILURE;
        }
    }

  if (errormsg)
    {
      fprintf (stderr, "%s: %s.\n", argv[0], errormsg);
      free (errormsg);
      return EXIT_FAILURE;
    }

  return EXIT_SUCCESS;
}

/* Be careful to save a copy of the error message,
   since the next API call may overwrite the original. */
static char *
dlerrordup (char *errormsg)
{
  char *error = (char *) dlerror ();
  if (error && !errormsg)
    errormsg = strdup (error);
  return errormsg;
}
```

You would compile this on a GNU/Linux machine as follows:

```
$ gcc -o simple-loader simple-loader.c -ldl
```

However, despite making reasonable effort with this loader, and ignoring features which could easily be added, it still has some seemingly insoluble problems:

1. It fails if the user's platform doesn't have the `dlopen` API. This also includes platforms that have no shared libraries.

2. It relies on the implementation to provide a working self-opening mechanism. `'dlopen (NULL, RTLD_NOW)'` is very often unimplemented, or buggy, and without that, it is impossible to access the symbols of the main program through the `'dlsym'` mechanism.

3. It is quite difficult to figure out at compile time whether the target host needs `'libdl.so'` to be linked.

The following chapter shows how to use GNU Autotools to tackle these problems.

16.5 A Simple GNU/Linux Dynamic Module

As an appetizer for working with dynamic loadable modules, here is a minimal module written for the interface used by the loader in the preceding section:

```
#include <stdio.h>

int
run (const char *argument)
{
  printf ("Hello, %s!\n", argument);
  return 0;
}
```

Again, to compile on a GNU/Linux machine:

```
$ gcc -fPIC -c simple-module.c
$ gcc -shared -o simple-module.so simple-module.o
```

Having compiled both loader and module, a test run looks like this:

```
$ ./simple-loader simple-module World
Hello, World!
        => 0
```

If you have a GNU/Linux system, you should experiment with the simple examples from this chapter to get a feel for the relationship between a dynamic module loader and its modules—tweak the interface a little; try writing another simple module. If you have a machine with a different dynamic loading API, try porting these examples to that machine. By doing so, you will get a feel for the kinds of problems you would encounter if you wanted a module system that would work with both APIs.

The next chapter does just that, developing these examples into a fully portable module loading system with the aid of GNU Autotools. Section 17.2.3, "Module Loader," adds a more realistic module loader into the Sic project last discussed in Chapter 11, "A Large GNU Autotools Project."

17

Using GNU libltdl

Now that you are conversant with the mechanics and advantages of using dynamic runtime modules in your projects, you can probably already imagine 101 uses for a plug-in architecture. As I described in the preceding chapter, there are several gratuitously different architecture-dependent dynamic loading APIs, and yet several more shortcomings in many of those. If you have Libtool installed on your machine, you almost certainly have libltdl, which has shipped as part of the standard Libtool distribution since release 1.3. This chapter describes *GNU libltdl*, the Libtool dynamic loading library, and explains some of its features and how to make use of them.

17.1 Introducing libltdl

Probably the best known and supported Unix runtime-linking API is the `'dlopen'` interface, used by Solaris and GNU/Linux among others, and discussed earlier in Chapter 16, "Dynamic Loading." libltdl is based on the `'dlopen'` API, with a few small differences and several enhancements.

The following libltdl API functions are declared in `'ltdl.h'`:

lt_dlhandle **lt_dlopen** (const char *filename)   Function
  This function brings the code from a named module into the address space of the running program that calls it and returns a handle used by the other API functions. If *filename* is not an absolute path, libltdl searches for it in directories named in the `'LTDL_LIBRARY_PATH'` environment variable, and then in the standard library directories before giving up. It is safe to call this function many times; libltdl keeps track of the number of calls made, but requires the same number of calls to `'lt_dlclose'` to actually unload the module.

lt_ptr_t **lt_dlsym** (lt_dlhandle *handle*, const char *name)   Function
  Returns the address of the named symbol in the module that returned *handle* when it was lt_dlopen'ed. You must cast the returned address to a known type before using it.

---

int **lt_dlclose** (lt_dlhandle *handle*)   Function
  After you have finished with a particular module, you can remove it from
  memory using this function.

const char * **lt_dlerror** (void)   Function
  If any of the libltdl API calls fail, this function returns a string that describes
  the last error that occurred.

To use these functions, you must #include <ltdl.h> for the function prototypes
and link with '-lltdl' to provide the API implementation. Assuming you link
your application with libtool, and that you call the necessary macros from
your 'configure.in' (see Section 17.2, "Using libltdl"), any host-specific-
dependent libraries (for example, 'libdl' on GNU/Linux) are automatically
added to the final link line by libtool.

You do not limit yourself to using only Libtool-compiled modules when you
use libltdl. A carefully written module loader will be able to load native
modules, too —although you cannot preload non-Libtool modules (see
Section 17.4, "dlpreopen Loading"). The loader in Section 17.2.3, "Module
Loader," is written in this way. It is useful to be able to load modules flexibly
like this, because you don't tie your users into using Libtool for any modules
they write.

Compare the descriptions of the previous functions with the API described in
Section 16.2, "Module Access Functions." You will notice that they are very
similar.

Back Linking

*Back linking is the process of resolving any remaining symbols by referencing
back into the application that loads the library at runtime—a mechanism implemented on almost all modern Unices.*

*For instance, your main application might provide some utility function,
'my_function', to which you want a module to have access. You can accomplish
this in two ways:*

- *You can use Libtool to link your application, using the '-export-dynamic'
  option to ensure that the global application symbols are available to
  modules. When libltdl loads a module into an application compiled like
  this, it back links symbols from the application to resolve any otherwise-
  undefined symbols in a module. When the module is 'ltdlopen'ed, libltdl
  arranges for calls to 'my_function' in the module, to execute the
  'my_function' implementation in the application.*

If you have need of this functionality, relying on back linking is the simplest way to achieve it. Unfortunately, this simplicity is at the expense of portability: Some platforms have no support for back linking at all, and others do not allow a module to be created with unresolved symbols. Nevertheless, libltdl enables you to do this if you want to.

- *You can split the code that implements the symbols you need to share with modules into a separate library. This library is then used to resolve the symbols you want to share, by linking them into modules and applications alike. The definition of* `'my_function'` *is compiled separately into a library,* `'libmy_function.la'`*. References to* `'my_function'` *from the application are resolved by linking it with* `'libmy_function.la'`*, and the library is installed so that modules that need to call* `'my_function'` *can resolve the symbol by linking with* `'-lmy_function'`*.*

  This method requires support for neither back linking nor unresolved link-time symbols from the host platform. The disadvantage is that when you realize you need this functionality, it may be quite complicated to extract the shared functionality from the application to be compiled in a standalone library.◆

On those platforms that support *back linking,* you can configure libltdl to resolve external symbol references in a dynamic module with any global symbols already present in the main application. This has two implications for the libltdl API:

- There is no need to pass `'RTLD_GLOBAL'` (or the equivalent) to `lt_dlopen` as might be necessary with the native module-loading API.
- You should be aware that your application will not work on some platforms—most notably, Windows and AIX—if you rely on a back linking.

Similarly, there is no need to specify whether the module should be integrated into the application core before `lt_dlopen` returns or, on the other hand, when the symbols it provides are first referenced. libltdl uses *lazy loading* if it is supported, because this is a slight performance enhancement; otherwise, it falls back to loading everything immediately. Between this feature and the support of back linking, there is no need to pass flags into `lt_dlopen` as there is with most native `dlopen` APIs.

You need a couple of other important API functions when using libltdl:

int **lt_dlinit** (void)   Function
> You must call this function to initialize libltdl before calling any of the other libltdl API functions. It is safe to call this function many times; libltdl keeps track of the number of calls made, but requires the same number of calls to 'lt_dlexit' to actually recycle the library resources. If you don't call 'lt_dlinit' before any other API call, the other calls, including 'lt_dlerror', return their respective failure codes ('NULL' or '1', as appropriate).

int **lt_dlexit** (void)   Function
> After you have finished with libltdl and all dynamic modules have been unloaded, you can call this function to finalize the library and recycle its resources. If you forget to unload any modules, the call to 'lt_dlexit' will 'lt_dlclose' them for you.

Another useful departure that the libltdl API makes from a vanilla dlopen implementation is that it will work correctly with old K&R C compilers as well, by virtue of not relying on 'void *' pointers. libltdl uses lt_dlhandles to pass references to loaded modules, and this also improves ANSI C compiler's type checking compared to the untyped addresses typically used by native dlopen APIs.

17.2 Using libltdl

Various aspects of libltdl are addressed in the following subsections, starting with a step-by-step guide to adding libltdl to your own GNU Autotools projects (see Section 17.2.1, "Configury") and an explanation of how to initialize libltdl's memory management (see Section 17.2.2, "Memory Management"). After this comes a simple libltdl module loader that you can use as the basis for a module loader in your own projects (see Section 17.2.3, "Module Loader"), including an explanation of how libltdl finds and links any native dynamic module library necessary for the host platform. Section 17.2.4, "Dependent Libraries," deals with the similar problem of dynamic modules that depend on other libraries—take care not to confuse the problems discussed in the two subsections preceding that one. Following that, the source code for and use of a simple dynamic module for use with this section's module loader is detailed (see Section 17.2.5, "Dynamic Module").

17.2.1 Configury

Because libltdl supports so many different platforms[1], it needs to be configured for the host platform before it can be used.

> **Note**
>
> *The path of least resistance to successfully integrating libltdl into your own project dictates that the project use Libtool for linking its module loader with libltdl. This is certainly the method I use and recommend, and is the method discussed in this chapter. I have seen projects that did not use Libtool (specifically because Libtool's poor C++ support made it difficult to adopt), however, but which wanted the advantages of libltdl. It is possible to use libltdl entirely without Libtool, provided you take care to use the configuration macros described here and use the results of those running these macros to determine how to link your application with libltdl.*◆

The easiest way to add libltdl support to your own projects is by following these simple steps:

1. You must add the libltdl sources to your project distribution. If you are not already using Libtool in some capacity for your project, you should add `'AC_PROG_LIBTOOL'`[2] to your `'configure.in'`. That done, move to the top-level directory of the project, and execute the following:

    ```
    $ libtoolize --ltdl
    $ ls -F
    aclocal.m4    configure.in    libltdl/
    $ ls libltdl/
    COPYING.LIB   README       aclocal.m4   configure.in   stamp-h.in
    Makefile.am   acconfig.h   config.h.in  ltdl.c
    Makefile.in   acinclude.m4 configure    ltdl.h
    ```

2. libltdl has its own configuration to run in addition to the configuration for your project, so you must be careful to call the subdirectory configuration from your top-level `'configure.in'`:

    ```
    AC_CONFIG_SUBDIRS(libltdl)
    ```

    And you must ensure that Automake knows that it must descend into the libltdl source directory at make time, by adding the name of that subdirectory to the `'SUBDIRS'` macro in your top-level `'Makefile.am'`:

    ```
    SUBDIRS = libltdl src
    ```

---

[1] *As I always like to say, "From BeOS to Windows!" And yes, I do think that it is a better catch-phrase than "From AIX to Xenix!"*

[2] *Use `'AM_PROG_LIBTOOL'` if you have Automake version 1.4 or older or a version of Libtool earlier than 1.4.*

3. You must also arrange for the code of libltdl to be linked into your application. You can do this in two ways: as a regular Libtool library, or as a convenience library (see Section 9.2.4, "Creating Convenience Libraries"). Either way you must be aware of certain catches, which will be addressed in a future release. Until libltdl is present on the average user's machine, I recommend building a convenience library. You can do that in 'configure.in':

```
AC_LIBLTDL_CONVENIENCE
AC_PROG_LIBTOOL
```

The main thing to be aware of when you follow these steps is that you can have only one copy of the code from libltdl in any application. Once you link the objects into a library, that library will not work with any other library that has also linked with libltdl or any application that has its own copy of the objects. If you were to try, the libltdl symbol names would clash.

The alternative is to substitute 'AC_LIBLTDL_CONVENIENCE' with 'AC_LIBLTDL_INSTALLABLE'. Unfortunately there are currently many potential problems with this approach. This macro tries to find an already installed libltdl and use that, or else the embedded libltdl will be built as a standard shared library, which must be installed along with any libraries or applications that use it. There is no testing for version compatibility, so it is possible that two or more applications which use this method will overwrite one another's copies of the installed libraries and headers. Also, the code that searches for the already installed version of libltdl tends not to find the library on many hosts, due to the native libraries it depends on being difficult to predict.

Both of the 'AC_LIBLTDL_...' macros set the values of 'INCLTDL' and 'LIBLTDL' so that they can be used to add the correct include and library flags to the compiler in your Makefiles. They are not substituted by default. If you need to use them, you must also add the following macros to your 'configure.in':

```
AC_SUBST(INCLTDL)
AC_SUBST(LIBLTDL)
```

Many of the libltdl-supported hosts require that a separate shared library be linked into any application that uses dynamic runtime loading. libltdl is wrapped around this native implementation on these hosts, so it is important to link that library too. Adding support for module loading through the wrapped native implementation is independent of Libtool's determination of how shared objects are compiled. On GNU/Linux, you would need to link your program with libltdl and 'libdl', for example.

Libtool installs a macro, `'AC_LIBTOOL_DLOPEN'`, which adds tests to your `'configure'` that searches for this native library. Whenever you use libltdl, you should add this macro to your `'configure.in'` before `'AC_PROG_LIBTOOL'`:

```
AC_LIBTOOL_DLOPEN
AC_LIBLTDL_CONVENIENCE
AC_PROG_LIBTOOL
...
AC_SUBST(INCLTDL)
AC_SUBST(LIBLTDL)
```

`'AC_LIBTOOL_DLOPEN'` takes care to substitute a suitable value of `'LIBADD_DL'` into your `'Makefile.am'` so that your code will compile correctly wherever the implementation library is discovered:

```
INCLUDES        += @INCLTDL@

bin_PROGRAMS     = your_app
your_app_SOURCES = main.c support.c
your_app_LDADD   = @LIBLTDL@ @LIBADD_DL@
```

Libtool 1.4 has much improved interlibrary-dependency tracking code that no longer requires `'@LIBADD_DL@'` to be explicitly referenced in your `'Makefile.am'`. When you install libltdl, Libtool 1.4 (or better) makes a note of any native library that libltdl depends on—linking it automatically, provided that you link `'libltdl.la'` with libtool. You might want to omit the `'@LIBADD_DL@'` from your `'Makefile.am'` in this case, if seeing the native library twice (once as a dependee of libltdl, and again as an expansion of `'@LIBADD_DL@'`) on the link line bothers you.

Beyond this basic configury setup, you will also want to write some code to form a module-loading subsystem for your project, and of course some modules! That process is described in Sections 17.2.3 ("Module Loader") and 17.2.5 ("Dynamic Module").

17.2.2 Memory Management

Internally, libltdl maintains a list of loaded modules and symbols on the heap. If you find that you want to use it with a project that has an unusual memory-management API, or if you just want to use a debugging `'malloc'`, libltdl provides hook functions for you to set the memory routines it should call.

The way to use these hooks is to point them at the memory allocation routines you want libltdl to use before calling any of its API functions:

```
lt_dlmalloc = (lt_prt_t (*) PARAMS((size_t))) mymalloc;
lt_dlfree   = (void (*) PARAMS((lt_ptr_t))) myfree;
```

Notice that the function names need to be cast to the correct type before assigning them to the hook symbols. You need to do this because the prototypes of the functions you want libltdl to use will vary slightly from libltdls own function pointer types—libltdl uses `'lt_ptr_t'` for compatibility with K&R compilers, for example.

17.2.3 Module Loader

This section contains a fairly minimal libltdl-based dynamic module loader that you can use as a base for your own code. It implements the same API as the simple module loader in Section 16.5, "A Simple GNU/Linux Dynamic Module," and because of the way libltdl is written is able to load modules written for that loader, too. The only part of this code arguably more complex than the equivalent from the previous example loader is that `'lt_dlinit'` and `lt_dlexit` must be called in the appropriate places. In contrast, the module search path initialization is much simplified thanks to another relative improvement in the libltdl API:

---

int **lt_dlsetsearchpath** (const char *path)   Function
This function takes a colon-separated list of directories, which will be the first directories libltdl searches when trying to locate a dynamic module.

Another new API function is used to actually load the module:

---

lt_dlhandle **lt_dlopenext** (const char *filename)   Function
This function is used in precisely the same way as `lt_dlopen`. If the search for the named module by exact match against *filename* fails, however, it will try again with a `'.la'` extension, and then the native shared library extension (`'.sl'` on HP-UX, for example).

The advantage of using `lt_dlopenext` to load dynamic modules is that it works equally well when loading modules not compiled with Libtool. Also, by passing the module name parameter with no extension, this function allows module coders to manage without Libtool:

```
#include <stdio.h>
#include <stdlib.h>
#ifndef EXIT_FAILURE
#  define EXIT_FAILURE    1
#  define EXIT_SUCCESS    0
#endif

#include <limits.h>
#ifndef PATH_MAX
#  define PATH_MAX 255
#endif
```

```
#include <string.h>
#include <ltdl.h>

#ifndef MODULE_PATH_ENV
#  define MODULE_PATH_ENV        "MODULE_PATH"
#endif

typedef int entrypoint (const char *argument);

/* Save and return a copy of the dlerror() error  message,
   since the next API call may overwrite the original. */
static char *dlerrordup (char *errormsg);

int
main (int argc, const char *argv[])
{
  char *errormsg = NULL;
  lt_dlhandle module = NULL;
  entrypoint *run = NULL;
  int errors = 0;

  if (argc != 3)
    {
      fprintf (stderr, "USAGE: main MODULENAME ARGUMENT\n");
      exit (EXIT_FAILURE);
    }

  /* Initialize libltdl. */
  errors = lt_dlinit ();

  /* Set the module search path. */
  if (!errors)
    {
      const char *path = getenv (MODULE_PATH_ENV);

      if (path != NULL)
        errors = lt_dlsetsearchpath (path);
    }

  /* Load the module. */
  if (!errors)
    module = lt_dlopenext (argv[1]);

  /* Find the entry point. */
  if (module)
    {
      run = (entrypoint *) lt_dlsym (module, "run");

      /* In principle, run might legitimately be NULL, so
         I don't use run == NULL as an error indicator
         in general. */
      errormsg = dlerrordup (errormsg);
      if (errormsg != NULL)
```

```
              {
                errors = lt_dlclose (module);
                module = NULL;
              }
          }
      else
        errors = 1;

      /* Call the entry point function. */
      if (!errors)
        {
          int result = (*run) (argv[2]);
          if (result < 0)
            errormsg = strdup ("module entry point execution failed");
          else
            printf ("\t=> %d\n", result);
        }

      /* Unload the module, now that we are done with it. */
      if (!errors)
        errors = lt_dlclose (module);

      if (errors)
        {
          /* Diagnose the encountered error. */
          errormsg = dlerrordup (errormsg);

          if (!errormsg)
            {
              fprintf (stderr, "%s: dlerror() failed.\n", argv[0]);
              return EXIT_FAILURE;
            }
        }

      /* Finished with ltdl now. */
      if (!errors)
        if (lt_dlexit () != 0)
          errormsg = dlerrordup (errormsg);

      if (errormsg)
        {
          fprintf (stderr, "%s: %s.\n", argv[0], errormsg);
          free (errormsg);
          exit (EXIT_FAILURE);
        }

      return EXIT_SUCCESS;
}

/* Be careful to save a copy of the error message,
   since the  next API call may overwrite the original. */
static char *
dlerrordup (char *errormsg)
```

```
{
  char *error = (char *) lt_dlerror ();
  if (error && !errormsg)
    errormsg = strdup (error);
  return errormsg;
}
```

This file must be compiled with libtool so that the dependent libraries ('libdl.so' on my GNU/Linux machine) are handled correctly and so that the dlpreopen support is compiled in correctly (see Section 17.4, "dlpreopen Loading"):

```
$ libtool --mode=link gcc -g -o ltdl-loader -dlopen self \
-rpath /tmp/lib ltdl-loader.c -lltdl
gcc -g -o ltdl-loader -Wl,--rpath,/tmp/lib ltdl-loader.c -lltdl -ldl
```

By using *both* lt_dlopenext and lt_dlsetsearchpath, this module loader will make a valiant attempt at loading anything you pass to it—including the module I wrote for the simple GNU/Linux module loader earlier (see Section 16.5). Here, you can see the new ltdl-loader loading and using the 'simple-module' module from Section 16.5:

```
$ ltdl-loader simple-module World
Hello, World!
        => 0
```

17.2.4 Dependent Libraries

On modern Unices (architectures that use ELF and ECOFF binary format, for example), the binary format used for the shared library architecture is smart enough to encode all the other libraries that a dynamic module depends on. On these architectures, when you lt_dlopen a module, if any shared libraries it depends on are not already loaded into the main application, the system runtime loader ensures that they too are loaded so that all the module's symbols are satisfied.

Less-well-endowed systems (those that use a.out binary format, for example) cannot do this by themselves. Since Libtool release 1.4, libltdl uses the record of interlibrary dependencies in the Libtool pseudo-library (see Chapter 9, "Introducing GNU Libtool") to manually load dependent libraries as part of the lt_dlopen call.

An example of the sort of difficulties that can arise from trying to load a module that has a complex library-dependency chain is typified by a problem I encountered with GNU Guile a few years ago: Earlier releases of the libXt Athena widget wrapper library for GNU Guile failed to load on my a.out-based GNU/Linux system. When I tried to load the module into a running Guile interpreter, it could not resolve any of the symbols that referred to libXt. I soon discovered that the libraries which the module depended on were not loaded by virtue of loading the module itself. I needed to build the interpreter itself with libXt and rely on back linking to resolve the 'Xt' references when I loaded the module. This pretty much defeated the whole point of having the wrapper library as a module. Had Libtool been around in those days, it could have loaded libXt as part of the process of loading the module.

If you program with the X Window system, you know that the list of libraries you need to link into your applications soon grows to be very large. Worse, if you want to load an X extension module into a non-X-aware application, you will encounter the problems I found with Guile, unless you link your module with libtool and dynamically load it with libltdl. At the moment, the various X Window libraries are not built with Libtool, so you must be sure to list all the dependencies when you link a module. By doing this, Libtool can use the list to check that all the libraries required by a module are loaded correctly as part of the call to 'lt_dlopen', like this:

```
$ libtool --mode=link gcc -o module.so -module -avoid-version \
source.c -L/usr/X11R6/lib -lXt -lX11
...
$ file .libs/module.so
.libs/module.so: ELF 32-bit LSB shared object, Intel 80386,
version 1, not stripped
$ ldd .libs/module.so
        libX11.so.6 => /usr/X11R6/lib/libX11.so.6 (0x4012f00)
        libXt.so.6 => /usr/X11R6/lib/libXt.so.6 (0x4014500)
```

Or, if you are using Automake:

```
...
lib_LTLIBRARIES   = module.la
module_la_SOURCES = source.c
module_la_LDFLAGS = -module -avoid-version -L$(X11LIBDIR)
module_la_LIBADD  = -lXt -lX11
...
```

It is especially important to be aware of this if you develop on a modern platform that correctly handles these dependencies natively (as in the preceding example), because the code may still work on your machine even if you don't correctly note all the dependencies. It will break only if someone tries to use it on a machine that needs Libtool's help for it to work, thus reducing the portability of your project.

17.2.5 Dynamic Module

Writing a module for use with the libltdl-based dynamic module loader is no more involved than before: It must provide the correct entry points, as expected by the simple API I designed—the 'run' entry point described in Section 16.5. Here is such a module, 'ltdl-module.c':

```c
#include <stdio.h>
#include <math.h>

#define run ltdl_module_LTX_run

int
run (const char *argument)
{
  char *end = NULL;
  long number;

  if (!argument || *argument == '\0')
    {
      fprintf (stderr, "error: invalid argument, \"%s\".\n",
               argument ? argument : "(null)");
      return -1;
    }

  number = strtol (argument, &end, 0);
  if (end && *end != '\0')
    {
      fprintf (stderr, "warning: trailing garbage \"%s\".\n",
               end);
    }

  printf ("Square root of %s is %f\n", argument, sqrt (number));

  return 0;
}
```

To take full advantage of the new module loader, the module itself *must* be compiled with Libtool, otherwise dependent libraries will not have been stored when libltdl tries to load the module on an architecture that doesn't load them natively, or which doesn't have shared libraries at all (see Section 17.4, "dlpreopen Loading"):

```
$ libtool --mode=compile gcc -c ltdl-module.c
rm -f .libs/ltdl-module.lo
gcc -c ltdl-module.c  -fPIC -DPIC -o .libs/ltdl-module.lo
gcc -c ltdl-module.c -o ltdl-module.o >/dev/null 2>&1
mv -f .libs/ltdl-module.lo ltdl-module.lo

$ libtool --mode=link gcc -g -o ltdl-module.la -rpath `pwd` \
-no-undefined -module -avoid-version ltdl-module.lo -lm
rm -fr .libs/ltdl-module.la .libs/ltdl-module.* .libs/ltdl-module.*
gcc -shared  ltdl-module.lo  -lm -lc  -Wl,-soname \
-Wl,ltdl-module.so -o .libs/ltdl-module.so
ar cru .libs/ltdl-module.a  ltdl-module.o
creating ltdl-module.la
(cd .libs && rm -f ltdl-module.la && ln -s ../ltdl-module.la \
ltdl-module.la)
```

You can see from the following interaction that 'ltdl-loader' does not load
the math library, 'libm', and that the shared part of the Libtool module,
'ltdl-module', does have a reference to it. The pseudo-library also has a note
of the 'libm' dependency so that libltdl will be able to load it even on architectures that cannot do it natively:

```
$ libtool --mode=execute ldd ltdl-loader
        libltdl.so.0 => /usr/lib/libltdl.so.0 (0x4001a000)
        libdl.so.2 => /lib/libdl.so.2 (0x4001f000)
        libc.so.6 => /lib/libc.so.6 (0x40023000)
        /lib/ld-linux.so.2 => /lib/ld-linux.so.2 (0x40000000)

$ ldd .libs/ltdl-module.so
        libm.so.6 => /lib/libm.so.6 (0x40008000)
        libc.so.6 => /lib/libc.so.6 (0x40025000)
        /lib/ld-linux.so.2 => /lib/ld-linux.so.2 (0x80000000)


$ fgrep depend ltdl-module.la
# Libraries that this one depends upon.
dependency_libs=' -lm'
```

This module is now ready to load from 'ltdl-loader':

```
$ ltdl-loader ltdl-module 9
Square root of 9 is 3.000000
        => 0
```

17.3 Portable Library Design

When partitioning the functionality of your project into libraries, and particularly loadable modules, it is easy to inadvertently rely on modern shared library
features such as *back linking* or *dependent library loading*. If you do accidentally use any of these features, you probably won't find out about it until
someone first tries to use your project on an older or less-featureful host.

I have already used the '-module' and '-avoid-version' Libtool linking options when compiling the libltdl module in the preceding section; the others are useful to know also. All these are used with the 'link' mode of libtool ('libtool --mode=link'):

-module	This option tells libtool that the target is a dynamically loadable module (as opposed to a conventional shared library) and as such does not need to have the 'lib' prefix.
-avoid-version	When linking a dynamic module, this option can be used rather than the '-version-info' option, so that the module is not subject to the usual shared library version-number suffixes.
-no-undefined	This is an extremely important option when you are aiming for maximum portability. It declares that all the symbols required by the target are resolved at link time. Some shared library architectures do not allow undefined symbols by default (Tru64 Unix), and others do not allow them at all (AIX). By using this switch and ensuring that all symbols really are resolved at link time, your libraries will work on even these platforms. See Section 10.2.1, "Creating Libtool Libraries with Automake."
-export-dynamic	Almost the opposite of '-no-undefined', this option compiles the target so that the symbols it exports can be used to satisfy unresolved symbols in subsequently loaded modules. Not all shared library architectures support this feature, and many that do support it do so by default regardless of whether this option is supplied. If you rely on this feature, you should use this option, in the knowledge that your project will not work correctly on architectures that have no support for the feature. For maximum portability, you should neither rely on this feature nor use the '-export-dynamic' option—but, on the occasions you do need the feature, this option is necessary to ensure that the linker is called correctly.

When you have the option to do so, I recommend that you design your project so that each of the libraries and modules is self-contained, except for a minimal number of dependent libraries, arranged in a directional graph shaped like a tree. That is, by relying on back linking, or mutual or cyclic dependencies, you reduce the portability of your project.

In Figure 17.1, an arrow indicates that the compilation object relies on symbols from the objects to which it points.

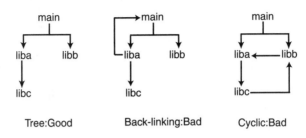

Figure 17.1   Library Dependency Architectures.

17.4 dlpreopen Loading

On machines that do not have any facility for shared libraries or dynamic modules, libltdl allows an application to lt_dlopen modules, provided that the modules are known at link time. This works by linking the code for the modules into the application in advance, and then looking up the addresses of the already loaded symbols when lt_dlsym is called. We call this mechanism *dlpreopening*—so named because the modules must be loaded at link time, not because the API to use modules loaded in this way is any different.

This feature is extremely useful for debugging, enabling you to make a fully statically linked application from the executable and module objects, without changing any source code to work around the module-loading calls. As far as the code outside the libltdl API can tell, these modules really are being loaded dynamically. Driving a symbolic debugger across module boundaries is much easier, however, when blocks of code are not moving in and out of memory during execution.

The following line appears in the dynamic module code later in this chapter in Section 17.2.5, "Dependent Libraries." You might be wondering why:

```
#define run ltdl_module_LTX_run
```

The reason for redefining the entry point symbol in this way is to prevent a symbol clash when two or more modules that provide identically named entry-point functions are preloaded into an executable. It would be otherwise impossible to preload both 'simple-module.c' and 'ltdl-module.c', for example, because each defines the symbol 'run'. To enable us to write dynamic modules that are potentially preloaded, lt_dlsym will first try to look up the address of a named symbol with a prefix consisting of the canonicalized name of the module being searched, followed by the characters '_LTX_'. The module name part of this prefix is canonicalized by replacing all non-alphanumeric characters with an underscore. If that fails, lt_dlsym resorts to the unadorned symbol name, which is how 'run' was found in 'simple-module.la' by 'ltdl-loader' earlier.

Supporting this feature in your module loading code is a simple matter of initializing the address lookup table, and 'ltdl.h' defines a convenient macro to do exactly that:

LTDL_SET_PRELOADED_SYMBOLS ()	Add this macro to the code of your module loading code, before the first call to a libltdl function, to ensure that the dlopen address lookup table is populated.

Now change the contents of 'ltdl-loader.c', and add a call to this macro, so that it looks like this:

```
/* Initialize preloaded symbol lookup table. */
LTDL_SET_PRELOADED_SYMBOLS();

/* Initialize libltdl. */
errors = lt_dlinit ();
```

Libtool can now fall back to using preloaded static modules if you tell it to, or if the host platform doesn't support native dynamic loading.

Note

If you use 'LTDL_SET_PRELOADED_SYMBOLS' *in your module loader, you* must *also specify something to preload to avoid compilation failure due to undefined* 'lt_preloaded_symbols'. *You can name modules on the Libtool link command line using either* '-dlopen' *or* '-dlpreopen'. *This includes support for accessing the symbols of the main executable opened with* 'lt_dlopen(NULL)'*—you can ask Libtool to fall back to preopening the main modules like this:*

```
$ libtool gcc -g -o ltdl-loader -dlopen self -rpath /tmp/lib \
ltdl-loader.c -lltdl
rm -f .libs/ltdl-loader.nm .libs/ltdl-loader.nmS \
.libs/ltdl-loader.nmT
creating .libs/ltdl-loaderS.c
(cd .libs && gcc -c -fno-builtin -fno-rtti -fno-exceptions
"ltdl-loaderS.c")
rm -f .libs/ltdl-loaderS.c .libs/ltdl-loader.nm .libs/ltdl-loader.nmS
.libs/ltdl-loader.nmT
gcc -o ltdl-loader .libs/ltdl-loaderS.o ltdl-loader.c
-Wl,--export-dynamic /usr/lib/libltdl.so -ldl -Wl,--rpath -Wl,/tmp/lib
rm -f .libs/ltdl-loaderS.o
```

continues ▶

▶ *continued*

> *It doesn't make sense to add preloaded module support to a project, when you
> have no modules to preopen, so the compilation failure in that case is actually a
> feature of sorts.*✦

The 'LTDL_SET_PRELOADED_SYMBOLS' macro does not interfere with the normal
operation of the code when modules are dynamically loaded, provided you use
the '-dlopen' option on the link line. The advantage of referencing the macro
by default is that you can recompile the application with or without preloaded
modules, and all without editing the sources.

If you have no modules to link in by default, you can force Libtool to populate
the preload symbol table by using the '-dlopen force' option. This is the
option used to preload the symbols of the main executable so that you can
subsequently call 'lt_dlopen(NULL)'. Multiple modules can be preloaded;
although at the time of writing, only Libtool-compiled modules can be used. If
there is a demand, Libtool will be extended to include native library preloading
in a future revision.

To illustrate, I have recompiled the 'simple-module.c' module with libtool:

```
$ libtool --mode=compile gcc -c simple-module.c
rm -f .libs/simple-module.lo
gcc -c simple-module.c  -fPIC -DPIC -o .libs/simple-module.lo
gcc -c simple-module.c -o simple-module.o >/dev/null 2>&1
mv -f .libs/simple-module.lo simple-module.lo

$ libtool --mode=link gcc -g -o simple-module.la -rpath `pwd`
-no-undefined -module -avoid-version simple-module.lo
rm -fr .libs/simple-module.la .libs/simple-module.*
.libs/simple-module.*
gcc -shared simple-module.lo  -lc  -Wl,-soname \
-Wl,simple-module.so -o .libs/simple-module.so
ar cru .libs/simple-module.a  simple-module.o
creating simple-module.la
(cd .libs && rm -f simple-module.la && ln -s ../simple-module.la \
simple-module.la)
```

The names of the modules that may be subsequently lt_dlopen'ed are added to
the application link line. I am using the '-static' option to force a static only
link, which must use dlpreopened modules by definition. I am specifying this
only because my host has native dynamic loading and Libtool will use that
unless I force a static only link, like this:

```
$ libtool --mode=link gcc -static -g -o ltdl-loader ltdl-loader.c \
-lltdl -dlopen ltdl-module.la -dlopen simple-module.la
rm -f .libs/ltdl-loader.nm .libs/ltdl-loader.nmS \
.libs/ltdl-loader.nmT
creating .libs/ltdl-loaderS.c
extracting global C symbols from ./.libs/ltdl-module.a
extracting global C symbols from ./.libs/simple-module.a
(cd .libs && gcc -c -fno-builtin -fno-rtti -fno-exceptions \
"ltdl-loaderS.c")
rm -f .libs/ltdl-loaderS.c .libs/ltdl-loader.nm \
.libs/ltdl-loader.nmS .libs/ltdl-loader.nmT
gcc -g -o ltdl-loader ltdl-loader.c .libs/ltdl-loaderS.o \
./.libs/ltdl-module.a -lm ./.libs/simple-module.a \
/usr/lib/libltdl.a -ldl
rm -f .libs/ltdl-loaderS.o

$ ./ltdl-loader ltdl-module 345
Square root of 345 is 18.574176
        => 0

$ ./ltdl-loader simple-module World
Hello, World!
        => 0
```

Note that the current release of Libtool requires that the pseudo-library be present for any libltdl-loaded module, even preloaded ones. Once again, if there is sufficient demand, this may be fixed in a future release. Until then, if the pseudo-library was deleted or cannot be found, this will happen:

```
$ rm -f simple-module.la
$ ./ltdl-loader simple-module World
./ltdl-loader: file not found.
```

A side effect of using the 'LTDL_SET_PRELOADED_SYMBOLS' macro is that if you subsequently link the application without Libtool, you will get an undefined symbol for the Libtool-supplied 'lt_preloaded_symbols'. If you need to link in this fashion, you need to provide a stub that supplies the missing definition. Conversely, you must be careful not to link the stub file when you *do* link with Libtool, because it will clash with the Libtool-generated table it is supposed to replace:

```
#include <ltdl.h>
const lt_dlsymlist lt_preloaded_symbols[] = { { 0, 0 } };
```

Of course, if you use this stub, and link the application without the benefits of Libtool, you cannot use any preloaded modules—even if you statically link them—because there is no preloaded symbol lookup table in this case.

17.5 User Module Loaders

While writing the module-loading code for GNU M4 1.5, I found that libltdl did not provide a way to load modules in exactly the way I required. As good as the preloading feature of libltdl may be, and as useful as it is for simplifying debugging, it does not have all the functionality of full dynamic module loading when the host platform is limited to static linking. After all, you can only ever load modules that were specified at link time, so for access to user-supplied modules the whole application must be relinked to preload these new modules before lt_dlopen can make use of the additional module code.

In this situation, it would be useful to be able to automate this process. That is, if a libltdl-using process cannot lt_dlopen a module in any other fashion, but can find a suitable static archive in the module search path, it should relink itself along with the static archive (using libtool to preload the module), and then exec the new executable. Assuming all this is successful, the attempt to lt_dlopen can be tried again—if the "suitable" static archive was chosen correctly it should now be possible to access the preloaded code.

17.5.1 Loader Mechanism

Since Libtool 1.4, libltdl has provided a generalized method for loading modules, which the user can extend. libltdl has a default built-in list of module-loading mechanisms—some of which are peculiar to a given platform, others of which are more general. When the 'libltdl' subdirectory of a project is configured, the list is narrowed to include only those *mechanisms*, or simply *loaders*, that can work on the host architecture. When 'lt_dlopen' is called, the loaders in this list are tried, in order, until the named module has loaded, or until all the loaders in the list have been exhausted. The entries in the final list of loaders each have a unique name, although there may be several candidate loaders for a single name before the list is narrowed. For example, the 'dlopen' loader is implemented differently on BeOS and Solaris—for a single host, there can be only one implementation of any named loader. The name of a module loader is something entirely different from the name of a loaded module, something that should become clearer as you read on.

In addition to the loaders supplied with libltdl, your project can add more loaders of its own. New loaders can be added to the end of the existing list or immediately before any other particular loader, thus giving you complete control of the relative priorities of all the active loaders in your project.

In your module-loading API, you might even support the dynamic loading of user-supplied loaders: That is, your users would be able to create dynamic modules that added more loading mechanisms to the existing list of loaders!

Version 1.4 of Libtool has a default list that potentially contains an implementation of the following loaders (assuming all are supported by the host platform):

dlpreopen	If the named module was preloaded, use the preloaded symbol table for subsequent lt_dlsym calls.
dlopen	If the host machine has a native dynamic loader API, use that to try and load the module.
dld	If the host machine has GNU dld (see http://www.gnu.org/software/dld), use that to try and load the module.

Note that loader names with a 'dl' prefix are reserved for future use by Libtool, so you should choose something else for your own module names to prevent a name clash with future Libtool releases.

17.5.2 Loader Management

The API supplies all the functions you need to implement your own module-loading mechanisms to solve problems just like this:

lt_dlloader_t * **lt_dlloader_find** (const char *loader_name)   Function

Each of the module loaders implemented by libltdl is stored according to a unique name, which can be used to look up the associated handle. These handles operate in much the same way as lt_dlhandles: They are used for passing references to modules in and out of the API, except that they represent a kind of *module-loading* method, as opposed to a loaded module instance. This function finds the 'lt_dlloader_t' handle associated with the unique name passed as the only argument, or else returns 'NULL' if there is no such module loader registered.

int **lt_dlloader_add** (lt_dlloader_t *place, lt_user_   Function
dlloader *dlloader, const char *loader_name)

This function is used to register your own module-loading mechanisms with libltdl. If *place* is given, it must be a handle for an already registered module loader, which the new loader *dlloader* will be placed in front of for the purposes of which order to try loaders in. If *place* is 'NULL', on the other hand, the new *dlloader* will be added to the end of the list of loaders to try when loading a module instance. In either case, *loader_name* must be a unique name for use with lt_dlloader_find.

The *dlloader* argument must be a C structure of the following format, populated with suitable function pointers that determine the functionality of your module loader:

```
struct lt_user_dlloader {
    const char          *sym_prefix;
    lt_module_open_t    *module_open;
    lt_module_close_t   *module_close;
    lt_find_sym_t       *find_sym;
    lt_dlloader_exit_t  *dlloader_exit;
    lt_dlloader_data_t  dlloader_data;
};
```

---

int **lt_dlloader_remove** (const char *loader_name)   Function

When there are no more loaded modules that were opened by the given module loader, the loader itself can be removed using this function.

When you come to set the fields in the lt_user_dlloader structure, they must each be of the correct type, as described here:

const char * **sym_prefix**   Variable

If a particular module loader relies on a prefix to each symbol being looked up (for example, the Windows module loader necessarily adds a '_' prefix to each symbol name passed to lt_dlsym), it should be recorded in the 'sym_prefix' field.

lt_module_t **lt_module_open_t** (lt_dlloader_data_t *loader_data*,   Function
const char *module_name)

When lt_dlopen has reached your registered module loader when attempting to load a dynamic module, this is the type of the module_open function that will be called. The name of the module that libltdl is attempting to load, along with the module loader instance data associated with the loader being used currently, are passed as arguments to such a function call.

The lt_module_t returned by functions of this type can be anything at all that can be recognized as unique to a successfully loaded module instance when passed back into the module_close or find_sym functions in the lt_user_dlloader module-loader structure.

int **lt_module_close_t** (lt_dlloader data_t *loader_data*,   Function
lt_module_t *module*)

In a similar vein, a function of this type will be called by lt_dlclose, where *module* is the returned value from the 'module_open' function that loaded this dynamic module instance.

lt_ptr_t **lt_find_sym_t** (lt_dlloader data_t *loader_data*,   Function
lt_module_t *module*, const char *symbol_name)

In a similar vein once more, a function of this type will be called by lt_dlsym, and must return the address of *symbol_name* in *module*.

int **lt_dlloader_exit_t** (lt_dlloader_data_t *loader_data*)   Function

When a user module loader is lt_dlloader_remove'd, a function of this type will be called. That function is responsible for releasing any resources that were allocated during the initialization of the loader, so that they are not "leaked" when the lt_user_dlloader structure is recycled.

Note that there is no initialization function type: The initialization of a user module loader should be performed before the loader is registered with lt_dlloader_add.

`lt_dlloader_data_t` **`dlloader_data`**   Variable
The *dlloader_data* is a spare field that can be used to store or pass any data specific to a particular module loader. That data will always be passed as the value of the first argument to each of the implementation functions above.

17.5.3 Loader Errors

When writing the code to fill out each of the functions needed to populate the `lt_user_dlloader` structure, you will often need to raise an error of some sort. The set of standard errors that might be raised by the internal module loaders are available for use in your own loaders, and should be used where possible for the sake of uniformity if nothing else. On the odd occasion where that is not possible, libltdl has API calls to register and set your own error messages, so that users of your module loader can call `lt_dlerror` and have the error message you set returned:

---

int **`lt_dlseterror`** (int *errorcode*)   Function
By calling this function with one of the error codes enumerated in the header file, 'ltdl.h', lt dlerror will return the associated diagnostic until the error code is changed again.

int **`lt_dladderror`** (const char *diagnostic*)   Function
Often you will find that the existing error diagnostics do not describe the failure you have encountered. By using this function, you can register a more suitable diagnostic with libltdl, and subsequently use the returned integer as an argument to lt dlseterror.

The next chapter discusses the more complex features of Automake, before moving on to show you how to use those features and add libltdl module loading to the Sic project from Chapter 11, "A Large GNU Autotools Project," in the chapter after that.

18

Advanced GNU Automake Usage

This chapter covers a few seemingly unrelated Automake features that are commonly considered "advanced": conditionals, user-added language support, and automatic dependency tracking.

18.1 Conditionals

Automake conditionals are a way to omit or include different parts of the 'Makefile', depending on what configure discovers. A conditional is introduced in 'configure.in' using the 'AM_CONDITIONAL' macro. This macro takes two arguments: The first is the name of the condition, and the second is a shell expression that returns true when the condition is true.

For instance, here is how to make a condition named 'TRUE' that is always true:

```
AM_CONDITIONAL(TRUE, true)
```

As another example, here is how to make a condition named 'DEBUG' that is true when the user has given the '--enable-debug' option to configure:

```
AM_CONDITIONAL(DEBUG, test "$enable_debug" = yes)
```

After you have defined a condition in 'configure.in', you can refer to it in your 'Makefile.am' using the 'if' statement. Here is a part of a sample 'Makefile.am' that uses the conditions defined above:

```
if TRUE
## This is always used.
bin_PROGRAMS = foo
endif

if DEBUG
AM_CFLAGS = -g -DDEBUG
endif
```

It is important to remember that Automake conditionals are *configure-time* conditionals. They don't rely on any special feature of make, and there is no way for the user to affect the conditionals from the make command line. Automake conditionals work by rewriting the 'Makefile'—make is unaware that these conditionals even exist.

Traditionally, Automake conditionals have been considered an advanced feature. However, practice has shown that they are often easier to use and understand than other approaches to solving the same problem. I now recommend the use of conditionals to everyone.

For instance, consider this example:

```
bin_PROGRAMS = echo
if FULL_ECHO
echo_SOURCES = echo.c extras.c getopt.c
else
echo_SOURCES = echo.c
endif
```

In this case, the equivalent code without conditionals is more confusing and correspondingly more difficult for the new Automake user to figure out:

```
bin_PROGRAMS = echo
echo_SOURCES = echo.c
echo_LDADD    = @echo_extras@
EXTRA_echo_SOURCES = extras.c getopt.c
```

> **Note**
>
> *Automake conditionals have some limitations. One known problem is that conditionals don't interact properly with '+=' assignment. For instance, consider this code:*
>
> ```
> bin_PROGRAMS = z
> z_SOURCES = z.c
> if SOME_CONDITION
> z_SOURCES += cond.c
> endif
> ```
>
> *This code appears to have an unambiguous meaning, but Automake 1.4 doesn't implement this and will give an error. This bug will be fixed in the next major Automake release.*◆

18.2 Language Support

Automake comes with built-in knowledge of the most common compiled languages: C, C++, Objective C, Yacc, Lex, Assembly, and Fortran. However, programs are sometimes written in an unusual language, or in a custom language translated into something more common. Automake enables you to handle these cases in a natural way.

Automake's notion of a "language" is tied to the suffix appended to each source file written in that language. You must inform Automake of each new suffix you introduce. You do so by listing them in the 'SUFFIXES' macro. Suppose, for instance, that you are writing part of your program in the language 'M', which is compiled to object code by a program named mc. The typical suffix for an 'M' source file is '.m'. In your 'Makefile.am', you would write the following:

```
SUFFIXES = .m
```

This differs from ordinary make usage, where you would use the special .SUFFIX target to list suffixes.

Now you need to tell Automake (and make) how to compile a '.m' file to a '.o' file. You do this by writing an ordinary make suffix rule:

```
MC = mc
.m.o:
        $(MC) $(MCFLAGS) $(AM_MCFLAGS) -c $<
```

Note that we introduced the 'MC', 'MCFLAGS', and 'AM_MCFLAGS' variables. Although not required, this is good style in case you want to override any of these later (for instance, from the command line).

Automake understands enough about suffix rules to recognize that '.m' files can be treated just like any file it already understands, so now you can write the following:

```
bin_PROGRAMS = myprogram
myprogram_SOURCES = foo.c something.m
```

Note that Automake does not really understand chained suffix rules; however, frequently the right thing happens anyway. If you have a '.m.c' rule, for instance, Automake naively assumes that '.m' files should be turned into '.o' files—and then it proceeds to rely on make to do the real work. In this example, if the translation takes three steps—from '.m' to '.x', and then from '.x' to '.c', and finally to '.o'—Automake's simplistic approach breaks. Fortunately, these cases are very rare.

18.3 Automatic Dependency Tracking

Keeping track of dependencies for a large program is tedious and error-prone. Many edits require the programmer to update dependencies; for some changes, however, such as adding a #include to an existing header, the change is large enough that he just refuses (or does it incorrectly). To fix this problem, Automake supports automatic dependency tracking.

The implementation of automatic dependency tracking in Automake 1.4 requires gcc and GNU make. These programs are required only for maintainers; the 'Makefile's generated by make dist are completely portable. If you can't use gcc or GNU make for your project, you are just out of luck; you have to disable dependency tracking.

Automake 1.5 will include a completely new dependency-tracking implementation. This new implementation will work with any compiler and any version of make.

Another limitation of the current scheme is that the dependencies included into the portable 'Makefile's by make dist are derived from the current build environment. First, this means that you must use make all before you can meaningfully run make dist (otherwise the dependencies won't have been created). Second, this means that any files not built in your current tree will not have dependencies in the distributed 'Makefile's. The new implementation will avoid both of these shortcomings as well.

Automatic dependency tracking is on by default; you don't have to do anything special to get it. To turn it off, either run automake -i rather than plain automake, or put 'no-dependencies' into the 'AUTOMAKE_OPTIONS' macro in each 'Makefile.am'.

19

A Complex GNU Autotools Project

This chapter polishes the worked example introduced in Chapter 7, "A Small GNU Autotools Project," and developed in Chapter 11, "A Large GNU Autotools Project." As always, the ideas presented here are my own views and not necessarily the only way to do things. Everything I present here has, however, served me well for quite some time, and you should find plenty of interesting ideas for your own projects.

Herein, I add a libltdl module loading system to Sic, as well as some sample modules to illustrate how extensible such a project can be. I also explain how to integrate the 'dmalloc' library into the development of a project and show why this is important.

If you noticed that, as it stands, Sic is useful only as an interactive shell unable to read commands from a file, go to the top of the class! For it to be of genuine use, I extend it to interpret commands from a file, too.

19.1 A Module-Loading Subsystem

As you saw in Chapter 17, "Using GNU libltdl," I need to put an invocation of the macro 'AC_LIBTOOL_DLOPEN' just before 'AC_PROG_LIBTOOL', in the file 'configure.in'. But, as well as being able to use libtoolize --ltdl, which adds libltdl in a subdirectory with its own subconfigure, you can also manually copy just the ltdl source files into your project[1], and use AC_LIB_LTDL in your existing 'configure.in'. At the time of writing, this is still a very new and (as yet) undocumented feature, with a few kinks that need to be ironed out. In any case, you probably should not use this method to add 'ltdl.lo' to a C++

---

[1] *If you have an early 1.3c snapshot of Libtool, you also need to copy the* 'ltdl.m4' *file into your distribution.*

library, because 'ltdl.c' is written in C. If you do want to use libltdl with a
C++ library, things will work much better if you build it in a subdirectory
generated with libtoolize --ltdl.

For this project, let's do the following:

```
$ cp /usr/share/libtool/libltdl/ltdl.[ch] sic/
```

The Sic module loader is probably as complicated as any you will ever need to
write, because it must support two kinds of modules: modules that contain
additional built-in commands for the interpreter, and modules that extend the
Sic syntax table. A single module can also provide both syntax extensions *and*
additional built-in commands.

19.1.1 Initializing the Module Loader

Before using this code (or any other libltdl-based module loader for that
matter), a certain amount of initialization is required:

- libltdl itself requires initialization.

  1. libltdl should be told to use the same memory allocation routines
     used by the rest of Sic.

  2. Any preloaded modules (see Section 17.4, "dlpreopen Loading")
     need to be initialized with LTDL_SET_PRELOADED_SYMBOLS().

  3. ltdl_init() must be called.

- The module search path needs to be set. Here I allow the installer to
  specify a default search path to correspond with the installed Sic
  modules at compile time, but search the directories in the runtime environment variable 'SIC_MODULE_PATH' first.

- The internal error handling needs to be initialized.

Here is the start of the module loader, 'sic/module.c', including the initialization code for libltdl:

```
#if HAVE_CONFIG_H
#  include <config.h>
#endif

#include "common.h"
#include "builtin.h"
#include "eval.h"
#include "ltdl.h"
#include "module.h"
#include "sic.h"
```

```
#ifndef SIC_MODULE_PATH_ENV
#  define SIC_MODULE_PATH_ENV    "SIC_MODULE_PATH"
#endif

int
module_init (void)
{
  static int initialised = 0;
  int errors = 0;

  /* Only perform the initialization once. */
  if (!initialised)
    {
      /* ltdl should use the same mallocation as us. */
      lt_dlmalloc = (lt_ptr_t (*) (size_t)) xmalloc;
      lt_dlfree = (void (*) (lt_ptr_t)) free;

      /* Make sure preloaded modules are initialised. */
      LTDL_SET_PRELOADED_SYMBOLS();

      last_error = NULL;

      /* Call ltdl initialization function. */
      errors = lt_dlinit();


      /* Set up the module search directories. */
      if (errors == 0)
        {
          const char *path = getenv (SIC_MODULE_PATH_ENV);

          if (path != NULL)
            errors = lt_dladdsearchdir(path);
        }

      if (errors == 0)
        errors = lt_dladdsearchdir(MODULE_PATH);

      if (errors != 0)
        last_error = lt_dlerror ();

      ++initialised;

      return errors ? SIC_ERROR : SIC_OKAY;
    }

  last_error = multi_init_error;
  return SIC_ERROR;
}
```

19.1.2 Managing Module-Loader Errors

The error handling is a very simplistic wrapper for the libltdl error functions, with the addition of a few extra errors specific to this module loader code[2]. Here are the error messages from 'module.c':

```
static char multi_init_error[]
              = "module loader initialised more than once";
static char no_builtin_table_error[]
              = "module has no builtin or syntax table";
static char builtin_unload_error[]
              = "builtin table failed to unload";
static char syntax_unload_error[]
              = "syntax table failed to unload";
static char module_not_found_error[]
              = "no such module";
static char module_not_unloaded_error[]
              = "module not unloaded";

static const char *last_error = NULL;

const char *
module_error (void)
{
  return last_error;
}
```

19.1.3 Loading a Module

Individual modules are managed by finding specified *entry points* (prescribed exported symbols) in the module:

const Builtin * **builtin_table**   Variable
  An array of names of built-in commands implemented by a module, with associated handler functions.

void **module_init** (Sic *sic)   Function
  If present, this function is called when the module is loaded.

void **module_finish** (Sic *sic)   Function
  If supplied, this function is called just before the module is unloaded.

const Syntax * **syntax_table**   Variable
  An array of syntactically significant symbols, and associated handler functions.

int **syntax_init** (Sic *sic)   Function
  If specified, Sic calls this function before the syntax of each input line is analyzed.

int **syntax_finish** (Sic *sic, BufferIn *in, BufferOut *out) Function
  Similarly, this function is called after the syntax analysis of each line has completed.

---

[2]*This differs significantly from the way errors are managed when writing a custom loader for libltdl. Compare this section with Section 17.5.3, "Loader Errors."*

libltdl performs all the hard work in locating and loading the module and extracting addresses for the symbols described here. The following `module_load` function just registers these symbols with the Sic interpreter so that they are called at the appropriate times—or diagnoses any errors if things don't go according to plan:

```
int
module_load (Sic *sic, const char *name)
{
  lt_dlhandle module;
  Builtin *builtin_table;
  Syntax *syntax_table;
  int status = SIC_OKAY;

  last_error = NULL;

  module = lt_dlopenext (name);

  if (module)
    {
      builtin_table = (Builtin*) lt_dlsym (module, "builtin_table");
      syntax_table = (Syntax *) lt_dlsym (module, "syntax_table");
      if (!builtin_table && !syntax_table)
        {
          lt_dlclose (module);
          last_error = no_builtin_table_error;
          module = NULL;
        }
    }

  if (module)
    {
      ModuleInit *init_func
        = (ModuleInit *) lt_dlsym (module, "module_init");
      if (init_func)
        (*init_func) (sic);
    }

  if (module)
    {
      SyntaxFinish *syntax_finish
        = (SyntaxFinish *) lt_dlsym (module, "syntax_finish");
      SyntaxInit *syntax_init
        = (SyntaxInit *) lt_dlsym (module, "syntax_init");

      if (syntax_finish)
        sic->syntax_finish = list_cons (list_new (syntax_finish),
                                        sic->syntax_finish);
      if (syntax_init)
        sic->syntax_init = list_cons (list_new (syntax_init),
                                      sic->syntax_init);
    }
```

```
if (module)
  {
    if (builtin_table)
      status = builtin_install (sic, builtin_table);

    if (syntax_table && status == SIC_OKAY)
      status = syntax_install (sic, module, syntax_table);

    return status;
  }

last_error = lt_dlerror();
if (!last_error)
  last_error = module_not_found_error;

return SIC_ERROR;
}
```

Notice that the generalized List data type introduced earlier (see Chapter 7) is reused to keep a list of accumulated module initialization and finalization functions.

19.1.4 Unloading a Module

When unloading a module, several things must be done:

- Any built-in commands implemented by this module must be unregistered so that Sic doesn't try to call them after the implementation has been removed.

- Any syntax extensions implemented by this module must be similarly unregistered, including syntax_init and syntax_finish functions.

- If there is a finalization entry point in the module, 'module_finish', it must be called (see Section 19.1.3, "Loading a Module").

My first-cut implementation of a module subsystem kept a list of the entry points associated with each module so that they could be looked up and removed when the module was subsequently unloaded. It also kept track of multiple loaded modules so that a module wasn't unloaded prematurely. libltdl already does all this, however, and it is wasteful to duplicate all that work. This system uses lt_dlforeach and lt_dlgetinfo to access libltdl's records of loaded modules and to save on duplication. These two functions are described fully in "Libltdl Interface" in The Libtool Manual.

```
static int unload_ltmodule (lt_dlhandle module, lt_ptr_t data);

struct unload_data { Sic *sic; const char *name; };

int
module_unload (Sic *sic, const char *name)
{
  struct unload_data data;

  last_error = NULL;

  data.sic = sic;
  data.name = name;

  /* Stopping might be an error, or we may have unloaded the module. */
  if (lt_dlforeach (unload_ltmodule, (lt_ptr_t) &data) != 0)
    if (!last_error)
      return SIC_OKAY;

  if (!last_error)
    last_error = module_not_found_error;

  return SIC_ERROR;
}
```

This function asks libltdl to call the function unload_ltmodule for each of the
modules it has loaded, along with some details of the module it wants to
unload. The tricky part of the following callback function is recalculating the
entry-point addresses for the module to be unloaded and then removing all
matching addresses from the appropriate internal structures. Otherwise, the
balance of this callback is involved in informing the calling lt_dlforeach loop
of whether a matching module has been found and handled:

```
static int userdata_address_compare (List *elt, void *match);

/* This callback returns 0 if the module was not yet found.
   If there is an error, LAST_ERROR will be set, otherwise the
   module was successfully unloaded. */
static int
unload_ltmodule (lt_dlhandle module, void *data)
{
  struct unload_data *unload = (struct unload_data *) data;
  const lt_dlinfo *module_info = lt_dlgetinfo (module);

  if ((unload == NULL)
      || (unload->name == NULL)
      || (module_info == NULL)
      || (module_info->name == NULL)
      || (strcmp (module_info->name, unload->name) != 0))
    {
      /* No match, return 0 to keep searching */
      return 0;
    }
```

```
if (module)
  {
    /* Fetch the addresses of the entrypoints into the module. */
    Builtin *builtin_table
      = (Builtin*) lt_dlsym (module, "builtin_table");
    Syntax *syntax_table
      = (Syntax *) lt_dlsym (module, "syntax_table");
    void *syntax_init_address
      = (void *) lt_dlsym (module, "syntax_init");
    void **syntax_finish_address
      = (void *) lt_dlsym (module, "syntax_finish");
    List *stale;

    /* Remove all references to these entry points in the internal
       data structures, before actually unloading the module. */
    stale = list_remove (&unload->sic->syntax_init,
                 syntax_init_address, userdata_address_compare);
    XFREE (stale);

    stale = list_remove (&unload->sic->syntax_finish,
                 syntax_finish_address, userdata_address_compare);
    XFREE (stale);

    if (builtin_table
        && builtin_remove (unload->sic, builtin_table) != SIC_OKAY)
      {
        last_error = builtin_unload_error;
        module = NULL;
      }

    if (syntax_table
        && SIC_OKAY != syntax_remove (unload->sic, module,
                                      syntax_table))
      {
        last_error = syntax_unload_error;
        module = NULL;
      }
  }

if (module)
  {
    ModuleFinish *finish_func
      = (ModuleFinish *) lt_dlsym (module, "module_finish");

    if (finish_func)
      (*finish_func) (unload->sic);
  }

if (module)
  {
    if (lt_dlclose (module) != 0)
      module = NULL;
  }
```

```
/* No errors?  Stop the search! */
if (module)
  return 1;

/* Find a suitable diagnostic. */
if (!last_error)
  last_error = lt_dlerror();
if (!last_error)
  last_error = module_not_unloaded_error;

/* Error diagnosed. Stop the search! */
return -1;
}

static int
userdata_address_compare (List *elt, void *match)
{
  return (int) (elt->userdata - match);
}
```

The userdata_address_compare helper function at the end is used to compare the address of recalculated entry points against the already registered functions and handlers to find which items need to be unregistered.

There is also a matching header file to export the module interface, so that the code for loadable modules can make use of it:

```
#ifndef SIC_MODULE_H
#define SIC_MODULE_H 1

#include <sic/builtin.h>
#include <sic/common.h>
#include <sic/sic.h>

BEGIN_C_DECLS

typedef void ModuleInit     (Sic *sic);
typedef void ModuleFinish   (Sic *sic);

extern const char *module_error (void);
extern int module_init     (void);
extern int module_load     (Sic *sic, const char *name);
extern int module_unload   (Sic *sic, const char *name);

END_C_DECLS

#endif /* !SIC_MODULE_H */
```

This header also includes some of the other Sic headers; so in most cases, the source code for a module needs only '#include <sic/module.h>'.

To make the module-loading interface useful, I have added built ins for `'load'`
and `'unload'`. Naturally, these must be compiled into the bare sic executable so
that it can load additional modules:

```
#if HAVE_CONFIG_H
#  include <config.h>
#endif

#include "module.h"
#include "sic_repl.h"

/* List of built in functions. */
#define builtin_functions                \
        BUILTIN(exit,          0, 1)  \
        BUILTIN(load,          1, 1)  \
        BUILTIN(unload,        1, -1)

BUILTIN_DECLARATION (load)
{
  int status = SIC_ERROR;

  if (module_load (sic, argv[1]) < 0)
    {
      sic_result_clear (sic);
      sic_result_append (sic, "module \"", argv[1], "\" not loaded: ",
                         module_error (), NULL);
    }
  else
    status = SIC_OKAY;

  return status;
}

BUILTIN_DECLARATION (unload)
{
  int status = SIC_ERROR;
  int i;

  for (i = 1; argv[i]; ++i)
    if (module_unload (sic, argv[i]) != SIC_OKAY)
      {
        sic_result_clear (sic);
        sic_result_append (sic, "module \"", argv[1],
                           "\" not unloaded: ", module_error (), NULL);
      }
    else
      status = SIC_OKAY;

  return status;
}
```

These new built-in commands are just wrappers around the module loading
code in `'module.c'`.

As with `'dlopen'`, you can use libltdl to `'lt_dlopen'` the main executable, and then look up *its* symbols. I have simplified the initialization of Sic by replacing the sic_init function in `'src/sic.c'` by "loading" the executable itself as a module. This works because I was careful to use the same format in `'sic_builtin.c'` and in `'sic_syntax.c'` as would be required for a genuine loadable module, as follows:

```
/* initialise the module subsystem */
if (module_init () != SIC_OKAY)
    sic_fatal ("module initialization failed");

if (module_load (sic, NULL) != SIC_OKAY)
    sic_fatal ("sic initialization failed");
```

19.2 A Loadable Module

A feature of the Sic interpreter is that it will use the `'unknown'` built in to handle any command line not handled by any of the other registered built-in callback functions. This mechanism is very powerful and enables me to look up unhandled built ins in the user's `'PATH'`, for instance.

Before adding any modules to the project, I have created a separate subdirectory, `'modules'`, to put the module source code into. Not forgetting to list this new subdirectory in the AC_OUTPUT macro in `'configure.in'`, and the SUBDIRS macro in the top-level `'Makefile.am'`, a new `'Makefile.am'` is needed to build the loadable modules:

```
## Makefile.am — Process this file with automake to produce Makefile.in
INCLUDES     = -I$(top_builddir) -I$(top_srcdir) \
               -I$(top_builddir)/sic -I$(top_srcdir)/sic \
               -I$(top_builddir)/src -I$(top_srcdir)/src

pkglib_LTLIBRARIES = unknown.la
```

pkglibdir is a Sic-specific directory in which modules will be installed (see Chapter 13, "Installing and Uninstalling Configured Packages").

Note

For a library to be maximally portable, it should be written so that it does not require back linking to resolve its own symbols (see Section 17.1, "Introducing libltdl"). That is, if at all possible you should design all your libraries (not just dynamic modules) so that all their symbols can be resolved at link time. Sometimes, it is impossible or undesirable to architect your libraries and modules in this way. In that case, you sacrifice the portability of your project to platforms such as AIX and Windows. ♦

The key to building modules with Libtool is in the options specified when the module is linked. This is doubly true when the module must work with libltdl's dlpreopening mechanism:

```
unknown_la_SOURCES = unknown.c
unknown_la_LDFLAGS = -no-undefined -module -avoid-version
unknown_la_LIBADD  = $(top_builddir)/sic/libsic.la
```

Sic modules are built without a 'lib' prefix ('-module'), and without version suffixes ('-avoid-version'). 'libsic.la' resolves all the undefined symbols at link time, hence '-no-undefined'.

Having added 'ltdl.c' to the 'sic' subdirectory, and called the AC_LIB_LTDL macro in 'configure.in', 'libsic.la' cannot build correctly on those architectures that do not support back linking. This is because 'ltdl.c' just abstracts the native dlopen API with a common interface, and that local interface often requires that a special library be linked—'-ldl' on Linux, for example. AC_LIB_LTDL probes the system to determine the name of any such dlopen library, and enables you to depend on it in a portable way by using the configure substitution macro, '@LIBADD_DL@'. If I were linking a libtool-compiled libltdl at this juncture, the system library details would have already been taken care of. In this project, I have bypassed that mechanism by compiling and linking 'ltdl.c' myself, so I have altered 'sic/Makefile.am' to use '@LIBADD_DL@':

```
lib_LTLIBRARIES        = libcommon.la libsic.la

libsic_la_LIBADD       = $(top_builddir)/replace/libreplace.la \
                         libcommon.la @LIBADD_DL@
libsic_la_SOURCES      = builtin.c error.c eval.c list.c ltdl.c \
                         module.c sic.c syntax.c
```

Having put all this infrastructure in place, the code for the 'unknown' module is a breeze (helper functions omitted for brevity):

```
#if HAVE_CONFIG_H
#  include <config.h>
#endif

#include <sys/types.h>
#include <sys/wait.h>
#include <sic/module.h>

#define builtin_table    unknown_LTX_builtin_table

static char *path_find  (const char *command);
static int path_execute (Sic *sic, const char *path, char *const argv[]);

/* Generate prototype. */
SIC_BUILTIN (builtin_unknown);
```

```
Builtin builtin_table[] = {
  { "unknown", builtin_unknown, 0, -1 },
  { 0, 0, -1, -1 }
};

BUILTIN_DECLARATION(unknown)
{
  char *path = path_find (argv[0]);
  int status = SIC_ERROR;

  if (!path)
    sic_result_append (sic, "command \"", argv[0], "\" not found",
                       NULL);
  else if (path_execute (sic, path, argv) != SIC_OKAY)
    sic_result_append (sic, "command \"", argv[0],"\" failed: ",
                       strerror (errno), NULL);
  else
    status = SIC_OKAY;

  return status;
}
```

In the first instance, notice that I have used the preprocessor to redefine the entry-point functions to be compatible with libltdl's dlpreopen, hence the unknown_LTX_builtin_table cpp macro. The 'unknown' handler function itself looks for a suitable executable in the user's path, and if something suitable *is* found, executes it.

Notice that Libtool does not relink dependent libraries ('libsic' depends on 'libcommon', for example) on my GNU/Linux system, because they are not required for the static library in any case, and because the dependencies are also encoded directly into the shared archive, 'libsic.so', by the original link. On the other hand, Libtool *does* relink the dependent libraries if necessary for the target host:

```
$ make
/bin/sh ../libtool --mode=compile gcc -DHAVE_CONFIG_H -I. -I. -I.. \
-I.. -I.. -I../sic -I../sic -I../src -I../src    -g -O2 -c unknown.c
mkdir .libs
gcc -DHAVE_CONFIG_H -I. -I. -I.. -I.. -I.. -I../sic -I../sic -I../src \
-I../src -g -O2 -Wp,-MD,.deps/unknown.pp -c unknown.c  -fPIC -DPIC \
-o .libs/unknown.lo
gcc -DHAVE_CONFIG_H -I. -I. -I.. -I.. -I.. -I../sic -I../sic -I../src \
I../src -g -O2 -Wp,-MD,.deps/unknown.pp -c unknown.c -o unknown.o \
>/dev/null 2>&1
mv -f .libs/unknown.lo unknown.lo
/bin/sh ../libtool --mode=link gcc  -g -O2   -o unknown.la -rpath \
/usr/local/lib/sic -no-undefined -module -avoid-version unknown.lo \
../sic/libsic.la
rm -fr .libs/unknown.la .libs/unknown.* .libs/unknown.*
```

```
gcc -shared  unknown.lo -L/tmp/sic/sic/.libs ../sic/.libs/libsic.so \
-lc  -Wl,-soname -Wl,unknown.so -o .libs/unknown.so
ar cru .libs/unknown.a  unknown.o
creating unknown.la
(cd .libs && rm -f unknown.la && ln -s ../unknown.la unknown.la)
$ ./libtool --mode=execute ldd ./unknown.la
        libsic.so.0 => /tmp/sic/.libs/libsic.so.0 (0x40002000)
        libc.so.6 => /lib/libc.so.6 (0x4000f000)
        libcommon.so.0 => /tmp/sic/.libs/libcommon.so.0 (0x400ec000)
        libdl.so.2 => /lib/libdl.so.2 (0x400ef000)
        /lib/ld-linux.so.2 => /lib/ld-linux.so.2 (0x80000000)
```

After compiling the rest of the tree, I can now use the 'unknown' module:

```
$ SIC_MODULE_PATH=`cd ../modules; pwd` ./sic
] echo hello!
command "echo" not found.
] load unknown
] echo hello!
hello!
] unload unknown
] echo hello!
command "echo" not found.
] exit
$
```

19.3 Interpreting Commands from a File

For all practical purposes, any interpreter is pretty useless if it works only inter-
actively. I have added a 'source' built-in command to 'sic_builtin.c', which
takes lines of input from a file and evaluates them using 'sic_repl.c' in much
the same way as lines typed at the prompt are evaluated otherwise. Here is the
built-in handler:

```
/* List of built in functions. */
#define builtin_functions            \
        BUILTIN(exit,       0, 1)  \
        BUILTIN(load,       1, 1)  \
        BUILTIN(source,     1, -1)  \
        BUILTIN(unload,     1, -1)

BUILTIN_DECLARATION (source)
{
  int status = SIC_OKAY;
  int i;

  for (i = 1; status == SIC_OKAY && argv[i]; ++i)
    status = source (sic, argv[i]);

  return status;
}
```

And the 'source' function from 'sic_repl.c':

```c
int
source (Sic *sic, const char *path)
{
  FILE *stream;
  int result = SIC_OKAY;
  int save_interactive = is_interactive;

  SIC_ASSERT (sic && path);

  is_interactive = 0;

  if ((stream = fopen (path, "rt")) == NULL)
    {
      sic_result_clear (sic);
      sic_result_append (sic, "cannot source \"", path, "\": ",
                         strerror (errno), NULL);
      result = SIC_ERROR;
    }
  else
    result =  evalstream (sic, stream);

  is_interactive = save_interactive;

  return result;
}
```

You separate the 'source' function in this way to make it easy for the startup sequence in main to evaluate a startup file. In traditional UNIX fashion, the startup file is named '.sicrc' and is evaluated if present in the user's home directory:

```c
static int
evalsicrc (Sic *sic)
{
  int result = SIC_OKAY;
  char *home = getenv ("HOME");
  char *sicrcpath, *separator = "";
  int len;

  if (!home)
    home = "";

  len = strlen (home);
  if (len && home[len -1] != '/')
    separator = "/";

  len += strlen (separator) + strlen (SICRCFILE) + 1;

  sicrcpath = XMALLOC (char, len);
  sprintf (sicrcpath, "%s%s%s", home, separator, SICRCFILE);
```

```
if (access (sicrcpath, R_OK) == 0)
  result = source (sic, sicrcpath);

return result;
}
```

19.4 Integrating Dmalloc

Mismanagement of memory causes a huge number of bugs in C and C++ code. Using the wrapper functions described earlier (see the section "Memory Management" in Section 7.2.1, "Portability Infrastructure"), or their equivalent can help immensely in reducing the occurrence of such bugs. Ultimately, you will introduce a difficult-to-diagnose memory bug despite these measures.

That is where Dmalloc[3] comes in. I recommend using it routinely in all your projects; you will find all sorts of leaks and bugs that might otherwise have lain dormant for some time. Automake has explicit support for Dmalloc to make using it in your own projects as painless as possible. The first step is to add the macro 'AM_WITH_DMALLOC' to 'configure.in'. Citing this macro adds a '--with-dmalloc' option to configure, which, when specified by the user, adds '-ldmalloc' to 'LIBS' and defines 'WITH_DMALLOC'.

The usefulness of Dmalloc is much increased by compiling an entire project with the header 'dmalloc.h'—easily achieved in Sic by conditionally adding it to 'common-h.in':

```
BEGIN_C_DECLS

#define XCALLOC(type, num)                              \
        ((type *) xcalloc ((num), sizeof(type)))
#define XMALLOC(type, num)                              \
        ((type *) xmalloc ((num) * sizeof(type)))
#define XREALLOC(type, p, num)                          \
        ((type *) xrealloc ((p), (num) * sizeof(type)))
#define XFREE(stale)                   do {             \
        if (stale) { free ((void *) stale);  stale = 0; }  \
                             } while (0)

extern void *xcalloc        (size_t num, size_t size);
extern void *xmalloc        (size_t num);
extern void *xrealloc       (void *p, size_t num);
extern char *xstrdup        (const char *string);

END_C_DECLS

#if WITH_DMALLOC
#  include <dmalloc.h>
#endif
```

---

[3]*Dmalloc is distributed from* http://www.dmalloc.com.

I have been careful to include the `'dmalloc.h'` header from the end of this file so that it overrides my own *definitions* without renaming the function *prototypes*. Similarly, I must be careful to accomodate Dmalloc's redefinition of the mallocation routines in `'sic/xmalloc.c'` and `'sic/xstrdup.c'`, by putting each file inside an `'#ifndef WITH_DMALLOC'`. That way, when compiling the project, if `'--with-dmalloc'` is specified and the `'WITH_DMALLOC'` preprocessor symbol is defined, Dmalloc's debugging definitions of xstrdup and others will be used in place of the versions I wrote.

Enabling Dmalloc is now just a matter of reconfiguring the whole package using the `'--with-dmalloc'` option, and disabling it again is a matter of reconfiguring without that option.

The use of Dmalloc is beyond the scope of this book, and is in any case described very well in the documentation that comes with the package. I strongly recommend you become familiar with it; the time you invest will pay dividends many times over in the time you save debugging.

This chapter completes the description of the Sic library project, and indeed this part of the book. All the infrastructure for building an advanced command-line shell is in place now—you need add only the built-in and syntax function definitions to create a complete shell of your own.

Each of the chapters in the next part of the book explores a more specialized application of the GNU Autotools, starting with a discussion of M4, a major part of the implementation of Autoconf.

20
GNU M4

M4 is a general-purpose tool for processing text and has existed on Unix systems of all kinds for many years, rarely catching the attention of users. Text generation through macro processing is not a new concept. Originally M4 was designed as the preprocessor for the Rational Fortran system and was influenced by the *General Purpose Macro* generator (GPM), first described by Stratchey in 1965! GNU M4 is the GNU project's implementation of M4 and was written by Rene Seindal in 1990.

In recent years, awareness of M4 has grown through its use by popular free software packages. The Sendmail package incorporates a configuration system that uses M4 to generate its complex `sendmail.cf` file from a simple specification of the desired configuration. Autoconf uses M4 to generate output files such as a `configure` script.

It is somewhat unfortunate that users of GNU Autotools need to know so much about M4, because it has been too exposed. Many of these tools' implementation details were just left up to M4, forcing the user to know about M4 in order to use them. It is a well-known problem and there is a movement among the development community to improve this shortcoming in the future. This deficiency is the primary reason that this chapter exists; it is important to have a good working knowledge of M4 in order to use the GNU Autotools and to extend it with your own macros (see Chapter 22, "Writing New Macros for Autoconf").

The GNU M4 manual provides a thorough tutorial on M4. Refer to it for additional information.

20.1 What Does M4 Do?

m4 is a general-purpose tool suitable for all kinds of text processing applications—not unlike the C preprocessor, cpp, with which you are probably familiar. Its obvious application is as a front end for a compiler—m4 is in many ways superior to cpp.

Briefly, m4 reads text from the input and writes processed text to the output. Symbolic macros may be defined which have replacement text. As macro invocations are encountered in the input, they are replaced ("expanded") with the macro's definition. Macros may be defined with a set of parameters and the definition can specify where the actual parameters will appear in the expansion. Section 20.3, "Fundamentals of M4 Processing," expands on these concepts.

M4 includes a set of predefined macros that make it substantially more useful. The most important ones are discussed in Section 20.4, "Features of M4." These macros perform functions such as arithmetic, conditional expansion, string manipulation, and running external shell commands.

20.2 How GNU Autotools Uses M4

The GNU Autotools may all appear to use M4, but in actual fact, it all boils down to autoconf, which invokes m4 to generate your 'configure' script. You might be surprised to learn that the shell code in 'configure' does not use m4 to generate a final 'Makefile' from 'Makefile.in'. Instead, it uses sed, because that is more likely to be present on an end-user's system and thereby removes the dependency on m4.

Automake and Libtool include a lot of M4 input files. These are macros provided with each package that you can use directly (or indirectly) from your 'configure.in'. These packages don't invoke m4 themselves.

If you have already installed Autoconf on your system, you may have encountered problems resulting from its strict M4 requirements. Autoconf *demands* to use GNU M4, mostly due to it exceeding limitations present in other M4 implementations. As noted by The Autoconf Manual, this is not an onerous requirement, because it affects only package maintainers who must regenerate 'configure' scripts.

Autoconf's own 'Makefile' freezes some of the Autoconf '.m4' files containing macros as it builds Autoconf. When M4 freezes an input file, it produces another file that represents the internal state of the M4 processor so that the input file does not need to be parsed again. This helps to reduce the startup time for autoconf.

20.3 Fundamentals of M4 Processing

When properly understood, M4 seems like child's play. It is common to learn M4 in a piecemeal fashion, however, and to have an incomplete or inaccurate understanding of certain concepts. Ultimately, this leads to hours of furious debugging. It is important to understand the fundamentals well before progressing to the details.

20.3.1 Token Scanning

m4 scans its input stream, generating (often, just copying) text to the output stream. The first step that m4 performs in processing is to recognize *tokens*. There are three kinds of tokens:

Names	A name is a sequence of characters that starts with a letter or an underscore and may be followed by additional letters, characters, and underscores. The end of a name is recognized by the occurrence of a character that is not any of the permitted characters (for example, a period). A name is always a candidate for macro expansion (see Section 20.3.2, "Macros and Macro Expansion"), whereby the name will be replaced in the output by a macro definition of the same name.
Quoted strings	A sequence of characters may be *quoted* (see Section 20.3.3, "Quoting") with a starting quote at the beginning of the string and a terminating quote at the end. The default M4 quote characters are ' ` ' and ' ´ ', however Autoconf reassigns them to ' [' and '] ', respectively. Suffice to say, M4 removes the quote characters and passes the inner string to the output.
Other tokens	All other tokens are those single characters not recognized as belonging to any of the other token types. They are passed through to the output unaltered.

Like most programming languages, M4 enables you to write comments in the input that will be ignored. Comments are delimited by the '#' character and by the end of a line. Comments in M4 differ from most languages, however, in that the text within the comment, including delimiters, is passed through to the output unaltered. Although the user can reassign the comment-delimiting characters, this is highly discouraged. Doing so may break GNU Autotools' macros, which rely on this fact to pass Bourne shell comment lines—which share the same comment delimiters—through to the output unaffected.

20.3.2 Macros and Macro Expansion

Macros are definitions of replacement text and are identified by a name—as defined by the syntax rules given in Section 20.3.1, "Token Scanning." M4 maintains an internal table of macros, some of which are built-ins defined when m4 starts. When a name is found in the input that matches a name registered in

M4's macro table, the macro *invocation* in the input is replaced by the macro's definition in the output. This process is known as *expansion*—even if the new text may be shorter! Many beginners to M4 confuse themselves the moment they start to use phrases such as "I am going to call this particular macro, which returns this value." As you will see, macros differ significantly from *functions* in other programming languages, regardless of how similar their syntax may seem. You should instead use phrases such as "If I invoke this macro, it will expand to this text."

Suppose M4 knows about a simple macro called `foo` that is defined to be `bar`. Given the following input, m4 would produce the corresponding output:

```
That is one big foo.
➡That is one big bar.
```

The period character at the end of this sentence is not permitted in macro names; therefore, m4 knows when to stop scanning the `foo` token and consult the table of macro definitions for a macro named `foo`.

Curiously, macros are defined to m4 using the built-in macro define. The preceding example would be defined to m4 with the following input:

```
define(`foo', `bar')
```

Because define is itself a macro, it too must have an expansion—by definition, it is the empty string, or *void*. Therefore, m4 will appear to consume macro invocations like these from the input. The ` and ' characters are M4's default quote characters and play an important role (see Section 20.3.3, "Quoting"). Additional built-in macros exist for managing macro definitions (see Section 20.4.2, "Macro Management").

You have now explored the simplest kind of macros that exist in M4. To make macros substantially more useful, M4 extends the concept to macros that accept a number of arguments[1]. If a macro is given arguments, the macro may address its arguments using the special macro names `$1` through to `$n`, where `n` is the maximum number of arguments that the macro cares to reference. When such a macro is invoked, the argument list must be delimited by commas and enclosed in parentheses. Any white space that precedes an argument is discarded, but trailing white space (for example, before the next comma) is preserved. Here is an example of a macro that expands to its third argument:

```
define(`foo', `$3')
That is one big foo(3, `0x', `beef').
➡That is one big beef.
```

---

[1] *GNU M4 permits an unlimited number of arguments, whereas other versions of M4 limit the number of addressable arguments to nine.*

Arguments in M4 are just text, so they have no type. If a macro that accepts arguments is invoked, m4 expands the macro regardless of how many arguments are provided. M4 does not produce errors resulting from conditions such as a mismatched number of arguments, or arguments with malformed values/types. It is the responsibility of the macro to validate the argument list, and this is an important practice when writing GNU Autotools macros. Some common M4 idioms have developed for this purpose and are covered in Section 20.4.3, "Conditionals." A macro that expects arguments can still be invoked without arguments—the number of arguments seen by the macro will be zero:

```
This is still one big foo.
➥That is one big .
```

A macro invoked with an empty argument list is not empty at all, but rather is considered to be a single empty string:

```
This is one big empty foo().
➥That is one big .
```

It is also important to understand how macros are expanded. It is here that you will see why an M4 macro is not the same as a function in any other programming language. The explanation you have been reading about macro expansion thus far is a little bit simplistic: Macros are not exactly matched in the input and expanded in the output. In actual fact, the macro's expansion replaces the invocation in the input stream and it is *rescanned* for further expansions until none are remaining. Here is an example:

```
define(`foobar', `FUBAR')
define(`f', `foo')
f()bar
➥FUBAR
```

If the token 'a1' were to be found in the input, m4 would replace it with 'a2' in the input stream and rescan. This continues until no definition can be found for a4, at which point the literal text 'a4' is sent to the output. This is by *far the biggest point of misunderstanding* for new M4 users.

The same principles apply for the collection of arguments to macros that accept arguments. Before a macro's actual arguments are handed to the macro, they are expanded until no more expansions are left. Here is an example, using the built-in `define` macro (where the problems are no different), which highlights the consequences of this. Usually, `define` redefines any existing macro:

```
define(foo, bar)
define(foo, baz)
```

In this example, we expect `'foo'` to be defined to `'bar'`, and then redefined to `'baz'`. Instead, we have defined a new macro `'bar'` that is defined to be `'baz'`! Why? The second `define` invocation has its arguments expanded prior to expanding the `define` macro. At this stage, the name `'foo'` is expanded to its original definition, `bar`. In effect, we have stated the following:

```
define(foo, bar)
define(bar, baz)
```

Sometimes this can be a very useful property, but mostly it serves to thoroughly confuse the GNU Autotools macro writer. The key is to know that m4 will expand as much text as it can as early as possible in its processing. You can prevent expansion by quoting[2], which is discussed in detail in the following section.

20.3.3 Quoting

You have seen how m4 expands macros when it encounters a name that matches a defined macro in the input. At times, however, you will want to defer expansion. Principally, there are three situations when this is so:

Free-form text	You might want free-form text to appear at the output—and as such, be unaltered by any macros that may be inadvertently invoked in the input. It is not always possible to know whether some particular name is defined as a macro, so it should be quoted.
Overcoming syntax rules	Sometimes you may want to form strings that would violate M4's syntax rules—for example, you might want to use leading white space or a comma in a macro argument. The solution is to quote the entire string.
Macro arguments	This is the most common situation for quoting: when arguments to macros are to be taken literally and not expanded as the arguments are collected. The preceding section provided an example that demonstrated the effects of not quoting the first argument to `define`. Quoting macro arguments is considered a good practice that you should emulate.

Strings are quoted by surrounding the quoted text with the `'` ` ` `'` and `'` ` ` `'` characters. When m4 encounters a quoted string—as a type of token (see Section 20.3.1, "Token Scanning")—the quoted string is expanded to the string itself, with the outermost quote characters removed.

---

[2] *Which is precisely what the* `'` ` ` `'` *and* `'` ` ` `'` *characters in all the examples in this section are.*

Here is an example of a string that is triple quoted:

```
```foo'''
➡``foo''
```

The following is a more concrete example using quoting to demonstrate how to prevent unwanted expansion within macro definitions:

```
define(`foo', ``bar'')dnl
define(`bar', `zog')dnl
foo
➡bar
```

When the macro `foo' is defined, m4 strips off the outermost quotes and registers the definition `bar'.

As the macro `foo' is expanded, the next pair of quote characters are stripped off and the string is expanded to `bar'. Because the expansion of the quoted string is the string itself (minus the quote characters), we have prevented unwanted expansion from the string `bar' to `zog'.

As mentioned in Section 20.3.1, "Token Scanning," the default M4 quote characters are '`' and '''. Because these are two commonly used characters in Bourne shell programming[3], Autoconf reassigns these to the '[' and ']' characters—a symmetric looking pair of characters least likely to cause problems when writing GNU Autotools macros. From this point forward, we use '[' and ']' as the quote characters and you can forget about the default M4 quotes.

Autoconf uses M4's built-in changequote macro to perform this reassignment and, in fact, this built-in is still available to you. In recent years, the common practice when needing to use the quote characters '[' or ']' or to quote a string with an legitimately imbalanced number of the quote characters has been to invoke changequote and temporarily reassign them around the affected area:

```
dnl Uh-oh, we need to use the apostrophe! And even worse, we have two
dnl opening quote marks and no closing quote marks.
changequote(<<, >>)dnl
perl -e 'print "$]\n";'
changequote([, ])dnl
```

This leads to a few potential problems, the least of which is that it is easy to reassign the quote characters and then forget to reset them, leading to total chaos! Moreover, it is possible to entirely disable M4's quoting mechanism by blindly changing the quote characters to a pair of empty strings.

---

[3] *The '`' is used in grave redirection and ''' for the shell's own quote character!*
```

In hindsight, the overwhelming conclusion is that using `changequote` within the GNU Autotools framework is a bad idea. Instead, leave the quote characters assigned as `'['` and `']'` and use the special strings `@<:@` and `@:>@` anywhere you want real square brackets to appear in your output. This is an easy practice to adopt, because it is faster and less error-prone than using `changequote`:

```
perl -e 'print "$@:>@\n";'
```

This and other guidelines for using M4 in the GNU Autotools framework are covered in detail in Section 20.5, "Writing Macros Within the GNU Autotools Framework."

20.4 Features of M4

M4 includes a number of predefined macros that make it a powerful preprocessor. This section takes you on a tour of the most important features provided by these macros. Although some of these features are not very relevant to GNU Autotools users, Autoconf is implemented using most of them. For this reason, it is useful to understand the features to better understand Autoconf's behavior and for debugging your own `'configure'` scripts.

20.4.1 Discarding Input

A macro called `dnl` discards text from the input. The `dnl` macro takes no arguments and expands to the empty string, but it has the side effect of discarding all input up to and including the next newline character. Here is an example of `dnl` from the Autoconf source code:

```
# AC_LANG_POP
# --------.
# Restore the previous language.
define([AC_LANG_POP],
[popdef([_AC_LANG])dnl
ifelse(_AC_LANG, [_AC_LANG],
       [AC_FATAL([too many $0])])dnl
AC_LANG(_AC_LANG)])
```

It is important to remember `dnl`'s behavior: It discards the newline character, which can have unexpected effects on generated `'configure'` scripts! If you want a newline to appear in the output, you must add an extra blank line to compensate.

`dnl` need not appear in the first column of a given line; it begins discarding input at any point that it is invoked in the input file. Be aware, however, of the newline eating problem again! In the preceding example of `AC_TRY_LINK_FUNC`, note the deliberate use of `dnl` to remove surplus newline characters.

In general, dnl makes sense for macro invocations that appear on a single line, where you would expect the whole line to just vanish from the output. In the following subsections, dnl is used to illustrate where it makes sense to use it.

20.4.2 Macro Management

A number of built-in macros exist in M4 to manage macros. This section examines the most common ones that you are likely to encounter. There are others, and you should consult the GNU M4 manual for further information.

The most obvious one is define, which defines a macro. It expands to the empty string:

```
define([foo], [bar])dnl
define([combine], [$1 and $2])dnl
```

It is worth highlighting again the liberal use of quoting. We want to define a pair of macros whose names are *literally* foo and combine. If another macro had been previously defined with either of these names, m4 would have expanded the macro immediately and passed the definition of foo to define, giving unexpected results.

The undefine macro removes a macro's definition from M4's macro table. It also expands to the empty string:

```
undefine([foo])dnl
undefine([combine])dnl
```

Recall that once removed from the macro table, unmatched text is once more passed through to the output.

The defn macro expands to the definition of a macro, named by the single argument to defn. It is quoted so that it can be used as the body of a new, renamed macro:

```
define([newbie], defn([foo]))dnl
undefine([foo])dnl
```

You can use the ifdef macro to determine whether a macro name has an existing definition. If it does exist, ifdef expands to the second argument; otherwise, it expands to the third:

```
ifdef([foo], [yes], [no])dnl
```

Again, yes and no have been quoted to prevent expansion due to any preexisting macros with those names. *Always* consider this a real possibility!

Finally, a word about built-in macros: These macros are all defined for you when m4 is started. One common problem with these macros is that they are not in any kind of namespace, so it is easier to accidentally invoke them or want to define a macro with an existing name. One solution is to use the define and defn combination shown earlier to rename all the macros, one by one. This is how Autoconf makes the distinction clear.

20.4.3 Conditionals

Macros that can expand to different strings based on runtime tests are extremely useful—they are used extensively throughout macros in GNU Autotools and third-party macros. The macro that this section examines closely is ifelse. This macro compares two strings and expands to a different string based on the result of the comparison. The first form of ifelse is akin to the if/then/else construct in other programming languages:

```
ifelse(string1, string2, equal, not-equal)
```

The other form is unusual to a beginner because it actually resembles a case statement from other programming languages:

```
ifelse(string1, string2, equala, string3, string4, equalb, default)
```

If string1 and string2 are equal, this macro expands to equala. If they are not equal, m4 shifts the argument list three positions to the left and tries again:

```
ifelse(string3, string4, equalb, default)
```

If 'string3' and 'string4' are equal, this macro expands to 'equalb'. If they are not equal, it expands to 'default'. The number of cases that may be in the argument list is unbounded.

As mentioned in Section 20.3.2, "Macros and Macro Expansion," macros that accept arguments may access their arguments through specially named macros such as '$1'. If a macro has been defined, no checking of argument counts is performed before it is expanded and the macro may examine the number of arguments given through the '$#' macro. This has a useful result: You may invoke a macro with too few (or too many) arguments and the macro will still be expanded. In the following example, '$2' expands to the empty string.

```
define([foo], [$1 and $2])dnl
foo([a])
➡a and
```

This is useful because m4 expands the macro and gives the macro the opportunity to test each argument for the empty string. In effect, we have the equivalent of default arguments from other programming languages. The macro can use ifelse to provide a default value if, say, '$2' is the empty string. You will notice in much of the documentation for existing Autoconf macros that arguments may be left blank to accept the default value. This is an important idiom that you should practice in your own macros.

In this example, we want to accept the default shell code fragment for the case where `/etc/passwd` is found in the build system's file system, but output `Big trouble!` if it is not.

```
AC_CHECK_FILE([/etc/passwd], [], [echo "Big trouble!"])
```

20.4.4 Looping

There is no support in M4 for doing traditional iterations (that is, `for-do` loops); however, macros may invoke themselves. Therefore, it is possible to iterate using recursion. The recursive definition can use conditionals to terminate the loop at its completion by providing a trivial case (see Section 20.4.3, "Conditionals"). The GNU M4 manual provides some clever recursive definitions, including a definition for a forloop macro that emulates a `for-do` loop.

It is conceivable that you might want to use these M4 constructs when writing macros to generate large amounts of in-line shell code or arbitrarily nested if; then; fi statements.

20.4.5 Diversions

Diversions are a facility in M4 for diverting text from the input stream into a holding buffer. GNU M4 has a large number of diversion buffers, limited only by available memory. Text can be diverted into any one of these buffers and then "undiverted" back to the output (diversion number 0) at a later stage.

Text is diverted and undiverted using the divert and undivert macros. They expand to the empty string, with the side effect of setting the diversion. Here is an illustrative example:

```
divert(1)dnl
This goes at the end.
divert(0)dnl
This goes at the beginning.
undivert(1)dnl
➡This goes at the beginning.
➡This goes at the end.
```

It is unlikely that you will want to use diversions in your own macros, and it is difficult to do so reliably without understanding the internals of Autoconf. It is interesting to note, however, that this is how autoconf generates fragments of shell code on-the-fly that must precede shell code at the current point in the `configure` script.

20.4.6 Including Files

M4 permits you to include files into the input stream using the `include` and `sinclude` macros. They just expand to the contents of the named file. Of course, the expansion will be rescanned as the normal rules dictate (see Section 20.3, "Fundamentals of M4 Processing").

The difference between `include` and `sinclude` is subtle: If the filename given as an argument to `include` is not present, an error is raised. The `sinclude` macro instead expands to the empty string—presumably the "s" stands for "silent."

Older GNU Autotools macros that tried to be modular would use the `include` and `sinclude` macros to import libraries of macros from other sources. Although this is still a workable mechanism, there is an active effort within the GNU Autotools development community to improve the packaging system for macros. An `'--install'` option is being developed to improve the mechanism for importing macros from a library.

20.5 Writing Macros Within the GNU Autotools Framework

With a good grasp of M4 concepts, you can now turn your attention to applying these principles to writing `'configure.in'` files and new `'.m4'` macro files. There are some differences between writing generic M4 input files and macros within the GNU Autotools framework and these are covered in this section, along with some useful hints on working within the framework. This section ties in closely with Chapter 22, "Writing New Macros for Autoconf."

Now that you are familiar with the capabilities of M4, you can forget about the names of the built-in M4 macros—they should be avoided in the GNU Autotools framework. Where appropriate, the framework provides a collection of macros laid on top of the M4 built-ins. For instance, the macros in the AC_ family are just regular M4 macros that take a number of arguments and rely on an extensive library of AC_ support macros.

20.5.1 Syntactic Conventions

Some conventions have grown over the life of the GNU Autotools, mostly as a disciplined way of avoiding M4 pitfalls. These conventions are designed to make your macros more robust, your code easier to read, and, most importantly, improve your chances for getting things to work the first time! A brief list of recommended conventions follows:

- Do not use the M4 built-in `changequote`. Any good macro will already perform sufficient quoting.

- Never use the argument macros (for example, '$1') within shell comments and dnl remarks. If such a comment were to be placed within a macro definition, M4 will expand the argument macros, leading to strange results. Instead, quote the argument number to prevent unwanted expansion. For instance, you would use '$[1]' in the comment.

- Quote the M4 comment character, '#'. This can appear often in shell code fragments and can have undesirable effects if M4 ignores any expansions in the text between the '#' and the next newline.

- In general, macros invoked from 'configure.in' should be placed one per line. Many of the GNU Autotools macros conclude their definitions with a dnl to prevent unwanted white space from accumulating in 'configure'.

- Many of the AC_ macros, and others that emulate their good behavior, permit default values for unspecified arguments. It is considered good style to explicitly show your intention to use an empty argument by using a pair of quotes, such as '[]'.

- Always quote the names of macros used within the definitions of other macros.

- When writing new macros, generate a small 'configure.in' that uses (and abuses!) the macro—particularly with respect to quoting. Generate a 'configure' script with autoconf and inspect the results.

20.5.2 Debugging with M4

After writing a new macro or a 'configure.in' template, the generated 'configure' script may not contain what you expect. Frequently this is due to a problem in quoting (see Section 20.3.3, "Quoting"), but the interactions between macros can be complex. When you consider that the arguments to GNU Autotools macros are often shell scripts, things can get rather hairy. A number of techniques exist for helping you to debug these kinds of problems.

Expansion problems due to over-quoting and under-quoting can be difficult to pinpoint. Autoconf half-heartedly tries to detect this condition by scanning the generated 'configure' script for any remaining invocations of the AC_ and AM_ families of macros. This works only for the AC_ and AM_ macros, however, and not for third-party macros.

M4 provides a comprehensive facility for tracing expansions. This makes it possible to see how macro arguments are expanded and how a macro is finally expanded. Often, this can be half the battle in discovering whether the macro

definition or the invocation is at fault. Autoconf 2.15 will include this tracing
mechanism. To trace the generation of 'configure', Autoconf can be invoked
as follows:

```
$ autoconf --trace=AC_PROG_CC
```

Autoconf provides fine control over which macros are traced and the format of
the trace output. You should refer to the Autoconf manual for further details.

GNU m4 also provides a debugging mode that can be helpful in discovering
problems such as infinite recursion. This mode is activated with the '-d'
option. To pass options to m4, invoke Autoconf like this:

```
$ M4='m4 -dV' autoconf
```

Another situation that can arise is the presence of shell syntax errors in the
generated 'configure' script. These errors are usually obvious, because the shell
aborts 'configure' when the syntax error is encountered. The task of then
locating the troublesome shell code in the input files can be potentially quite
difficult. If the erroneous shell code appears in 'configure.in', it should be easy
to spot—presumably because you wrote it recently! If the code is imported
from a third-party macro, however, it may be present only because you invoked
that macro. A trick to help locate these kinds of errors is to place some magic
text (__MAGIC__) throughout 'configure.in':

```
AC_INIT
AC_PROG_CC
__MAGIC__
MY_SUSPECT_MACRO
__MAGIC__
AC_OUTPUT(Makefile)
```

After autoconf has generated 'configure', you can search through it for the
magic text to determine the extremities of the suspect macro. If your erroneous
code appears within the magic text markers, you have found the culprit! Don't
be afraid to hack up 'configure'. It can easily be regenerated.

Finally, because of an error on your part, m4 may generate a 'configure' script
that contains semantic errors. Something as simple as inverted logic may lead to
a nonsense test result:

```
checking for /etc/passwd... no
```

Semantic errors of this kind are usually easy to solve once you can spot them. A fast and simple way of tracing the shell execution is to use the shell's '-x' and '-v' options to turn on its own tracing. This can be done by explicitly placing the required set commands into 'configure.in':

```
AC_INIT
AC_PROG_CC
set -x -v
MY_BROKEN_MACRO
set +x +v
AC_OUTPUT(Makefile)
```

This kind of tracing is invaluable in debugging shell code containing semantic errors.

21

Writing Portable Bourne Shell

This chapter is a whistle-stop tour of the accumulated wisdom of the free software community, with respect to best practices for portable shell scripting, as encoded in the sources for Autoconf and Libtool, as interpreted and filtered by me. It is by no means comprehensive—entire books have been devoted to the subject—although it is, I hope, authoritative.

21.1 Why Use the Bourne Shell?

Unix has been around for more than 30 years and has splintered into hundreds of small and not-so-small variants (see Section 1.1, "The Diversity of Unix Systems"). Much of the subject matter of this book is concerned with how best to approach writing programs that will work on as many of these variants as possible. One of the few programming tools absolutely guaranteed to be present on every flavor of Unix in use today is Steve Bourne's original shell, sh—the Bourne shell. That is why Libtool is written as a Bourne shell script, and why the configure files generated by Autoconf are Bourne shell scripts: They can be executed on all known Unix flavors, and as a bonus on most POSIX-based non-Unix operating systems too.

However, there are complications. Over the years, OS vendors have improved Steve Bourne's original shell or have re-implemented it in an almost, but not quite, compatible way. A great number of Bourne compatible shells are also often used as a system's default '/bin/sh': ash, bash, bsh, ksh, sh5, and zsh are some that you may come across. For the rest of this chapter, when I say "shell," I mean a Bourne-compatible shell.

This leads us to the black art known as _portable shell programming_, the art of writing a single script that will run correctly through all these varying implementations of '/bin/sh'. Of course, Unix systems are constantly evolving and new variations are being introduced all the time (and very old systems that have fallen into disuse can perhaps be ignored by the pragmatic). The amount of system knowledge required to write a truly portable shell script is vast, and a great deal of the information that sets a precedent for a given idiom is necessarily second or third (or tenth) hand. Practically, this means that some of the knowledge accumulated in popular portable shell scripts is very probably folklore. That doesn't really matter too much, however; the important thing is that if you adhere to these idioms, you shouldn't have any problems from people who cannot run your program on their system.

21.2 Implementation

By their very nature, a sizable part of the functionality of shell scripts is provided by the many utility programs that they routinely call to perform important subsidiary tasks. Addressing the portability of the script involves issues of portability in the host operating system environment and portability of the utility programs as well as the portability of the shell implementation itself.

This section discusses differences between shell implementations to which you must cater when writing a portable script. It is broken into several subsections, each covering a single aspect of shell programming that needs to be approached carefully to avoid pitfalls with unexpected behavior in some shell implementations. The following section discusses how to cope with the host environment in a portable fashion. The last section in this chapter addresses the portability of common shell utilities.

21.2.1 Size Limitations

Quite a lot of the Unix vendor implementations of the Bourne shell have a fixed buffer for storing command lines, as small as 512 characters in the worst cases. You may have an error akin to this:

```
$ ls -d /usr/bin/* | wc -l
sh: error: line too long
```

Notice that the limit applies to the *expanded* command line, not just the characters typed in for the line. A portable way to write this is as follows:

```
$ ( cd /usr/bin && ls | wc -l )
   1556
```

21.2.2 #!

When the kernel executes a program from the file system, it checks the first few bytes of the file and compares them to its internal list of known *magic numbers*, which encode how the file can be executed. This is a similar, but distinct, system to the '/etc/magic' magic number list used by user space programs.

Having determined that the file is a script by examining its magic number, the kernel finds the path of the interpreter by removing the '#!' and any intervening space from the first line of the script. One optional argument is allowed (additional arguments are not ignored; they constitute a syntax error), and the resulting command line is executed. There is a 32-character limit to the significant part of the '#!' line, so you must ensure that the full path to the interpreter plus any switches you need to pass to it do not exceed this limit. Also, the interpreter must be a real binary program; it cannot be a '#!' file itself.

It used to be thought that the semantics between different kernels' idea of the magic number for the start of an interpreted script varied slightly between implementations. In actual fact, all look for '#!' in the first 2 bytes—in spite of commonly held beliefs, there is no evidence that there are others that require '#! /'.

A portable script must give an absolute path to the interpreter, which causes problems when, for example, some machines have a better version of Bourne shell in an unusual directory—'/usr/sysv/bin/sh', for instance. See Section 21.2.3, ":," for a way to re-execute the script with a better interpreter.

Imagine, for example, a script file called '/tmp/foo.pl' with the following first line:

```
#! /usr/local/bin/perl
```

Now, the script can be executed from the 'tmp' directory, with the following sequence of commands:

```
$ cd /tmp
$ ./foo.pl
```

When executing these commands, the kernel actually executes the following from the '/tmp' directory:

```
/usr/local/bin/perl ./foo.pl
```

This can pose problems of its own, however. A script such as the one just described does not work on a machine on which the Perl interpreter is installed as '/usr/bin/perl'. You can circumvent this problem by using the env program to find the interpreter by looking in the user's 'PATH' environment variable. Change the first line of the 'foo.pl' to read as follows:

```
#! /usr/bin/env perl
```

This idiom does rely on the env command being installed as '/usr/bin/env' and that, in this example, perl can be found in the user's 'PATH'. But that is indeed the case on the great majority of machines. In contrast, perl is installed in 'usr/local/bin' as often as '/usr/bin', so using env like this is a net win overall. You can also use this method to get around the 32-character limit if the path to the interpreter is too long.

Unfortunately, you lose the capability to pass an option flag to the interpreter if you choose to use env. For example, you can't do the following, because it requires two arguments:

```
#! /usr/bin/env guile -s
```

21.2.3:

In the beginning, the magic number for Bourne shell scripts used to be a colon followed by a newline. Most Unices still support this, and correctly pass a file with a single colon as the first line to '/bin/sh' for interpretation. Nobody uses this any more, and I suspect some very new Unices may have forgotten about it entirely; so you should stick to the more usual '#! /bin/sh' syntax for your own scripts. You might occasionally come across a very old script that starts with a ':', however, and it is nice to know why!

In addition, all known Bourne-compatible shells have a built-in command, ':', which always returns success. It is equivalent to the system command /bin/true, but can be used from a script without the overhead of starting another process. When setting a shell variable as a flag, it is good practice to use the commands,: and false as values, and choose the sense of the variable to be ':' in the common case. When you come to test the value of the variable, you will avoid the overhead of additional processes most of the time:

```
var=:
if $var; then
  foo
fi
```

The : command just described can take any number of arguments, which it will fastidiously ignore. This allows the ':' character to double up as a comment leader of sorts. Be aware that the characters that follow are not discarded, they are still interpreted by the shell; so metacharacters can have unexpected effects:

```
$ cat foo
:
: echo foo
: `echo bar`
: `echo baz >&2`
$ ./foo
baz
```

You might find very old shell scripts that are commented using ':' or new scripts that exploit this behavior in some esoteric fashion. My advice is, don't: It will bite you later.

21.2.4 ()

A great number of shells, like Steve Bourne's original implementation, do not have functions! So, strictly speaking, you can't use shell functions in your scripts. Luckily, in this day and age, even though '/bin/sh' itself may not support shell functions, it is not too far from the truth to say that almost every machine will have *some* shell that does.

Taking this assumption to its logical conclusion, it is a simple matter of writing your script to find a suitable shell, and then feed itself to that shell so that the rest of the script can use functions with impunity:

```
#! /bin/sh

# Zsh is not Bourne compatible without the following:
if test -n "$ZSH_VERSION"; then
  emulate sh
  NULLCMD=:
fi

# Bash is not POSIX compliant without the following:
test -n "$BASH_VERSION" && set -o posix

SHELL="${SHELL-/bin/sh}"
if test x"$1" = x--re-executed; then
  # Functional shell was found. Remove option and continue
  shift
elif "$SHELL" -c 'foo () { exit 0; }; foo' 2>/dev/null; then
  # The current shell works already!
  :
else
  # Try alternative shells that (sometimes) support functions
  for cmd in sh bash ash bsh ksh zsh sh5; do
    set IFS=:; X="$PATH:/bin:/usr/bin:/usr/afsws/bin:/usr/ucb"; echo $X`
    for dir
    do
      shell="$dir/$cmd"
      ...
    done
    if (test -f "$shell" || test -f "$shell.exe") &&
      "$shell" -c 'foo () { exit 0; }; foo 2>/dev/null
    then
      # Re-execute with discovered functional shell
      SHELL="$shell" exec "$shell" "$0" --re-executed ${1+"$"}
    fi
  done
done
echo "Unable to locate a shell interpreter with function support" >&2
exit 1
fi
```

```
foo () {
    echo "$SHELL: ta da!"
}

foo

exit 0
```

Note that this script finds a shell that supports functions of the following syntax, because the use of the `function` keyword is much less widely supported:

```
foo () { ... }
```

A notable exception to the assertion that all machines have a shell that can handle functions is 4.3BSD, which has only a single shell: a shell-function-deprived Bourne shell. You can deal with this in two ways:

1. Ask 4.3BSD users of your script to install a more featureful shell, such as bash, so that the technique above will work.
2. Have your script run itself through sed, chopping itself into pieces, with each function written to its own script file, and then feed what is left into the original shell. Whenever a function call is encountered, one of the fragments from the original script will be executed in a subshell.

If you decide to split the script with sed, you need to be careful not to rely on shell variables to communicate between functions, because each "function" will be executed in its own subshell.

21.2.5 .

The semantics of '.' are rather peculiar to say the least. Here is a simple script—it just displays its positional parameters:

```
#! /bin/sh
echo "$0" ${1+"$@"}
```

Put this in a file, 'foo'. Here is another simple script—it calls the first script. Put this in another file, 'wrapper':

```
#! /bin/sh
. ./foo
. ./foo bar baz
```

Observe what happens when you run this from the command line:

```
$ ./wrapper
./wrapper
./wrapper bar baz
```

So '$0' is inherited from the calling script, and the positional parameters are as passed to the command. Observe what happens when you call the wrapper script with arguments:

```
$ ./wrapper 1 2 3
./wrapper 1 2 3
./wrapper bar baz
```

So the sourced script has access to the calling scripts positional parameters, *unless you override them in the '.' command.*

This can cause no end of trouble if you are not expecting it, so you must either be careful to omit all parameters to any '.' command, or else don't reference the parameters inside the sourced script. If you are re-executing your script with a shell that understands functions, the best use for the '.' command is to load libraries of functions that can subsequently be used in the calling script.

Most importantly, don't forget that if you call the exit command in a script that you load with '.', it will cause the calling script to exit too!

21.2.6 [

Although technically equivalent, test is preferable to [in shell code written in conjunction with Autoconf, because '[' is also used for M4 quoting in Autoconf. Your code will be much easier to read (and write) if you abstain from the use of '['.

Except in the most degenerate shells, test is a shell built in to save the overhead of starting another process, and is no slower than '['. It does mean, however, that there is a huge range of features not implemented often enough that you can use them freely within a truly portable script. The less obvious ones to avoid are '-a' and '-o'—the logical "and" and "or" operations. A good litmus test for the portability of any shell feature is to see whether that feature is used in the source of Autoconf; and it turns out that '-a' and '-o' *are* used here and there, but never more than once in a single command. All the same, to avoid any confusion, I always avoid them entirely. I would not use the following, for example:

```
test foo -a bar
```

Instead I would run test twice, like this:

```
test foo && test bar
```

The negation operator of test is quite portable and can be used in portable shell scripts. For example:

```
if test ! foo; then bar; fi
```

The negation operator of `if` is not at all portable and should be avoided. The following generates a syntax error on some shell implementations:

```
if ! test foo; then bar; fi
```

An implication of this axiom is that when you need to branch if a command fails, and that command is not `test`, you cannot use the negation operator. The easiest way to work around this is to use the `'else'` clause of the un-negated `if`, like this:

```
if foo; then :; else bar; fi
```

Notice the use of the `:` built-in as a null operation when `foo` doesn't fail.

The `test` command does not cope with missing or additional arguments, so you must take care to ensure that the shell does not remove arguments or introduce new ones during variable and quote expansions. The best way to do that is to enclose any variables in double quotation marks. You should also add a single character prefix to both sides in case the value of the expansion is a valid option to `test`:

```
$ for foo in "" "!" "bar" "baz quux"; do
>     test x"$foo" = x"bar" && echo 1 || echo 0
> done
0
0
1
0
```

Here, you can see that using the `'x'` prefix for the first operand saves `test` from interpreting the `'!'` argument as a real option or from choking on an empty string—something you must always be aware of, or else the following behavior will ensue:

```
$ foo=!
$ test "$foo" = "bar" && echo 1 || echo 0
test: argument expected
0
$ foo=""
$ test "$foo" = "bar" && echo 1 || echo 0
test: argument expected
0
```

Also, the double quotation marks help `test` cope with strings that contain white space. Without the double quotation marks, you will see this error:

```
$ foo="baz quux"
$ test x$foo = "bar" && echo 1 || echo 0
test: too many arguments
0
```

You should not rely on the default behavior of test (to return "true" if its single argument has non-zero length); use the '-n' option to force that behavior if it is what you want. Beyond that, the other thing you need to know about test is that if you use operators other than those following here, you are reducing the portability of your code:

'-n' *string*	*string* is nonempty.
'-z' *string*	string is empty.
string1 = *string2*	Both strings are identical.
string1 != *string2*	The strings are not the same.
'-d' *file*	*file* exists and is a directory.
'-f' *file*	*file* exists and is a regular file.

You can also use the following, provided that you don't mix them within a single invocation of test:

expression '-a' *expression*	Both expressions evaluate to "true."
expression '-o' *expression*	Neither expression evaluates to "false."

21.2.7 $

When using shell variables in portable scripts, you need to write them in a somewhat stylized fashion to maximize the number of shell implementations that will interpret your code as expected:

- Convenient though it is, the POSIX '$(command parameters)' syntax for command substitution is not remotely portable. Despite it being more difficult to nest, you must use 'command parameters' instead.

- The most portable way to set a default value for a shell variable is as follows:
  ```
  $ echo ${no_such_var-"default value"}
  default value
  ```

  If there is any white space in the default value, as there is here, you must be careful to quote the entire value, because some shells will raise an error:
  ```
  $ echo ${no_such_var-default value}
  sh: bad substitution
  ```

- The unset command is not available in many of the degenerate Bourne shell implementations. Generally, it is not too difficult to get by without it; but following the logic that led to the shell script in Section 21.2.3, it would be trivial to extend the test case for confirming a shell's suitability to include a check for unset. Although it has not been put to the test, the theory is that all the interesting machines in use today have *some* shell that supports unset.

- Be religious about double quoting variable expansions. By using `"$foo"`, you avoid trouble with unexpected spaces in filenames and compression of all white space to a single space in unquoted variable expansions.

- To avoid accidental interpretation of variable expansions as command options, you can use the following technique:

```
$ foo=-n
$ echo $foo
$ echo x"$foo" | sed -e 's/^x//'
-n
```

- If it is set, IFS splits words on white space by default. If you change it, be sure to put it back when you are done; otherwise, the shell may behave very strangely from that point. For example, when you need to examine each element of `'$PATH'` in turn:

```
# The white space at the end of the following line is a space
# followed by a literal tab and newline characters.
save_IFS="${IFS=
}"; IFS=":"
set dummy $PATH
IFS="$save_IFS"
shift
```

Alternatively, you can take advantage of the fact that command substitutions occur in a separate subshell and do not corrupt the environment of the calling shell:

```
set dummy `IFS=:; echo $PATH`
shift
```

Strictly speaking, the `'dummy'` argument is required to stop the set command from interpreting the first word of the expanded backquote expression as a command option. Realistically, no one is going to have `'-x'`, for example, as the first element of his `'PATH'` variable, so the `'dummy'` could be omitted—as I did earlier in the script in Section 21.2.4.

- Some shells expand `'$@'` to the empty string, even when there are no actual parameters (`'$#'` is 0). If you need to replicate the parameters that were passed to the executing script—when feeding the script to a more suitable interpreter, for example—you must use the following:

```
    ${1+"$@"}
```

Similarly, although all known shells do correctly use `'$@'` as the default argument to a for command, you must write it like this:

```
for arg
do
  stuff
done
```

When you rely on implicit '$@' like this, it is important to write the do keyword on a separate line. Some degenerate shells cannot parse the following:

```
for arg; do
    stuff
done
```

21.2.8 * versus .*

This section compares *file globbing* with *regular expression matching*. Many Unix commands are regularly used from shell scripts and provide some sort of pattern-matching mechanism: expr, egrep, and sed, to name a few. Unfortunately they each have different quoting rules regarding whether particular metacharacters must be backslash escaped to revert to their literal meaning and vice versa. There is no real logic to the particular dialect of regular expressions accepted by these commands. To confirm the correctness of each regular expression, you should always check them from the shell prompt with the relevant tool before committing to a script, so I won't belabor the specifics.

Shell globbing is much more regular (no pun intended), however, and provides a reasonable and sometimes more CPU-efficient solution to many shell-matching problems. The key is to make good use of the case command, which is easier to use (because it uses globbing rules) and doesn't require additional processes to be spawned. Unfortunately, GNU Bash doesn't handle backslashes correctly in glob character classes—the backslash must be the first character in the class; otherwise, it will never match. If you want to detect absolute directory paths on Unix and Windows using case, for example, you should write the code like this:

```
case $dir in
  [\\/]* | ?:[\\/]* ) echo absolute ;;
  * )                 echo relative ;;
esac
```

Even though expr uses regular expressions rather than shell globbing, it is often[1] a shell built-in, so using it to extract sections of strings can be faster than spawning a sed process to do the same. As with echo and set, for example, you must be careful that variable or command expansions for the first argument to expr are not accidentally interpreted as reserved keywords. As with echo, you can work around this problem by prefixing any expansions with a literal 'x', as follows:

```
$ foo=substr
$ expr $foo : '.*\(str\)'
expr: syntax error
```

---

[1] *Notable exceptions are GNU Bash, and both Ksh and the Bourne shell on Solaris.*

```
$ expr x$foo : '.*\(str\)'
str
```

21.3 Environment

In addition to the problems with portability in shell implementations discussed in the preceding section, the behavior of the shell can also be drastically affected by the contents of certain environment variables and the operating environment provided by the host machine.

It is important to be aware of the behavior of some of the operating systems within which your shell script might run. Although not directly related to the implementation of the shell interpreter, the characteristics of some of target architectures do influence what is considered to be portable. To ensure your script will work on as many shell implementations as possible, you must observe the following points.

SCO Unix doesn't like LANG=C and friends, but without LC_MESSAGES=C, Solaris translates variable values in 'set'! Similarly, without LC_CTYPE=C, compiled C code can behave unexpectedly. The trick is to set the values to 'C', except for if they are not already set at all:

```
for var in LANG LC_ALL LC_MESSAGES LC_CTYPES LANGUAGES
do
  if eval test x"\${$var+set}" = xset; then
    eval $var=C; eval export $var
  fi
done
```

HP-UX ksh and all POSIX shells print the target directory to standard output if 'CDPATH' is set:

```
if test x"${CDPATH+set}" = xset; then CDPATH=:; export CDPATH; fi
```

The target architecture file system might impose limits on your scripts. If you want your scripts to run on the architectures that impose these limits, your script must adhere to these limits:

- The ISO9660 file system, as used on most CD-ROMs, limits nesting of directories to a maximum depth of 12 levels.
- Many old Unix file systems place a 14-character limit on the length of any filename. If you care about portability to DOS, *that* has an 8-character limit with an optional extension of 3 or fewer characters (known as 8.3 notation).

A useful idiom when you need to determine whether a particular path name is relative or absolute, which works for DOS targets, follows:

```
case "$file" in
  [\\/]* | ?:[\\/]*) echo absolute ;;
  *)                 echo default ;;
esac
```

21.4 Utilities

The utility programs commonly executed by shell scripts can have a huge impact on the portability of shell scripts, and it is important to know which utilities are universally available and any differences certain implementations of these utilities may exhibit. According to the GNU standards document, you can rely on having access to these utilities from your scripts:

```
cat cmp cp diff echo egrep expr false grep install-info
ln ls mkdir mv pwd rm rmdir sed sleep sort tar test touch true
```

You must be aware of the following things when using some of these tools:

cat	Host architectures supply cat implementations with conflicting interpretations of, or entirely missing, the various command-line options. You should avoid using any command-line options to this command.
cp and mv	Unconditionally duplicated or otherwise open file descriptors cannot be deleted on many operating systems, and worse on Windows, the destination files cannot even be moved. Constructs such as this must be avoided, for example:
	`exec > foo` `mv foo bar`
echo	The echo command has at least two flavors: The one takes a '-n' option to suppress the automatic newline at the end of the echoed string; the other uses an embedded '\c' notation as the last character in the echoed string for the same purpose.
	If you need to emit a string without a trailing newline character, you can use the following script fragment to discover which flavor of echo you are using:

```
case echo "testing\c"`,`echo -n testing` in
  *c,*)   echo_n=-n echo_c= ;;
  *,-n*)  echo_n= echo_c='\c' ;;
  *)      echo_n= echo_c='
'2
          '
  ;;
esac
```

---

[2] *This is a literal newline.*

Any echo command after the preceding shell fragment, which should not move the cursor to a new line, can now be written like this:

```
echo $echo_n "prompt:$echo_c"
```

In addition, you should try to avoid backslashes in echo arguments unless the shell expands them. Some implementations interpret them and effectively perform another backslash expansion pass, whereas equally many implementations do not. This can become a really hairy problem if you need to have an echo command that does not perform backslash expansion; and in fact the first 150 lines of the ltconfig script distributed with Libtool are devoted to finding such a command.

ln

Not all systems support soft links. You should use the Autoconf macro 'AC_PROG_LN_S' to discover what the target architecture supports and assign the result of that test to a variable. Whenever you subsequently need to create a link, you can use the command stored in the variable to do so:

```
LN_S=@LN_S@
...
$LN_S $top_srcdir/foo $dist_dir/foo
```

Also, you cannot rely on support for the 'f' option from all implementations of ln. Use rm before calling ln instead.

mkdir

Unfortunately, 'mkdir -p' is not as portable as we might like. You must either create each directory in the path in turn or use the mkinstalldirs script supplied by Automake.

sed

When you resort to using sed (rather, use case or expr if you can), there is no need to introduce command-line scripts using the '-e' option. Even when you want to supply more than one script, you can use ';' as a command separator. The following two lines are equivalent, although the latter is cleaner:

```
$ sed -e 's/foo/bar/g' -e '12q' < infile > outfile
$ sed 's/foo/bar/g;12q' < infile > outfile
```

Some portability zealots still go to great lengths to avoid *here documents* of more than 12 lines. The 12-line limit is actually a limitation in some implementations of sed, which has gradually seeped into the portable shell folklore as a general limit in all here documents. Autoconf, however, includes many here documents with far more than 12 lines and has not generated any complaints from users. This is testament to the fact that at worst the limit is encountered only in very obscure cases (and most likely that it is not a real limit after all).

Also, be aware that branch labels of more than eight
characters are not portable to some implementations
of sed.

Note

*Here documents are a way of redirecting literal strings into the standard input of a
command. You have certainly seen them before if you have looked at other
people's shell scripts, although you may not have realized what they were called:*

```
cat >> /tmp/file$$ << _EOF_
This is the text of a "here document"
_EOF_
```

Something else to be aware of is that the temporary files created by your scripts
can become a security problem if they are left in '/tmp' or if the names are
predictable. A simple way around this is to create a directory in '/tmp' that is
unique to the process and owned by the process user. Some machines have a
utility program for just this purpose: `mktemp -d`; otherwise, you can always fall
back to `umask 077 && mkdir /tmp/$$`. Having created this directory, all the
temporary files for this process should be written to that directory, and its
contents removed as soon as possible.

Armed with the knowledge of how to write shell code in a portable fashion as
discussed in this chapter, in combination with the M4 details from the
preceding chapter, the specifics of combining the two to write your own
Autoconf macros are covered in the next chapter.

22

Writing New Macros for Autoconf

Autoconf is an extensible system that permits new macros to be written and shared among Autoconf users. Although it is possible to perform custom tests by placing fragments of shell code into your 'configure.in' file, it is better practice to encapsulate that test in a macro. This encourages macro authors to make their macros more general-purpose, easier to test, and easier to share with other users.

This chapter presents some guidelines for designing and implementing good Autoconf macros. It concludes with a discussion of the approaches being considered by the Autoconf development community for improving the creation and distribution of macros. You can find a more general discussion of macros in Section 20.3.2, "Macros and Macro Expansion."

22.1 Autoconf Preliminaries

In a small package that uses only Autoconf, your own macros are placed in the 'aclocal.m4' file—this includes macros that you may have obtained from third parties, such as the Autoconf macro archive (see Section 22.5.1, "Autoconf Macro Archive"). If your package additionally uses Automake, these macros should be placed in 'acinclude.m4'. The aclocal program from Automake reads in macro definitions from 'acinclude.m4' when generating 'aclocal.m4'. When using Automake, for instance, 'aclocal.m4' includes the definitions of AM_ macros needed by Automake.

In larger projects, it is advisable to keep your custom macros in a more organized structure. Autoconf version 2.15 will introduce a new facility to explicitly include files from your 'configure.in' file. The details have not solidified yet, but it will almost certainly include a mechanism to automatically include files with the correct filename extension from a subdirectory ('m4/', for example).

22.2 Reusing Existing Macros

It goes without saying that it makes sense to reuse macros where possible—indeed, a search of the Autoconf macro archive might turn up a macro that does exactly what you want, alleviating the need to write a macro at all (see Section 22.5.1, "Autoconf Macro Archive").

It is more likely, however, that you can use generic, parameterized tests to help you get your job done. Autoconf's "generic" tests provide one such collection of macros. A macro that wants to test for support of a new language keyword, for example, should rely on the AC_TRY_COMPILE macro. You can use this macro to attempt to compile a small program and detect a failure resulting from, say, a syntax error.

In any case, it is good practice when reusing macros to adhere to their publicized interface. Do *not* rely on implementation details such as shell variables used to record the test's result unless this is explicitly mentioned as part of the macro's behavior. Macros in the Autoconf core can, and do, change their implementation from time to time.

Reusing a macro does not imply that the macro is necessarily invoked from within the definition of your macro. Sometimes you might just want to rely on some action performed by a macro earlier in the configuration run—this is still a form of reuse. In these cases, it is necessary to ensure that this macro has indeed run at least once before your macro is invoked. It is possible to state such a dependency by invoking the 'AC_REQUIRE' macro at the beginning of your macro's definition.

Should you need to write a macro from scratch, the following sections provide guidelines for writing better macros.

22.3 Guidelines for Writing Macros

You should follow some guidelines when writing a macro. The criteria for a well-written macro are that it should be easy to use, well documented, and, most importantly, portable. Portability is a difficult problem that requires much anticipation on the part of the macro writer. This section discusses the design considerations for using a static Autoconf test at compile time versus a test at runtime. It also covers some of the characteristics of a good macro, including noninteractive behavior, properly formatted output, and a clean interface for the user of the macro.

22.3.1 Noninteractive Behavior

Autoconf's generated 'configure' scripts are designed to be noninteractive—they should not prompt the user for input. Many users like the fact that 'configure' can be used as part of an automated build process. By introducing code into 'configure' which prompts a user for more information, you prohibit unattended operation. Instead, you should use the AC_ARG_ENABLE macro in 'configure.in' to add extra options to 'configure' or consider runtime configuration.

22.3.2 Testing System Features at Application Runtime

When pondering how to handle a difficult portability problem or configurable option, consider whether the problem is better solved by performing tests at runtime or by providing a configuration file to customize the application. Keep in mind that the results of tests that Autoconf can perform ultimately affect how the program will be built (and can limit the number of machines that the program can be moved to without recompiling it). In the following example, this consideration had to be made in a real-life project:

The *pthreads for Win32* project has sought to provide a standards-compliant implementation for the POSIX threads API. It does so by mapping the POSIX API functions into small functions that achieve the desired result using the Win32 thread API. Windows 95, Windows 98, and Windows NT have different levels of support for a system call primitive that attempts to enter a critical section without blocking. The TryEnterCriticalSection function is missing on Windows 95, is an inoperative stub on Windows 98, and works as expected on Windows NT. If this behavior were to be checked by 'configure' at compile time, the resultant library would work only on the variant of Windows for which it was compiled. Because it is more common to distribute packages for Windows in binary form, this would be an unfortunate situation. Instead, it is sometimes preferable to handle this kind of portability problem with a test, performed by your code at runtime.

22.3.3 Output from Macros

Users who run 'configure' expect a certain style of output as tests are performed. As such, you should use the well-defined interface to the existing Autoconf macros for generating output. Your tests should not arbitrarily echo messages to the standard output.

Autoconf provides the following macros to output the messages for you in a consistent way (see Chapter 2, "How to Run Configure, and The Most Useful Standard Makefile Targets"). They are introduced here with a brief description of their purpose and are documented in more detail in in Appendix D, "Autoconf Macro Reference." Typically, a test starts by invoking AC_MSG_CHECKING to describe to the user what the test is doing and AC_MSG_RESULT is invoked to output the result of the test.

'AC_MSG_CHECKING'	This macro is used to notify the user that a test is commencing. It prints the text 'checking' followed by your message and ends with '...'. You should use 'AC_MSG_RESULT' after this macro to output the result of the test.
'AC_MSG_RESULT'	This macro notifies the user of a test result. In general, the result should be the word 'yes' or 'no' for Boolean tests, or the actual value of the result, such as a directory or filename.
'AC_MSG_ERROR'	This macro emits a hard-error message and aborts 'configure'; this should be used for fatal errors.
'AC_MSG_WARN'	This macro emits a warning to the user and proceeds.

22.3.4 Naming Macros

Just like functions in a C program, it is important to choose a good name for your Autoconf macros. A well-chosen name helps to unambiguously describe the purpose of the macro. Macros in M4 are all named within a single namespace and, therefore, it is necessary to follow a convention to ensure that names retain uniqueness. This reasoning goes beyond just avoiding collisions with other macros—if you happen to choose a name already known to M4 as a definition of any kind, your macro's name could be rewritten by the prior definition during macro processing.

One naming convention has emerged: prefixing each macro name with the name of the package that the macro originated in or the initials of the macro's author. Macros are usually named in a hierarchical fashion, with each part of the name separated by underscores. As you move left-to-right through each component of the name, the description becomes more detailed. The Autoconf Manual suggests some high-level categories of macros that you may want to use when forming a descriptive name for your own macro. If your macro tries to discover the existence of a particular C structure, for example, you might want to use C and STRUCT as components of its name.

`'C'`	Tests related to constructs of the C programming language.
`'DECL'`	Tests for variable declarations in header files.
`'FUNC'`	Tests for functions present in (or absent from) libraries.
`'HEADER'`	Tests for header files.
`'LIB'`	Tests for libraries.
`'PATH'`	Tests to discover absolute filenames (especially programs).
`'PROG'`	Tests to determine the base names of programs.
`'STRUCT'`	Tests for definitions of C structures in header files.
`'SYS'`	Tests for operating system features, such as restartable system calls.
`'TYPE'`	Tests for built-in or declared C data types.
`'VAR'`	Tests for C variables in libraries.

Some examples of macro names formed in this way include the following:

`'AC_PROG_CC'`	A test that looks for a program called cc.
`'AC_C_INLINE'`	A test that discovers if the C keyword inline is recognized.
`'bje_CXX_MUTABLE'`	A test, written by "bje," that discovers whether the C++ keyword mutable is recognized.

22.3.5 Macro Interface

When designing your macro, it is worth spending some time deciding on what your macro's interface (the macro's name and argument list) will be. Often, you can extract general-purpose functionality into a generic macro and write a second macro that is a client of the generic one. Like planning the prototype for a C function, this is usually a straightforward process of deciding what arguments the macro requires to perform its function. You should, however, consider a couple of other things as well.

M4 macros refer to their arguments by number with a syntax such as $1. It is typically more difficult to read an M4 macro definition and understand what each argument's designation is than in a C function body, where the formal argument is referred to by its name. Therefore, it is a good idea to include a standard comment block above each macro, documenting the macro and giving an indication of what each argument is for. The Autoconf source code provides the following example:

```
# AC_CHECK_FILE(FILE, [ACTION-IF-FOUND], [ACTION-IF-NOT-FOUND])
# ------------------------------------.
#
# Check for the existence of FILE.
```

To remain general-purpose, the existing Autoconf macros follow the convention of keeping side effects outside the definition of the macro. Here, when a user invokes 'AC_CHECK_FILE', he must provide shell code to implement the side effect that he wants to occur if the 'FILE' is found or is not found. Some macros implement a basic and desirable action (defining a symbol such as 'HAVE_UNISTD_H', for example) if no user-defined actions are provided. In general, your macros should provide an interface consistent with the interfaces provided by the core Autoconf macros.

M4 macros may have variable argument lists, so it is possible to implement macros that have defaults for arguments. By testing each individual argument against the empty string with 'ifelse', users can accept the default behavior for individual arguments by passing empty values:

```
AC_CHECK_FILE([/etc/passwd], [],
              [AC_MSG_ERROR([something is really wrong])])
```

One final point to consider when designing the interface for a macro is how to handle macros that are generic in nature and, for example, want to set a cache variable whose name is based on one of the arguments. Consider the 'AC_CHECK_HEADER' macro. It defines a symbol and makes an entry in the cache that reflects the result of the test it performs. 'AC_CHECK_HEADER' takes an argument, namely the name of a header file to look for. This macro cannot just make a cache entry with a name such as ac_cv_check_header, because it would work only once; any further uses of this macro in 'configure.in' would cause an incorrect result to be drawn from the cache. Instead, the name of the symbol that is defined and the name of the cache variable that is set need to be computed from one of the arguments: the name of the header file being sought. What you really need is to define HAVE_UNISTD_H and set the cache variable ac_cv_header_unistd_h. This can be achieved with some sed and tr magic in the macro, which transforms the filename into uppercase characters for the call to AC_DEFINE and into lowercase for the cache variable name. Unknown characters such as '.' need to be transformed into underscores.

Some existing macros also enable the user to pass in the name of a cache variable name so that the macro does not need to compute a name. In general, this should be avoided, because it makes the macro harder to use and exposes details of the caching system to the user.

22.4 Implementation Specifics

This section provides some tips about how to actually go about writing your macros after you have decided what it is that you want to test and how to go about testing for it. It covers writing shell code for the test and optionally caching the results of those tests.

22.4.1 Writing Shell Code

It is necessary to adopt a technique of writing portable Bourne shell code. Often, shell programming tricks you might have learned are actually extensions provided by your favorite shell and are non-portable. When in doubt, check documentation or try the construct on another system's Bourne shell. For a thorough treatment of this topic, see Chapter 21, "Writing Portable Bourne Shell."

22.4.2 Using M4 Correctly

Writing macros involves interacting with the M4 macro processor, which expands your macros when they are used in `configure.in`. It is crucial that your macros use M4 correctly—and in particular, that they quote strings correctly. Refer to Chapter 20, "GNU M4," for a thorough treatment of this topic.

22.4.3 Caching Results

Autoconf provides a caching facility, whereby the results of a test may be stored in a cache file. The cache file is itself a Bourne shell script sourced by the `configure` script to set any "cache variables" to values present in the cache file.

The next time `configure` is run, the cache is consulted for a prior result. If there is a prior result, the value is reused and the code that performs that test is skipped. This speeds up subsequent runs of `configure` and configuration of deep trees, which can share a cache file in the top-level directory (see Chapter 2).

A custom macro is not required to perform caching, although it is considered best practice. Sometimes it doesn't make sense for a macro to perform caching—tests for system aspects that may frequently change should not be cached. For example, a test for free disk space should not employ caching because it is a dynamic characteristic.

The 'AC_CACHE_CHECK' macro is a convenient wrapper for caching the results of tests. You just provide a description of the test, the name of a cache variable to store the test result to, and the body of the test. If the test has not been run before, the cache is primed with the result. If the result is already in the cache, the cache variable is set and the test is skipped. Note that the name of the cache variable must contain '_cv_' in order to be saved correctly.

The following Autoconf macro code ties together many of the concepts introduced in this chapter:

```
# AC_PROG_CC_G
# — — — — — —
AC_DEFUN(AC_PROG_CC_G,
[AC_CACHE_CHECK(whether ${CC-cc} accepts -g, ac_cv_prog_cc_g,
[echo 'void f(){}' > conftest.c
if test -z "${CC-cc} -g -c conftest.c 2>&1`"; then
  ac_cv_prog_cc_g=yes
else
  ac_cv_prog_cc_g=no
fi
rm -f conftest*
])]) # AC_PROG_CC_G
```

22.5 Future Directions for Macro Writers
A future trend for Autoconf is to make it easier to write reliable macros and to reuse macros written by others. This section describes some of the ideas currently being explored by those actively working on Autoconf.

22.5.1 Autoconf Macro Archive
In mid-1999, an official Autoconf macro archive was established on the World Wide Web by Peter Simons in Germany. The archive collects Autoconf macros that might be useful to some users, but are not sufficiently general-purpose to include in the core Autoconf distribution. You can find the macro archive at http://www.gnu.org/software/ac-archive.

It is possible to retrieve macros that perform different kinds of tests from this archive. The macros can then be inserted, in line, into your 'aclocal.m4' or 'acinclude.m4' file. The archive has been steadily growing since its inception. Please try and submit your macros to the archive!

22.5.2 Primitive Macros to Aid in Building Macros

Writing new macros is one aspect of Autoconf that has proven troublesome to users in the past, because this is one area where Autoconf's implementation details leak out. Autoconf extensively uses m4 to perform the translation of 'configure.in' to 'configure'. Therefore, it is necessary to understand implementation details, such as M4's quoting rules, to write Autoconf macros (see Chapter 20).

Another aspect of macro writing that is extremely hard to get right is scripting portable Bourne shell scripts (see Chapter 21). Writing portable software, be it in Bourne shell or C++, is something that can only be mastered with years of experience—and exposure to many different kinds of machines! Rather than expect all macro writers to acquire this experience, it makes sense for Autoconf to become a "knowledge base" for this experience.

With this in mind, one future direction for Autoconf will be to provide a library of low-level macros to assist in writing new macros. By way of hypothetical example, consider the benefit of using a macro named AC_FOREACH instead of needing to learn the hard way that some vendor's implementation of Bourne shell has a broken for loop construct. This idea will be explored in future versions of Autoconf.

When migrating existing packages to the GNU Autotools, which is the topic of the next chapter, remember these guidelines for best practices as you write the necessary tests to make those packages portable.

23

Migrating an Existing Package to GNU Autotools

Sometimes you have to take an existing package and wrap it in an Autoconf framework. This is called *autoconfiscating*[1] a package.

This chapter gives an overview of various approaches that have been taken when autoconfiscating, explains some important points through examples, and discusses some potential pitfalls. It is not an exhaustive guide to autoconfiscation, because this process is much more art than it is science.

23.1 Why Autoconfiscate?

There are a few reasons to autoconfiscate a package. You might be porting your package to a new platform for the first time, or you might have outstripped the capabilities of an ad hoc system. Or, you might be assuming maintenance of a package and you want to make it fit in with other packages that use the GNU Autotools.

For instance, for libgcj, we wanted to distribute some libraries needed for proper operation, such as the zip archiving program and the Boehm garbage collector. In neither case was an Autoconf framework available. We thought one was required, however, to give the overall package a seamless and easy-to-use configuration and build system. This attention to ease of install by users is important; it is one reason that the GNU Autotools were written.

In another case, a group I worked with was taking over maintenance of a preexisting package. We preferred an Autoconf-based solution to the home-grown one already in use by the package—the existing system was based on platform tests, not feature tests, and was difficult to navigate and extend.

---

[1]*A term coined by Noah Friedman in the early days of Autoconf to denote the process of converting a package that configures itself without Autoconf to one that does.*

23.2 Overview of the Two Approaches

There are two fundamental approaches to autoconfiscation: "quick and dirty" and the "full pull." In practice, each project is a mix of the two.

There are no hard-and-fast rules when autoconficating an existing package, particularly when you are planning to track future releases of the original source. Because Autoconf is so flexible, however, it is usually possible to find some reasonable way to implement whatever is required. Automake isn't as flexible, and with "strangely" constructed packages you're sometimes required to make a difficult choice: restructure the package or avoid Automake.

- **Quick and dirty.** In the quick-and-dirty approach, the goal is to get the framework up and running with the least effort. This is the approach we took when we autoconfiscated both zip and the Boehm garbage collector. Our reasons were simple: We knew we would be tracking the original packages closely, so we wanted to minimize the amount of work involved in importing the next release and subsequently merging our changes. Also, both packages were written to be portable (but in very different ways), so major modifications to the source were not required.

- **Full pull.** Sometimes you would rather completely convert a package to GNU Autotools. For instance, you might have just assumed maintenance of a package. Or, you might read this book and decide that your company's internal projects should use a state-of-the-art configuration system.

  The full pull is more work than the quick-and-dirty approach, but in the end it yields a more easily understood and more idiomatic package. This in turn has maintenance benefits due to the relative absence of quirks, traps, and special cases—oddities that creep into quick-and-dirty ports due to the need, in that case, to structure the build system around the package instead of having the ability to restructure the package to fit the build system.

23.3 Example: Quick and Dirty

As part of the `libgcj` project (see `http://sourceware.cygnus.com/java/`), I had to incorporate the `zip` program into our source tree. Because this particular program is used only in one part of the build, and because this program was already fairly portable, I decided to take a quick-and-dirty approach to autoconfiscation.

First I read through the `'README'` and `'install.doc'` files to see how `'zip'` is ordinarily built. From there I learned that `'zip'` came with a `'Makefile'` used to build all Unix ports (and, for the initial autoconfiscation, Unix was all I was interested in), so I read that. This file indicated that `zip` had few configurability options.

Running `ifnames` on the sources, both Unix and generic, confirmed that the `zip` sources were mostly self-configuring, using system-specific `'#defines'`—a practice that we recommend against; for a quicky-and-dirty port, however, it is not worth cleaning up:

```
$ ifnames *.[ch] unix/*.[ch] ¦ grep ^__ ¦ head
__386BSD__ unix/unix.c
__CYGWIN32__ unix/osdep.h
__CYGWIN__ unix/osdep.h
__DATE__ unix/unix.c zipcloak.c zipnote.c zipsplit.c
__DEBUG_ALLOC__ zip.c
__ELF__ unix/unix.c
__EMX__ fileio.c ttyio.h util.c zip.c
__FreeBSD__ unix/unix.c
__G ttyio.h
__GNUC__ unix/unix.c zipcloak.c zipnote.c zipsplit.c
```

Based on this information, I wrote my initial `'configure.in'`, which is the one still in use today:

```
AC_INIT(ziperr.h)
AM_INIT_AUTOMAKE(zip, 2.1)
AM_MAINTAINER_MODE

AC_PROG_CC

AC_HEADER_DIRENT
AC_DEFINE(UNIX)

AC_LINK_FILES(unix/unix.c, unix.c)

AC_OUTPUT(Makefile)
```

The one mysterious part of this `'configure.in'` is the define of the `'UNIX'` preprocessor macro. This define came directly from `zip`'s `'unix/Makefile'` file; `zip` uses this define to enable certain Unix-specific pieces of code.

In this particular situation, I lucked out. `zip` was unusually easy to autoconficate. Typically more actual checks are required in `'configure.in'`, and more than a single iteration is required to get a workable configuration system.

From `'unix/Makefile'` I also learned which files were expected to be built to produce the `zip` executable. This information enabled me to write my `'Makefile.am'`:

```
## Process this file with Automake to create Makefile.in.

## Note: This file doesn't really try to be complete. In particular
## 'make dist' won't work at all. We're just aiming to get the
## program built. We also don't bother trying to assemble code, or
## anything like that.

AUTOMAKE_OPTIONS = no-dependencies

INCLUDES = -I$(srcdir)/unix

bin_PROGRAMS = zip

zip_SOURCES = zip.c zipfile.c zipup.c fileio.c util.c globals.c \
    crypt.c ttyio.c unix.c crc32.c crctab.c deflate.c trees.c bits.c

## This isn't really correct, but we don't care.
$(zip_OBJECTS) : zip.h ziperr.h tailor.h unix/osdep.h crypt.h \
    revision.h ttyio.h unix/zipup.h
```

This file provides a good look at some of the tradeoffs involved. In my case,
I didn't care about full correctness of the resulting 'Makefile.am'—I wasn't
planning to maintain the project, I just wanted it to build in my particular
set of environments.

So, I sacrificed 'dist' capability to make my work easier. Also, I decided
to disable dependency tracking and instead make all the resulting object
files depend on all the headers in the project. This approach is inefficient,
but in my situation perfectly reasonable, because I was not planning to do
any actual development on this package—I was just looking to make it
build so that it could be used to build the parts of the package I was
actually hacking.

23.4 Example: The Full Pull

Suppose instead that I wanted to fully autoconfiscate zip. Let's ignore for
now that zip can build on systems to which the GNU Autotools have not
been ported (TOPS-20, for example)—perhaps a big problem back in the
real world.

The first step should always be to run autoscan. autoscan is a program that
examines your source code and then generates a file called 'configure.scan',
which can be used as a rough draft of a 'configure.in'. autoscan is not perfect,
and in fact in some situations can generate a 'configure.scan' that autoconf
won't directly accept, so you should examine this file by hand before renaming
it to 'configure.in'.

autoscan doesn't take into account macro names used by your program. If autoscan decides to generate a check for '<fcntl.h>', for instance, it just generates ordinary autoconf code, which in turn might define 'HAVE_FCNTL_H' at configure time. This just means that autoscan is not a panacea—you will probably have to modify your source to take advantage of the code that autoscan generates.

Here is the 'configure.scan' I get when I run autoscan on zip:

```
dnl Process this file with autoconf to produce a configure script.
AC_INIT(bits.c)

dnl Checks for programs.
AC_PROG_AWK
AC_PROG_CC
AC_PROG_CPP
AC_PROG_INSTALL
AC_PROG_LN_S
AC_PROG_MAKE_SET

dnl Checks for libraries.
dnl Replace `main' with a function in -lx:
AC_CHECK_LIB(x, main)

dnl Checks for header files.
AC_HEADER_DIRENT
AC_HEADER_STDC
AC_CHECK_HEADERS(fcntl.h malloc.h sgtty.h strings.h sys/ioctl.h \
termio.h unistd.h)

dnl Checks for typedefs, structures, and compiler characteristics.
AC_C_CONST
AC_TYPE_SIZE_T
AC_STRUCT_ST_BLKSIZE
AC_STRUCT_ST_BLOCKS
AC_STRUCT_ST_RDEV
AC_STRUCT_TM

dnl Checks for library functions.
AC_PROG_GCC_TRADITIONAL
AC_FUNC_MEMCMP
AC_FUNC_MMAP
AC_FUNC_SETVBUF_REVERSED
AC_TYPE_SIGNAL
AC_FUNC_UTIME_NULL
AC_CHECK_FUNCS(getcwd mktime regcomp rmdir strstr)

AC_OUTPUT(acorn/makefile unix/Makefile Makefile atari/Makefile)
```

As you can see, this is not suitable for immediate use as 'configure.in'. For instance, it generates several 'Makefile's that we know we won't need. At this point, there are two ways to fix this file.

First, we must fix outright flaws in 'configure.scan', add checks for libraries, and the like. For instance, we might also add code to see whether we are building on Windows and set a variable appropriately:

```
AC_CANONICAL_HOST
case "$target" in
  *-cygwin* | *-mingw*)
    INCLUDES='-I$(srcdir)/win32'
    ;;
  *)
    # Assume Unix.
    INCLUDES='-I$(srcdir)/unix'
    ;;
esac
AC_SUBST(INCLUDES)
```

Second, we must make sure that the zip sources use the results we compute. So, for instance, we would check the zip source to see whether we should use 'HAVE_MMAP', which is the result of calling AC_FUNC_MMAP.

At this point, you might also consider using a configuration header such as is generated by AC_CONFIG_HEADER. Typically this involves editing all your source files to include the header, but in the long run this is probably a cleaner way to go than using many -D options on the command line. If you are making major source changes to fully adapt your code to autoconf's output, adding a '#include' to each file will not be difficult.

Editing the source can be quite difficult if done thoroughly, as it can involve radical changes. After this, you have a minimal but functional 'configure.in' and a knowledge of what portability information your program has already incorporated.

Next, you want to write your 'Makefile.am's. This might involve restructuring your package so that it can more easily conform to what Automake expects. This work might also involve source code changes if the program makes assumptions about the layout of the install tree—these assumptions might very well break if you follow the GNU rules about the install layout.

At the same time as you are writing your 'Makefile.am's, you might consider *libtoolizing* your package. This makes sense if you want to export shared libraries, or if you have libraries that several executables in your package use.

In our example, because no library is involved, we won't use Libtool. The 'Makefile.am' used in the minimal example is nearly sufficient for our use, but not quite. Here's how we change it to add dependency tracking and dist support:

```
## Process this file with automake to create Makefile.in.

bin_PROGRAMS = zip

if UNIX
bin_SCRIPTS = unix/zipgrep
os_sources = unix/unix.c
else
os_sources = win32/win32.c win32zip.c
endif
zip_SOURCES = zip.c zipfile.c zipup.c fileio.c util.c globals.c \
              crypt.c ttyio.c crc32.c crctab.c deflate.c trees.c \
              bits.c $(os_sources)

## It was easier to just list all the source files than to pick out the
## non-source files.
EXTRA_DIST = algorith.doc README TODO Where crc_i386.S bits.c crc32.c \
acorn/RunMe1st acorn/ReadMe acorn/acornzip.c acorn/makefile \
acorn/match.s acorn/osdep.h acorn/riscos.c acorn/riscos.h \
acorn/sendbits.s acorn/swiven.h acorn/swiven.s acorn/zipup.h crctab.c \
crypt.c crypt.h deflate.c ebcdic.h fileio.c globals.c history \
...
wizdll/wizdll.def wizdll/wizmain.c wizdll/wizzip.h wizdll/zipdll16.mak \
wizdll/zipdll32.mak
```

The extremely long 'EXTRA_DIST' macro here has be truncated for brevity, denoted by the '...' line.

Note that we no longer define INCLUDES; configure now automatically defines it. Note also that, because of a small technicality, this 'Makefile.am' won't really work with Automake 1.4. Instead, we must modify things so that we don't try to compile 'unix/unix.c' or other files from subdirectories.

24

Using GNU Autotools with Cygnus' Cygwin

The GNU Autotools enable users to build software packages on Windows. Because the tools were developed on Unix, it is easier to get them to work using Cygnus Solutions' Cygwin distribution, which provides a POSIX wrapper for the Win32 API (see Section 1.1, "The Diversity of Unix Systems"), but it is certainly possible to run the tools within other Windows environments, notably Colin Peters' *Mingw32* and D.J. Delorie's DJGPP. These development environments are freely available on the Internet on the Mingw32 home page (http://www.mingw.org) and DJGPP home page (http://www.delorie.com/djgpp/). Unlike Cygwin, these other environments are designed for developing with the Win32 API directly, and consequently they are not as useful for porting Unix projects to Windows or writing code that works on both Windows and Unix. (For more details, see Section 14.3, "Unix/Windows Portability.")

This chapter describes the process of using GNU Autotools with Cygwin, although some of this advice also applies to employing some of the other GNU-based Windows development environments.

> ### Which API?
>
> *Recent Cygwin ports of GCC and* binutils *can produce binaries that will run with the* 'cygwin1.dll' *emulation layer, or linked against* 'CRTDLL.DLL' *(the Windows native C RunTime Dynamic Link Library), depending on the needs of particular source code. Recent versions (since Cygwin-b20.1, I believe) of the* binutils *implement the PE-COFF binary format used by Windows. Therefore, by specifying the* '-mno-cygwin' *compiler option to the Cygwin compiler and using only the API from* 'CRTDLL.DLL', *you can build binaries that are independent of the* 'cygwin1.dll *DLL. Such binaries generally run faster, because they bypass the*

continues ▶

▶ *continued*

> *POSIX emulation and provide easier access to Windows-specific things such as drive letters. Source code designed to be compiled this way does not compile on Unix, however, because it is limited to the Win32 API provided by* 'CRTDLL.DLL'. ◆

This chapter teaches you how to install and use GNU Autotools *natively* under Windows using Cygnus Solutions' Cygwin environment, both to develop your own packages with the aid of Cygwin and to compile, install, and to a certain degree port other people's packages for use with Cygwin. As a Unix package developer, you will learn how to write your configury to be Windows friendly, and to be aware of certain Windows quirks that can affect the portability of packages that need to work on Windows in addition to your Unix development machine.

24.1 Preliminaries

As explained in Section 24.2, "Installing GNU Autotools on Cygwin," GNU Autotools requires several other tools to operate. Most Unices provide the majority, if not all, of these prerequisites by default. Windows, unfortunately, does not. Cygwin is better than most in this respect, and only a few extras are required. The latest net release of Cygwin (1.1.1 at the time of writing) has a packaging mechanism that downloads and installs various Unix tools that have been precompiled for the Cygwin environment by the Cygnus folks. To develop with GNU Autotools and Cygwin, you need to install all these packages to make sure you have all the necessary header files and compiler tools.

Bourne shell	Cygwin provides a port of *ash*, which is smaller and faster than bash, but sometimes rejects arcane Bourne shell scripts. If you can stand to sacrifice a little speed, it is worth copying the supplied bash.exe to '/bin/sh.exe' to forestall any such problems.
GNU M4	Cygwin provides a port of GNU M4.
GNU Make	At the time of writing, developers need GNU Make to perform dependency tracking (see Section 18.3, "Automatic Dependency Tracking"), although this is set to change in a future release of Automake. Cygwin version 1.1.1 comes with a port of GNU make-3.77, with which I have personally never had any problems. The received wisdom from users is to manually upgrade to the latest version, make-3.79 (see ftp://ftp.gnu.org/gnu/make/make-3.79.tar.gz), which compiles and installs from source without modifi-

	cation. Should you experience (or anticipate) any Make-related problems, you might try upgrading to this version or later.
GNU GCC	At the time of writing, GNU GCC is also needed by Automake to perform dependency tracking. Cygwin version 1.1.1 comes with a port of the latest GNU GCC compiler.
Perl	The current implementation of Automake (1.4) is written in perl4, although it is likely that perl5 will be needed for Automake 1.5. The very latest versions of Perl now compile out of the box on Cygwin, and you can get a precompiled package from http://cygutils.netpedia.net/, an excellent resource for other packages ported to Cygwin.

There are other pitfalls to installing a fully working Cygwin environment on your Windows machine, but these are beyond the scope of this chapter. Cygnus hosts a mailing list archive and an FAQ at http://sourceware.cygnus.com/cygwin/ to provide some level of support, and you should make these your first port of call in case the installation does not go according to plan.

24.2 Installing GNU Autotools on Cygwin

With all the previously described infrastructure in place, each of the GNU Autotools can be built natively and installed from source right out of the box. Take care with the installation directories, however, because there is no package management under Cygwin, and it is easy to let everything get thrown into a big pile in '/usr/local', which makes it relatively difficult to upgrade and remove packages.

Support for Cygwin has been in Autoconf for several years, as far back as version 2.0 (as best as I can tell). Building it has never been a problem as long as GNU M4 and a Bourne shell are available; the macros themselves offer this support. Of course, you must carefully design any Autoconf macros that you write and not make any assumptions about them being executed on Unix if the Cygwin compatibility is to remain. A binary package of Autoconf for Cygwin version 1.1.1 is available from the CygUtils Web site at http://cygutils.netpedia.net/V1.1/.

Automake joined the fray much later than the Cygwin support code was added to Autoconf, and has consequently always supported Cygwin. Until the last release of Cygwin, the stumbling block has always been finding (or building) a Cygwin-compatible Perl interpreter for Automake to use. Thanks to the work of Eric Fifer, Perl 5.6.0 builds right out of the box on Cygwin, removing this problem entirely. Ready-built packages of Perl and Automake are available from the CygUtils Web site.

Ian Lance Taylor of Cygnus Solutions wrote the initial Libtool support for
Windows, when Cygwin was at release b18 (see Section 1.6, "Microsoft
Windows"). More recent releases of Cygwin in general, and GCC in particular,
have much better facilities for building and linking with Windows DLLs, to the
extent that with a little perseverance it is possible to build DLLs with GCC
from C++ sources, and to have those DLLs interoperate with DLLs built with
Windows development environments. In time, automation of these facilities will
make their way into Libtool. The method that Libtool currently uses to build
DLLs works with Cygwin releases at least as far back as b18, and at least as far
forward as the version I am now using, Cygwin-1.1.1. The same code also
builds DLLs correctly with Mingw32. There are certainly simpler ways to
assemble a DLL, but Libtool aims to combine two goals that are somewhat in
contention with Windows' treatment of DLLs; Libtool is aiming for maximum
portability across the various flavors of DLL—using Windows build environments; not forgetting Libtool's raîson d'être, which is to abstract the many and
varied ways of building libraries on different targets behind a single unified
interface. To meet these two goals, Libtool must use only tools that exist across
the range of versions it supports, and must at the same time try to make DLLs
appear to have the same characteristics as a modern ELF shared library, such as
the shared libraries under GNU/Linux. This is no mean feat, and in fact Libtool
still has some way to go to be able to do this convincingly. It turns out that
Windows DLLs lack many, many features that packages developed on Unix are
likely to take for granted. Emulation of these missing features is making their
way into Libtool. Although support for DLLs is improving steadily with every
release, some severe technical problems with the Windows library architecture
will prevent Libtool from ever being able to build DLLs completely transparently. The details are extremely technical and beyond the scope of this book.

As noted in Section A.3, "Installing the Tools," things will work correctly only
if Autoconf, Automake, and Libtool are installed with the same '--prefix'
argument, because they all share a macro directory in '$prefix/share/aclocal'.

24.3 Writing a Cygwin-Friendly Package

One approach to using the Cygwin support, offered by GNU Autotools
in your own package, is to have an eye for having it compile nicely on
Unix and on Windows, or indeed, for tweaking the configuration of existing
packages that use GNU Autotools, but do not compile under Cygwin, or do
not behave quite right after compilation. You need to be aware of several
things to design a package to work seamlessly under Cygwin, and several

more if portability to DOS and (non-Cygwin) Windows is important too. Section 14.3.5, "Unix/Windows Issues," discussed many of these things.

This section expands on those issues with ways in which GNU Autotools can help deal with them.

If you need to build only executables and static libraries, Cygwin provides an environment close enough to Unix that any packages which ship with a relatively recent configuration will compile pretty much out of the box, except for a few peculiarities of Windows (which are discussed throughout the rest of this section). If you want to build a package that has not been maintained for a while, and that consequently uses an old Autoconf, it is usually just a matter of removing the generated files, rebootstrapping the package with the installed (up-to-date!) Autoconf, and rerunning the 'configure' script. On occasion, some tweaks will be needed in the 'configure.in' to satisfy the newer autoconf, but autoconf will almost always diagnose these for you while it is being run.

24.3.1 Text Versus Binary Modes

As discussed in Section 14.3.5, "Unix/Windows Issues," text and binary files differ on Windows. Lines in a Windows text file end in a carriage-return/line-feed pair, but a C program reading the file in text mode sees a single line feed.

Cygwin has several ways to hide this dichotomy, and the solution(s) you choose depend on how you plan to use your program. The following relative tradeoffs apply to each choice you make:

What Is Mounting

Before installing an operating system to your hard drive, you must first organize the disk into partitions. Under Windows, you might have only a single partition on the disk, which would be called 'C:'[1]. Provided that some media is present, Windows enables you to access the contents of any drive letter—that is, you can access 'A:' when there is a floppy disk in the drive, and 'F:' provided you divided your available drives into sufficient partitions for that letter to be in use. With Unix, things differ somewhat: Hard disks are still divided into partitions (typically several), but there is only a single file system mounted under the root directory. You can use the mount *command to hook a partition (or floppy drive, or CD-ROM, or so on) into a subdirectory of the root file system:*

```
$ mount /dev/fd0 /mnt/floppy
$ cd /mnt/floppy
```

---

[1] *Typically you would also have a floppy drive named* 'A:', *and a CD-ROM named* 'D:'.

Until the directory is unmounted, the contents of the floppy disk are available as part of the single Unix file system in the directory, `'/mnt/floppy'`. This is in contrast with Windows' multiple root directories, which can be accessed by changing the file system root—to access the contents of a floppy disk:

```
C:\WINDOWS\> A:
A:> DIR
...
```

Mounting

Cygwin has a mounting facility to allow Cygwin applications to see a single unified file system starting at the root directory, by mounting drive letters to subdirectories. When mounting a directory, you can set a flag to determine whether the files in that partition should be treated the same whether they are TEXT or BINARY mode files. Mounting a file system to treat TEXT files the same as BINARY files means that Cygwin programs can behave in the same way as they might on Unix and treat all files as equal. Mounting a file system to treat TEXT files properly causes Cygwin programs to translate between Windows CR-LF line-end sequences and Unix CR line endings, which plays havoc with file seeking, and many programs that make assumptions about the size of a char in a FILE stream. However `'binmode'` is the default method because it is the only way to interoperate between Windows binaries and Cygwin binaries. You can get a list of which drive letters are mounted to which directories, and the modes they are mounted with, by running the mount command without arguments:

```
BASH.EXE-2.04$ mount
Device              Directory        Type      flags
C:\cygwin           /                user      binmode
C:\cygwin\bin       /usr/bin         user      binmode
C:\cygwin\lib       /usr/lib         user      binmode
D:\home             /home            user      binmode
```

As you can see, the Cygwin mount command enables you to "mount" arbitrary Windows directories as well as simple drive letters into the single file system seen by Cygwin applications.

binmode

The CYGWIN environment variable holds a space-separated list of setup options that exert some minor control over the way the `'cygwin1.dll'` (or `'cygwinb19.dll'`) behaves. One such option is the `'binmode'` setting; if CYGWIN contains the `'binmode'` option, files opened through `'cygwin1.dll'` without an explicit text or binary mode default to binary mode, which is closest to how Unix behaves.

System calls

`'cygwin1.dll'`, GNU libc, and other modern C API implementations accept extra flags for fopen and open calls to determine in which mode a file is opened. On Unix it makes no difference, and sadly most Unix programmers are not aware of this subtlety; therefore, this tends to be the first thing that needs to be fixed when porting a Unix program to Cygwin. The best way to use these calls portably is to use the following macros with a package's `'configure.in'` to be sure that the extra arguments are available:

```
# _AB_AC_FUNC_FOPEN(b | t, USE_FOPEN_BINARY | USE_FOPEN_TEXT)
# — — — — — — — — — — — — — — — — — — — — — — — — — — —.
define([_AB_AC_FUNC_FOPEN],
[AC_CACHE_CHECK([whether fopen accepts "$1" mode], [ab_cv_func_fopen_$1],
[AC_TRY_RUN([[#include <stdio.h>
int
main ()
{
   FILE *fp = fopen ("conftest.bin", "w$1");
   fprintf (fp, "\n");
   fclose (fp);
   return 0;
}]],
            [ab_cv_func_fopen_$1=yes],
            [ab_cv_func_fopen_$1=no],
            [ab_cv_func_fopen_$1=no])])
if test x$ab_cv_func_fopen_$1 = xyes; then
  AC_DEFINE([$2], 1,
            [Define this if we can use the "$1" mode for fopen safely.])
fi[]dnl
])# _AB_AC_FUNC_FOPEN


# AB_AC_FUNC_FOPEN_BINARY
# — — — — — — — — — — —.
# Test whether fopen accepts a "" in the mode string for binary file
# opening.  This makes no difference on most unices, but some OSes
# convert every newline written to a file to two bytes (CR LF), and
# every CR LF read from a file is silently converted to a newline.
AC_DEFUN([AB_AC_FUNC_FOPEN_BINARY], [_AB_AC_FUNC_FOPEN(b, USE_FOPEN_BINARY)])


# AB_AC_FUNC_FOPEN_TEXT
# — — — — — — — — — —.
# Test whether open accepts a "t" in the mode string for text file
# opening.  This makes no difference on most unices, but other OSes
# use it to assert that every newline written to a file writes two
# bytes (CR LF), and every CR LF read from a file are silently
# converted to a newline.
AC_DEFUN([AB_AC_FUNC_FOPEN_TEXT],   [_AB_AC_FUNC_FOPEN(t, USE_FOPEN_TEXT)])



# _AB_AC_FUNC_OPEN(O_BINARY|O_TEXT)
# — — — — — — — — — — — — — — — —.
AC_DEFUN([_AB_AC_FUNC_OPEN],
[AC_CACHE_CHECK([whether fcntl.h defines $1], [ab_cv_header_fcntl_h_$1],
[AC_EGREP_CPP([$1],
              [[#include <sys/types.h>
#include <sys/stat.h>
#include <fcntl.h>
$1
]],
            [ab_cv_header_fcntl_h_$1=no],
            [ab_cv_header_fcntl_h_$1=yes])
```

```
    if test "x$ab_cv_header_fcntl_h_$1" = xno; then
      AC_EGREP_CPP([_$1],
                       [#include <sys/types.h>
#include <sys/stat.h>
#include <fcntl.h>
_$1
],
                       [ab_cv_header_fcntl_h_$1=0],
                       [ab_cv_header_fcntl_h_$1=_$1])
    fi])
    if test "x$ab_cv_header_fcntl_h_$1" != xyes; then
      AC_DEFINE_UNQUOTED([$1], [$ab_cv_header_fcntl_h_$1],
        [Define this to a usable value if the system provides none])
    fi[]dnl
])# _AB_AC_FUNC_OPEN


# AB_AC_FUNC_OPEN_BINARY
# – – – – – – – – – –
# Test whether open accepts O_BINARY in the mode string for binary
# file opening.  This makes no difference on most unices, but some
# OSes convert every newline written to a file to two bytes (CR LF),
# and every CR LF read from a file is silently converted to a newline.
#
AC_DEFUN([AB_AC_FUNC_OPEN_BINARY], [_AB_AC_FUNC_OPEN([O_BINARY])])


# AB_AC_FUNC_OPEN_TEXT
# – – – – – – – – – –
# Test whether open accepts O_TEXT in the mode string for text file
# opening.  This makes no difference on most unices, but other OSes
# use it to assert that every newline written to a file writes two
# bytes (CR LF), and every CR LF read from a file are silently
# converted to a newline.
#
AC_DEFUN([AB_AC_FUNC_OPEN_TEXT],   [_AB_AC_FUNC_OPEN([O_TEXT])])
```

Add the following preprocessor code to a common header file that will be included by any sources that use fopen calls:

```
#define fopen    rpl_fopen
```

Save the following function to a file, and link that into your program so that in combination with the preprocessor magic above, you can always specify text or binary mode to open and fopen, and let this code take care of removing the flags on machines that do not support them:

```
#if HAVE_CONFIG_H
#  include <config.h>
#endif
```

```
#include <stdio.h>

/* Use the system size_t if it has one, or fallback to config.h */
#if STDC_HEADERS || HAVE_STDDEF_H
#  include <stddef.h>
#endif
#if HAVE_SYS_TYPES_H
#  include <sys/types.h>
#endif

/* One of the following headers will have prototypes for malloc
   and free on most systems.  If not, we don't add explicit
   prototypes which may generate a compiler warning in some
   cases — explicit  prototypes would certainly cause
   compilation to fail with a type clash on some platforms. */
#if STDC_HEADERS || HAVE_STDLIB_H
#  include <stdlib.h>
#endif
#if HAVE_MEMORY_H
#  include <memory.h>
#endif

#if HAVE_STRING_H
#  include <string.h>
#else
#  if HAVE_STRINGS_H
#    include <strings.h>
#  endif /* !HAVE_STRINGS_H */
#endif /* !HAVE_STRING_H */

#if ! HAVE_STRCHR

/* BSD based systems have index() instead of strchr() */
#  if HAVE_INDEX
#    define strchr index
#  else /* ! HAVE_INDEX */

/* Very old C libraries have neither index() or strchr() */
#    define strchr rpl_strchr

static inline const char *strchr (const char *str, int ch);

static inline const char *
strchr (const char *str, int ch)
{
  const char *p = str;
  while (p && *p && *p != (char) ch)
    {
      ++p;
    }
```

```
    return (*p == (char) ch) ? p : 0;
}
#  endif /* HAVE_INDEX */

#endif /* HAVE_STRCHR */

/* BSD based systems have bcopy() instead of strcpy() */
#if ! HAVE_STRCPY
# define strcpy(dest, src)          bcopy(src, dest, strlen(src) + 1)
#endif

/* Very old C libraries have no strdup(). */
#if ! HAVE_STRDUP
# define strdup(str)                strcpy(malloc(strlen(str) + 1), str)
#endif

char*
rpl_fopen (const char *pathname, char *mode)
{
   .char *result = NULL;
    char *p = mode;

    /* Scan to the end of mode until we find 'b' or 't'. */
    while (*p && *p != 'b' && *p != 't')
      {
        ++p;
      }

    if (!*p)
      {
        fprintf(stderr,
            "*WARNING* rpl_fopen called without mode 'b' or 't'\n");
      }

#if USE_FOPEN_BINARY && USE_FOPEN_TEXT
    result = fopen(pathname, mode);
#else
    {
        char ignore[3]= "bt";
        char *newmode = strdup(mode);
        char *q       = newmode;

        p = newmode;

#  if ! USE_FOPEN_TEXT
        strcpy(ignore, "b")
#  endif
#  if ! USE_FOPEN_BINARY
        strcpy(ignore, "t")
#  endif

        /* Copy characters from mode to newmode missing out
            b and/or t. */
```

```
        while (*p)
          {
            while (strchr(ignore, *p))
              {
                ++p;
              }
            *q++ = *p++;
          }
        *q = '\0';

        result = fopen(pathname, newmode);

        free(newmode);
      }
#endif /* USE_FOPEN_BINARY && USE_FOPEN_TEXT */

    return result;
  }
```

The correct operation of the preceding file relies on several things having been checked by the 'configure' script, so you also need to confirm the presence of the following macros in your 'configure.in' before you use this code:

```
# configure.in — Process this file with autoconf to produce configure
AC_INIT(rpl_fopen.c)

AC_PROG_CC
AC_HEADER_STDC
AC_CHECK_HEADERS(string.h strings.h, break)
AC_CHECK_HEADERS(stdlib.h stddef.h sys/types.h memory.h)

AC_C_CONST
AC_TYPE_SIZE_T

AC_CHECK_FUNCS(strchr index strcpy strdup)
AB_AC_FUNC_FOPEN_BINARY
AB_AC_FUNC_FOPEN_TEXT
```

24.3.2 File System Limitations

We discussed some differences between Unix and Windows filesystems in Section 14.3.5, "Unix/Windows Issues." You learned about some of the differences between Unix and Windows filesystems. This section expands on that discussion, covering filename differences and separator and drive letter distinctions.

8.3 Filenames

As discussed earlier, DOS file systems have severe restrictions on possible filenames: They *must* follow an 8.3 format (see the section "DOS Filename Restrictions" in Chapter 14).

This is quite a severe limitation, and affects some of the inner workings of GNU Autotools in two ways. The first is handled automatically, in that if .libs isn't a legal directory name on the host system, Libtool and Automake use the directory _libs instead. The other is that the traditional 'config.h.in' file is not legal under this scheme, and it must be worked around with a little-known feature of Autoconf:

```
AC_CONFIG_HEADER(config.h:config.hin)
```

Separators and Drive Letters

As discussed earlier in the section "Windows Separators and Drive Letters" in Chapter 14, the Windows file systems use different delimiters for separating directories and path elements than their Unix cousins. This has an effect in three places:

the shell command line

Up until Cygwin b20.1, it was possible to refer to drive-letter-prefixed paths from the shell using the '//c/path/to/file' syntax to refer to the directory root at 'C:\path\to\file'. Unfortunately, the Windows kernel confused this with its own network share notation, causing the shell to pause for a short while to look for a machine named 'c' in its network neighborhood. Since release 1.0 of Cygwin, the '//c/path/to/file' notation now really does refer to a machine named 'c' from Cygwin as well as from Windows. To refer to drive-letter-rooted paths on the local machine from Cygwin, there is a new hybrid 'c:/path/to/file' notation. This notation also works in Cygwin b20, and is probably the system you should use.

On the other hand, using the new hybrid notation in shell scripts means that they won't run on old Cygwin releases. Shell code embedded in 'configure.in' scripts should test whether the hybrid notation works, and use an alternate macro to translate hybrid notation to the old style if necessary.

I must confess that from the command line I now use the longer '/cygdrive/c/path/to/file' notation, because tab-completion doesn't yet work for the newer hybrid notation. It is important to use the new notation in shell scripts; otherwise, they will fail on the latest releases of Cygwin.

shell scripts

For a shell script to work correctly on non-Cygwin development environments, it needs to be aware of and handle Windows path and directory separators and drive letters. The Libtool scripts use the following idiom:

```
case "$path" in
# Accept absolute paths.
[\\/]* | [A-Za-z]:[\\/]*)
```

```
# take care of absolute paths
insert some code here
;;
*)
# what is left must be a relative path
insert some code here
;;
esac
```

source code

When porting Unix software to Cygwin, this is much less of an issue because these differences are hidden beneath the emulation layer and by the mount command respectively; although I have found that GCC, for example, returns a mixed mode ' / ' and ' \' delimited include path that upsets Automake's dependency tracking on occasion.

Cygwin provides convenient functions to convert back and forth between the different notations, called here *POSIX* paths or path lists, and *WIN32 paths* or path lists:

int **posix_path_list_p** (const char *path)   Function
    Return '0', unless *path* is a ' / '- and ' : '-separated path list. The determination is rather simplistic, in that a string that contains a ' ; ' or begins with a single letter followed by a ' : ' causes the '0' return.

void **cygwin_win32_to posix_path_list**   Function
(const char *win32, char *posix)
    Converts the ' \ ' and ' ; ' delimiters in   *win32* into the equivalent ' / ' and ' : ' delimiters while copying into the buffer at address *posix*. This buffer must be preallocated before calling the function.

void **cygwin_conv_to full_posix_path**   Function
(const char *path, char *posix_path)
    If *path* is a, possibly relative, ' \ '-delimited path, the equivalent, absolute, '/'-delimited path is written to the buffer at address *posix_path*. This buffer must be preallocated before calling the function.

void **cygwin_posix_to win32_path_list**   Function
(const char *posix, char *win32)
    This function converts the ' / ' and ' : '   delimiters in *posix* into the equivalent ' \ ' and ' ; ' delimiters while copying into the buffer at address *win32*. This buffer must be preallocated before calling the function.

void **cygwin_conv_to win32_path** (const char   Function
*path, char *win32_path)
    If *path* is a ' / '-delimited path, the equivalent ' \ '-delimited path is written to the buffer at address *win32_path*. This buffer must be preallocated before calling the function.

void **cygwin_conv_to_full win32_path** (const char   Function
*path, char *win32_path)
    If *path* is a, possibly relative, ' / ' delimited path, the equivalent, absolute, ' \ '-delimited path is written to the buffer at address *win32_path*. This buffer must be preallocated before calling the function.

You can use these functions something like this:

```
void
display_canonical_path(const char *maybe_relative_or_win32)
{
    char buffer[MAX_PATH];
    cygwin_conv_to_full_posix_path(maybe_relative_or_win32,
                                   buffer);
    printf("canonical path for %s:  %s\n",
           maybe_relative_or_win32, buffer);
}
```

For your code to be fully portable, however, you cannot rely on these Cygwin functions, because they are not implemented on Unix, or even Mingw or DJGPP. Instead you should add the following to a shared header, and be careful to use it when processing and building paths and path lists:

```
#if defined __CYGWIN32__ && !defined __CYGWIN__
    /* For backwards compatibility with Cygwin b19 and
       earlier, we define __CYGWIN__ here, so that
       we can rely on checking just for that macro. */
#  define __CYGWIN__    __CYGWIN32__
#endif

#if defined _WIN32 && !defined __CYGWIN__
    /* Use Windows separators on all _WIN32 defining
       environments, except Cygwin. */
#  define DIR_SEPARATOR_CHAR        '\\'
#  define DIR_SEPARATOR_STR         "\\"
#  define PATH_SEPARATOR_CHAR       ';'
#  define PATH_SEPARATOR_STR        ";"
#endif
#ifndef DIR_SEPARATOR_CHAR
    /* Assume that not having this is an indicator that all
       are missing. */
#  define DIR_SEPARATOR_CHAR        '/'
#  define DIR_SEPARATOR_STR         "/"
#  define PATH_SEPARATOR_CHAR       ':'
#  define PATH_SEPARATOR_STR        ":"
#endif /* !DIR_SEPARATOR_CHAR */
```

With this in place, you can use the macros previously defined to write code that compiles and works just about anywhere:

```
char path[MAXBUFLEN];
snprintf(path, MAXBUFLEN, "%ctmp%c%s\n",
         DIR_SEPARATOR_CHAR, DIR_SEPARATOR_CHAR, foo);
file = fopen(path, "tw+");
```

24.3.3 Executable Filename Extensions

As noted in Section 24.5, "Package Installation," the fact that Windows requires that all program files be named with the extension '.exe' is the cause of several inconsistencies in package behavior between Windows and Unix.

Where Libtool is involved, for example, if a package builds an executable linked against an as-yet-uninstalled library, libtool puts the real executable in the '.libs' (or '_libs') subdirectory, and writes a shell script to the original destination of the executable (see Section 9.5, "Executing Uninstalled Binaries"), which ensures the runtime library search paths are adjusted to find the correct (uninstalled) libraries that it depends on. On Windows, only a PE-COFF executable is allowed to bear the '.exe' extension, so the wrapper script has to be named differently from the executable for which it is substituted. (That is, the script is only executed correctly by the operating system if it does *not* have an .exe extension.) The result of this confusion is that the 'Makefile' can't see some of the executables it builds with Libtool because the generated rules assume an '.exe' extension will be in evidence. This problem will be addressed in some future revision of Automake and Libtool. In the meantime, it is sometimes necessary to move the executables from the '.libs' directory to their install destination by hand. The continual rebuilding of wrapped executables at each invocation of make is another symptom of using wrapper scripts with a different name to the executable that they represent.

It is very important to correctly add the '.exe' extension to program filenames in your 'Makefile.am'; otherwise, many of the generated rules will not work correctly while they await a file without the '.exe' extension. Fortunately, Automake does this for you wherever it can tell that a file is a program—everything listed in 'bin_PROGRAMS', for example. Occasionally you will find cases in which there is no way for Automake to be sure of this, in which case you must be sure to add the '$(EXEEXT)' suffix. By structuring your 'Makefile.am' carefully, you can avoid this in the majority of cases:

```
TESTS = $(check_SCRIPTS) script-test bin1-test$(EXEEXT)
```

could be rewritten as:

```
check_PROGRAMS = bin1-test
TESTS = $(check_SCRIPTS) script-test $(check_PROGRAMS)
```

The value of 'EXEEXT' is always set correctly with respect to the host machine if you use Libtool in your project. If you don't use Libtool, you must manually call the Autoconf macro, 'AC_EXEEXT' in your 'configure.in', to make sure that it is initialized correctly. If you don't call this macro (either directly or implicitly with 'AC_PROG_LIBTOOL'), your project will almost certainly not build correctly on Cygwin.

24.4 DLLs with Libtool

Windows' DLLs are very different from their nearest equivalent on Unix: shared libraries. This makes Libtool's job of hiding both behind the same abstraction extremely difficult—it is not fully implemented at the time of writing. As a package author who wants to use DLLs on Windows with Libtool, you must construct your packages very carefully to enable them to build and link with DLLs in the same way that they build and link with shared libraries on Unix.

Some of the difficulties that must be addressed are as follows:

- At link time, a DLL effectively consists of two parts: the DLL itself, which contains the shared object code; and an import library, which consists of the stub[2] functions that are actually linked into the executable, at a rate of one stub per entry point. Unix has a run-time loader that links shared libraries into the main program as it is executed, so the shared library is but a single file.

- Pointer comparisons do not always work as expected when the pointers cross a DLL boundary, because you can be comparing the addresses of the stubs in the import library rather than the addresses of the actual objects in the DLL. GCC provides the __declspec extension to alleviate this problem a little.

- The search algorithm for the runtime library loader is very different from the algorithms typically used on Unix. Section 24.4.5, "Runtime Loading of DLLs," explains how to deal with this.

- All the symbols required by a DLL at runtime must be resolved at link time. With some creative use of import libraries, it is usually possible to work around this shortcoming; it is easy to forget this limitation, however, if you are developing on a modern system that has lazy symbol resolution. Be sure to keep it at the back of your mind if you intend to have your package portable to Windows.

---

[2] *In general, a stub function satisfies the linker's requirements to resolve an undefined symbol at link time, but has no functionality of its own. In this context, the stubs do have some boilerplate code to pass execution flow into the correct full function in the DLL.*

- Worst of all is that it is impossible to reference a non-pointer item imported from a DLL. In practice, when you think you have exported a data item from a DLL, you are actually exporting its address (in fact, the address of the address if you take the import library into consideration), and it is necessary to add an extra level of indirection to any non-pointers imported from a DLL to take this into account. The GNU GCC __declspec extension can handle this automatically too, at the expense of obfuscating your code a little.

Cygwin support in Libtool is very new, and is being developed very quickly, so newer versions generally improve vastly over their predecessors when it comes to Cygwin. Therefore, you should get the newest release you can. The rest of this section is correct with respect to Libtool version 1.3.5.

In some future version, Libtool might be able to work as transparently as Autoconf and Automake. For now, however, designing your packages as described in this chapter will help Libtool to help us have DLLs and Unix shared libraries from the same code base.

The bottom line here is that setting a package up to build and use modules and libraries as both DLLs *and* Unix shared libraries is not straightforward. The remainder of this section provides a recipe that I have used successfully in several projects, including the module loader for GNU m4 1.5, which works correctly with DLLs on Windows. Let's create *hello world* as a DLL, and an executable where the runtime loader loads the DLL.

24.4.1 DLL Support with GNU Autotools

Here are the contents of the three source files used as an example for the remainder of this chapter (for brevity, they are missing most of the special code one would normally use to maximize portability).

'hello.h' documents the interface to 'libhello.dll':

```
#ifndef HELLO_H
#define HELLO_H 1

extern int hello (const char *who);

#endif /* !HELLO_H */
```

'hello.c' is the implementation of 'libhello.dll':

```
#if HAVE_CONFIG_H
#  include <config.h>
#endif

#include <stdio.h>
```

```
#include "hello.h"

int
hello (const char *who)
{
    printf("Hello, %s!\n", who);
    return 0;
}
```

'main.c' is the source for the executable that uses 'libhello.dll':

```
#if HAVE_CONFIG_H
#  include <config.h>
#endif

#include "hello.h"

int
main (int argc, const char *const argv[])
{
    return hello("World");
}
```

24.4.2 A Makefile.am for DLLs

First of all, we *autoconfiscate*[3] the previous source files with a minimal setup:

'Makefile.am' is used to generate the 'Makefile.in' template for the 'configure' script:

```
## Process this file with automake to produce Makefile.in.

lib_LTLIBRARIES       = libhello.la
libhello_la_SOURCES   = hello.c
libhello_la_LDFLAGS   = -no-undefined -version-info 0:0:0

include_HEADERS       = hello.h

bin_PROGRAMS          = hello
hello_SOURCES         = main.c
hello_LDADD           = libhello.la
```

The new feature introduced in this file is the use of the '-no-undefined' flag in the libhello_la_LDFLAGS value. This flag is required for Windows DLL builds. It asserts to the linker that there are no undefined symbols in the 'libhello.la' target, which is one of the requirements for building a DLL outlined earlier. (See Section 10.2.1, "Creating Libtool Libraries with Automake.")

---

[3] *Some people prefer to use the term* autoconfuse—*if you should meet any, be sure to tell them about this book.*

For an explanation of the contents of the rest of this `Makefile.am`, refer Chapter 6, "Introducing GNU Automake."

24.4.3 A configure.in for DLLs

configure.in is used to generate the `configure` script:

```
# Process this file with autoconf to create configure.

AC_INIT(hello.h)
AM_CONFIG_HEADER(config.h:config.hin)
AM_INIT_AUTOMAKE(hello, 1.0)

AC_PROG_CC
AM_PROG_CC_STDC
AC_C_CONST
AM_PROG_LIBTOOL

AC_OUTPUT(Makefile)
```

The `AC_PROG_CC` and `AM_PROG_CC_STDC` macros in the preceding `configure.in` will conspire to find a suitable compiler for the C code in this example and to discover any extra switches required to put that compiler into an ANSI mode. I have used the const keyword in the sources, so I need to specify the `AC_C_CONST` macro, in case the compiler doesn't understand it, and finally I have specified the `AM_PROG_LIBTOOL` macro because I want the library to be built with Libtool.

To set the build environment up, you need to create the autogenerated files:

```
$ ls
Makefile.in    hello.c    main.c
configure.in   hello.h
$ aclocal
$ autoheader
$ libtoolize --force --copy
$ automake --foreign --add-missing --copy
automake: configure.in: installing ./install-sh
automake: configure.in: installing ./mkinstalldirs
automake: configure.in: installing ./missing
$ autoconf
$ ls
Makefile.am    config.hin    hello.c       ltmain.sh      stamp-h.in
Makefile.in    config.sub     hello.h       main.c
aclocal.m4     configure      install-sh    missing
config.guess   configure.in   ltconfig      mkinstalldirs
```

If you have already tried to build DLLs with Libtool, you have probably noticed that the first point of failure is during the configuration process. For example, running the new configure script you might see the following:

```
...
checking if libtool supports shared libraries... yes
checking if package supports dlls... no
checking whether to build shared libraries... no
...
```

libtool provides a macro, 'AC_LIBTOOL_WIN32_DLL', which must be added to a package's configure.in to communicate to the libtool machinery that the package supports DLLs. Without this macro, libtool never tries to build a DLL on Windows. Add this macro to configure.in before the 'AM_PROG_LIBTOOL' macro, and try again:

```
$ make
cd . && aclocal
cd . && automake --foreign Makefile
cd . && autoconf

...

checking if libtool supports shared libraries... yes
checking if package supports dlls... yes
checking whether to build shared libraries... yes

...

gcc -DHAVE_CONFIG_H -I. -I. -I. -g -O2 -Wp,-MD,.deps/hello.pp \
-c -DDLL_EXPORT -DPIC hello.c -o .libs/hello.lo
gcc -DHAVE_CONFIG_H -I. -I. -I. -g -O2 -Wp,-MD,.deps/hello.pp \
-c hello.c -o hello.o >/dev/null 2>&1
mv -f .libs/hello.lo hello.lo
...
gcc -g -O2 -o ./libs/hello main.o .libs/libimp-hello-0-0-0.a \
-Wl,--rpath -Wl,/usr/local/lib
creating hello
...
$ ./hello
Hello, World!
```

If you run this and watch the full output of the 'make' command, Libtool uses a rather contorted method of building DLLs, with several invocations each of dlltool and gcc. I have omitted these from the preceding example, because they really are very ugly, and in any case are almost incomprehensible to most people. To see it all in its full horror, you can always examine the output after running the commands yourself! In a future release of Cygwin, recent work on the bin-utils linker by D.J. Delorie will allow gcc to link DLLs in a single pass using the same syntax used on other systems to produce shared libraries. Libtool will adopt this method when it becomes available, deprecating the use of dlltool.

I have extracted the interesting lines from among the many calls to dlltool[4] and gcc generated by make in the shell log. The main thing to notice is that we have a 'hello' binary, which is executable and which gives the right result when we run it! From the preceding partial log, it certainly appears that it has built 'libhello' as a DLL and linked that into 'hello'; just to double-check, however, you can use ldd. (This shell script for Cygwin emulates the behavior of ldd on GNU/Linux, and is available online from http://www.oranda.demon.co.uk/dist/ldd.)

```
$ libtool --mode=execute ldd ./hello
lt-hello.exe    -> /tmp/.libs/lt-hello.exe
libhello-0-0-0.dll      -> /tmp/.libs/libhello-0-0-0.dll
cygwin1.dll     -> /usr/bin/cygwin1.dll
kernel32.dll    -> /WINNT/system32/kernel32.dll
ntdll.dll       -> /WINNT/system32/ntdll.dll
advapi32.dll    -> /WINNT/system32/advapi32.dll
user32.dll      -> /WINNT/system32/user32.dll
gdi32.dll       -> /WINNT/system32/gdi32.dll
rpcrt4.dll      -> /WINNT/system32/rpcrt4.dll
```

So now you know how to build and link a simple Windows DLL using GNU Autotools: You add '-no-undefined' to the Libtool library 'LDFLAGS', and include the 'AC_LIBTOOL_WIN32_DLL' macro in your 'configure.in'.

24.4.4 Handling Data Exports from DLLs

Unfortunately, things are not quite that simple in reality, except in the rare cases in which no data symbols are exported across a DLL boundary. If you look back at the example in Section 24.4.3, "A configure.in for DLLs," you will notice that the Libtool object, 'hello.lo', was built with the preprocessor macro 'DLL_EXPORT' defined. Libtool does this deliberately so that it is possible to distinguish between a static object build and a Libtool object build from within the source code.

Let's add a data export to the DLL source to illustrate.

You must change the 'hello.h' header quite significantly:

```
#ifndef HELLO_H
#define HELLO_H 1

#if HAVE_CONFIG_H
#  include <config.h>
#endif
```

---

[4] *Part of the Binutils port to Windows, and necessary to massage compiler objects into a working DLL.*

```
#ifdef _WIN32
#  ifdef DLL_EXPORT
#    define HELLO_SCOPE          __declspec(dllexport)
#  else
#    ifdef LIBHELLO_DLL_IMPORT
#      define HELLO_SCOPE        extern __declspec(dllimport)
#    endif
#  endif
#endif
#ifndef HELLO_SCOPE
#  define HELLO_SCOPE            extern
#endif

HELLO_SCOPE const char *greet;
extern int hello (const char *who);

#endif /* !HELLO_H */
```

The nasty block of preprocessor would need to be shared among all the source files that comprise the 'libhello.la' Libtool library, which in this example is just 'hello.c'. It needs to take care of five different cases:

Compiling 'hello.lo'	When compiling the Libtool object that will be included in the DLL, you need to tell the compiler which symbols are exported data so that it can perform the automatic extra dereference required to refer to that data from a program that uses this DLL. You need to flag the data with __declspec(dllexport). (For more information, see Section 24.4, "DLLs with Libtool.")
Compilation unit that will link with 'libhello-0-0-0.dll'	When compiling an object that will import data from the DLL, again you need to tell the compiler so that it can perform the extra dereference, except this time you use extern __declspec(dllimport). From the preprocessor block, notice that you need to define 'LIBHELLO_DLL_IMPORT' to get this define (described shortly).
Compiling 'hello.o'	When compiling the object for inclusion in the static archive, you must be careful to hide the __declspec() declarations from the compiler; otherwise, it will start dereferencing variables for you by mistake at runtime, and in all likelihood cause a segmentation fault. In this case, you want the compiler to see a simple extern declaration.

Compilation unit that will link with 'libhello.a'	Similarly, an object that references a data symbol that will be statically linked into the final binary from a static archive must not see any of the __declspec() code, and requires a simple extern.
Non-Windows host	It seems obvious, but you must also be careful not to contaminate the code when it is compiled on a machine that doesn't need to jump through the DLL hoops.

The changes to 'hello.c' do not differ from what is required on a Unix machine. I have declared the greet variable to enable the caller to override the default greeting:

```
#if HAVE_CONFIG_H
#  include <config.h>
#endif

#include <stdio.h>

#include "hello.h"

const char *greet = "Hello";

int
hello (const char *who)
{
    printf("%s, %s!\n", greet, who);
    return 0;
}
```

Again, because the DLL-specific changes have been encapsulated in the 'hello.h' file, enhancements to 'main.c' are unsurprising too:

```
#if HAVE_CONFIG_H
#  include <config.h>
#endif

#include "hello.h"

int
main (int argc, const char *const argv[])
{
    if (argc > 1)
      {
        greet = argv[1];
      }
    return hello("World");
}
```

The final thing to be aware of is to be careful about ensuring that
`'LIBHELLO_DLL_IMPORT'` is defined when you link an executable against the
`'libhello'` DLL, but not defined if you link it against the static archive. It is
impossible to automate this completely, particularly when the executable in
question is from another package and is using the installed `'hello.h'` header.
In that case, it is the responsibility of the author of that package to probe
the system with `configure` to decide whether it will be linking with the DLL
or the static archive, and defining `'LIBHELLO_DLL_IMPORT'` as appropriate.

Things are a little simpler when everything is under the control of a single
package, but even then it isn't quite possible to tell for sure whether Libtool
is going to build a DLL or only a static library. If some dependencies are
dropped for being static, Libtool may disregard `-no-undefined` (see Section
10.2.1, "Creating Libtool Libraries with Automake"). The following is one
possible solution:

1. Define a function in the library that invokes `'return 1'` from a DLL.
   Fortunately that's easy to accomplish thanks to `-DDLL_EXPORT` (in this
   case, by adding the following to `'hello.c'`):
   ```
   #if defined WIN32 && defined DLL_EXPORT
   char
   libhello_is_dll (void)
   {
     return 1;
   }
   #endif /* WIN32 && DLL_EXPORT */
   ```

2. Link a program with the library, and check whether it is a DLL by
   seeing whether the link succeeded.

3. To get cross builds to work, you must, in the same vein, test whether
   linking a program that calls `'libhello_is_dll'` succeeds to tell whether
   to define `'LIBHELLO_DLL_IMPORT'`.

As an example of building the `'hello'` binary, you can add the following code
to `'configure.in'`, just before the call to `'AC_OUTPUT'`:

```
# ----------------------------------------
# Win32 objects need to tell the header whether they will be linking
# with a dll or static archive in order that everything is imported
# to the object in the same way that it was exported from the
# archive (extern for static, __declspec(dllimport) for dlls)
# ----------------------------------------
LIBHELLO_DLL_IMPORT=
case "$host" in
```

```
*-*-cygwin* | *-*-mingw* )
  if test X"$enable_shared" = Xyes; then
    AC_TRY_LINK_FUNC([libhello_is_dll],
                    [LIBHELLO_DLL_IMPORT=-DLIBHELLO_DLL_IMPORT])
  fi
  ;;
esac
AC_SUBST(LIBHELLO_DLL_IMPORT)
```

You must also arrange for the flag to be passed while compiling any objects that will end up in a binary that links with the DLL. For this simple example, only 'main.c' is affected, and you can add the following rule to the end of 'Makefile.am':

```
main.o: main.c
        $(COMPILE) @LIBHELLO_DLL_IMPORT@ -c main.c
```

In a more realistic project, dozens of files would probably be involved, in which case it would probably be easier to move them all to a separate subdirectory and give them a 'Makefile.am' of their own, which could include the following:

```
CPPFLAGS       = @LIBHELLO_DLL_IMPORT@
```

Now, let's put all this into practice, and check that it works:

```
$ make
cd . && aclocal
cd . && automake --foreign Makefile
cd . && autoconf
...
checking for gcc option to produce PIC ... -DDLL_EXPORT
checking if gcc PIC flag  -DDLL_EXPORT works... yes
...
checking whether to build shared libraries... yes
...
gcc -DHAVE_CONFIG_H -I. -I. -I. -g -O2 -Wp,-MD,.deps/hello.pp \
-c  -DDLL_EXPORT -DPIC hello.c -o .libs/hello.lo
gcc -DHAVE_CONFIG_H -I. -I. -I. -g -O2 -Wp,-MD,.deps/hello.pp \
-c hello.c -o hello.o >/dev/null 2>&1
...
gcc -DHAVE_CONFIG_H -I. -I. -I.      -g -O2 -DLIBHELLO_DLL_IMPORT \
-c main.c
...
gcc -g -O2 -o ./libs/hello main.o .libs/libimp-hello-0-0-0.a \
-Wl,--rpath -Wl,/usr/local/lib
creating hello
...
$ ./hello
Hello, World!
$ ./hello Howdy
Howdy, World!
```

The recipe also works if you use only the static archives:

```
$ make clean
...
$ ./configure --disable-shared
...
checking whether to build shared libraries... no
...

$ make
...
gcc -DHAVE_CONFIG_H -I. -I. -I. -f -O2 -Wp,-MD,.deps/hello.pp \
-c hello.c -o hello.o
...
ar cru ./libs/libhello.a  hello.o
...
gcc -DHAVE_CONFIG_H -I. -I. -I.     -g -O2 -c main.c
...
gcc -g -O2 -o hello main.o ./.libs/libhello.a
$ ./hello
Hello, World!
$ ./hello "G'Day"
G'day, World!
```

To be certain that you are really testing a new statically linked executable, run
the following:

```
$ ldd ./hello
hello.exe        -> /tmp/hello.exe
cygwin1.dll      -> /usr/bin/cygwin1.dll
kernel32.dll     -> /WINNT/system32/kernel32.dll
ntdll.dll        -> /WINNT/system32/ntdll.dll
advapi32.dll     -> /WINNT/system32/advapi32.dll
user32.dll       -> /WINNT/system32/user32.dll
gdi32.dll        -> /WINNT/system32/gdi32.dll
rpcrt4.dll       -> /WINNT/system32/rpcrt4.dll
```

24.4.5 Runtime Loading of DLLs

DLLs built using the formula described in this chapter can be loaded at runtime
in at least three different ways:

- Using the Cygwin emulation of the POSIX `dlopen/dlclose/dlsym`
  API. Note, however, that the emulation is broken up until at least
  version b20.1, and `dlopen(NULL)` doesn't work at all.

- Using the Windows `LoadLibrary/FreeLibrary/GetProcAddress` API.

- Using `libltdl`, which is covered in more detail in Chapter 17, "Using
  GNU libltdl."

24.5 Package Installation

Having successfully built a GNU Autotools–managed package, a systems administrator will typically want to install the binaries, libraries, and headers of the package. The GNU standards dictate that this be done with the command `make install`, and indeed Automake always generates `'Makefile'`s, which work in this way.

Unfortunately, this `make install` command is often thwarted by the peculiarities of Windows' file system. Often after an apparently successful installation, the Windows installation conventions are not always satisfied; therefore, the installed package may not work, even though the uninstalled build is fully operational.

A couple of issues merit discussion:

Prior to release 1.1.0, the Cygwin `install` program did not understand the `'.exe'` file extension. Fixing it was only a matter of writing a shell script wrapper for the `install` binary. Even though the current release is well-behaved in this respect, `'.exe'` handling is still the cause of some complications. (For more information, see Section 24.3.3, "Executable Filename Extensions.")

If a package builds any DLLs with `libtool`, they are installed to `$prefix/lib` by default, because this is where shared libraries would be installed on Unix. Windows searches for DLLs at runtime using the user's executable search path (`$PATH`), which generally doesn't contain library paths. The first evidence you will see of this problem is when DLLs you have installed are not found by executables that depend on them. You have two ways to fix it: The installed DLLs can be moved by hand from their installation directory into the equivalent executable destination (from '/usr/local/lib' to '/usr/local/bin'), or better, you can extend your binary search path to include library directories. Adding the following to your `'.profile'` would be a good start:

```
PATH=$PATH:/usr/local/lib:/usr/lib:/lib
```

When you are comfortable with setting up your packages like this, they will be relatively well-behaved on Windows and Unix. Of course, you must also write portable code. (For more information, see Chapter 14.)

25

Cross-Compilation with GNU Autotools

When you build a program, it usually runs on the system on which you built it. If you compile a simple program, for example, you can immediately run it on the same machine.

This is normally how GNU Autotools are used as well. You run the 'configure' script on a particular machine, you run make on the same machine, and the resulting program also runs on the same machine. In some cases, however, it proves useful to build a program on one machine and run it on another.

One common example is a program that runs on an *embedded system*. An embedded system is a special-purpose computer, often part of a larger system, such as the computers found within modern automobiles. An embedded system often does not support a general programming environment, so there is no way to run a shell or a compiler on the embedded system. However, it is still necessary to write programs to run on the embedded system. These programs are built on a different machine, usually a general-purpose computer. The resulting programs cannot be run directly on the general-purpose computer. Instead, they are copied onto the embedded system and run there. (The discussion omits many details and possibilities of programming embedded systems, but this should be enough to understand the points relevant to GNU Autotools.) For more information, see a book such as *Programming Embedded Systems in C and C++* by Michael Barr (O'Reilly and Associates).

Another example of when it proves useful to build a program on one machine and run it on another is the case when one machine is much faster. It can sometimes be useful to use the faster machine as a compilation server, to build programs that are then copied to the slower machine and run there.

Building a program on one type of system which runs on a different type of system is called *cross-compiling*. Doing this requires a specially configured compiler, known as a *cross-compiler*. Similarly, we speak of cross-assemblers, cross-linkers, and so on. When it is necessary to explicitly distinguish the ordinary sort of compiler, whose output runs on the same type of system, from a cross-compiler, this discussion refers to the ordinary compiler as a *native compiler*. Although the debugger is not (strictly speaking) a compilation tool, it is meaningful to speak of a cross-debugger: a debugger used to debug code that runs on another system.

GNU Autotools support cross-compilation in two distinct, though related ways. First, GNU Autotools support configuring and building a cross-compiler or other cross-compilation tools. Second, GNU Autotools support building tools using a cross-compiler (sometimes called a *Canadian Cross*). The remainder of this chapter explains how to use GNU Autotools to perform these tasks.

If you are not interested in performing cross-compilation, you might want to skip this chapter. If you are developing 'configure' scripts, however, you should at least skim this chapter to get some hints as to how to write them so that it is possible to build your package using a cross-compiler. Even if your package is useless for an embedded system, it is possible that somebody with a very fast compilation server will want to use it to cross-compile your package.

25.1 Host and Target

This discussion first focuses on using GNU Autotools to build cross-compilation tools. For example, the information in this section explains how to configure and build GCC as a cross-compiler.

When building cross-compilation tools, two different systems are involved: the system on which the tools will run, and the system for which the tools will generate code. The system on which the tools will run is called the *host* system. The system for which the tools generate code is called the *target* system.

Suppose, for example, that you have a compiler that runs on a GNU/Linux system and generates ELF programs for a MIPS-based embedded system. In this case, the GNU/Linux system is the host, and the MIPS ELF system is the target. Such a compiler could be called a GNU/Linux–cross–MIPS ELF compiler, or, equivalently, an 'i386-linux-gnu' cross-'mips-elf' compiler.

You learned about the latter sort of names earlier in Section 2.4, "Configuration Names." Naturally, most programs are not cross-compilation tools. For those programs, it does not make sense to speak of a target. It makes sense only to speak of a target for programs such as the GNU compiler or the GNU binutils, which actually produce running code. For example, it does not make sense to speak of the target of a program such as make.

Most cross-compilation tools can also serve as native tools. For a native compilation tool, it is still meaningful to speak of a target. For a native tool, the target is the same as the host. For a GNU/Linux native compiler, for example, the host is GNU/Linux, and the target is also GNU/Linux.

25.2 Specifying the Target

By default, the 'configure' script assumes that the target is the same as the host. This is the more common case; when the target is the same as the host, for example, you get a native compiler rather than a cross-compiler.

If you want to build a cross-compilation tool, you must specify the target explicitly by using the '--target' option when you run 'configure' (see Chapter 2). The argument to '--target' is the configuration name of the system for which you want to generate code (see Section 2.4, "Configuration Names"). To build tools that generate code for a MIPS ELF–embedded system, for example, you use '--target mips-elf'.

25.3 Using the Target Type

A 'configure' script for a cross-compilation tool uses the '--target' option to control how it is built, so that the resulting program will produce programs that run on the appropriate system. This section explains how you can write your own configure scripts to support the '--target' option.

You must start by putting 'AC_CANONICAL_SYSTEM' in 'configure.in'. 'AC_CANONICAL_SYSTEM' looks for a '--target' option and canonicalizes it using the 'config.sub' shell script. (For more information about configuration names, canonicalizing them, and 'config.sub', see Section 2.4, "Configuration Names.") 'AC_CANONICAL_SYSTEM' also runs 'AC_CANONICAL_HOST' to get the host information.

The host and target type are recorded in the following shell variables:

'host'	The canonical configuration name of the host. This is usually determined by running the 'config.guess' shell script, although the user is permitted to override this by using an explicit '--host' option.
'target'	The canonical configuration name of the target.

`'host_alias'`	The argument to the `'--host'` option, if used. Otherwise, the same as the `'host'` variable.
`'target_alias'`	The argument to the `'--target'` option. If the user did not specify a `'--target'` option, this is the same as `'host_alias'`.
`'host_cpu'` `'host_vendor'` `'host_os'`	The first three parts of the canonical host configuration name.
`'target_cpu'` `'target_vendor'` `'target_os'`	The first three parts of the canonical target configuration name.

Note that if `'host'` and `'target'` are the same string, you can assume a native configuration. If they differ, you can assume a cross-configuration.

It is possible for `'host'` and `'target'` to represent the same system, but for the strings to not be identical. If `'config.guess'` returns `'sparc-sun-sunos4.1.4'`, for example, and somebody configures with `'--target sparc-sun-sunos4.1'`, the slight differences between the two versions of SunOS may be unimportant for your tool. In the general case, however, it can be quite difficult to determine whether the differences between two configuration names are significant. Therefore, by convention, if the user specifies a `'--target'` option without specifying a `'--host'` option, it is assumed that the user wants to configure a cross-compilation tool.

The `'target'` variable should not be handled in the same way as the `'target_alias'` variable. In general, whenever the user may actually see a string, `'target_alias'` should be used. This includes anything that may appear in the file system, such as a directory name or part of a tool name. It also includes any tool output, unless it is clearly labeled as the canonical target configuration name. This permits the user to use the `'--target'` option to specify how the tool will appear to the outside world. On the other hand, when checking for characteristics of the target system, `'target'` should be used. This is because a wide variety of `'--target'` options may map into the same canonical configuration name. You should not attempt to duplicate the canonicalization done by `'config.sub'` in your own code.

By convention, cross tools are installed with a prefix of the argument used with the `'--target'` option, also known as `'target_alias'`. If the user does not use the `'--target'` option, and therefore is building a native tool, no prefix is used. If gcc is configured with `'--target mips-elf'`, the installed binary is named `'mips-elf-gcc'`. If gcc is configured without a `'--target'` option, the installed binary is named `'gcc'`.

The Autoconf macro `AC_ARG_PROGRAM` handles the names of binaries for you. If you are using Automake, no more need be done; the programs are automatically installed with the correct prefixes. Otherwise, see the Autoconf documentation for `AC_ARG_PROGRAM`.

25.4 Building with a Cross-Compiler

You can build a program that uses GNU Autotools on one system and run it on a different type of system. In other words, you can build programs using a cross-compiler. This section explains what this means, how to build programs this way, and how to write your `configure` scripts to support it. Building a program on one system and running it on another is sometimes referred to as a *Canadian Cross*.[1]

25.4.1 Canadian Cross Example

Let's start with an example of a Canadian Cross, to make sure that the concepts are clear. Using a GNU/Linux system, you can build a program that will run on a Solaris system. You would use a GNU/Linux cross Solaris compiler to build the program. You could not run the resulting programs on your GNU/Linux system. After all, they are Solaris programs. Instead, you would have to copy the result over to a Solaris system before you could run it.

Naturally, you could just build the program on the Solaris system in the first place. However, perhaps the Solaris system is not available for some reason; perhaps you don't actually have one, but you want to build the tools for somebody else to use. Or perhaps your GNU/Linux system is much faster than your Solaris system.

A Canadian Cross build is most frequently used when building programs to run on a non-Unix system, such as DOS or Windows. It may be simpler to configure and build on a Unix system than to support the GNU Autotools on a non-Unix system.

25.4.2 Canadian Cross Concepts

When building a Canadian Cross, at least two different systems are involved: the system on which the tools are being built, and the system on which the tools will run. The system on which the tools are being built is called the *build* system. The system on which the tools will run is called the *host* system. If you

---

[1] *The name Canadian Cross comes from the most complex case, in which three different types of systems are used. At the time that these issues were being hashed out, Canada had three national political parties.*

are building a Solaris program on a GNU/Linux system, as in the preceding example, the build system would be GNU/Linux, and the host system would be Solaris.

Note that you read about the host system earlier in Section 25.1, "Host and Target." It is, of course, possible to build a cross-compiler using a Canadian Cross (that is, build a cross-compiler using a cross-compiler). In this case, the system for which the resulting cross-compiler generates code is the target system.

An example of building a cross-compiler using a Canadian Cross is building a Windows cross MIPS ELF compiler on a GNU/Linux system. In this case, the build system is GNU/Linux, the host system is Windows, and the target system is MIPS ELF.

25.4.3 Build Cross Host Tools

To configure a program for a Canadian Cross build, you must first build and install the set of cross tools you will use to build the program. These tools will be build cross host tools. That is, they will run on the build system, and will produce code that runs on the host system. It is easy to confuse the meaning of build and host here. Always remember that the build system is where you are doing the build, and the host system is where the resulting program will run. Therefore, you need a build cross host compiler.

In general, you must have a complete cross environment to do the build. This usually means a cross-compiler, cross-assembler, and so forth, as well as libraries and header files for the host system. Setting up a complete cross environment can be complex, and is beyond the scope of this book. You may be able to get more information from the 'crossgcc' mailing list and FAQ (http://www.objsw.com/CrossGCC/).

25.4.4 Build and Host Options

When you run 'configure' for a Canadian Cross, you must use both the '--build' and '--host' options. The '--build' option is used to specify the configuration name of the build system. This can usually be the result of running the 'config.guess' shell script; and when using a Unix shell, it is reasonable to use '--build=`config.guess`'. The '--host' option is used to specify the configuration name of the host system.

As explained earlier, 'config.guess' is used to set the default value for the '--host' option (see Section 25.3, "Using the Target Type"). You can now see that because 'config.guess' returns the type of system on which it is run, it really identifies the build system. Because the host system is usually the same as the build system (or, in other words, people do not normally build using a cross-compiler), it is reasonable to use the result of 'config.guess' as the default for the host system when the '--host' option is not used.

It might seem that if the '--host' option were used without the '--build' option that the 'configure' script could run 'config.guess' to determine the build system, and presume a Canadian Cross if the result of 'config.guess' differed from the '--host' option. For historical reasons, however, some 'configure' scripts are routinely run using an explicit '--host' option rather than using the default from 'config.guess'. As noted earlier, it is difficult or impossible to reliably compare configuration names (see Section 25.3, "Using the Target Type"). Therefore, by convention, if the '--host' option is used, but the '--build' option is not used, the build system defaults to the host system. (This convention may be changing in the Autoconf 2.5 release. Check the release notes.)

25.4.5 Canadian Cross Tools

You must explicitly specify the cross tools that you want to use to build the program. You do so by setting environment variables before running the 'configure' script. You must usually set at least the environment variables 'CC', 'AR', and 'RANLIB' to the cross tools that you want to use to build. For some programs, you must set additional cross tools as well, such as 'AS', 'LD', or 'NM'. You set these environment variables to the build cross host tools that you are going to use.

If you are building a Solaris program on a GNU/Linux system, and your GNU/Linux cross Solaris compiler were named 'solaris-gcc', for example, you set the environment variable 'CC' to 'solaris-gcc'.

25.4.6 Supporting Building with a Cross Compiler

If you want to make it possible to build a program that you are developing using a cross compiler, you must take some care when writing your 'configure.in' and make rules. Simple cases usually work correctly. It is not hard to write configure tests that fail when building with a cross-compiler, however, so some care is required to avoid this.

You should write your 'configure' scripts to support building with a cross-compiler if you can, because that permits others to build your program on a fast compilation server.

Supporting Building with a Cross-Compiler in 'configure' Scripts

In a 'configure.in' file, after calling 'AC_PROG_CC', you can find out whether the program is being built by a cross-compiler by examining the shell variable 'cross_compiling'. If the compiler is a cross-compiler, which means that this is a Canadian Cross, 'cross_compiling' is 'yes'. In a normal configuration, 'cross_compiling' is 'no'.

Generally you do not need to know the type of the build system in a 'configure' script. If you do need that information, however, you can get it by using the macro 'AC_CANONICAL_SYSTEM', the same macro used to determine the target system. This macro sets the variables 'build', 'build_alias', 'build_cpu', 'build_vendor', and 'build_os', which correspond to the similar 'target' and 'host' variables, except that they describe the build system (see Section 25.3, "Using the Target Type").

When writing tests in 'configure.in', you must remember that you want to test the host environment, not the build environment. Macros that use the compiler, such as 'AC_CHECK_FUNCS', test the host environment. That is because the tests are done by running the compiler, which is actually a build cross host compiler. If the compiler can find the function, the function is present in the host environment.

Tests such as 'test -f /dev/ptyp0', on the other hand, test the build environment. Remember that the 'configure' script is running on the build system, not the host system. If your 'configure' scripts examine files, those files are on the build system. Whatever you determine based on those files may or may not be the case on the host system.

Most Autoconf macros work correctly when building with a cross-compiler. The main exception is 'AC_TRY_RUN'. This macro tries to compile and run a test program. This fails when building with a cross-compiler, because the program is compiled for the host system, which means that it will not run on the build system.

The 'AC_TRY_RUN' macro provides an optional argument to tell the 'configure' script what to do when building with a cross-compiler. If that argument is not present, you receive a warning when you run autoconf:

```
warning: AC_TRY_RUN called without default to allow cross compiling
```

This tells you that the resulting 'configure' script will not work when building with a cross-compiler.

In some cases, although it may better to perform a test at configure time, it is also possible to perform the test at runtime. (For more information, see Section 22.3.2, "Testing System Features at Application Runtime.") In such a case, you can use the cross-compiling argument to 'AC_TRY_RUN' to tell your program that the test could not be performed at configure time.

A few other Autoconf macros do not work correctly when building with a cross-compiler: a partial list is 'AC_FUNC_GETPGRP', 'AC_FUNC_SETPGRP', 'AC_FUNC_SETVBUF_REVERSED', and 'AC_SYS_RESTARTABLE_SYSCALLS'.

The 'AC_CHECK_SIZEOF' macro is generally not very useful when building with a cross-compiler; it permits an optional argument indicating the default size, but there is no way to know what the correct default should be.

Supporting Building with a Cross-Compiler in Makefiles

The main cross-compiling issue in a 'Makefile' arises when you want to use a subsidiary program to generate code or data that you will then include in your real program. If you compile this subsidiary program using '$(CC)' in the usual way, you cannot run it. This is because '$(CC)' builds a program for the host system, but the program is being built on the build system. You must instead use a compiler for the build system rather than for the host system. This compiler is conventionally called '$(CC_FOR_BUILD)'.

A 'configure' script should usually permit the user to define 'CC_FOR_BUILD' explicitly in the environment. Your 'configure' script should help by selecting a reasonable default value. If the 'configure' script is not being run with a cross-compiler (that is, the 'cross_compiling' shell variable is 'no' after calling 'AC_PROG_CC'), the proper default for 'CC_FOR_BUILD' is just '$(CC)'. Otherwise, a reasonable default is just 'cc'.   .

Note that you should not include 'config.h' in a file you are compiling with '$(CC_FOR_BUILD)'. The 'configure' script builds 'config.h' with information for the host system. However, you are compiling the file using a compiler for the build system (a native compiler). Subsidiary programs are usually simple filters that do no user interaction, and it is often possible to write them in a highly portable fashion so that the absence of 'config.h' is not crucial.

The gcc 'Makefile.in' shows a complex situation in which certain files, such as 'rtl.c', must be compiled into both subsidiary programs run on the build system and into the final program. This approach may be of interest for advanced GNU Autotools hackers. Note that, at least in GCC 2.95, the build system compiler is rather confusingly called 'HOST_CC'.

Installing GNU Autotools

The GNU Autotools may already be installed at your site, particularly if you are using a GNU/Linux system. If you don't have these tools installed, or do not have the most recent versions, this appendix will help you install them.

A.1 Prerequisite Tools

The GNU Autotools make use of a few additional tools to get their jobs done. This makes it necessary to gather all the prerequisite tools to get started. Before installing GNU Autotools, you need to obtain and install these tools.

The GNU Autotools are all built around the assumption that the system has a relatively functional version of the Bourne shell. If your system is missing a Bourne shell, or if your shell behaves differently from most (as is the case with the Bourne shell provided with Ultrix), you might want to obtain and install GNU bash. The following section explains how you can obtain GNU packages.

> **Note**
>
> *If you are using a Windows system, the easiest way to obtain a Bourne shell and all the shell utilities that you will need is to download and install Cygnus Solutions' Cygwin product. You can locate further information about Cygwin at* http://www.cygnus.com/cygwin/. ◆

Autoconf requires GNU M4. Vendor-provided versions of M4 have proven to be troublesome, so Autoconf checks that GNU M4 is installed on your system. (Again, the following section details how to obtain GNU packages such as M4.) At the time of writing, the latest version is 1.4. Earlier versions of GNU M4 will work, but they may not be as efficient.

Automake requires Perl version 5 or greater. You should download and install a version of Perl for your platform that meets these requirements.

A.2 Downloading GNU Autotools

The GNU Autotools are distributed as part of the GNU project, under the terms of the GNU General Public License. Each tool is packaged in a compressed archive that you can retrieve from sources such as Internet FTP archives and CD-ROM distributions. Although you may use any source convenient to you, it is best to use one of the recognized GNU mirror sites. You can find a current list of mirror sites at `http://www.gnu.org/order/ftp.html`.

The directory layout of the GNU archives has recently been improved to make it easier to locate particular packages. The new scheme places package archive files under a subdirectory whose name reflects the base name of the package. For example, GNU Autoconf 2.13 can be found at:

```
/gnu/autoconf/autoconf-2.13.tar.gz
```

The filenames corresponding to the latest versions of GNU Autotools, at the time of writing, are:

```
autoconf-2.13.tar.gz
automake-1.4.tar.gz
libtool-1.3.5.tar.gz
```

These packages are stored as `tar` archives and compressed with the `gzip` compression utility. After you have obtained all these packages, you should unpack them using the following commands:

```
gunzip TOOL-VERSION.tar.gz
tar xfv TOOL-VERSION.tar
```

GNU `tar` archives are created with a directory name prefixed to all the files in the archive. This means that files are tidily unpacked into an appropriately named subdirectory, instead of being written all over your current working directory.

A.3 Installing the Tools

When installing GNU Autotools, it is a good idea to install the tools in the same location (for example, `'/usr/local'`). This allows the tools to discover each other's presence at installation time. The location shown in the following examples is the default, `'/usr/local'`, because this choice makes the tools available to all users on the system.

Installing Autoconf is usually a quick and simple exercise, because Autoconf itself uses `'configure'` to prepare itself for building and installation. You can install Automake and Libtool using the same steps as for Autoconf. (As a matter of personal preference, I like to create a separate build tree when configuring packages to keep the source tree free of derived files such as object files.) Applying what we know about invoking 'configure' (see Section 2.1, "Configuring"), we can now configure and build Autoconf. The 'configure' option you are likely to want to use is '--prefix'; so if you want to install the tools in another location, include this option on the command line. When operating in networked environments, you might find it desirable to install the package elsewhere.

```
$ mkdir ac-build && cd ac-build
$ ~/autoconf-2.13/configure
```

You will see 'configure' running its tests and producing a 'Makefile' in the build directory:

```
creating cache ./config.cache
checking for gm4... no
checking for gnum4... no
checking for m4... /usr/bin/m4
checking whether we are using GNU m4... yes
checking for mawk... no
checking for gawk... gawk
checking for perl... /usr/bin/perl
checking for a BSD compatible install... /usr/bin/install -c
updating cache ./config.cache
creating ./config.status
creating Makefile
creating testsuite/Makefile
```

To build Autoconf, type the following:

```
$ make all
```

Autoconf has no architecture-specific files to be compiled, so this process finishes quickly. To install files into '/usr/local', you might need to become the root user before installing.

```
# make install
```

Autoconf is now installed on your system.

B
Platforms

This table lists platforms and toolchains known to be supported by Libtool. Each row represents completion of the self-test suite shipped with the Libtool distribution on the platform named in that row.

A 'PLATFORMS' file is maintained in the Libtool source tree, updated whenever a Libtool user volunteers updated information, or when the Libtool team runs prerelease tests on the platforms to which they individually have access.

The table from the latest source tree at the time of writing follows:

Canonical host name	This is the configuration triplet returned by 'config.guess' on each system for which the test suite was executed. Where the developer who ran the tests considered it to be significant, versions of tools in the compiler toolchain are named below the configuration triplet.
Compiler	The compiler used for the tests.
Libtool release	The version number of the Libtool distribution most recently tested for the associated configuration triplet. The GNU Autotools all use an alpha version numbering system in which "odd" letters (a, c, e, g, and so on) represent many CVS snapshots between the "even" lettered (b, d, f, and so on) alpha release versions. After version 1.4, the CVS revision number of the 'ChangeLog' file is appended to odd-lettered CVS snapshots ('1.4a 1.641.2.54', for example).
Results	Either 'ok' if the Libtool test suite passed all tests, or optionally 'NS' if the test suite would pass only when the distribution was configured with the '--disable-shared' option.

```
------------------------------------------------
canonical host name      compiler  libtool  results
  (tools versions)                 release
------------------------------------------------
```

canonical host name (tools versions)	compiler	libtool release	results
alpha-dec-osf4.0* (egcs-1.1.2)	gcc	1.3b	ok
alpha-dec-osf4.0*	cc	1.3b	ok
alpha-dec-osf3.2	gcc	0.8	ok
alpha-dec-osf3.2	cc	0.8	ok
alpha-dec-osf2.1	gcc	1.2f	NS
alpha*-unknown-linux-gnu (egcs-1.1.2, GNU ld 2.9.1.0.23)	gcc	1.3b	ok
hppa2.0w-hp-hpux11.00	cc	1.2f	ok
hppa2.0-hp-hpux10.20	cc	1.3.2	ok
hppa1.1-hp-hpux10.20	gcc	1.2f	ok
hppa1.1-hp-hpux10.20	cc	1.2f	ok
hppa1.1-hp-hpux10.10	gcc	1.2f	ok
hppa1.1-hp-hpux10.10	cc	1.2f	ok
hppa1.1-hp-hpux9.07	gcc	1.2f	ok
hppa1.1-hp-hpux9.07	cc	1.2f	ok
hppa1.1-hp-hpux9.05	gcc	1.2f	ok
hppa1.1-hp-hpux9.05	cc	1.2f	ok
hppa1.1-hp-hpux9.01	gcc	1.2f	ok
hppa1.1-hp-hpux9.01	cc	1.2f	ok
i*86-*-beos	gcc	1.2f	ok
i*86-*-bsdi4.0.1 (gcc-2.7.2.1)	gcc	1.3c	ok
i*86-*-bsdi4.0	gcc	1.2f	ok
i*86-*-bsdi3.1	gcc	1.2e	NS
i*86-*-bsdi3.0	gcc	1.2e	NS
i*86-*-bsdi2.1	gcc	1.2e	NS
i*86-pc-cygwin (egcs-1.1 stock b20.1 compiler)	gcc	1.3b	NS
i*86-*-dguxR4.20MU01	gcc	1.2	ok
i*86-*-freebsdelf4.0 (egcs-1.1.2)	gcc	1.3c	ok
i*86-*-freebsdelf3.2 (gcc-2.7.2.1)	gcc	1.3c	ok
i*86-*-freebsdelf3.1 (gcc-2.7.2.1)	gcc	1.3c	ok
i*86-*-freebsdelf3.0	gcc	1.3c	ok
i*86-*-freebsd3.0	gcc	1.2e	ok
i*86-*-freebsd2.2.8 (gcc-2.7.2.1)	gcc	1.3c	ok
i*86-*-freebsd2.2.6 (egcs-1.1 & gcc-2.7.2.1, native ld)	gcc	1.3b	ok
i*86-*-freebsd2.1.5	gcc	0.5	ok
i*86-*-gnu	gcc	1.3c	ok (1.602)
i*86-*-netbsd1.4 (egcs-1.1.1)	gcc	1.3c	ok
i*86-*-netbsd1.3.3 (gcc-2.7.2.2+myc2)	gcc	1.3c	ok
i*86-*-netbsd1.3.2	gcc	1.2e	ok

```
i*86-*-netbsd1.3I              gcc      1.2e    ok
  (egcs 1.1?)
i*86-*-netbsd1.2               gcc      0.9g    ok
i*86-*-linux-gnu               gcc      1.3b    ok
  (egcs-1.1.2, GNU ld 2.9.1.0.23)
i*86-*-linux-gnulibc1          gcc      1.2f    ok
i*86-*-openbsd2.5              gcc      1.3c    ok
  (gcc-2.8.1)
i*86-*-openbsd2.4              gcc      1.3c    ok
  (gcc-2.8.1)
i*86-*-solaris2.7              gcc      1.3b    ok
  (egcs-1.1.2, native ld)
i*86-*-solaris2.6              gcc      1.2f    ok
i*86-*-solaris2.5.1            gcc      1.2f    ok
i*86-ncr-sysv4.3.03            gcc      1.2f    ok
i*86-ncr-sysv4.3.03            cc       1.2e    ok
  (cc -Hnocopyr)
i*86-pc-sco3.2v5.0.5           cc       1.3c    ok
i*86-pc-sco3.2v5.0.5           gcc      1.3c    ok
  (gcc 95q4c)
i*86-pc-sco3.2v5.0.5           gcc      1.3c    ok
  (egcs-1.1.2)
i*86-UnixWare7.1.0-sysv5       cc       1.3c    ok
i*86-UnixWare7.1.0-sysv5       gcc      1.3c    ok
  (egcs-1.1.1)
m68k-next-nextstep3            gcc      1.2f    NS
m68k-sun-sunos4.1.1            gcc      1.2f    NS
  (gcc-2.5.7)
m88k-dg-dguxR4.12TMU01         gcc      1.2     ok
m88k-motorola-sysv4            gcc      1.3     ok
  (egcs-1.1.2)
mips-sgi-irix6.5               gcc      1.2f    ok
  (gcc-2.8.1)
mips-sgi-irix6.4               gcc      1.2f    ok
mips-sgi-irix6.3               gcc      1.3b    ok
  (egcs-1.1.2, native ld)
mips-sgi-irix6.3               cc       1.3b    ok
  (cc 7.0)
mips-sgi-irix6.2               gcc      1.2f    ok
mips-sgi-irix6.2               cc       0.9     ok
mips-sgi-irix5.3               gcc      1.2f    ok
  (egcs-1.1.1)
mips-sgi-irix5.3               gcc      1.2f    NS
  (gcc-2.6.3)
mips-sgi-irix5.3               cc       0.8     ok
mips-sgi-irix5.2               gcc      1.3b    ok
  (egcs-1.1.2, native ld)
mips-sgi-irix5.2               cc       1.3b    ok
  (cc 3.18)
mipsel-unknown-openbsd2.1      gcc      1.0     ok
powerpc-ibm-aix4.3.1.0         gcc      1.2f    ok
  (egcs-1.1.1)
powerpc-ibm-aix4.2.1.0         gcc      1.2f    ok
  (egcs-1.1.1)
```

```
powerpc-ibm-aix4.1.5.0          gcc      1.2f     ok
  (egcs-1.1.1)
powerpc-ibm-aix4.1.5.0          gcc      1.2f     NS
  (gcc-2.8.1)
powerpc-ibm-aix4.1.4.0          gcc      1.0      ok
powerpc-ibm-aix4.1.4.0          xlc      1.0i     ok
rs6000-ibm-aix4.1.5.0           gcc      1.2f     ok
  (gcc-2.7.2)
rs6000-ibm-aix4.1.4.0           gcc      1.2f     ok
  (gcc-2.7.2)
rs6000-ibm-aix3.2.5             gcc      1.0i     ok
rs6000-ibm-aix3.2.5             xlc      1.0i     ok
sparc-sun-solaris2.7            gcc      1.3b     ok
  (egcs-1.1.2, GNU ld 2.9.1 & native ld)
sparc-sun-solaris2.6            gcc      1.3.2    ok
  (egcs-1.1.2, GNU ld 2.9.1 & native ld)
sparc-sun-solaris2.5.1          gcc      1.2f     ok
sparc-sun-solaris2.5            gcc      1.3b     ok
  (egcs-1.1.2, GNU ld 2.9.1 & native ld)
sparc-sun-solaris2.5            cc       1.3b     ok
  (SC 3.0.1)
sparc-sun-solaris2.4            gcc      1.0a     ok
sparc-sun-solaris2.4            cc       1.0a     ok
sparc-sun-solaris2.3            gcc      1.2f     ok
sparc-sun-sunos4.1.4            gcc      1.2f     ok
sparc-sun-sunos4.1.4            cc       1.0f     ok
sparc-sun-sunos4.1.3_U1         gcc      1.2f     ok
sparc-sun-sunos4.1.3C           gcc      1.2f     ok
sparc-sun-sunos4.1.3            gcc      1.3b     ok
  (egcs-1.1.2, GNU ld 2.9.1 & native ld)
sparc-sun-sunos4.1.3            cc       1.3b     ok
sparc-unknown-bsdi4.0           gcc      1.2c     ok
sparc-unknown-linux-gnulibc1    gcc      1.2f     ok
sparc-unknown-linux-gnu         gcc      1.3b     ok
  (egcs-1.1.2, GNU ld 2.9.1.0.23)
sparc64-unknown-linux-gnu       gcc      1.2f     ok
```

You too can contribute to this file, either if you use a platform missing from the table entirely, or if you are using a newer release of Libtool than the version listed in the table.

---

ok *means "all tests passed".*

NS *means "Not Shared", but OK for static libraries.*

From a freshly unpacked release, do the following:

```
$ cd libtool-1.4
$ ./configure
...

_ _ _ _ _ _ _ _ _ _ _ _ _ _ _ _ _ _ _ _ _ _ _ _ _ _ _ _ _ _ _.
Configuring libtool 1.4a (1.641.2.54 2000/06/18 03:02:52)
_ _ _ _ _ _ _ _ _ _ _ _ _ _ _ _ _ _ _ _ _ _ _ _ _ _ _ _ _ _ _.

...
checking host system type... i586-pc-linux-gnu
checking build system type... i586-pc-linux-gnu
...
$ make
...
$ make check
...
===================
All 76 tests passed
===================
...
```

If no test failures occur, and you see a message similar to the message above, send a short note to libtool@gnu.org stating what you did, the configuration triplet for your platform as reported for the 'host system' by configure (see the preceding example), and the precise version number of the release you have tested as reported by 'libtool --version':

```
$ pwd
/tmp/cvs/libtool
$ ./libtool --version
ltmain.sh (GNU libtool) 1.4a (1.641.2.41 2000/05/29 10:40:46)
```

The official 'PLATFORMS' file will be updated shortly thereafter.

C

Generated File Dependencies

These diagrams show the data flows associated with each of the tools you
might need to use when bootstrapping a project with GNU Autotools. A lot of
files are consumed and produced by these tools, and it is important that all the
required input files are present (and correct) at each stage—configure requires
'Makefile.in' and produces 'Makefile', for example. There are many of these
relationships, and these diagrams should help you to visualize the dependencies.
They will be invaluable while you learn your way around GNU Autotools, but
before long you will find that you need to refer to them rarely, if at all.

They do not show how the individual files are laid out in a project directory
tree, because some of them ('config.guess', for example) have no single place
at which they must appear, and others ('Makefile.am', for example) may be
present in several places, depending on how you want to structure your
project directories.

The key to the diagrams in this appendix follows:

- The boxes are the individual tools that comprise GNU Autotools.
- Where multiple interlinked boxes appear in a single diagram, this
  represents one tool itself running other helper programs. If a box is
  behind another box, it is a (group of) helper program(s) that may be
  automatically run by the boxes in front.
- Dotted arrows are for optional files, which may be a part of the process.
- Where an input arrow and output arrow are aligned horizontally, the
  output is created from the input by the process between the two.
- Words in parentheses, "()", are for deprecated files that are supported
  but no longer necessary.

Notice that in some cases a file output during one stage of the whole process
becomes the driver for a subsequent stage.

Each of the following diagrams represents the execution of one of the tools in GNU Autotools; they are presented in the order that we recommend you run them, although some stages may not be required for your project. You should not run `libtoolize` if your project doesn't use `libtool`, for example.

C.1 *aclocal*

The `aclocal` program creates the file `'aclocal.m4'` by combining stock-installed macros, user-defined macros, and the contents of `'acinclude.m4'` to define all the macros required by `'configure.in'` in a single file. `aclocal` was created as a fix for some missing functionality in Autoconf, and as such we consider it a wart. In due course, `aclocal` itself will disappear, and Autoconf will perform the same function unaided.

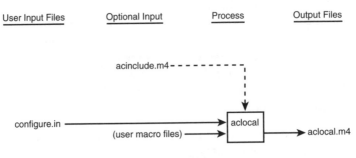

Figure C.1   *aclocal.*

C.2 *autoheader*

`autoheader` runs `m4` over `'configure.in'`, but with key macros defined differently from when `autoconf` is executed, such that suitable `cpp` definitions are output to `'config.h.in'`.

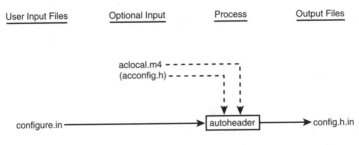

Figure C.2   *autoheader.*

C.3 *automake* and *libtoolize*

automake calls libtoolize to generate some extra files if the macro
'AC_PROG_LIBTOOL' is used in 'configure.in'. If it is not present, automake
installs 'config.guess' and 'config.sub' by itself. libtoolize can also be
run manually if desired; automake runs libtoolize automatically only if
'ltmain.sh' and 'ltconfig' are missing.

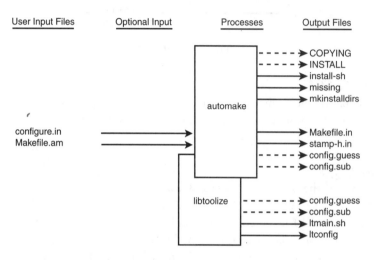

Figure C.3 *automake* and *libtoolize*.

'config.guess' *and* 'config.sub'

The versions of 'config.guess' *and* 'config.sub' *installed differ between
releases of Automake and Libtool, and might be different depending on whether*
libtoolize *is used to install them. Before releasing your own package, you
should get the latest versions of these files from* ftp://ftp.gnu.org/gnu/config,
in case there have been changes since releases of the GNU Autotools. ◆

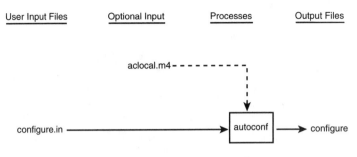

Figure C.4   *autoconf.*

C.4 *autoconf*

autoconf expands the m4 macros in 'configure.in', perhaps using macro definitions from 'aclocal.m4', to generate the configure script.

C.5 *configure*

The purpose of the preceding processes was to create the input files necessary for configure to run correctly. You would ship your project with the generated script and the files in columns, *other input* and *processes* (except 'config.cache'), but configure is designed to be run by the person installing your package. Naturally, you will run it too while you develop your project, but the files it produces are specific to your development machine, and are not shipped with your package—the person installing it later runs configure and generates *output files* specific to his or her own machine.

Running the configure script on the build host executes the various tests originally specified by the 'configure.in' file, and then creates another script, 'config.status'. This new script generates the 'config.h' header file from 'config.h.in', and 'Makefile's from the named 'Makefile.in's. After 'config.status' has been created, it can be executed by itself to regenerate files without rerunning all the tests. Additionally, if 'AC_PROG_LIBTOOL' was used, ltconfig is used to generate a libtool script.

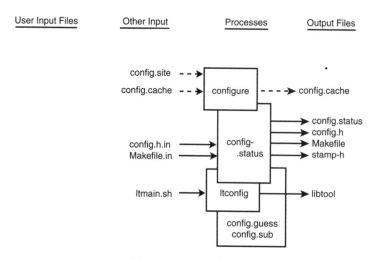

Figure C.5   *configure.*

C.6 *make*

The final tool to be run is make. Like configure, it is designed to execute on the build host. make uses the rules in the generated 'Makefile' to compile the project sources with the aid of various other scripts generated earlier on.

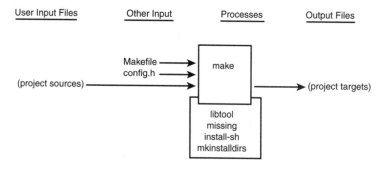

Figure C.6   *make.*

Autoconf Macro Reference

This is an alphabetic list of each Autoconf macro used in this book, along with a description of what each does. They are provided for your reference while reading this book. The descriptions are only brief; see the appropriate reference manual for a complete description.

`AC_ARG_ENABLE(feature, help-text, [if-given], [if-not-given])`	This macro allows the maintainer to specify additional package options accepted by 'configure'--for example, '--enable-zlib'. The action shell code may access any arguments to the option in the shell variable enableval. For example, '--enable-buffers=128' would cause 'configure' to set enableval to '128'.
`AC_ARG_PROGRAM`	This macro places a sed transformation program into the output variable program_transform_name that can be used to transform the filenames of installed programs. If the '--program-prefix', '--program-suffix' or '--program-transform-name' options are passed to 'configure', an appropriate transformation program will be generated. If no options are given, but the type of the host system differs from the type of the target system, program names are transformed by prefixing them with the type of the target (for example, arm-elf-gcc).
`AC_ARG_WITH(package, help-text, [if-given], [if-not-given])`	This macro allows the maintainer to specify additional packages that this package should work with (for example, a library to manipulate shadow passwords). The user indicates this preference by invoking 'configure' with an option such as '--with-shadow'. If an optional argument is given, this value is available to shell code in the shell variable withval.

AC_CACHE_CHECK
(*message*, *cache-variable*, *commands*)

This macro is a convenient front end to the AC_CACHE_VAL macro that takes care of printing messages to the user, including whether the result was found in the cache. It should be used in preference to AC_CACHE_VAL.

AC_CACHE_VAL
(*cache-variable*, *commands*)

This is a low-level macro that implements the Autoconf cache feature. If the named variable is set at runtime (for instance, if it was read from 'config.cache'), this macro does nothing. Otherwise, it runs the shell code in commands, which is assumed to set the cache variable.

AC_CANONICAL_HOST

This macro determines the type of the host system and sets the output variable 'host', as well as other more obscure variables.

AC_CANONICAL_SYSTEM

This macro determines the type of the build, host, and target systems and sets the output variables 'build', 'host', and 'target', among other more obscure variables.

AC_CHECK_FILE(*file*, [*if-found*], [*if-not-found*])

This macro tests for the existence of a file in the file system of the build system, and runs the appropriate shell code depending on whether the file is found.

AC_CHECK_FUNCS(*function-list*, [*if-found*], [*if-not-found*])

This looks for a series of functions. If the function quux is found, the C preprocessor macro HAVE_QUUX will be defined. In addition, if the *if-found* argument is given, it will be run (as shell code) when a function is found—this code can use the sh break command to prevent AC_CHECK_FUNCS from looking for the remaining functions in the list. The shell code in *if-not-found* is run if a function is not found.

AC_CHECK_HEADER(*header*, [*if-found*], [*if-not-found*])

This macro executes some specified shell code if a header file exists. If it is not present, alternative shell code is executed instead.

AC_CHECK_HEADERS(*header-list*, [*if-found*], [*if-not-found*])

This looks for a series of headers. If the header quux.h is found, the C preprocessor macro HAVE_QUUX_H will be defined. In addition, if the *if-found* argument is given, it will be run (as shell code) when a header is found—this code can use the sh break command to prevent AC_CHECK_HEADERS from looking for the remaining headers in the list. The shell code in *if-not-found* is run if a header is not found.

AC_CHECK_LIB(*library*, *function*, [*if-found*], [*if-not-found*], [*other-libraries*])	This looks for the named function in the named library specified by its base name. For instance, the math library, 'libm.a', would be named just 'm'. If the function is found in the library 'foo', the C pre-processor macro HAVE_LIBFOO is defined.
AC_CHECK_PROG (*variable*, *program-name*, *value-if-found*, [*value-if-not-found*], [*path*], [*reject*])	Checks to see whether the program named by *program-name* exists in the path *path*. If found, it sets the shell variable *variable* to the value *value-if-found*; if not, it uses the value *value-if-not-found*. If *variable* is already set at runtime, this macro does nothing.
AC_CHECK_SIZEOF(*type*, [*size-if-cross-compiling*])	This macro determines the size of C and C++ built-in types and defines SIZEOF_type to the size, where type is transformed—all characters to uppercase, spaces to underscores, and '*' to 'P'. If the type is unknown to the compiler, the size is set to 0. An optional argument specifies a default size when cross-compiling. The 'configure' script aborts with an error message if it tries to cross-compile without this default size.
AC_CONFIG_AUX_DIR(*directory*)	This macro allows an alternative directory to be specified for the location of auxil-iary scripts such as 'config.guess', 'config.sub', and 'install-sh'. By default, '$srcdir', '$srcdir/..', and '$srcdir/../..' are searched for these files.
AC_CONFIG_HEADER(*header-list*)	This indicates that you want to use a config header, as opposed to having all the C preprocessor macros defined via -D options in the DEFS 'Makefile' variable. Each header named in *header-list* is created at runtime by 'configure' (via AC_OUTPUT). There are a variety of optional features for use with config headers (different naming schemes and so forth); see the reference manual for more information.
AC_C_CONST	This macro defines the C preprocessor macro const to the string const if the C compiler supports the const keyword. Otherwise it is defined to be the empty string.
AC_C_INLINE	This macro tests whether the C compiler can accept the inline keyword. It defines the C preprocessor macro inline to be the keyword accepted by the compiler or the empty string if it is not accepted at all.

`AC_DEFINE(variable, [value], [description])`	This is used to define C preprocessor macros. The first argument is the name of the macro to define. The *value* argument, if given, is the value of the macro. The final argument can be used to avoid adding an '#undef' for the macro to 'acconfig.h'.
`AC_DEFINE_UNQUOTED(variable, [value], [description])`	This is like `AC_DEFINE`, but it handles the quoting of *value* differently. This macro is used when you want to compute the value instead of having it used verbatim.
`AC_DEFUN(name, body)`	This macro is used to define new macros. It is similar to M4's `define` macro, except that it performs additional internal functions.
`AC_DISABLE_FAST_INSTALL`	This macro can be used to disable Libtool's "fast install" feature.
`AC_DISABLE_SHARED`	This macro changes the default behavior of `AC_PROG_LIBTOOL` so that shared libraries will not be built by default. The user can still override this new default by using '--enable-shared'.
`AC_DISABLE_STATIC`	This macro changes the default behavior of `AC_PROG_LIBTOOL` so that static libraries will not be built by default. The user can still override this new default by using '--enable-static'.
`AC_EXEEXT`	Sets the output variable EXEEXT to the extension of executables produced by the compiler. It is usually set to the empty string on Unix systems and '.exe' on Windows.
`AC_FUNC_ALLOCA`	This macro defines the C preprocessor macro HAVE_ALLOCA if the various tests indicate that the C compiler has built-in alloca support. If there is an alloca.h header file, this macro defines HAVE_ALLOCA_H. If, instead, the alloca function is found in the standard C library, this macro defines C_ALLOCA and sets the output variable ALLOCA to alloca.o.
`AC_FUNC_GETPGRP`	This macro tests whether the getpgrp function takes a process ID as an argument. If it does not, the C preprocessor macro GETPGRP_VOID is defined.
`AC_FUNC_MEMCMP`	This macro tests for a working version of the memcmp function. If absent, or if it does not work correctly, 'memcmp.o' is added to the LIBOBJS output variable.

`AC_FUNC_MMAP`	Defines the C preprocessor macro `HAVE_MMAP` if the `mmap` function exists and works.
`AC_FUNC_SETVBUF_REVERSED`	On some systems, the order of the `mode` and `buf` arguments is reversed with respect to the ANSI C standard. If so, this macro defines the C preprocessor macro `SETVBUF_REVERSED`.
`AC_FUNC_UTIME_NULL`	Defines the C preprocessor macro `HAVE_UTIME_NULL` if a call to `utime` with a `NULL utimbuf` pointer sets the file's time stamp to the current time.
`AC_FUNC_VPRINTF`	Defines the C preprocessor macro `HAVE_VPRINTF` if the `vprintf` function is available. If not and the `_doprnt` function is available instead, this macro defines `HAVE_DOPRNT`.
`AC_HEADER_DIRENT`	This macro searches a number of specific header files for a declaration of the C type `DIR`. Depending on which header file the declaration is found in, this macro may define one of the C preprocessor macros `HAVE_DIRENT_H`, `HAVE_SYS_NDIR_H`, `HAVE_SYS_DIR_H`, or `HAVE_NDIR_H`. Refer to The Autoconf Manual for an example of how these macros should be used in your source code.
`AC_HEADER_STDC`	This macro defines the C preprocessor macro `STDC_HEADERS` if the system has the ANSI standard C header files. It determines this by testing for the existence of the `'stdlib.h'`, `'stdarg.h'`, `'string.h'`, and `'float.h'` header files and testing whether `'string.h'` declares `memchr`, `'stdlib.h'` declares `free`, and `'ctype.h'` macros such as `isdigit` work with 8-bit characters.
`AC_INIT(filename)`	This macro performs essential initialization for the generated `'configure'` script. An optional argument may provide the name of a file from the source directory to ensure that the directory has been specified correctly.
`AC_LIBTOOL_DLOPEN`	Call this macro before `AC_PROG_LIBTOOL` to indicate that your package wants to use Libtool's support for `dlopen`'ed modules.
`AC_LIBTOOL_WIN32_DLL`	Call this macro before `AC_PROG_LIBTOOL` to indicate that your package has been written to build DLLs on Windows. If this macro is not called, Libtool will build only static libraries on Windows.

`AC_LIB_LTDL`	This macro does the `configure`-time checks needed to cause `'ltdl.c'` to be compiled correctly. That is, this is used to enable dynamic loading via `libltdl`.
`AC_LINK_FILES(source-list, dest-list)`	Use this macro to create a set of links; if possible, symlinks are made. The two arguments are parallel lists: The first element of *dest-list* is the name of a to-be-created link whose target is the first element of *source-list*.
`AC_MSG_CHECKING(message)`	This macro outputs a message to the user in the usual style of `'configure'` scripts: leading with the word `'checking'` and ending in `'...'`. This message gives the user an indication that the `'configure'` script is still working. A subsequent invocation of `AC_MSG_RESULT` should be used to output the result of a test.
`AC_MSG_ERROR(message)`	This macro outputs an error message to standard error and aborts the `'configure'` script. It should be used only for fatal error conditions.
`AC_MSG_RESULT(message)`	This macro should be invoked after a corresponding invocation of `AC_MSG_CHECKING` with the result of a test. Often the result string can be as simple as `'yes'` or `'no'`.
`AC_MSG_WARN(message)`	This macro outputs a warning to standard error, but allows the `'configure'` script to continue. It should be used to notify the user of abnormal, but non-fatal, conditions.
`AC_OBJEXT`	Sets the output variable `OBJEXT` to the extension of object files produced by the compiler. Usually, it is set to `'.o'` on Unix systems and `'.obj'` on Windows.
`AC_OUTPUT(files, [extra-commands], [init-commands])`	This macro must be called at the end of every `'configure.in'`. It creates each file listed in *files*. For a given file, by default, `configure` reads the template file whose name is the name of the input file with `'.in'` appended—for instance, `'Makefile'` is generated from `'Makefile.in'`. This default can be overridden by using a special naming convention for the file. For each name `'foo'` given as an argument to `AC_SUBST`, `configure` will replace any occurrence of `'@foo@'` in the template file with the value of the shell variable `'foo'` in the generated file. This macro also generates the config header, if

	AC_CONFIG_HEADER was called, and any links, if AC_LINK_FILES was called. The additional arguments can be used to further tailor the output processing.
AC_OUTPUT_COMMANDS (extra-commands, [init-commands])	This macro works like the optional final arguments of AC_OUTPUT, except that it can be called more than once from 'configure.in'. (This makes it possible for macros to use this feature and yet remain modular.) See the reference manual for the precise definition of this macro.
AC_PROG_AWK	This macro searches for an awk program and sets the output variable AWK to be the best one it finds.
AC_PROG_CC	This checks for the C compiler to use and sets the shell variable CC to the value. If the GNU C compiler is being used, this sets the shell variable GCC to 'yes'. This macro sets the shell variable CFLAGS if it has not already been set. It also calls AC_SUBST on CC and CFLAGS.
AC_PROG_CC_STDC	This macro attempts to discover a necessary command-line option to have the C compiler accept ANSI C. If so, it adds the option to the CC. If it was not possible to get the C compiler to accept ANSI, the shell variable ac_cv_prog_cc_stdc will be set to 'no'.
AC_PROG_CPP	This macro sets the output variable CPP to a command that runs the C preprocessor. If '$CC -E' does not work, it will set the variable to '/lib/cpp'.
AC_PROG_CXX	This is like AC_PROG_CC, but it checks for the C++ compiler, and sets the variables CXX, GXX, and CXXFLAGS.
AC_PROG_GCC_TRADITIONAL	This macro determines whether GCC requires the '-traditional' option to compile code that uses ioctl and, if so, adds '-traditional' to the CC output variable. This condition is rarely encountered (mostly on old systems).
AC_PROG_INSTALL	This looks for an install program and sets the output variables INSTALL, INSTALL_DATA, INSTALL_PROGRAM, and INSTALL_SCRIPT. This macro assumes that if an install program cannot be found on the system, your package will have 'install-sh' available in the directory chosen by AC_CONFIG_AUX_DIR.

`AC_PROG_LEX`	This looks for a lex-like program and sets the 'Makefile' variable LEX to the result. It also sets LEXLIB to whatever might be needed to link against lex output.
`AC_PROG_LIBTOOL`	This macro is the primary way to integrate Libtool support into 'configure'. If you are using Libtool, you should call this macro in 'configure.in'. Among other things, it adds support for the '--enable-shared' configure flag.
`AC_PROG_LN_S`	This sets the 'Makefile' variable LN_S to 'ln -s' if symbolic links work in the current working directory. Otherwise it sets LN_S to just 'ln'.
`AC_PROG_MAKE_SET`	Some versions of make need to have the 'Makefile' variable MAKE set in 'Makefile' for recursive builds to work. This macro checks whether this is needed, and, if so, it sets the 'Makefile' variable SET_MAKE to the result. AM_INIT_AUTOMAKE calls this macro, so if you are using Automake, you don't need to call it or use SET_MAKE in 'Makefile.am'.
`AC_PROG_RANLIB`	This searches for the ranlib program. It sets the 'Makefile' variable RANLIB to the result. If ranlib is not found, or not needed on the system, the result is :.
`AC_PROG_YACC`	This searches for the yacc program—it tries bison, byacc, and yacc. It sets the 'Makefile' variable YACC to the result.
`AC_REPLACE_FUNCS(function list)`	This macro takes a single argument, which is a list of functions. For a given function 'func', 'configure' will do a link test to try to find it. If the function cannot be found, 'func.o' will be added to LIBOBJS. If the function can be found, 'configure' will define the C preprocessor symbol HAVE_FUNC.
`AC_REQUIRE(macro-name)`	This macro takes a single argument, which is the name of another macro. (Note that you must quote the argument correctly: AC_REQUIRE([FOO]) is correct, whereas AC_REQUIRE(FOO) is not.) If the named macro has already been invoked, AC_REQUIRE does nothing. Otherwise, it invokes the named macro with no arguments.
`AC_REVISION(revision)`	This macro takes a single argument, a version string. Autoconf will copy this string into the generated 'configure' file.

`AC_STRUCT_ST_BLKSIZE`	Defines the C preprocessor macro `HAVE_ST_BLKSIZE` if struct stat has an st_blksize member.
`AC_STRUCT_ST_BLOCKS`	Defines the C preprocessor macro `HAVE_ST_BLOCKS` if struct stat has an st_blocks member.
`AC_STRUCT_ST_RDEV`	Defines the C preprocessor macro `HAVE_ST_RDEV` if struct stat has an st_rdev member.
`AC_STRUCT_TM`	This macro looks for struct tm in 'time.h' and defines TM_IN_SYS_TIME if it is not found there.
`AC_SUBST(name)`	This macro takes a single argument, which is the name of a shell variable. When configure generates the files listed in AC_OUTPUT (for example, 'Makefile'), it substitutes the variable's value (at the end of the configure run—the value can be changed after AC_SUBST has been called) anywhere a string of the form '@VARNAME@' is seen.
`AC_TRY_COMPILE(includes, body, [if-ok], [if-not-ok])`	This macro is used to try to compile a given function, whose body is given in *body*. *includes* lists any '#include' statements needed to compile the function. If the code compiles correctly, the shell commands in *if-ok* are run; if not, *if-not-ok* is run. Note that this macro does not try to link the test program—it tries only to compile it.
`AC_TRY_LINK(includes, body, [if-found], [if-not-found])`	This is used like AC_TRY_COMPILE, but it tries to link the resulting program. The libraries and options in the LIBS shell variable are passed to the link.
`AC_TRY_RUN(program, [if-true], [if-false], [if-cross-compiling])`	This macro tries to compile and link the program whose text is in *program*. If the program compiles, links, and runs successfully, the shell code *if-true* is run. Otherwise, the shell code *if-false* is run. If the current configure is a cross-configure, the program is not run, and on a successful compile and link, the shell code *if-cross-compiling* is run.
`AC_TYPE_SIGNAL`	This macro defines the C preprocessor macro RETSIGTYPE to be the correct return type of signal handlers. For instance, it might be 'void' or 'int'.
`AC_TYPE_SIZE_T`	This macro looks for the type size_t. If not defined on the system, it defines it (as a macro) to be 'unsigned'.

`AM_CONDITIONAL(name, testcode)`

This Automake macro takes two arguments: the name of a conditional and a shell statement used to determine whether the conditional should be true or false. If the shell code returns a successful (0) status, the conditional will be true. Any conditional in your `'configure.in'` is automatically available for use in any `'Makefile.am'` in that project.

`AM_CONFIG_HEADER(header)`

This is just like `AC_CONFIG_HEADER`, but does some additional setup required by Automake. If you are using Automake, use this macro. Otherwise, use `AC_CONFIG_HEADER`.

`AM_INIT_AUTOMAKE(package, version, [nodefine])`

This macro is used to do all the standard initialization required by Automake. It has two required arguments: the package name and the version number. This macro sets and calls `AC_SUBST` on the shell variables `PACKAGE` and `VERSION`. By default it also defines these variables (via `AC_DEFINE_UNQUOTED`). However, this macro also accepts an optional third argument that, if not empty, means that the `AC_DEFINE_UNQUOTED` calls for `PACKAGE` and `VERSION` should be suppressed.

`AM_MAINTAINER_MODE`

This macro is used to enable a special Automake feature, maintainer mode, which we have documented elsewhere (see Section 4.3, "Maintaining Input Files").

`AM_PROG_CC_STDC`

This macro takes no arguments. It is used to try to get the C compiler to be ANSI-compatible. It does this by adding different options known to work with various system compilers. This macro is most typically used in conjunction with Automake when you want to use the automatic de-ANSI-fication feature.

`AM_PROG_LEX`

This is like `AC_PROG_LEX`, but it does some additional processing used by Automake-generated `'Makefile'`s. If you are using Automake, you should use this. Otherwise, you should use `AC_PROG_LEX` (and perhaps `AC_DECL_YYTEXT`, which `AM_PROG_LEX` calls).

`AM_WITH_DMALLOC`

This macro adds support for the `'--with-dmalloc'` flag to `configure`. If the user chooses to enable `dmalloc` support, this macro will define the preprocessor symbol `'WITH_DMALLOC'` and will add `'-ldmalloc'` to the `'Makefile'` variable `'LIBS'`.

E

Open Publication License

OPEN PUBLICATION LICENSE Draft v0.4, 8 June 1999

I. REQUIREMENTS ON BOTH UNMODIFIED AND MODIFIED VERSIONS

The Open Publication works may be reproduced and distributed in whole or in part, in any medium physical or electronic, provided that the terms of this license are adhered to, and that this license or an incorporation of it by reference (with any options elected by the author(s) and/or publisher) is displayed in the reproduction.

Proper form for an incorporation by reference is as follows:

> Copyright ©<year> by <author's name or designee>. This material may be distributed only subject to the terms and conditions set forth in the Open Publication License, vX.Y or later (the latest version is presently available at <http://www.opencontent.org/openpub/>).

The reference must be immediately followed with any options elected by the author(s) and/or publisher of the document (see section VI).

Commercial redistribution of Open Publication-licensed material is permitted.

Any publication in standard (paper) book form shall require the citation of the original publisher and author. The publisher and author's names shall appear on all outer surfaces of the book. On all outer surfaces of the book the original publisher's name shall be as large as the title of the work and cited as possessive with respect to the title.

II. COPYRIGHT

The copyright to each Open Publication is owned by its author(s) or designee.

III. SCOPE OF LICENSE

The following license terms apply to all Open Publication works, unless otherwise explicitly stated in the document.

Mere aggregation of Open Publication works or a portion of an Open Publication work with other works or programs on the same media shall not cause this license to apply to those other works. The aggregate work shall contain a notice specifying the inclusion of the Open Publication material and appropriate copyright notice.

SEVERABILITY. If any part of this license is found to be unenforceable in any jurisdiction, the remaining portions of the license remain in force.

NO WARRANTY. Open Publication works are licensed and provided "as is" without warranty of any kind, express or implied, including, but not limited to, the implied warranties of merchantability and fitness for a particular purpose or a warranty of non-infringement.

IV. REQUIREMENTS ON MODIFIED WORKS

All modified versions of documents covered by this license, including translations, anthologies, compilations and partial documents, must meet the following requirements:

1. The modified version must be labeled as such.
2. The person making the modifications must be identified and the modifications dated.
3. Acknowledgement of the original author and publisher if applicable must be retained according to normal academic citation practices.
4. The location of the original unmodified document must be identified.
5. The original author's (or authors') name(s) may not be used to assert or imply endorsement of the resulting document without the original author's (or authors') permission.

V. GOOD-PRACTICE RECOMMENDATIONS

In addition to the requirements of this license, it is requested from and strongly recommended of redistributors that:

1. If you are distributing Open Publication works on hardcopy or CD-ROM, you provide email notification to the authors of your intent to redistribute at least thirty days before your manuscript or media freeze, to give the authors time to provide updated documents. This notification should describe modifications, if any, made to the document.

2. All substantive modifications (including deletions) be either clearly marked up in the document or else described in an attachment to the document.

3. Finally, while it is not mandatory under this license, it is considered good form to offer a free copy of any hardcopy and CD-ROM expression of an Open Publication-licensed work to its author(s).

VI. LICENSE OPTIONS

The author(s) and/or publisher of an Open Publication-licensed document may elect certain options by appending language to the reference to or copy of the license. These options are considered part of the license instance and must be included with the license (or its incorporation by reference) in derived works.

A. To prohibit distribution of substantively modified versions without the explicit permission of the author(s). "Substantive modification" is defined as a change to the semantic content of the document, and excludes mere changes in format or typographical corrections. To accomplish this, add the phrase `Distribution of substantively modified versions of this document is prohibited without the explicit permission of the copyright holder.' to the license reference or copy.

B. To prohibit any publication of this work or derivative works in whole or in part in standard (paper) book form for commercial purposes is prohibited unless prior permission is obtained from the copyright holder.

To accomplish this, add the phrase "Distribution of the work or derivative of the work in any standard (paper) book form is prohibited unless prior permission is obtained from the copyright holder." to the license reference or copy.

OPEN PUBLICATION POLICY APPENDIX
(This is not considered part of the license.)

Open Publication works are available in source format via the Open Publication home page at http://www.opencontent.org.

Open Publication authors who want to include their own license on Open Publication works may do so, as long as their terms are not more restrictive than the Open Publication license.

If you have questions about the Open Publication License, please contact David Wiley, and/or the Open Publication Authors' List at opal@opencontent.org, via email.

To **subscribe** to the Open Publication Authors' List:
Send E-mail to opal-request@opencontent.org with the word "subscribe" in the body.

To **post** to the Open Publication Authors' List:
Send E-mail to opal@opencontent.org or simply reply to a previous post.

To **unsubscribe** from the Open Publication Authors' List:
Send E-mail to opal-request@opencontent.org with the word "unsubscribe" in the body.

Index

Symbols

A

B

C

M

Advanced Information on Networking & Developer Technologies

New Riders Books Offer Advice and Experience

LANDMARK

We know how important it is to have access to detailed, solution-oriented information on core technologies. *Landmark Series* books contain the essential information you need to solve technical problems. Written by experts and subjected to rigorous peer and technical reviews, our *Landmark* books are hard-core resources for practitioners like you.

ESSENTIAL REFERENCE

The *Essential Reference* series from New Riders provides answers when you know what you want to do but need to know how to do it. Each title skips extraneous material and assumes a strong base of knowledge. These are indispensable books for the practitioner who wants to find specific features of a technology quickly. Avoiding fluff and basic material, these books present solutions in an innovative, clean format—and at a great value.

CERTIFICATION

New Riders offers a complete line of test preparation materials to help you achieve your certification. With books like the *Training Guide* and software like the revolutionary *ExamGear*, New Riders offers comprehensive products built by experienced professionals who have passed the exams and instructed hundreds of candidates.

Open Source Books for Professionals

MySQL
By Paul DuBois
1st Edition
800 pages, $49.99
ISBN: 0-7357-0921-1

MySQL teaches readers how to use the tools provided by the MySQL distribution, covering installation, setup, daily use, security, optimization, maintenance, and troubleshooting. It also discusses important third-party tools, such as the Perl DBI and Apache/PHP interfaces that provide access to MySQL.

Web Application Development with PHP 4.0
By Till Gerken, et al.
1st Edition
416 pages, $39.99
ISBN: 0-7357-0997-1

Web Application Development with PHP 4.0 explains PHP's advanced syntax including classes, recursive functions, and variables. The authors present software development methodologies and coding conventions, which are a must-know for industry quality products and make software development faster and more productive. Included is coverage on Web applications and insight into user and session management, e-commerce systems, XML applications, and WDDX.

PHP Functions Essential Reference
By Landon Bradshaw, Till Gerken, Graeme Merrall, and Tobias Ratschiller
1st Edition
500 pages, $35.00
ISBN: 0-7357-0970-X
April 2001

This carefully crafted title covers the latest developments through PHP 4.0, including coverage of Zend. These authors share their knowledge not only of the development of PHP, but also how they use it daily to create dynamic Web sites. Covered as well is instruction on using PHP alongside MySQL.

Python Essential Reference
By David Beazley
1st Edition
352 pages, $34.95
ISBN: 0-7357-0901-7

Avoiding the dry and academic approach, the goal of *Python Essential Reference* is to concisely describe the Python programming language and its large library of standard modules, collectively known as the Python programming environment. This informative reference covers Python's lexical conventions, datatypes, control flow, functions, statements, classes, and execution model—a truly essential reference for any Python programmer!

Linux System Administration

By M Carling, James T. Dennis, and Stephen Degler
1st Edition
368 pages, $29.99
ISBN: 1-56205-934-3

Today's overworked sysadmins are looking for ways to keep their networks running smoothly and achieve enhanced performance. Users are always looking for more storage, more services, and more Speed. *Linux System Administration* guides the reader through the many intricacies of maintaining a secure, stable system.

Linux Firewalls

By Robert Ziegler
1st Edition
496 pages, $39.99
ISBN: 0-7357-0900-9

This book details security steps that a small, non-enterprise business user might take to protect his system. These steps include packet-level firewall filtering, IP masquerading, proxies, tcp wrappers, system integrity checking, and system security monitoring with an overall emphasis on filtering and protection. The goal of *Linux Firewalls* is to help people get their Internet security measures in place quickly, without the need to become experts in security or firewalls.

Linux Essential Reference

By Ed Petron
1st Edition
368 pages, $24.95
ISBN: 0-7357-0852-5

This title is all about getting things done by providing structured organization to the plethora of available Linux information. Providing clear and concise instructions on how to perform important administration and management tasks, as well as how to use some of the more powerful commands and more advanced topics, the scope of *Linux Essential Reference* includes the best way to implement the most frequently used commands, manage shell scripting, administer your own system, and utilize effective security.

UnixWare 7 System Administration

By Gene Henriksen and Melissa Henriksen
1st Edition
560 pages, $40.00
ISBN: 1-57870-080-9

In great technical detail, this title presents the latest version of SCO UnixWare and is the definitive operating system resource for SCO engineers and administrators. SCO troubleshooting notes and tips are integrated throughout the text, as are tips specifically designed for those who are familiar with other UNIX variants.

Developing Linux Applications with GTK+ and GDK
By Eric Harlow
1st Edition
512 pages, $34.99
ISBN: 0-7357-0021-4

This handbook is for developers who are moving to the Linux platform, and those using the GTK+ library, including Glib and GDK using C. All the applications and code the author developed for this book have been released under the GPL.

GTK+/Gnome Application Development
By Havoc Pennington
1st Edition
528 pages, $39.99
ISBN: 0-7357-0078-8

More than one million Linux users are also application developers. *GTK+/Gnome Application Development* provides the experienced programmer with the knowledge to develop X Windows applications with the popular GTK+ toolkit. It contains reference information for more experienced users who are already familiar with usage, but require function prototypes and detailed descriptions.

KDE Application Development
By Uwe Thiem
1st Edition
190 pages, $39.99
ISBN: 1-57870-201-1

KDE Application Development offers a head start on KDE and Qt. The book covers the essential widgets available in KDE and Qt, and offers a strong start without the "first try" annoyances which sometimes make strong developers and programmers give up.

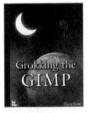

Grokking the GIMP
By Carey Bunks
1st Edition
342 pages, $45.00
ISBN: 0-7357-0924-6

Grokking the GIMP is a technical reference that covers the intricacies of the GIMP's functionality. The material gives the reader the ability to get up to speed quickly and start creating great graphics using the GIMP. Included as a bonus are step-by-step cookbook features that can be used for advanced effects.

GIMP Essential Reference
By Alex Harford
1st Edition
400 pages, $24.95
ISBN: 0-7357-0911-4

As the use of the Linux OS gains steam, so does the use of the GIMP. Many Photoshop users are starting to use the GIMP, recognized for its power and versatility. Taking this into consideration, GIMP Essential Reference has shortcuts exclusively for Photoshop users and puts the power of this program into the palm of the reader's hand.

Solaris System Administrator's Guide
By Janice Winsor
2nd Edition
324 pages, $34.99
ISBN: 1-57870-040-X

Designed to work as both a practical tutorial and quick reference, this book provides UNIX administrators complete, detailed descriptions of the most frequently performed tasks for Solaris. Learn how to employ the features of Solaris to meet these needs of your users, and get tips on how to make administration easier.

Solaris Advanced System Administrator's Guide
By Janice Winsor
2nd Edition
587 pages, $39.99
ISBN: 1-57870-039-6

This officially authorized tutorial provides indispensable tips, advice, and quick-reference tables to help you add system components, improve service access, and automate routine tasks. This book also includes updated information on Solaris 2.6 topics.

Solaris Essential Reference
By John Mulligan
1st Edition
304 pages, $24.95
ISBN: 0-7357-0023-0

A great companion to the solarisguide.com website, *Solaris Essential Reference* assumes readers are well-versed in general UNIX skills and simply need some pointers on how to get the most out of Solaris. This book provides clear and concise instructions on how to perform important administration and management tasks.

Networking

Cisco Router Configuration & Troubleshooting
By Mark Tripod
2nd Edition
330 pages, $39.99
ISBN: 0-7357-0999-8

A reference for the network and system administrator who finds himself having to configure and maintain existing Cisco routers, as well as get new hardware up and running. By providing advice and preferred practices, instead of just rehashing Cisco documentation, this book gives networking professionals information they can start using today.

Understanding the Network: A Practical Guide to Internetworking
By Michael Martin
1st Edition
690 pages, $39.99
ISBN: 0-7357-0977-7

Understanding the Network addresses the audience in practical terminology, and describes the most essential information and tools required to build high-availability networks in a step-by-step implementation format. Each chapter could be read as a standalone, but the book builds progressively toward a summary of the essential concepts needed to put together a wide-area network.

Understanding Directory Services
By Beth Sheresh and Doug Sheresh
1st Edition
390 pages, $39.99
ISBN: 0-7357-0910-6

Understanding Directory Services provides the reader with a thorough knowledge of the fundamentals of directory services: what Directory Services are, how they are designed, and what functionality they can provide to an IT infrastructure. This book provides a framework to the exploding market of directory services by placing the technology in context and helping people understand what directories can, and can't, do for their networks.

Understanding Data Communications
By Gilbert Held
6th Edition
620 pages, $39.99
ISBN: 0-7357-0036-2

Gil Held's book is ideal for those who want to get up to speed on technological advances as well as those who want a primer on networking concepts. This book is intended to explain how data communications actually work. It contains updated coverage on hot topics like thin client technology, x2 and 56Kbps modems, voice digitization, and wireless data transmission. Whatever your needs, this title puts perspective and expertise in your hands.

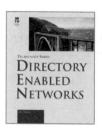

Directory Enabled Networks

By John Strassner
1st Edition
752 pages, $50.00
ISBN: 1-57870-140-6

Directory Enabled Networks is a comprehensive resource on the design and use of DEN. This book provides practical examples side-by-side with a detailed introduction to the theory of building a new class of network-enabled applications that will solve networking problems. DEN is a critical tool for network architects, administrators, and application developers.

Quality of Service in IP Networks

By Grenville Armitage
1st Edition
310 pages, $50.00
ISBN: 1-57870-189-9

Quality of Service in IP Networks presents a clear understanding of the architectural issues surrounding delivering QoS in an IP network, and positions the emerging technologies within a framework of solutions. The motivation for QoS is explained with reference to emerging real-time applications, such as Voice/Video over IP, VPN services, and supporting Service Level Agreements.

Differentiated Services for the Internet

By Kalevi Kilkki
1st Edition
400 pages, $50.00
ISBN: 1-57870-132-5

This book offers network architects, engineers, and managers of packet networks critical insight into the continuing development of Differentiated Services. It addresses the particular needs of a network environment as well as issues that must be considered in its implementation. Coverage allows networkers to implement DiffServ on a variety of networking technologies, including ATM, and to solve common problems related to TCP, UDP, and other networking protocols.

Designing Addressing Architectures for Routing and Switching

By Howard Berkowitz
1st Edition
500 pages, $45.00
ISBN: 1-57870-059-0

One of the greatest challenges for a network design professional is making the users, servers, files, printers, and other resources visible on their network. This title equips the network engineer or architect with a systematic methodology for planning the wide area and local area network "streets" on which users and servers live.

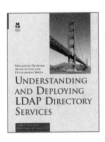

Understanding and Deploying LDAP Directory Services

By Tim Howes, Mark Smith, and Gordon Good
1st Edition
850 pages, $50.00
ISBN: 1-57870-070-1

This comprehensive tutorial provides the reader with a thorough treatment of LDAP directory services. Minimal knowledge of general networking and administration is assumed, making the material accessible to intermediate and advanced readers alike. The text is full of practical implementation advice and real-world deployment examples to help the reader choose the path that makes the most sense for his specific organization.

Switched, Fast, and Gigabit Ethernet

By Sean Riley and Robert Breyer
3rd Edition
615 pages, $50.00
ISBN: 1-57870-073-6

Switched, Fast, and Gigabit Ethernet, Third Edition is the one and only solution needed to understand and fully implement this entire range of Ethernet innovations. Acting both as an overview of current technologies and hardware requirements as well as a hands-on, comprehensive tutorial for deploying and managing switched, fast, and gigabit ethernet networks, this guide covers the most prominent present and future challenges network administrators face.

Wide Area High Speed Networks

By Dr. Sidnie Feit
1st Edition
624 pages, $50.00
ISBN: 1-57870-114-7

Networking is in a transitional phase between long-standing conventional wide area services and new technologies and services. This book presents current and emerging wide area technologies and services, makes them understandable, and puts them into perspective so that their merits and disadvantages are clear.

Local Area High Speed Networks

By Dr. Sidnie Feit
1st Edition
655 pages, $50.00
ISBN: 1-57870-113-9

There is a great deal of change happening in the technology being used for local area networks. As Web intranets have driven bandwidth needs through the ceiling, inexpensive Ethernet NICs and switches have come into the market. As a result, many network professionals are interested in evaluating these new technologies for implementation. This book provides real-world implementation expertise for these technologies, including traces, so that users can realistically compare and decide how to use them.

The DHCP Handbook

By Ralph Droms and Ted Lemon
1st Edition
535 pages, $55.00
ISBN: 1-57870-137-6

The DHCP Handbook is an authoritative overview and expert guide to the setup and management of a DHCP server. This title discusses how DHCP was developed and its interaction with other protocols. Learn how DHCP operates, its use in different environments, and the interaction between DHCP servers and clients. Network hardware, inter-server communication, security, SNMP, and IP mobility are also discussed. Also, included in the book are several appendices that provide a rich resource for networking professionals working with DHCP.

Designing Routing and Switching Architectures for Enterprise Networks

By Howard Berkowitz
1st Edition
992 pages, $55.00
ISBN: 1-57870-060-4

This title provides a fundamental understanding of how switches and routers operate, enabling the reader to use them effectively to build networks. The book walks the network designer through all aspects of requirements, analysis, and deployment strategies, strengthens readers' professional abilities, and helps them develop skills necessary to advance in their profession.

Wireless LANs: Implementing Interoperable Networks

By Jim Geier
1st Edition
432 pages, $40.00
ISBN: 1-57870-081-7

Wireless LANs covers how and why to migrate from proprietary solutions to the 802.11 standard, and explains how to realize significant cost savings through wireless LAN implementation for data collection systems.

Network Performance Baselining

By Daniel Nassar
1st Edition
736 pages, $50.00
ISBN: 1-57870-240-2

Network Performance Baselining focuses on the real-world implementation of network baselining principles and shows not only how to measure and rate a network's performance, but also how to improve the network performance. This book includes chapters that give a real "how-to" approach for standard baseline methodologies along with actual steps and processes to perform network baseline measurements. In addition, the proper way to document and build a baseline report will be provided.

The Economics of Electronic Commerce
By Soon-Yong Choi, Andrew Whinston, and Dale Stahl
1st Edition
656 pages, $49.99
ISBN: 1-57870-014-0

This is the first electronic commerce title to focus on traditional topics of economics applied to the electronic commerce arena. While all other electronic commerce titles take a "how-to" approach, this focuses on what it means from an economic perspective.

Intrusion Detection
By Rebecca Gurley Bace
1st Edition
340 pages, $50.00
ISBN: 1-57870-185-6

Intrusion detection is a critical new area of technology within network security. This comprehensive guide to the field of intrusion detection covers the foundations of intrusion detection and system audit. *Intrusion Detection* provides a wealth of information, ranging from design considerations to how to evaluate and choose the optimal commercial intrusion detection products for a particular networking environment.

Understanding Public-Key Infrastructure
By Carlisle Adams and Steve Lloyd
1st Edition
300 pages, $50.00
ISBN: 1-57870-166-X

This book is a tutorial on, and a guide to the deployment of, Public-Key Infrastructures. It covers a broad range of material related to PKIs, including certification, operational considerations and standardization efforts, as well as deployment issues and considerations. Emphasis is placed on explaining the interrelated fields within the topic area, to assist those who will be responsible for making deployment decisions and architecting a PKI within an organization.

Network Intrusion Detection: An Analyst's Handbook
By Stephen Northcutt and Judy Novak
2nd Edition
480 pages, $45.00
ISBN: 0-7357-1008-2

Get answers and solutions from someone who has been in the trenches. Author Stephen Northcutt, original developer of the Shadow intrusion detection system and former Director of the United States Navy's Information System Security Office, gives his expertise to intrusion detection specialists, security analysts, and consultants responsible for setting up and maintaining an effective defense against network security attacks.

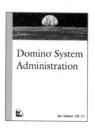

Domino System
Administration

Domino System Administration

By Rob Kirkland
1st Edition
860 pages, $49.99
ISBN: 1-56205-948-3

Need a concise,
practical explana-
tion about the new features of
Domino, and how to make some
of the advanced stuff really work?
Domino System Administration is the
first book on Domino that attacks
the technology at the professional
level, with practical, hands-on assistance to get Domino 5 running in
your organization.

Lotus Notes & Domino
ESSENTIAL REFERENCE

Lotus Notes & Domino Essential Reference

By Dave Hatter, and
Tim Bankes
1st Edition
675 pages, $45.00
ISBN: 0-7357-0007-9

If you need something to facilitate
your creative and technical abilities—
something to perfect your Lotus
Notes and Domino programming
skills—this is the book for you. This
title includes all of the objects, classes,
functions, and methods found if you
work with Lotus Notes and Domino.
It shows the object hierarchy and the
overlying relationship between each
one, organized the way the language
is designed.

Software Architecture and Engineering

Designing Flexible Object-Oriented Systems with UML
By Charles Richter
1st Edition
416 pages, $40.00
ISBN: 1-57870-098-1

Designing Flexible Object-Oriented Systems with UML details the UML, which is a notation system for designing object-oriented programs. The book follows the same sequence that a development project might employ, starting with requirements of the problem using UML case diagrams and activity diagrams. The reader is shown ways to improve the design as the author moves through the transformation of the initial diagrams into class diagrams and interaction diagrams.

Constructing Superior Software
By Paul Clements, et al.
1st Edition
285 pages, $40.00
ISBN: 1-57870-147-3

Published in cooperation with the Software Quality Institute at the University of Texas, Austin, this title presents a set of fundamental engineering strategies for achieving a successful software solution, with practical advice to ensure that the development project is moving in the right direction. Software designers and development managers can improve the development speed and quality of their software, and improve the processes used in development.

A UML Pattern Language
By Paul Evitts
1st Edition
260 pages, $40.00
ISBN: 1-57870-118-X

While other books focus only on the UML notation system, this book integrates key UML modeling concepts and illustrates their use through patterns. It provides an integrated, practical, step-by-step discussion of UML and patterns, with real-world examples to illustrate proven software modeling techniques.

Other Books By New Riders Press

Microsoft Technologies

ADMINISTRATION

Inside Windows 2000 Server
1-56205-929-7 • $49.99

Windows 2000 Essential Reference
0-7357-0869-X • $35.00

Windows 2000 Active Directory
0-7357-0870-3 • $29.99

Windows 2000 Routing and Remote Access Service
0-7357-0951-3 • $34.99

Windows 2000 Deployment & Desktop Management
0-7357-0975-0 • $34.99

Windows 2000 DNS
0-7357-0973-4 • $39.99

Windows 2000 User Management
1-56205-886-X • $34.99

Windows 2000 Professional
0-7357-0950-5 • $34.99

Planning for Windows 2000
0-7357-0048-6 • $29.99

Windows 2000 Server Professional Reference
0-7357-0952-1 • $75.00

Windows 2000 Security
0-7357-0991-2 • $39.99

Windows 2000 TCP/IP
0-7357-0992-0 • $39.99
Available August 2000

Windows 2000 Registry
0-7357-0944-0 • $34.99

Windows 2000 Terminal Services and Citrix MetaFrame
0-7357-1005-8 • $39.99

Windows NT/2000 Network Security
1-57870-253-4 • $45.00

Windows NT/2000 Thin Client Solutions
1-57870-239-9 • $45.00

Windows 2000 Virtual Private Networking
1-57870-246-1 • $45.00

Windows 2000 Active Directory Design & Deployment
1-57870-242-9 • $45.00

Windows 2000 and Mainframe Integration
1-57870-200-3 • $40.00

Windows 2000 Server: Planning and Migration
1-57870-023-X • $40.00

Windows 2000 Quality of Service
1-57870-115-5 • $45.00

Windows NT Power Toolkit
0-7357-0922-X • $49.99

Windows NT Terminal Server and Citrix MetaFrame
1-56205-944-0 • $29.99

Windows NT Performance: Monitoring, Benchmarking, and Tuning
1-56205-942-4 • $29.99

Windows NT Registry: A Settings Reference
1-56205-941-6 • $29.99

Windows NT Domain Architecture
1-57870-112-0 • $38.00

SYSTEMS PROGRAMMING

Windows NT/2000 Native API Reference
1-57870-199-6 • $50.00

Windows NT Device Driver Development
1-57870-058-2 • $50.00

DCE/RPC over SMB: Samba and Windows NT Domain Internals
1-57870-150-3 • $45.00

APPLICATION PROGRAMMING

Delphi COM Programming
1-57870-221-6 • $45.00

Windows NT Applications: Measuring and Optimizing Performance
1-57870-176-7 • $40.00

Applying COM+
ISBN 0-7357-0978-5 • $49.99

SCRIPTING

Windows Script Host
1-57870-139-2 • $35.00

Windows NT Shell Scripting
1-57870-047-7 • $32.00

Windows NT Win32 Perl Programming: The Standard Extensions
1-57870-067-1 • $40.00

Windows NT/2000 ADSI Scripting for System Administration
1-57870-219-4 • $45.00

Windows NT Automated Deployment and Customization
1-57870-045-0 • $32.00

Open Source

MySQL
0-7357-0921-1 • $49.99

Web Application Development with PHP 4.0
0-7357-0997-1 • $45.00

PHP Functions Essential Reference
0-7357-0970-X • $35.00
Available February 2001

Python Essential Reference
0-7357-0901-7 • $34.95

GNU Autoconf, Automake, and Libtool
1-57870-190-2 • $35.00

Linux/Unix

ADMINISTRATION

Linux System Administration
1-56205-934-3 • $29.99

Linux Firewalls
0-7357-0900-9 • $39.99

Linux Essential Reference
0-7357-0852-5 • $24.95

UnixWare 7 System Administration
1-57870-080-9 • $40.00

DEVELOPMENT

Developing Linux Applications with GTK+ and GDK
0-7357-0021-4 • $34.99

GTK+/Gnome Application Development
0-7357-0078-8 • $39.99

KDE Application Development
1-57870-201-1 • $39.99

GIMP

Grokking the GIMP
0-7357-0924-6 • $39.99

GIMP Essential Reference
0-7357-0911-4 • $24.95

SOLARIS

Solaris Advanced System Administrator's Guide, Second Edition
1-57870-039-6 • $39.99

Solaris System Administrator's Guide, Second Edition
1-57870-040-X • $34.99

Solaris Essential Reference
0-7357-0023-0 • $24.95

Networking

STANDARDS & PROTOCOLS

Cisco Router Configuration & Troubleshooting, Second Edition
0-7357-0999-8 • $34.99

Understanding Directory Services
0-7357-0910-6 • $39.99

Understanding the Network: A Practical Guide to Internetworking
0-7357-0977-7 • $39.99

Understanding Data Communications, Sixth Edition
0-7357-0036-2 • $39.99

LDAP: Programming Directory Enabled Applications
1-57870-000-0 • $44.99

Gigabit Ethernet Networking
1-57870-062-0 • $50.00
Supporting Service Level
Agreements on IP Networks
1-57870-146-5 • $50.00
Directory Enabled Networks
1-57870-140-6 • $50.00
Differentiated Services for the
Internet
1-57870-132-5 • $50.00
Quality of Service on IP Networks
1-57870-189-9 • $50.00
Designing Addressing
Architectures for
Routing and Switching
1-57870-059-0 • $45.00
Understanding & Deploying
LDAP Directory Services
1-57870-070-1 • $50.00
Switched, Fast and Gigabit
Ethernet, Third Edition
1-57870-073-6 • $50.00
Wireless LANs: Implementing
Interoperable Networks
1-57870-081-7 • $40.00
Wide Area High Speed Networks
1-57870-114-7 • $50.00
The DHCP Handbook
1-57870-137-6 • $55.00
Designing Routing and Switching
Architectures for Enterprise
Networks
1-57870-060-4 • $55.00
Local Area High Speed Networks
1-57870-113-9 • $50.00
Network Performance Baselining
1-57870-240-2 • $50.00
Economics of Electronic
Commerce
1-57870-014-0 • $49.99

SECURITY

Intrusion Detection
1-57870-185-6 • $50.00
Understanding Public-Key
Infrastructure
1-57870-166-X • $50.00
Network Intrusion Detection: An
Analyst's Handbook, 2nd Edition
0-7357-1008-2 • $39.99
Linux Firewalls
0-7357-0900-9 • $39.99

LOTUS NOTES/DOMINO

Domino System Administration
1-56205-948-3 • $49.99
Lotus Notes & Domino Essential
Reference
0-7357-0007-9 • $45.00

Software Architecture & Engineering

Designing Flexible Object-
Oriented Systems with UML
1-57870-098-1 • $40.00
Constructing Superior Software
1-57870-147-3 • $40.00
A UML Pattern Language
1-57870-118-X • $45.00

Professional Certification

TRAINING GUIDES

MCSE Training Guide:
Networking Essentials, 2nd Ed.
156205919X • $49.99
MCSE Training Guide: Windows
NT Server 4, 2nd Ed.
1562059165 • $49.99
MCSE Training Guide: Windows
NT Workstation 4, 2nd Ed.
1562059181 • $49.99
MCSE Training Guide: Windows
NT Server 4 Enterprise, 2nd Ed.
1562059173 • $49.99
MCSE Training Guide: Core
Exams Bundle, 2nd Ed.
1562059262 • $149.99
MCSE Training Guide: TCP/IP,
2nd Ed.
1562059203 • $49.99
MCSE Training Guide: IIS 4,
2nd Ed.
0735708657 • $49.99
MCSE Training Guide: SQL
Server 7 Administration
0735700036 • $49.99

MCSE Training Guide: SQL
Server 7 Database Design
0735700044 • $49.99
CLP Training Guide: Lotus
Notes 4
0789715058 • $59.99
MCSD Training Guide: Visual
Basic 6 Exams
0735700028 • $69.99
MCSD Training Guide: Solution
Architectures
0735700265 • $49.99
MCSD Training Guide: 4-in-1
Bundle
0735709122 • $149.99
A+ Certification Training Guide,
2nd Ed.
0735709076 • $49.99
Network+ Certification Guide
073570077X • $49.99

Solaris 2.6 Administrator
Certification Training Guide,
Part I
157870085X • $40.00
Solaris 2.6 Administrator
Certification Training Guide,
Part II
1578700868 • $40.00
Solaris 7 Administrator
Certification Training Guide, Part
I and II
1578702496 • $49.99
MCSE Training Guide: Windows
2000 Professional
0735709653 • $49.99
MCSE Training Guide:
Windows 2000 Server
0735709688 • $49.99
MCSE Training Guide: Windows
2000 Network Infrastructure
0735709661 • $49.99
MCSE Training Guide: Windows
2000 Network Security Design
073570984X • $49.99
MCSE Training Guide: Windows
2000 Network Infrastructure
Design
0735709823 • $49.99
MCSE Training Guide: Windows
2000 Directory Services.
Infrastructure
0735709769 • $49.99
MCSE Training Guide: Windows
2000 Directory Services Design
0735709831 • $49.99
MCSE Training Guide: Windows
2000 Accelerated Exam
0735709793 • $69.99
MCSE Training Guide: Windows
2000 Core Exams Bundle
0735709882 • $149.99

Java 2 Certification Training
Guide
1562059505 • $39.99

FAST TRACKS

CLP Fast Track: Lotus
Notes/Domino 5 System
Administration.
0735708789 • $39.99
CLP Fast Track: Lotus
Notes/Domino 5 Application
Development
0735708789 • $39.99
MCSD Fast Track: Solution
Architectures
073570029X • $29.99
MCSD Fast Track: Visual Basic 6,
Exam 70-175
0735700184 • $19.99
MCSD Fast Track: Visual Basic 6,
Exam 70-176
0735700192 • $19.99

 # How to Contact Us

Visit Our Web Site

www.newriders.com

On our Web site you'll find information about our other books, authors, tables of contents, indexes, and book errata. You can also place orders for books through our Web site.

Email Us

Contact us at this address:

editors@newriders.com

- If you have comments or questions about this book
- To report errors that you have found in this book
- If you have a book proposal to submit or are interested in writing for New Riders
- If you would like to have an author kit sent to you
- If you are an expert in a computer topic or technology and are interested in being a technical editor who reviews manuscripts for technical accuracy

sales@newriders.com

- To find a distributor in your area, please contact our international department at the address above.

pr@newriders.com

- For instructors from educational institutions who wish to preview New Riders books for classroom use. Email should include your name, title, school, department, address, phone number, office days/hours, text in use, and enrollment in the body of your text along with your request for desk/examination copies and/or additional information.

Write to Us

New Riders Publishing

201 W. 103rd St.

Indianapolis, IN 46290-1097

Call Us

Toll-free (800) 571-5840 + 9 +7477

If outside U.S. (317) 581-3500. Ask for New Riders.

Fax Us

(317) 581-4663

New Riders

We Want to Know What You Think

To better serve you, we would like your opinion on the content and quality of this book. Please complete this card and mail it to us or fax it to 317-581-4663.

Name _____

Address _____

City_____State_____Zip_____

Email Address _____

Occupation _____

What influenced your purchase of this book?
- ❑ Recommendation
- ❑ Cover Design
- ❑ Table of Contents
- ❑ Index
- ❑ Magazine Review
- ❑ Advertisement
- ❑ New Rider's Reputation
- ❑ Author Name

How would you rate the contents of this book?
- ❑ Excellent
- ❑ Very Good
- ❑ Good
- ❑ Fair
- ❑ Below Average
- ❑ Poor

How do you plan to use this book?
- ❑ Quick reference
- ❑ Self-training
- ❑ Classroom
- ❑ Other

What do you like most about this book?
Check all that apply.
- ❑ Content
- ❑ Writing Style
- ❑ Accuracy
- ❑ Examples
- ❑ Listings
- ❑ Design
- ❑ Index
- ❑ Page Count
- ❑ Price
- ❑ Illustrations

What do you like least about this book?
Check all that apply.
- ❑ Content
- ❑ Writing Style
- ❑ Accuracy
- ❑ Examples
- ❑ Listings
- ❑ Design
- ❑ Index
- ❑ Page Count
- ❑ Price
- ❑ Illustrations

Can you name a similar book that you like better than this one, or one that is as good? Why?

_____

_____

How many New Riders books do you own?_____

What are your favorite computer books? _____

What other titles would you like to see us develop? _____

Any comments for us? _____

_____

_____

_____

GNU Autoconf, Automake and Libtool, 1-57870-190-2

www.newriders.com • Fax 317-581-4663

Fold here and tape to mail

- -

Place
Stamp
Here

New Riders Publishing
201 W. 103rd St.
Indianapolis, IN 46290